Anne M. Mallberg
P. O. Box 713, 120 East 8th Street
Pierre, South Dakota 57501-0713

Dumbing Down

Dumbing Down
Essays on the Strip Mining of American Culture

Edited by
KATHARINE WASHBURN
and
JOHN F. THORNTON

Introduction by
JOHN SIMON

W · W · NORTON & COMPANY · *NEW YORK* · *LONDON*

To my parents (KW)

To Katharine and Sarah (JT)

The Spider and the Bee

. . . In short, the question comes all to this—Whether is the
nobler being of the two, that which, by a lazy contemplation
of four inches round, by an overweening pride, which feeding and
engendering on itself, turns all into excrement and venom, produces
nothing at last but flybane and a cobweb; or that which, by an
universal range, with long search, much study, true judgment,
and distinction of things, brings home honey and wax.

Jonathan Swift, *The Battle of the Books* (1704)

Contents

PART FOUR Public Life

PART FIVE Private Life

Foreword

by THE EDITORS

> All, all of a piece throughout:
> Thy chase had a beast in view;
> Thy wars brought nothing about;
> Thy lovers were all untrue.
> 'Tis well an old age is out,
> And time to begin a new.
>
> John Dryden, "The Secular Masque" (1700)

THIS BOOK BEGAN with a subway epiphany, a revelation on the F train early in the cold spring of 1994. While the radio two seats down poured out its stream of tuneless abuse, one of us, holding up a frail screen of newsprint against the visual bombardments of life underground, turned to the editorial pages of the *New York Times*. Two words leapt out from an Op-Ed piece on the fate of American planetariums. Its author, Ken Kalfus, casually alluded to the "dumbing down" of science museums in the United States, evoking displays of the constellations gone dark, as the lightbulbs have, quite literally, spluttered out, and lamented the deterioration of the grand exhibits of the cosmos into glitzy sideshows celebrating sci-fi dreams of extraterrestrial life. The editors of this book decided, after an extended series of conversations, memoranda, and solitary reflections at midnight, that perhaps we were, in fact, looking at a severe and demonstrable downward spiral of American life and culture. "Dumbing down" fused gerund and preposition into a nifty alliteration, and this neologism lurking at the edges of our awareness had now come into its own.

But what was the real provenance of our title? As a catchphrase, "dumbing down" seemed already to have worked its stealthy way through half a century. A check with the helpful lexicographers at Merriam-Webster yielded our first citation: Hollywood during the depression. It establishes an early link—and an ominous one—between American society and the entertainment industry. One H. T. Webster remarked in *Forum* in December 1933 that he could "cheer, too, for the Hollywood gag men in conference on a comedy which has been revealed as too subtle, when they determine to dumb it down. That phrase saves time and wearying gestures." (One of our essayists here, Phillip Lopate, would probably murmur that those dumbed-down comedies look, from the distance of seventy-odd years later, like the theater of Aristophanes, in contrast to many of the productions of American cinema in 1995. For although we seem to be looking at a culture in free fall, things still tend to fall in place.)

After the 1930s references to dumbing down fell into a period of latency, emerging briefly in the fifties with S. J. Perelman's aside to the effect that the bulk of the changes in the magazine trade "reflected an effort to dumb the piece down for the . . . reader." But by the early 1980s it had become idiomatic to refer to dumbing down as part of an inevitable process in textbook publishing, and thereafter the increase in usage was geometric. The term no longer stood for a predication, a prophecy, a sorry aberration: it was a *fait accompli,* and reflected a new reality: while we were looking the other way, someone appeared to have given away the store.

Our list of topics for inclusion continued to proliferate with every editorial discussion, and we began to wonder if dumbing down was in fact some deliberate cultural and commercial strategy, an active procedure with goals of its own rather than a passive experience. American culture has long existed in a complicated symbiosis with the marketplace, and the possibility that markets thrive on endless segmentation, on divisions of taste and judgment rather than on communality and inherited consensus, continued to shape our thinking about this book, its catalogue of issues, and the writers whom we proposed to match to a burgeoning table of contents. But whether we looked at the very central subject of how we raise and educate our children or the seemingly marginal one of food and culinary culture, we kept an eye on the gloomy trajectory of our title.

Meanwhile, jeremiads on national decline seemed to be rolling in from every political position in American society, right, left, and center, when a magazine piece by our editor, Gerald Howard, supplied a subtitle and a subtheme. We took his phrase—"strip mining"—as a governing metaphor for the opportunistic process of dumbing down and cashing in on the decline of American culture, yoking the terms together into a working title, and we set out to assemble a chorus of contributors. From the cantankerous to the merely somber, from the witty to the morose, even allowing for the occasional dissenter to our thesis, we looked for writers already vocal on this subject, for the familiar (but by no means predictable) curmudgeons who had sounded the early warnings, but we scouted as well for those still sulking in their tents yet likely to respond persuasively to our summons.

The authors whose essays constitute this book share a central premise: that American society, for some time fallen into disarray, has somehow begun sliding down a long, steep chute into nullity. Many of them worry the question of how, without slipping through the trapdoor of a facile nostalgia, it would be possible, nonetheless, to speak with candor about a collective sense of loss. If these writers can be said to compose a chorus, it's one which unites in a lament, stated with great poignancy here in Cynthia Ozick's essay, over the recent primacy of a soft culture in a nation which once circulated a hard currency, however painfully. Moreover, once earned, if necessary over several generations, such hard currency could be salted away for the next to enjoy.

We proceeded warily, with some real distrust of our own perceptions, given the tendency of the middle-aged to look back with longing to the orderly world of their youth, to the immediate past and the well-burnished glow of its genial arrangements and to the safety of those hierarchies which at least we understood, however we might resent them. If this book's intention was to diagnose rather than to describe, were we looking for identifiable perpetrators, villains, and late-twentieth-century demons? As our list of cultural casualties grew longer, the roster of possible causes dwindled, and we were left mainly with the sense that something had imperceptibly shifted in American society while we were protesting the Vietnam War, studying Middle High German or minoring in Women's Film Studies, vacationing in Dubrovnik and mortgaging the grand piano for the rock guitar—all the while counting on someone else to maintain what we had inherited.

Perhaps, assuming that the complicated interaction between the high, the low, and the much-abused middle would last forever, we were living off capital. Reading the essays in this book, we came to realize what had happened was the collapse of a social pyramid in which the highbrow condescended to the low, while the low and the high took shots together at the middle. Only when it was almost irrevocably gone, did we begin to miss its stolid, stuffy, and perhaps parental legacy of striving, cultural assimilation, and notion of a common good. The bottom of the social pyramid may, as a consequence of its forced economic isolation from the rest, have taken subtle revenge at last, by making those manners, mores, and habits of mind, which never served it well in the first place, part of the mainstream. (W. H. Auden, in his last collection of essays, *The Dyers Hand,* suggested this as the inevitable outcome of the democracy which he sought, and still cherished, in the United States.) In a post-sixties America which witnessed a major assault on class distinctions, we may have cast away our ability to make distinctions of *any* kind, as words like "elitist" and "judgmental," heavily laden with negative meaning, began to enter the language: Joseph Epstein, who has written here on the future of the arts, has remarked in another of his essays that in our age vulgarity consists in the inability to make distinctions.

Trolling for topics, we found that a few, which initially seemed intrinsic to this impossibly broad subject, later fell off the line. Every area seemed in a state of devolution, whether we surveyed the scorched earth of literary criticism, the educational system which became an early hostage to the cultural wars, or the carnival of American litigation in which psychiatrist and lawyer became united as entrepreneurs, co-exhibitors of the freakish and novel defense in which every crime is linked to a certifiable disorder, a fresh entitlement, and a swift enrollment in what Benjamin Barber has called "the aristocracy of everyone." Barber means, above all, victims. At the same time, the compensations being awarded these plaintiffs guaranteed that the victim's coronet was no hollow honorific. Staggering stipends are attached to the rewards of entering what appears, at times, to be a mass lottery (greasily publicized by the afternoon talk shows) in which bad luck, poor judgment, and the claims of *ressentiment* are the winning tickets in a new kind of national sweepstakes.

A number of recent books have amply covered the explosion of litigation in American life, the demise of common sense and its displacement by the instant expertise of a class of *lumpen professionals* whose salaried wisdom walls us off from the necessity of thinking through a problem—let alone first articulating it—for ourselves. We let this subject go, engulfed as we are in the backwash of lawyer jokes anyway, but happily included Paul McHugh's essay on the training of psychiatrists in the cultural environment which gave us that Odd Couple of the nineties—lawyer and shrink—partnered in recording the testimony (from a front-page story in the *New York Times* last year) in a rape trial where a witness, suffering from multiple personality disorder, gave evidence from her experience as a canine. The transformation of the justice system has entered our literary life, and the utterance of an old theme—that character, in the American novel, is destiny—has succumbed to a new script: chance is destiny, pick a lottery number, and let's write an American *Bovary* in which Emma survives and sues Charles, her father, her lover, and the pharmacist alike for multiple damages.

We would also have liked to commission a piece on civility, that imperfect and fragile lattice of social behaviors that arises from ordinary good manners, a belief in hierarchy, and the notion of a common good. Even so, many of our contributors, while focusing on other subjects in their own essays, nonetheless gave its decay a vivid place on the map of their concerns. We ourselves observed that the problems of etiquette addressed in a 1940s edition of Emily Post, when contrasted with the issues raised in the 1980s by Judith Martin (Miss Manners), appear, by contrast, as the quaint, nuanced, and thoroughly benign predicaments of a population whose worst fault is the level of anxiety required to protect its claim to gentility.

Speculations on the passing of civility can be many-layered. Consider the noise of radios in public places where short utterances, often reduced to crass expletives, replace the kind of discourse we remember as conversation (an evolutionary adaptation which has gripped us unawares, as we live in an increasingly cacophonous silence). We shout, we speak in slogans, and we have apparently lost our tenuous grip on the compound/complex sentence and the kind of thinking which requires its syntactical structures. (Try coming out with a fifty-word utterance in most restaurants these days, where everyone's compelled to shout above the music. The soloist in our culture is a half-dead concept, so if you want to get heard, you'll have to try the Internet, where everyone enjoys equal opportunity, and everyone gets published.)

Connections between the topic of civility, as with every other, became clearer: we discovered a subtle rapport among the twenty-two writers whose work is represented in *Dumbing Down*, many of them arriving separately at an intricate consensus. John Simon's introductory essay hints at the (seeming) abolition of class distinctions in late American democracy, prompting our thought that this may have led inevitably to the collapse of "good manners," a system which developed, after all, to ease differences between men and women, old and young, rich and poor, while acknowledging their inevitability. Our speculation widened to include the possibility that the kind of violence we deplore in the media, in the streets, and even in the corporate workplace—where its sublimation into simple rudeness, jockeying for power, and "attitude" is celebrated as a model for survival and success!—is central to the problem: Has some ugly notion of egalitarian "empowerment" replaced every other virtue in human and civic relationships, at the expense of the common good?

Many of these essays point, sometimes obliquely, sometimes explicitly, to the cynical wisdom of Rhett Butler's remark to Scarlett O'Hara in *Gone with the Wind:* "What most people don't seem to realize is that there is just as much money to be made out of the wreckage of a civilization as from the upbuilding of one. . . . I'm making my fortune out of the wreckage." If American culture is dumbing down, a part of its citizenry is cashing in on our willful obtuseness, our turning away from common sense, and our cheerful submission to the micro-managed well-being designed for us by those phalanxes of experts who, after all, profit from our helplessness.

Even cooking, as contributor Nahum Waxman suggests, has become almost exclusively the terrain of professionals, as our own competence (and the confidence it engenders) ebbs away: When we cook, if we prepare our own food at all, we shakily perform the ritual in kitchens which are miracles of technology and design, spacious in some direct proportion to their infrequency of use—like those temples in late antiquity which increased in size and grandeur as the cult of the resident deity declined in observance. Designer kitchens seem still another manifestation of the virtual reality which increasingly claims so many aspects of the quotidian, from the simulated friendships available on the Internet, which Sven Birkerts's essay discusses, to the "explosion" in the arts, which, to the jaundiced eye of Joseph Epstein, looks more like cultural and intellectual entropy. There may be more orchestras in the United States than ever before, but the purchase of recordings of art music, as a percentage of recordings sold, has declined to a lower level than that of the provincial, philistine, and easily mocked 1940s and 1950s.

Education is always a ready target, but the essayists converging on this well-known catastrophe rejected the opportunity to indulge in hand-wringing over the "decline of standards" and the nimble distortions of the politically correct. Heather MacDonald locates in contemporary writing pedagogy a giddy cultivation of self-esteem over competence and of self-expression over the discipline of syntax. This resembles the symptoms of vacuity and aimlessness which David Klinghoffer has uncovered in our religious lives. We glumly suspected that this malaise was well under way around the time—in the 1970s—when the New Age term "spirituality," redolent of something vague, universal, and almost entirely formless, began to shoulder aside the very word "religion," with its older implication of tradition, dogma, and hierarchy.

The kitsch exposed in Klinghoffer's essay has invaded other areas of our society. The writers here detected, one after another, the advance of a ferocious literalism over a landscape where irony, nuance, and elegance of mind and soul once flourished. We are left in the postmodern schoolhouse with Gilbert Sewall, counting casualties which we must assume will reach not only into this generation, but into the next, stranding us on the doorstep of the Holocaust Museum. Jonathan Rosen's thoughtful piece makes it clear that good intentions are not enough; what we get in a dumbed-down context is the enshrinement of a glossy literalism, a monument where experience, memory, and empathy are formatted to do our thinking and feeling for us.

So the museum, the mall, and the educational cafeteria where multicultural fashions ensure that our children can consume the doubtful benefits of their parents' overdose of media culture—an un-nutritious but certifiably international kind of Lean Cuisine for the brain, selling McAsian, McIndian, and McMeso-American—all collaborate in appeasing our hunger for fresh stimulation and quick gratification, under the claim of expansion, but simply result in the contraction of the knowable world into a bland and homogeneous unletteredness. The mind of the middle-schooler is stretched to the desired paper-thinness, absorbing a sketchy impression of a vast number of things, savoring at an early age his middle-aged parents' surfeit of endlessly numbing—and finally dumbing—information. Skittish, distractible, and insatiable ourselves, we hustle our offspring into the antechambers of our own pseudo-so-phisticated, cocksure, and measureless ignorance, while attributing their shortcomings, as well as ours, to the mysterious ravages of attention deficit disorder.

We are the creatures of a marketing society, of carefully managed investigations into our tastes and preferences. Meanwhile, the politics of the last thirty years has divided our souls into ever newer, smaller, and more discrete identities. The goal is that we become consumers thus more easily manipulated into a variegated honeycomb of special needs. So in the end we are finally united only in that abundant ignorance which seems to be the main course, served up just after the hors d'oeuvres catering to our very particular requirements, anodynes for our carefully nurtured political, social, and intellectual allergies. We're snacking off our cheapest preferences, everyone at the table has his special caterer, and we eat and run, off into a boundless oblivion.

If a feast of ignorance is bliss, why isn't America blissed out? What is it that we must be ignorant of in order to achieve bliss? In *Dumbing Down* we try to test the ignorance = bliss hypothesis by comparing it with another one, namely, that within the span of one generation there has been a widespread and remarkable drop-off of intelligent words and deeds in this country. Thirty years ago, on a wave of unparalleled optimism of which he was the cynosure, President Kennedy prophesied, "I look forward to a world that will not only be safe for democracy and diversity but also for distinction." Why do we who live in that world foretold now seem left with almost no distinction and with precious few of the constructive aspects of either democracy or diversity?

Again, we sought a villain. Maybe it was television after all, which, following a deceptively promising start, had by the 1970s superseded much of what had formerly passed for real life in this country. Maybe the dream of global communication, of worldwide consciousness, was always doomed. Had the builders of the dream only built another Tower of Babel? To borrow an appraisal from one of our contributors, James Twitchell: "So television dulls perception, flattens consciousness, manipulates desire, breeds decadence, fosters escapism, insulates the senses, rebarbarizes, infantilizes, is a narcotic or a plug-in drug, mediates experience, colonizes, pollutes, encourages commodity fetishism, leads to psychic privitization, makes us narcissistic, passive, and superficial, and also increases aggression" (*Carnival Culture,* 1992). Twitchell's list reads like the scratch notes Aldous Huxley or George Orwell might have used to plot a novel about a world gone very wrong.

Are things really so bad? In the pages of *Dumbing Down*, we think you will find that they are, but at least their badness is a complex one, and therein may lie the seeds of hope. Why, then, given a groaning banquet of opportunity and resources, have we decided to catch flies for supper? Why haven't we, "instead of dirt and poison . . . rather chosen to fill our hives with honey and wax, thus furnishing mankind with the two noblest of things, which are sweetness and light"? This enigma troubled Jonathan Swift three centuries ago. And it troubled his friend Alexander Pope, whose *Dunciad*'s climactic lines offer us a checklist to ponder as the shadow of Dumbness slouches across the land of the free and the home of the brave:

> Art after Art goes out, and all is Night.
> See skulking Truth to her old Cavern fled,
> Mountains of Casuistry heap'd o'er her head!
> Philosophy, that lean'd on Heav'n before,
> Shrinks to her second cause, and is no more.
> Physic of Metaphysic begs defence,
> And Metaphysic calls for aid on Sense!
> See Mystery to Mathematics fly!
> In vain! they gaze, turn giddy, rave, and die.
> Religion blushing veils her sacred fires,
> And unawares Mortality expires.
> Nor public Flame, nor private, dares to shine
> Nor human Spark is left, nor Glimpse divine!
> Lo! thy dread Empire, Chaos! is restor'd;
> Light dies before thy uncreating word:
> Thy hand, great Anarch! lets the curtain fall;
> And Universal Darkness buries All.

But Pope was speaking about Dullness, not Dumbness. Aren't they the same? It might be well to open this debate—for it is that much more than a conversation or discussion—by trying to look at the history and dynamics of the ideas that inform this book's title, since they will recur throughout.

First, the notion of Culture, which we have reduced hitherto to its lowercase usage. Matthew Arnold opined in his then-renowned and now half-forgotten *Culture and Anarchy* (1869) that it was a word that had gotten itself all mixed up with the wrong associations: pedantry, bookishness, and futility. He saw it in a far nobler light as

the great help out of our present difficulties; culture being a pursuit of our total perfection by means of getting to know, on all the matters which most concern us, the best which has been thought and said in the world, and, through this knowledge, turning a stream of fresh and free thought upon our stock notions and habits, which we now follow staunchly but mechanically, vainly imagining that there is a virtue in following them staunchly which makes up for the mischief of following them mechanically.

In other words, in an age in which conventional wisdom ruled rigid and supreme, culture offered a spirit, a mode of acting that amounted to a way out of all the low, mean, stupid aspects of the everyday. Arnold didn't mean "my culture, not yours"; he didn't mean that the culture of the past must by its nature override the importance of the culture of the present; he didn't mean absolute ascendancy of high culture over all else; but he did mean that setting the mind and spirit on a search for the *best* would, as a habit and a discipline, have the natural effect of displacing large quantities of the worst or lowest elements. It would inevitably elevate us to express our highest human possibilities.

How did he think this would happen? It was very simple. He had become increasingly struck by how much "a man's life of each day depends for its solidity and value on whether he reads during that day, and far more still, on what he reads during it." Without this constant intake of the best reading he can find, the whole dynamic of culture as a process of absorption/reflection/action never begins. If, however, it is permitted to begin and is then fostered, its yield is a thousandfold.

Arnold's idealized expression, though impractical to implement in the highly stratified day of High Victorian culture, has, alas, gone from impractical to improbable in our own. The filters, the baffles, and the barriers currently interposed between the citizen and his or her culture today are formidable.

Another aspect of culture, specifically of culture in a democracy, was the fear Alexis de Tocqueville voiced in *Democracy in America* that the future would inevitably result in an egalitarian dismissal of excellence—seen by democratic man as an easily removable cause of envy and exclusiveness.

From there draw a straight line down to the 1920s and the Sage of Baltimore, Henry Louis Mencken, out of whose writing seeps the disdain for and disgust with the pernicious egalitarianism of his countrymen: "Democracy is depicted as brotherhood, even as altruism. All such notions are in error . . . there is only one sound argument for democracy, and that is the argument that it is a crime for any man to hold himself out as better than other men, and, above all, a most heinous offense for him to prove it." But Mencken realized only too clearly that the forces of barbarism had already advanced far beyond the perimeters of all he held sacred (Johann Sebastian Bach, for example, or malt liquor).

Still, in many ways, even after Mencken's passing four decades ago, the value of high culture, and its critical position as an exception, situated above the plane of pure market economics, continued to be respected. Even when the emergence of an educated middle class brought its inevitable demands that high culture be made easier to absorb, more related to current interests, and accessible to a broader audience, the very existence of a growing body of citizens open to experiencing "the better things in life" seemed to ensure that such things would continue to be protected.

One of the most withering critiques ever penned of this class of aspirants is to be found in Dwight Macdonald's "Masscult & Midcult," which appeared in the small-circulation but then-influential *Partisan Review* in 1960. Macdonald, a paradigm of the maverick public intellectual and withal a former staff writer for Henry Luce's *Fortune* magazine, set up the classic distinctions of high culture, mass culture, and, his own coinage, midcult, the newcomer, the dangerous virus that thrived on indiscriminately mixing the other two.

Seeing the basis of masscult in Marxian economic terms as a process that turns everything into a salable commodity, Macdonald compared it to the dairy process of homogenization (an American invention, he noted) whereby instead of floating on top, the cream gets distributed equally throughout the milk; in masscult, he noted, "the interesting difference is that whereas the cream is still in the homogenized milk, it disappears from homogenized culture. For the process destroys all values, since value judgments require discrimination, an ugly word in liberal-democratic America."

For Macdonald the hybrid midcult posed the greater danger to high culture, for while masscult happily enjoyed its lowbrow pursuits, midcult was always trying to replace them with modified, or mediated, versions of high culture. (This is what Hannah Arendt, soon to make her appearance here, called, with similar distaste, educated philistinism.)

Yanked out of its revered place—the concert stage, the museum gallery, the cathedral, or the university lecture hall—through cheap and usually poor modes of reproduction, high culture suddenly found itself strewn unrecognizably among the groundlings. Once that happens, Macdonald notes, masscult and midcult become a "reciprocating engine" whose stroke and counterstroke inevitably drive the whole culture *to* and *down* market.

Who is to blame? Is it the public, in its conspiratorial acquiescence to the cynical "Lords of Kitsch" Macdonald identifies as the media and entertainment moguls who grow rich through this degrading process? Ultimately, no. Macdonald doesn't believe in the notion of "the public" and appositely quotes Kierkegaard on the matter: "Only when the sense of association in society is no longer strong enough to give life to concrete realities is the Press able to create that abstraction, 'the public,' consisting of unreal individuals who never are and never can be united in an actual situation or organization—and yet be held together as a whole."

In the end, for Macdonald the best solution is to forget about the meddlesome improving aims of midcult with its destructive transformations of high culture, and let mass culture go its own mindless way; high culture then can do what it does best—exist apart from and above the fray. Let it start showing some *esprit de corps,* he exhorts, and set its standards high and be done with trying to coax or fool anybody out of a state of blissful ignorance.

Perhaps if the aristocracy of wealth in America coincided with the highest expressions of belief in high culture as a sacred trust apart from commerce, its transmission to future generations would be assured. But, dear reader, it does not. Too often the tastes of the rich and the powerful are at one with masscult and in practice deeply indifferent and even inimical to high culture.

This brings us to Hannah Arendt's analysis and a thought from your editors about what we need to do to stop (we almost wrote "retard"!) the dumbing down of this country's high culture. One year after Macdonald's essay, in 1961, Arendt published a characteristically brilliant essay of her own, "The Crisis in Culture," wherein she lays bare the mechanism of mass society as it feeds on culture. Despite its difficult technical Germanic prose often commingled with untranslated Latin and Greek terms, it points up the stark distinction between cultural objects, which by their nature stand outside time and pass unchanging from age to age, and mass society's demand for goods to consume—the famously described *panis et circenses.*

For Arendt high culture and mass culture are unalterably opposed. The modern efficiency of delivering mass entertainment has only served to create a gargantuan appetite for more. To prepare any form of high culture to fit mass culture's gaping maw is to alter it beyond recognition. This *functionalization* of high culture actually destroys it. Once used up, it is not easily restored. High culture, if respected for what it is, is a wellspring of inexhaustible value. But it must be permitted to speak to us directly in its own strong, clear voice and not in any substitute form of itself. Arendt herself describes a version of the reciprocating engine that dumbs us down:

> The relatively new trouble with mass society is perhaps even more serious, but not because of the masses themselves, but because this society is essentially a consumers' society where leisure time is used no longer for self-perfection or acquisition of more social status, but for more and more consumption and more and more entertainment. And since there are not enough consumer goods around to satisfy the growing appetites of a life process whose vital energy, no longer spent in the toil and trouble of a laboring body, must be used up by

consumption, it is as though life itself reached out and helped itself to things which were never meant for it. The result is, of course, not mass culture which, strictly speaking, does not exist, but mass entertainment, feeding on the cultural objects of the world. To believe that such a society will become more "cultured" as time goes on and education has done its work, is, I think, a fatal mistake. The point is that a consumers' society cannot possibly know how to take care of a world and the things which belong exclusively to the space of worldly appearances, because its central attitude toward all objects, the attitude of consumption, spells ruin to everything it touches.

In the end our best defense against the depletion of our national cultural legacy by dumbing down may be by choosing *not* to heed Dwight Macdonald's suggestion to separate, irrevocably, the two cultures, high and mass. Instead it may be that encouraging the return of the educated philistine in sufficient numbers—rather like the successful restocking of salmon in the rivers of our Northwest—such as seemed to exist until the early 1960s, may be our best hope to forfend a future diet of unrelieved mass entertainment of the dumbest sort. At least, in their Puritanical way, educated philistines do in principle stand up for cultural aspiration, for the well-stocked family bookshelf, the series tickets to the symphony, and they express their distaste for the mayhem which they never endorsed and for which they never felt bound to apologize.

If high culture continues to be shouldered aside at the present rate by the pandemic products of the mass-entertainment industrial complex, we will indeed be buried in Alexander Pope's "Universal Darkness." Will it be a world where history is forsaken for lessons in self-esteem and the great issues of the day are settled by interactive voting? where our conversation about books is really conversation about the celebrities we saw talking about books on television last night? where grammar and style are superseded by Spellcheck and adspeak? where Fourth of July oratory in the town square is replaced by a gangsta rap "concert" at the mall?

We hoped all along that two questions (followed by some redemptive answers, modest, polemical, but deeply engaged) would pervade *Dumbing Down:* How could such a vibrant legacy of knowledge, tradition, competency, and common sense be so rapidly squandered in seemingly so short a time? And how rapidly, given the extent of the damage, can it be replaced? It was with the intention of creating, if you will, a small but palpable speed bump on the Infobahn that these troubling essays have been written and presented for your inspection. We believe that in the aggregate they offer an agenda for doing something about the real (and we don't mean the virtually real) culture crisis now raging in America.

Katharine Washburn and John F. Thornton

Dumbing Down: Some Leading Indicators

THE EFFORT to build the case that the national intelligence is plummeting called for much poring over the daily press and much searching for presaging commentary in the writings of earlier scholars and littérateurs. The conclusions thereby reached seem incontrovertible: (1) the marginalization of formal culture we deplore in this book has been at work since the beginning of the modern period two and a half centuries ago; and (2) the feeling that *something particularly bad is happening in this country right now* is very widely shared by its artists- and pundits-in-chief. Some of this evidence follows, arrayed by source in simple alphabetical order to reveal that no matter how you slice it, the conclusions keep coming. Let us here openly call for remedies for this wasting disease.

The Editors

HANNAH ARENDT ◆ *On Violence* (New York: Harcourt Brace & Company, 1970):
. . . there are, indeed, few things that are more frightening than the steadily increasing prestige of scientifically minded brain trusters in the councils of government during the last decades. The trouble is not that they are cold-blooded enough to "think the unthinkable," but that they do not *think*. Instead of indulging in such an old-fashioned, uncomputerizable activity, they reckon with the consequences of certain hypothetically assumed constellations without, however, being able to test their hypotheses against actual occurrences. The logical flaw in these hypothetical constructions of future events is always the same: what first appears as a hypothesis—with or without its implied alternatives, according to the level of sophistication—turns immediately, usually after a few paragraphs, into a "fact," which then gives birth to a whole string of similar non-facts, with the result that the purely speculative character of the whole enterprise is forgotten. Needless to say, this is not science but pseudo-science, "the desperate attempt of the social and behavioral sciences," in the words of Noam Chomsky, "to imitate the surface fea-

tures of sciences that really have significant intellectual content." And the most obvious and "most profound objection to this kind of strategic theory is not its limited usefulness but its danger, for it can lead us to believe we have an understanding of events and control over their flow which we do not have. . . ."

JAMES ATLAS ◆ "When Fact Is Treated as Fiction," *New York Times* (7/24/95):

We live in a permissive time. In "All the President's Men," Woodward and Bernstein required *two* sources for anything they went with; with "The Agenda" it's down to one. Books come denuded of documentation, demanding that we accept their contents on faith.

H. BRANDT AYERS ◆ "The Death of Civility," *New York Times,* Op-Ed page (7/16/95):

Everett Dennis, director of the Media Center at Columbia University, is astounded by the casual arrogance among TV reporters. "There's open contempt for the Presidency with TV reporters saying on the air what they like and don't like—as if their opinion mattered," Mr. Dennis said. And in an interview, Mr. Neustadt [Richard Neustadt, author of *Presidential Power*] called the White House press "obnoxious, arrogant, pampered and self-important baby-boomers."

NICOLSON BAKER ◆ "Annals of Self-Esteem: Books as Furniture," *The New Yorker* (6/12/95):

What is it with all these books [appearing decoratively in mail-order-catalogue illustrations]? Isn't the Book supposed to be in decline—its authority eroding, its informational base fleeing to suburbs of impeccably edged and weeded silicon? . . . Catalogue designers know perfectly well that books, if we are fortunate enough to own any, should be out there somewhere, visible, shelved in motley ranks or heaped on tables as nodes of compacted linearity that arrest the causal eye and suggest wealths of partriarchal, or matriarchal, learnedness. . . .

There is a surprising further development in the history of the book and the bookcase. Not only is the book the prop of commonest resort in the world of mail order, but objects that resemble books—non-book items that carry bookishly antiquarian detailing—are suddenly popular. The book as a middle-class totem is in fashion to a degree not seen since Joseph Addison in 1711 encountered a private library containing dummy books of "All the Classick Authors in Wood," along with a silver snuffbox "made in the Shape of a little Book." . . . Our working notion of what books look like is on the verge of becoming frozen in a brownish fantasy phase that may estrange us from, and therefore weaken our resolve to read, the books we actually own. Hamlet, who was tolerant of bad puns, might have been tempted to point out that when a book turn faux it may cease to be a friend.

RUSSELL BAKER ◆ "Writing to Himself," *New York Times,* Op-Ed page (6/17/95):
When we hear of nobody reading anymore, the Dark Ages come to mind, and with them images of endless boredom. Nowadays of course, with so many things to do, boredom on a Dark Ages scale is unthinkable. That's because so many of the things we do encourage us to wallow in unthought.

JACQUES BARZUN ◆ on making substitutions in Columbia University's required course Contemporary Civilization, *New York Times* (11/16/94):
If you drop from the core a passage by John Calvin and substitute something by Martin Luther King, there's nothing wrong with that . . . but to take away a masterpiece like Tolstoy's "War and Peace" and substitute an only pretty-fair novel published last year is not a trade-off but a diminution of the idea.

SAUL BELLOW ◆ "Papuans and Zulus," *New York Times,* Op-Ed page (3/10/94):
Snowbound, I watched the blizzard impounding parked cars at midnight. The veering of the snowflakes under the street lights made me think how nice it would be if we were totally covered by white drifts. Give us a week's moratorium, dear Lord, from the idiocies that burn on every side and let the pure snows cool these overheated minds and dilute the toxins which have infected our judgments. Grant us a breather, merciful God.

Any sensible, feeling person, in the present state of things, might utter such a prayer in the dead of night. In my case, the immediate cause was an odd one. I had come under attack in the press and elsewhere for a remark I was alleged to have made about the Zulus and the Papuans. I had been quoted as saying that the Papuans had had no Proust and that the Zulus had not as yet produced a Tolstoy, and this was taken as an insult to Papuans and Zulus, and as a proof that I was at best insensitive and at worst an elitist, a chauvinist, a reactionary and a racist—in a word, a monster. . . .

WALTER BENJAMIN ◆ "The Work of Art in the Age of Mechanical Reproduction," reprinted in *Illuminations,* Hannah Arendt, ed. (New York: Harcourt, Brace & World, 1969; first published in German, 1936):
. . . that which withers in the age of mechanical reproduction is the aura of the work of art. This is a symptomatic process whose significance points beyond the realm of art. One might generalize by saying: the technique of reproduction detaches the reproduced object from the do-

main of tradition. By making many reproductions it substitutes a plurality of copies for a unique existence. And in permitting the reproduction to meet the beholder or listener in his own particular situation, it reactivates the object reproduced. These two processes lead to a tremendous shattering of tradition which is the obverse of the contemporary crisis and renewal of mankind. . . . To pry an object from its shell, to destroy its aura, is the mark of a perception whose "sense of the universal equality of things" has increased to such a degree that it extracts it even from a unique object by means of reproduction. Thus is manifested in the field of perception what in the theoretical sphere is noticeable in the increasing importance of statistics. The adjustment of reality to the masses and of the masses to reality is a process of unlimited scope. . . .

CATHOLIC NEWS SERVICE, ♦ quoted in *Catholic New York* article (2/16/95): . . . when Catholics were asked in a Times-CBS poll what best describes their belief about what happens to the bread and wine at Mass, most chose the answer that the bread and wine are "symbolic reminders of Christ" over the answer that they are "changed into the body and blood of Christ." Among Catholics under 45 years of age, 70 percent called the "symbolic reminders" description the best expression of what they believe.

RICH COHEN ♦ "The Dawn of Dumb," *New York Times,* Op-Ed page (3/11/95):
Being dumb is very American, very egalitarian. . . . There must be some kind of correlation between the onset of the dumb culture and the death of liberalism. . . . As the great intellectual movements of the century, behemoths like Communism and the New Deal, have collapsed or been brushed aside, stupidity has sometimes rushed to fill the vacuum.

CHARLES DICKENS ♦ *A Tale of Two Cities* (1859):
It was the best of times, it was the worst of times, it was the age of wisdom, it was the age of foolishness, it was the epoch of belief, it was the epoch of incredulity, it was the season of Light, it was the season of Darkness, it was the spring of hope, it was the winter of despair, we had everything before us, we had nothing before us, we were all going direct to Heaven, we were all going direct the other way. . . .

ASHLEY DUNN ♦ "The Net Is Getting, Like, Really Stupid," *New York Times* (3/19/95):
I have seen the future . . . and it is Tom's toilet.
It's nothing fancy, mind you, just a plain bowl, white ceramic, chrome flush handle, ashtray on top. But through the wonders of modern technology, Tom has placed a digital image of his toilet for the viewing pleasure of millions of computer users. . . .
Travelers along the Information Superhighway can now gaze at the Cyperstare, a picture of an eyeball that does nothing; browse the hURL

home page for several hundred expressions for the word "vomit"; see what Sho Kuwamoto, a Purdue University graduate student, is eating for lunch today; watch a video of Cindy Crawford morphing into Claudia Schiffer; click on a really big button that does nothing; and submit an electronic confession to some geeks in the computer sciences department of Carnegie Mellon University on a home page that boasts: "bringing the net to its knees since 1994."

STUART ELLIOTT ♦ "The Media Business: Advertising," *New York Times* (8/25/94):
If you can reed this, may bee its time too work on Maddison Avenue.

The advertising industry, as that worst-case sentence suggests, seems increasingly in need of spelling lessons. More advertisements are appearing in magazines and newspapers—and sometimes on television—replete with misspellings that range from minor mistakes in tiny type in the texts to major mishaps in large-type headlines.

The prevalence and frequency of these misspellings indicate they are not typographical errors. These are among some recent examples:

¶An eight-page insert in advertising and media trade publications from Paramount Communications, thanking the cast and crew of "Star Trek: The Next Generation" as that series ended its run, featured a quotation attributed to "T. S. Elliot."

¶Advertisements for the Psychic Friends Network telephone line in Cosmopolitan magazine included a description of a caller who lived in "Lancing, Michigan."

¶A newspaper advertisement for Continental Airlines showed one airline passenger addressing another as "Susy" and King Kong asking a woman "Say mam can you tell me the way to the Empire State Building?"

¶A commercial for Nobody Beats the Wiz praised the consumer electronics retailer for being "emminent" in its field.

JONATHAN FRANZEN ♦ "The Reader in Exile," *The New Yorker* (3/6/95):
The electronic apotheosis of mass culture has merely reconfirmed the élitism of literary reading, which was briefly obscured in the novel's heyday. I mourn the eclipse of the cultural authority that literature once possessed, and I rue the onset of an age so anxious that the pleasure of a text becomes difficult to sustain. I don't suppose that many other people will give away their TVs. I'm not sure I'll last long myself without buying a new one. But the first lesson reading teaches is how to be alone.

TRIP GABRIEL ♦ "Public Relations Has Potent Image," *New York Times* (3/17/95):
. . . At America's journalism and mass communications schools, there are more students majoring in public relations today than in print reporting and editing.

"A lot of the stories you see on the news are generated by public relations people," says Michael McHenry, a 21-year-old member of the N.Y.U. [p.r.] club. . . .

Susanne Shaw, a journalism professor at the University of Kansas, says, "If I have two or three students out of 15 or 20 in a basic reporting class today who want to be reporters, that's good. . . ."

[The N.Y.U. club's] adviser, Ms. Hauser, told them public relations people had no reason to apologize for their profession, which can trace its roots in America all the way to Samuel Adams, the revolutionary patriot and newspaper essayist. What was the Boston Tea Party, which Adams helped plan, but a publicity stunt? How about the way he hyped the shooting of a handful of colonists by labeling it the Boston Massacre? "Talk about spinning!" said Ms. Hauser, a peppy woman who used to be a guest host for a daytime talk show on Channel 5 in New York and is now an assistant professor.

DAVID GELERNTER ♦ "The End of Dignity," *New York Times,* Op-Ed page (3/5/95):
The American Museum of Natural History in New York City plans to tear down the old Hayden Planetarium and replace it with something snazzier: an 80-foot sphere in a glass box. The outside of the sphere will function as a giant projection screen, capable of flashing thousands of images simultaneously. . . .

In itself, the proposed new planetarium does no harm. I'll miss the old building, but not because it is an architectural masterpiece. In a larger sense, though, those bulldozers will be plowing calm dignity under and replacing it with glitz, hype and somersaults, and we will all be worse off for it. . . .

Before tearing down the Hayden Planetarium, the museum might stage one last exhibit in there. Call it "On the wisdom of the society that built this condemned planetarium." Forgo just this once (as a special favor to children) the tendentious recitation of American sins that has turned so many contemporary history books, articles and exhibits into sanctimonious rot. Tell us instead what our grandparents did right, which of their accomplishments we ought to treasure, what aspects of the society they built were noble—and are gone.

OLIVER GOLDSMITH ♦ the Dutch schoolmaster in *The Vicar of Wakefield* (1766):
I have ten thousand florins a year without Greek, I eat heartily without Greek, and in short, as I don't know Greek, I do not believe there is any good in it.

ADAM GOPNIK ♦ "Read All About It," *The New Yorker* (12/12/94):
In the past twenty years, the American press has undergone a transformation from an access culture to an aggression culture: the tradition,

developed after the Civil War, in which a journalist's advancement depended on his intimacy with power, has mutated into one in which his success can also depend on a willingness to stage visible, ritualized displays of aggression. The reporter used to gain status by dining with his subjects; now he gains status by dining on them. . . . Aggression has become a kind of abstract form, practiced in a void of ideas, or even of ordinary sympathy. In a grim paradox, the media in America, because their aggression has been kept quarantined from good ideas, have become surprisingly vulnerable to bad ideas. Having turned themselves into a forum for the sort of craziness that was previously kept to the margins of American life, the media have nothing left to do but watch the process, and act as though it were entertaining; the jaded tone and the prosecutorial tone are masks, switched quickly enough so that you can appear active and neutral at the same time. Or, to put it another way, the cynicism and the sanctimony turn out to be a little like electricity and magnetism—two aspects of a single field, perpetuating themselves in a thought-free vacuum.

STEPHEN JAY GOULD ♦ "The Monster's Human Nature," *Natural History* (7/94):
Shelley's *Frankenstein* is a rich book of many themes, but I can find little therein to support the Hollywood reading. The text is neither a diatribe on the dangers of technology nor a warning about overextended ambition against a natural order. We find no passages about disobeying God—an unlikely subject for Mary Shelley and her free-thinking friends (Percy had been expelled from Oxford in 1811 for publishing a defense of atheism). Victor Frankenstein (I do not know why Hollywood changed him to Henry) is guilty of a great moral failing, . . . but his crime is not technological transgression against a natural or divine order.

We can find a few passages about the awesome power of science, but these words are not negative. . . .

But Hollywood dumbed these subtleties down to the easy formula—"man must not go beyond what God and nature intended" . . .—and has been treading in its own footsteps ever since. The latest incarnation, *Jurassic Park*, substitutes a *Velociraptor*, re-created from old DNA, for Karloff, cobbled together from bits and pieces of corpses, but hardly alters the argument an iota. Spielberg's *Jurassic Park* also dumbs down Michael Crichton's book. . . .

CLEMENT GREENBERG ♦ "Avant-Garde and Kitsch," *Partisan Review* (1939):
Where there is an avant-garde, generally we also find a rear-guard. True enough—simultaneously with the entrance of the avant-garde, a second new cultural phenomenon appeared in the industrial West: that thing to which the Germans give the wonderful name of Kitsch: popular, commercial art and literature with their chromeotypes, magazine covers,

illustrations, ads, slick and pulp fiction, comics, Tin Pan Alley music, tap dancing, Hollywood movies, etc., etc. . . .

The precondition for kitsch, a condition without which kitsch would be impossible, is the availability close at hand of a fully matured cultural tradition, whose discoveries, acquisitions, and perfected self-consciousness kitsch can take advantage of for its own ends. It borrows from it devices, tricks, stratagems, rules of thumb, themes, converts them into a system, and discards the rest. It draws its life blood, so to speak, from this reservoir of accumulated experience. This is what is really meant when it is said that the popular art and literature of today were once the daring, esoteric art and literature of yesterday. Of course, no such thing is true. What is meant is that when enough time has elapsed the new is looted for new "twists," which are then watered down and served up as kitsch.

BARBARA GRIZZUTI HARRISON ◆ "P.C. on the Grill," *Harper's* (June 1992):

Why do people lap up [the Frugal Gourmet's] arts-and-craftsy pretentious approach to food, which owes nothing to art, science, or sensuality? The short answer is that we live in a debased intellectual climate. Why have they made him the guru cook of our troubled times? For an inspirational buzz that exacts no intellectual toll and obliges one to do nothing but be the passive recipient of factoids. . . . For the same reason people take guided tours: to take home fortune cookies, packaged wisdom, not too stressful on the brain. And, loving everybody, he gives us all somebody to hate: the Puritan, a bogeyman we never meet at the grocery store, a specter who never tries to rent our apartment or take away our job. Why is he beloved? The short answer is that people are stupid.

He is not stupid. He writes, he says, to satisfy "a hunger for meaning." People are *not* stupid; they are needy. And he panders, the result being spiritual and political malnutrition. . . . Why do people allow themselves to be patronized? Probably because, in spite of the fact that we are forever told that our trouble is lack of self-esteem, we are all indeed guilty of something; he's a minister—he knows this.

People like small, manageable worlds—hence our enduring fascination with dollhouses, our addiction to epigrammatic bestsellers, our attachment to slogans and buzzwords that address complexity without unraveling it. In a world of terrifying complexity we keep the furniture of our minds tidy, light, disposable, ready for the next change of fashion, the season's trend.

WILLIAM A. HENRY III ◆ *In Defense of Elitism* (New York: Doubleday, 1994):
The prevailing popular notion that high culture is hard brain-work is, in fact, true. That is part of its point, not necessarily to exclude the less able but certainly to challenge them to stretch themselves and to heighten their learning.

American popular culture does not embrace this certification of art as work. Indeed the word *art* is rarely used at all. The preferred signifier is the word *entertainment,* which correctly conveys that the aspirations are generally escapist, nostalgic, or anodyne. Entertainment promises to make you feel better, to help you forget your troubles, to liberate you from having to think. Even when entertainment touches deep feelings, it does so as a gesture of reassurance, a combination of sentiment and sloganeering. This is what most people say they want, and the market lets them have it without anyone in a position of intellectual or social leadership telling them that they should ask more of themselves—and might benefit thereby.

BOB HERBERT ♦ "A Nation of Nitwits," *New York Times,* Op-Ed page (3/1/95):
I turned on "Beavis and Butt-head" the other night, and it was so much worse—so much more stupid—than anything I had imagined that I just sat staring in astonishment. I had a notebook in my hand, which was ridiculous. You can't make notes about "Beavis and Butt-head." . . .

Some African-American students, unable to extricate themselves from the quicksand of self-defeat, have adopted the incredibly stupid tactic of harassing fellow blacks who have the temerity to take their studies seriously. According to the poisonous logic of the harassers, any attempt at acquiring knowledge is a form of "acting white," and that, of course, is to be shunned at all costs. . . .

Americans who willingly swim in a sea of ignorance can blame themselves when the quality of their lives deteriorates.

STEVEN A. HOLMES ♦ "Even if the Numbers Don't Add Up," *New York Times* (8/14/94):
If America is the land of the free, it is also the home of the telling statistic, numbers proffered by politicians, interest groups or businesses to cajole, comfort or frighten the public into accepting their particular view of the world. Increasingly, as in the examples just cited, the statistics are confusing, contradictory or just plain wrong. . . . [What concerns many is that] statistics, which were once held in high esteem, will go the way of television advertisement or promises by campaigning politicians—dismissed out of hand as lacking credibility. . . .

Advocacy groups say it is all well and good for academics to compose odes to the purity of data. In the highly charged world of interest group politics, the correct spin is important, and if gaining that means manipulating numbers or emphasizing one set of statistics over another, then so be it.

GERALD HOWARD ♦ "Divide and Deride," the *Nation* (12/20/93):
It seems to me that this nation's media elite—the people who make the

deals, create the networks, conceive, write and produce the shows, the albums, the books—are well along in their own meretricious form of strip mining. They are stripping away what was already a shallow overlay of national taste and intelligence in an incredibly lucrative dive down-market. The Flavor of the Month in the media supermarket is Stupid, preferably with generous toppings of Vulgar and Vicious. Stupid sells— does it ever. . . . And if the nation's cultural landscape eventually looks like the most ravaged sections of western Pennsylvania once did, and the number of people who can distinguish wit from witlessness and sexual allure from full-frontal exposure is reduced to a corporal's guard, well, that's the cost of doing business. The numbers say you are giving people what they want, and numbers, famously, don't lie.

PHILIP K. HOWARD ♦ "Put the Judges Back in Justice," *New York Times,* Op-Ed page (4/3/95):
Boiling water must be handled with care. Every day millions of Americans nonetheless heat water past 212 degrees and make coffee with it. Many then get into their cars, hot coffee in hand. Some may burn themselves.

Most people agree that this [is] an ordinary risk of life. That's why the $2.7 million punitive damages verdict against McDonald's for serving 180-degree coffee, now a part of American folklore, symbolizes the judicial excesses that the new Congress is rightly seeking to cure. . . .

Forty years ago, there were no lawsuits over hot coffee. Such claims were tossed out long before a jury was selected because judges acted as gatekeepers. Today, judges are reluctant to take on this role; they act more like referees. Any claim that can make it over a low threshold of conceivability can go before a jury.

Courts, supposedly the anchor of social sanity, have become a kind of theater, with Hollywood-sized riches available to those who give the best performance. Anyone with the good fortune to have a misfortune can get rich on unmeasurable claims of pain and suffering.

ROBERT HUGHES ♦ in *New York Review of Books* (2/16/95):
Reading is a collaborative act, in which your imagination goes halfway to meet the author's; you visualize the book as you read it, you participate in making up the characters and rounding them out—Captain Hook, Mowgli, Alice, and the rest. The effort of bringing something vivid out of the neutral array of black print is quite different, and in my experience far better for the imagination, than passive submission to the bright icons of television, which come complete and overwhelming, and tend to burn out the tender wiring of a child's imagination because they allow no reworking.

MICHAEL JANOFSKY ♦ "Mock Auction of Slaves: Education or Outrage?" *New York Times* (10/8/94):

WILLIAMSBURG, Va., Oct. 7—Here on Monday afternoon, four blacks— two men and two women—are scheduled to be auctioned to the highest bidder. They will stand outside a tavern while a dozen people look them over and call out how much they are willing to spend. The event is open to the public.

The "slaves" will be actors and the auction a drama, part of a three-day program called "Publick Times" designed to re-create life in Colonial Williamsburg. Organizers say the auction is intended only to educate visitors about a brutal yet important part of Black American history. But critics around the state contend that education could be trivialized into entertainment and that, in any case, slave auctions were too painful to revive in any form.

"Our phones have been ringing off the hook," said Salim Khalfani of the Virginia branch of the National Association for the Advancement of Colored People.

LEON JAROFF ♦ "Science: Teaching Reverse Racism," *Time* (4/4/94):

Afrocentrist myths have taken hold in higher education as well, extending beyond black-studies courses. In one of the required multicultural courses for freshmen at Southern Methodist University, for example, the Rev. Clarence Glover, director of intercultural education and minority affairs, tells students that melanin content generates certain emotional reactions. He suggests that those with little melanin and a Nordic background are "member-object" oriented: they rely on objects like warm clothing made of animal skins to survive. But Africans, with more melanin, he says, "have a 'member-member' orientation and value human relationships more than objects."

MICHIKO KAKUTANI ♦ "Art Is Easier the 2nd Time Around," *New York Times* (10/30/94):

Recycling is no longer confined to Diet Coke cans and Evian water bottles. It's become one of the dominant impulses in American culture today. . . . Whether you call it nostalgia, postmodernism or a simple vandalizing of the past, all this recycling essentially amounts to the same thing: a self-conscious repudiation of originality, a bemused preference for style over content and a boundless faith in the creative possibilities of irony and spin. . . . the current vogue has no real interest in using its borrowed references in the service of a larger artistic vision, no interest in participating in an intelligent conversation with the past.

WENDY KAMINER ♦ *I'm Dysfunctional, You're Dysfunctional* (Reading, Mass.: Addison-Wesley, 1992):

Some will call me an elitist for disdaining popular self-help literature

and the popular recovery movement; but a concern for literacy and critical thinking is only democratic. The popularity of books comprising
slogans, sound bites, and recipes for success is part of a larger, frequently
bemoaned trend blamed on television and the failures of public education and blamed for political apathy. Intellectuals, right and left, complain about the debasement of public discourse the way fundamentalist
preachers complain about sex. Still, to complain just a little—recently
the fascination with self-help has made a significant contribution to the
dumbing down of general interest books and begun changing the relationship between writers and readers; it is less collegial and collaborative
than <u>didactic.</u> Today, even critical books about ideas are expected to be
prescriptive, to conclude with simple, step-by-step solutions to whatever
crisis they discuss. Reading itself is becoming a way out of thinking.

ALFRED KAZIN ♦ "Big Apple, Falling," *New York Times,* Op-Ed page
(3/26/95):

   I was silent when the kid walking right in front of me spat through the
open window of a car parked on 97th Street. I was silent when the cop in
the squad car, impatient to roll on, yelled "Move it!" ("it" obviously
being me). I am in my 80th year and I was crossing Broadway too slowly
for his convenience. I was silent when the lady on 42nd Street just threw
off the wrappings of her chocolate bar. Silent when the brat in the M-104
bus captured the seat that had been given up by a young woman for an
old woman. When the young woman protested he jeered, "Does the seat
have your name on it? . . ."

   Actually, I was not always this silent, cowardly and apathetic in the
face of so much incivility—and worse—in the city of which I am a proud
citizen. (The words "city," "citizen" and "civility" all spring from the
same Sanskrit root, *siva,* meaning "friendly, hence dear to one," according to Eric Partridge's "Origins.") I once gently reminded a girl who had
left the remains of her lunch on the steps of her school that this was not
showing much consideration for others. There was no resentment or
anger in her reply. She just looked blankly back at me. . . .

   The problem, as always, is that while this is our city, the city of all, too
few remember what we owe to each other as fellow citizens.

GARRISON KEILLOR ♦ "New Yorker Magazine Goes to Dogs," *Los Angeles
Times* (4/6/95):

   Tina Brown hasn't changed the New Yorker, she has obliterated it.

   There is still a magazine, just as there is still a place in Manhattan
called Penn Station, but nobody confuses it with the old one. And now,
this past week—the April Fool's Day edition—you opened the magazine
to a portfolio of Annie Leibowitz photos of the O. J. Simpson trial and its
inhabitants and you heard the whoosh of an American institution suddenly getting smaller. . . .

Some people considered the magazine elitist because it published a few writers who wrote better than anybody else in the world, but great writing is truly democratic, open to all. What's really snooty is to put out commercial garbage for an audience that you yourself feel superior to. . . .

So long, Mr. Shawn, and good night, E. B. White.

ROGER KIMBALL ♦ "Art in the Mass Culture," *Literary Review* (2/95):
The hypertrophy of public relations efforts is not the only result of the commercialization of museums. In the effort to increase crowds, the "product" has been adulterated too. This has taken many forms. One especially worrying development has been the tendency of even major museums to compete or collaborate with art galleries in presenting "cutting edge" art. The result is that many art museums, which not so long ago functioned as custodians of tradition, are now slaves to novelty. The result, alas, is not greater artistic vitality, as the museums' PR departments would have us believe, but a sort of puerile unseemliness.

The replacement of traditional standards of aesthetic accomplishment by the fickle banner of novelty and radical chic is one problem. Another is the relentless "dumbing down" of museums. More and more exhibitions, it seems, are organized for shock value or crowd appeal. Conversely, the chances of mounting an exhibition that may draw only a moderate or small public are dwindling. "Quality" and "connoisseurship," once sacred words for museum curators, are these days routinely excoriated as politically incorrect holdovers from a period when museums were "elitist" institutions.

R. J. LAMBROSE ♦ "Why Johnny's Professor Can't Read," *Lingua Franca* (January/February 1995):
Columbia [University]'s D. A. Miller claimed to have "left literature" for Broadway musicals and muscle magazines, while a few miles away, NYU's Andrew Ross told a *New York* magazine reporter that he's "hardly got time to read books anymore," only "glossy magazines." And only last May Gridley Stoker wrote a column in the San Francisco fanzine, *h2so4*, devoted to "Reviews of Books I Haven't Read and Why I Haven't Read Them."

DWIGHT MACDONALD ♦ "Masscult & Midcult," *Partisan Review* (spring 1960):
Masscult is very, very democratic; it refuses to discriminate against or between anything or anybody. All is grist to its mill and all comes out finely ground indeed.

Life is a typical homogenized magazine, appearing on the mahogany library tables of the rich, the glass cocktail tables of the middle class, and the oilcloth kitchen tables of the poor. Its contents are as thoroughly homogenized as its circulation. The same issue will present a serious

exposition of atomic energy followed by a disquisition on Rita Hay-
worth's love life; photos of starving children picking garbage in Calcutta
and of sleek models wearing adhesive brassieres; an editorial hailing
Bertrand Russell's eightieth birthday (A GREAT MIND IS STILL ANNOYING AND
ADORNING OUR AGE) across from a full-page photo of a matron arguing
with a baseball umpire (MOM GETS THUMB); nine color pages of Renoir
paintings followed by a picture of a roller-skating horse; a cover announcing in the same size type two features: A NEW FOREIGN POLICY, BY
JOHN FOSTER DULLES and KERIMA: HER MARATHON KISS IS A MOVIE SENSATION.
Somehow these scramblings together seem to work all one way, degrading the serious rather than elevating the frivolous. Defenders of our
Masscult society . . . see phenomena like *Life* as inspiriting attempts at
popular education—just think, nine pages of Renoirs! But that roller-
skating horse comes along, and the final impression is that both Renoir
and the horse were talented.

MARY MCCARTHY ◆ quoted (from an unpublished prospectus) by Dwight
Macdonald in his essay "Masscult & Midcult," *Partisan Review* (spring
1960):

A great abstract force governing our present journalism is a concep-
tualized picture of the reader. The reader, in this view, is a person stupider than the editor whom the editor both fears and patronizes. He
plays the same role the child plays in the American home and school, the
role of an inferior being who must nevertheless be propitiated. *What our
readers will take* is the watchword. . . . When an article today is adulterated, this is not done out of respect for the editor's prejudices (which
might at least give us an individualistic and eccentric journalism) but in
deference to the reader's averageness and supposed stupidity. The fear
of giving offense to some hypothetical dolt and the fear of creating a
misunderstanding have replaced the fear of advertisers' reprisals.

NEW YORK TIMES ◆ "After a Money Hunt, a Library's Real Treasures Are
in Tatters" (4/8/94):

FORT WORTH, April 7—Classics by James Joyce, Alexandre Dumas and
Zane Grey lay atop stacks of irreparably damaged books at the Fort
Worth Central Library today. Their spines cracked, covers ripped and
pages torn, they seemed unlikely victims of a frenzied mob.

But these works of masters were among the thousands of books
hurled from shelves and mauled on Tuesday evening as more than 500
people stampeded through the downtown library looking for money.
They were responding to an announcement by a Dallas radio station that
it had placed $5 and $10 bills in books in the fiction section of the library.
The station, KYNG-FM, urged listeners to go on a treasure hunt. . . .

"Books were sailing, and elbows were flying, and people were climb-
ing the shelves," a spokeswoman for the library, Marsha Anderson, said.

She was preparing to leave work on Tuesday until people, ranging in age from youths [and] teens to the elderly, began streaming into the library after 5 P.M. for the money.

GUSTAVE NIEBUHR ♦ "The Minister as Marketer: Learning from Business," *New York Times* (4/18/95):

In a vivid encounter with the allures of secular culture a few years back, the Rev. Walt Kallestad, a Lutheran pastor in suburban Phoenix, found a hard lesson for the church.

At a shopping mall, he came across a long, snaking line of people waiting to see the movie "Batman."

"How in the world," he remembered asking a friend, "could we ever create something so exciting in church, where people would wait four and a half [h]ours to get in?

"Then I made a flippant comment," he added in a recent interview. "Entertainment is really the medium of the day."

With its electric bands playing contemporary music, its dramatic skits and its sermons that focus on the tough issues of everyday living, Pastor Kallestad's church, the Community Church of Joy, does not quite have the pull of "Batman." But it draws upward of 2,500 adults and 1,500 children a week, which places it in the ranks of the United States' megachurches.

DR. ARNO A. PENZIAS ♦ 1978 Nobel Prize winner and executive of Bell Labs, quoted in *New York Times* (6/20/95):
Dr. Penzias acknowledged that the emphasis at Bell Labs was now on the development of commercially valuable devices and systems, not the pursuit of scientific knowledge per se. "It's true that the changes have been made to benefit the shareholders and customers, not basic science . . . but that's as it should be, because the world has changed."

RETHA POWERS ♦ caption in "Brat Rap," *New York Times Magazine* (3/5/95):
Vicious Lyrics: *"Some gal a freak, some gal a freak a de week."* Promiscuous women, the subject of "Freaks," is a surprising topic for a 13-year-old, but Delores Riley, Vicious's mother, is unfazed. "Whether he sings dirty or not he knows exactly what he wants." A Sega Genesis video game was the only item he bought with his advance money from his first album, "Destination Brooklyn." The remainder went toward private school and what one hopes is not an occupational hazard—medical bills incurred when he was wounded in a crossfire shooting in 1992.

JUDITH REGAN ♦ quoted in *New York* (9/11/95):
GUSH OF THE WEEK: "I *do* think if someone were to read his book in 200 years, they would get a very good look at what was going on in late-twentieth-century American culture. I think he is a great social commen-

tator on the degenerate life we're living."—Judith Regan, editor of Howard Stern's still-untitled second book [*Miss America*], saying she wasn't kidding when she told the *New York Post*, "First there was Shakespeare, then Steinbeck, now there's Stern."

JOHN H. RICHARDSON ◆ "Dumb and Dumber," *New Republic* (4/10/95): So how did these smart guys [Ricardo Mestres, Harvard-educated head of Disney's Hollywood pictures, and Barry Josephson, producer of *The Last Action Hero*] wind up making such horrible movies? Ricardo talked about the culture of Disney, about being trapped by the high-concept, low-budget approach to comedy that worked so well for them early in the 1980s, about not having money for stars. And it all made sense, sort of.

Then I remembered a scene from *Taking Care of Business*. Jim Belushi and a Japanese businessman are at a lunch meeting with an obnoxious career woman. Finally Belushi puts the career woman in her place by walking out on this exit line: "Nice titties." Then the Japanese businessman walks out in solidarity, repeating the line. I think the joke is that he doesn't really know what he's saying, being Japanese. When I first saw this scene I had to rewind my VCR twice to make sure that I'd really seen it, and ever since I have tried to picture Ricardo and his hypersmart then-boss, Jeffrey Katzenberg, sitting in a screening room watching it. What did they say to each other? What did they think? Did their wives see this movie?

Ricardo explained it this way: they knew the picture wasn't working, but they couldn't stop it. "You hire the director, and the director owns the set."

HANNA ROSIN ◆ "Woolly Pulpit," *New Republic* (3/13/95): "People think of the church as a draconian thing of the past, with big towers and iron gates and frocked people who do weird things and speak a language no one understands," the pastor explains. "We get the message out that we are relevant," as relevant as, say, your local mall. "The shopping center makes you feel comfortable," clarifies Assistant Pastor Frank Bouts. "We want our church to be equally as customer-service oriented, or equally as sensitive to the needs of all the seekers, all the first-time visitors who come here."

SIMON SCHAMA ◆ "The Princess of Eco-Kitsch," *New York Times*, Op-Ed page (6/14/95): No one, though, is in much danger of confusing "Pochahantas" with a history lesson, not least because its makers have gone out of their way to avoid the less upbeat features of the true story. . . . Disney's determination to make its eco-historical fable all bright and shiny was symbolized by the prohibition of cigarettes at the premiere. This ban was apparently observed by the cast as well, so that the Powhatans are the only nicotine-free Native Americans ever shown on the big screen. A pity, really, since cultivating tobacco was one of the few practices that Europeans and natives had in common.

To show that tobacco was as much part of native life as corn would have been inconvenient. But then history, like nature, is full of awkward blemishes. They give its stories the pungency of truth, and they resist being rendered down to so much moral candy.

ARTHUR SCHOPENHAUER ♦ "On Books and Writing," *Essays and Aphorisms* (1851; Penguin trans., 1970):
And then again, there can be said to be three kinds of author. Firstly, there are those who write without thinking. They write from memory, from reminiscence, or even directly from other people's books. This class is the most numerous.—Secondly, there are those who think while writing. They think in order to write. Very common.—Thirdly, there are those who have thought before they started writing. They write simply because they have thought. Rare.

AMY E. SCHWARTZ ♦ "The Newest Fashion Accessory: Books," *Boston Globe* (7/8/94):
Surely it's an ad for a dress sale—on the cover is a gorgeous glossy shot of a model in flowing white pantsuit, posed against a Grecian blue sky and sea. Across the bottom, in white letters, runs this legend: "The LITERARY GUILD: The book club for all the women you are." . . .

Marketing creates weird hybrids, but the mating of the book club with Cosmopolitan and the Saks catalogue may be the weirdest yet. . . . The categories, though, are strangely random. . . . "At Home . . . for the Homebody in you" offers "Webster's New World Dictionary" and "Betty Crocker's New Choices Cookbook," but it's not clear how this differs from "Smart Moves . . . for the clever side of you," which has "Weight Watchers' Slim Way With Pasta" and Roget's "Thesaurus."

What are these books being sorted by—color? Or has somebody in publishing taken that final step and decided that selling books for their contents is hopelessly passé? [Editorial director Arlene] Friedman insists not: "We describe the books more than before. They're always the main attraction. But our creative director comes out of advertising, and he's a very high fashion oriented person."

JANNY SCOTT ♦ "Half a Wit Meets Technology," *New York Times* (5/14/95):
Anyway, who's to say what's dumb? Or, as Jack Romanos, president of Simon & Schuster Consumer Publishing Group, put it: "What makes anyone think Howard Stern is not an intellectual?" (Mr. Romano's company publishes Mr. Stern.)

JUSTICE DAVID H. SOUTER ◆ from the unanimous Supreme Court decision (6/19/95) to exclude gay marchers from the Boston St. Patrick's Day parade:
The very idea that a noncommercial speech restriction be used to produce thoughts and statements acceptable to some groups or, indeed, all people, grates on the First Amendment, for it amounts to nothing less than a proposal to limit speech in the service of orthodox expression.

PATRICIA MEYER SPACKS ◆ "The Simpson Jury's Right to Be Needy," *New York Times,* Op-Ed page (6/9/95):
What has led us to expect constant distraction? Our forebears proclaimed our inalienable right to the pursuit of happiness. They did not guarantee we would find it. Nor did they suggest a sense of grievance as the appropriate response to a lack of external stimulation. Today's consumers have established new emotional expectations and converted them into quasi-rights. The world rarely gives us what we want, yet we feel aggrieved by our unsatisfied desires. This sense of entitlement has even infected our required role as temporary arbiters of justice and other obligations of citizenship.

ROBERT J. THOMPSON ◆ Associate Professor of Television, Syracuse University, in *New York Times* (11/13/94):
If you back me against a wall, I would say ostensibly, as a piece of art "Hamlet" is in some ways superior to "Lou Grant."

KURT VONNEGUT ◆ from the story "Harrison Bergeron," *Welcome to the Monkey House* (Laurel paperback edition, 1988; first published in *Fantasy and Science Fiction Magazine*, 1961):
The Year was 2081, and everybody was finally equal. They weren't only equal before God and the law. They were equal every which way. Nobody was smarter than anybody else. Nobody was better looking than anybody else. Nobody was stronger or quicker than anybody else. All this equality was due to the 211th, 212th, and 213th Amendments to the Constitution, and to the unceasing vigilance of agents of the United States Handicapper General.

AUBERON WAUGH ◆ "You Don't Laugh When Your Friends Have a Virus," *Literary Review* (May 1995):
No, we must agree that the film *Forrest Gump* is an important document for the understanding of American culture, but the key statement in it is surely the announcement "Forrest, I got a virus," made by the female lead shortly before she dies of AIDS. It was that statement which had the American audiences weeping in the course of the film's $314 million run,

not the proposition about the box of chocolates. The reason their eyes pricked with sentimental self-pity was that they realized it was true. There is a sickness in American society and it may well prove fatal. It is called stupidity. A society which panders to the stupidity and ignorance of its lowest rungs and allows them to set the scene for the entire culture is bound to have its own in-built death factor, even without the symbolic presence of AIDS to cross every "t" and dot every "i." This may help to explain why my autobiography failed to find a publisher in America.

Tom Wicker and Gore Vidal ♦ "MM Interview," *Modern Maturity* (April–May 1994):
Modern Maturity: At breakfast you suggested that artistic achievement tends to be flat around the world.
Gore Vidal: All the arts seem to be on hold. Walt Whitman said that to have great poets, you must have great audiences. I think that holds true in all the arts. If there aren't people who can appreciate it, art withers and dies. Epic poetry is finished. The masque is gone, the verse play is gone, the serious novel is going. Novels by lawyers and thrillers by Stephen King should not have driven out serious books, but they have.
MM [Tom Wicker]: Why do we have more good writers today than good readers?
Vidal: The educational system. Fewer and fewer are addicted to reading. If they don't get into it from the time they are ten or 12 years old, they'll never enjoy reading. And if you don't *enjoy* reading, there goes literature. If a novel is any good it creates empathy—you're able to see what it was like to be somebody else. The standard of Roman education was to set a boy the problem of imagining he was a famous historical figure at a crucial moment in his career. An exiled Marius among the ruins of Carthage was a popular one. A marvelous exercise, highly developed. Literature is still the most profound of the arts, but its prognosis is very bad.

Leon Wieseltier ♦ "Against Identity," *New Republic* (11/28/94):
In the modern world, the cruelest thing that you can do to people is to make them ashamed of their complexity.

Garry Wills ♦ "The Tragic Pope?" *New York Review of Books* (12/22/94):
For most priests in the pulpit, the basic doctrines of the Church—the Trinity, the Incarnation—are "mysteries" in the sense that they are technical points of theology not "relevant" to Catholics' modern concerns. Sermons become therapeutic and empathetic, leveling farther down every day toward the *Oprah Winfrey Show*. . . .

But when I am asked whether I am a church-going Catholic and answer yes, no one inquires whether I really believe in such strange things as the Trinity, the Incarnation, the Resurrection. I am asked about ovaries and trimesters. The great mysteries of faith have become, for many inside the church as well as outside, the "doctrines" on contraception and abortion. These are hardly great concerns in the gospels and the letters of Saint Paul, which never mention them. But they crowd out most other talk of Catholic beliefs in modern conversation.

Introduction

by JOHN SIMON

John Simon was born in Yugoslavia and was educated there, in England, and at Harvard, where at his own measured pace he acquired a Ph.D. in comparative literature. He then misspent the remnant of his youth teaching at various universities before going into publishing. He ended up as a freelance writer and then film and drama critic for sundry magazines. He is now drama critic of *New York* magazine, film critic of *National Review,* and frequent contributor on literature and opera to *New Criterion.*

P ERHAPS the greatest epigraph I know is Ödön von Horváth's to his play *Stories from the Vienna Woods:* "Nichts gibt so sehr das Gefühl der Unendlichkeit als wie die Dummheit"—nothing gives you such a sense of the infinite as stupidity. Of interest, too, is the solecism in the phrasing: *als wie* for *wie* is demotic or dialectal and can be taken either to corroborate or to undermine the statement. And the hero of Georg Büchner's masterpiece, *Woyzeck,* exclaims, "Man is an abyss. You get dizzy looking down in it." Do-gooders might write these aperçus out a hundred times each and ponder them.

There are fashions in everything—from restaurants to crime, from beachwear to stupidity. The following essays will inform you about the prevalent dumbing down in numerous fields of human endeavor (I say "human" because other animals show signs of getting smarter). I shall try to give you my impressions as a generalist, an Americanized European, a writer on various arts, and a hapless lover of culture who has pursued her vanishing hem around countless frustrating corners. I also listen to or eavesdrop on people in public places: in bistros and record stores, at theater exits and art galleries, on buses and talk shows. It is disheartening but revelatory.

If I had to name the most striking change I've come across in well over a half-century's observing and spying, I would probably pick the ever more frequent comings and goings in auditoriums: movie theaters especially, but also opera houses and playhouses. It is impossible to attend even a good movie these days without noticing the number of people who get up and leave at any time, to return several minutes later. It is equally impossible to say whether they go to the toilet, to smoke, to phone, or to buy another bag of popcorn. But go they do—one here, one over there—and come back to sit down as if nothing had happened. But something has: they have missed a charming scene, a crucial plot point, the most amusing line, or the moment that breaks the heart.

Some few of them may have valid excuses: a bladder may turn anticultural and downright inconsiderate. But these walkers out, who can be pretty distracting to the rest of the audience, cannot all be in crisis situations, and almost seem motivated by the mere desire to step on your toes during sublime moments. Talking through a movie has been with us since time began, but this is something new. It may have been generated by the to-and-fro before a home television set, and the growing inability to distinguish between one's apartment and a cinema.

So add this new disturbance to the old ones of talking, candy unwrapping, popcorn crunching, pocketbook unzipping, etc., none of which anyone nowadays dares to shush. Today's movie audience is the perfect picture of insensitivity, indifference, the dumbed-down mind. It shows that understanding the film is not a primary concern: one can get the general idea and kill a couple of hours without that. Watching a movie recently in Bradentown, Florida, I had to move four times to escape the chatterers around me. Then, since there seemed to be no safe area left, I asked the two sixteen-or-seventeenish girls behind me to please stop talking. "Why don't *you* move somewhere else?" one of them snapped back as the other grinned. No question, of course, of respect for my gray head; in the movie-house night, all cats are gray.

Still, I wonder, why pay for a movie ticket if all you want is to hear yourself and your friend talk? But perhaps the movie is needed to stimulate one's conversation and to empower one to talk back at the screen. For talking back has come to pass for wit. Even *on* the screen, not just in front of it. Film dialogue now seldom has prolonged repartee; almost always (as Phillip Lopate also notes) it is, in fencing terms, thrust, parry, kill. As much as with anything else—or more—this has to do with the shortening of the attention span. If genius is a great aptitude for patience, as Buffon is supposed to have said, might not intelligence be a modest aptitude for patience? Patience, of course, in both the filmmaker and the audience. A mediocre movie such as *The Bridges of Madison County* nevertheless achieves some distinction merely by allowing a relatively speedy love affair to come about in what feels like natural time: just by not rushing things the film takes on an otherwise undeserved worthiness and sagacity.

Impatience is of the essence. The impatience of minorities, for example, to be fully recognized, revered, and rewarded in their multicultural, countercultural, or uncultured splendor. (A single member of a minority is now called "a minority" with perfect illiteracy, but then, who still has or wants literacy?) The symmetrical impatience of the under- and overprivileged to get their dreary school years over with and earn (earn?) the diploma that opens the Sesame of success and wealth. The impatience of the real or imaginary outsider in gender, sexual preference, linguistic prowess, or cultural achievement to become an insider, and impose his or her own beliefs and rules on the world. What has become of Pascal's discovery that all human unhappiness stems from one single thing, the inability to stay calmly put inside a room? What has become of the German concept of *Sitzfleisch*, the ability to remain seated and pursue some useful activity without fidgeting?

And then the higher fidgets! The universal current conviction that one deserves better, that one is employed beneath one's station. Everyone dreaming of the higher job he or she has so richly merited, while botching the one he is lucky to have. I can't be bothered to give you correct change, help you find the suit that really suits you, transport your furniture without breaking it; I'm made for finer things: movie star, chairman of the board, president of the United States. And as the waiter dreams his dream of upward mobility, he spills the soup downward into your lap.

But do not think that this impatience at least protects us from its opposite, sluggishness. No such luck: in many areas where flexibility, elasticity, springiness—even hyperactivity—might be of some use, sloth, slowness, and mental constipation have taken over. Nowhere is this more clearly discernible than in our language. Not so very long ago Mallarmé was complaining that language was debased to something like the drably utilitarian process of putting a coin into the other person's hand. But such a prosaically functional use of language still beats today's stutter and sputter, the shuffling and meandering on the road to communication.

Take, first, that dreadful piece of detritus, the meaningless *like*. The *I means*, *you know*s, *kind of*s, and *sort of*s are bad enough; but they at least form a hesitation waltz to give the speaker time to gather his next thought, or focus more tightly on the current one. That bit of verbal litter, *like*, however, is something else—"something else" in the slang sense as well: something unconscionable, weird. It must not be mistaken for a more elegant synonym of *er*, with which speakers formerly tried to carpet the interstices of thought. It is too frequent to be that; nobody *er*red that consistently—not even a lighter-than-airhead on Hollywood Boulevard. That *like* is, rather, an attempt at emphasis or embellishment.

To a muddled mind, *like* may constitute a grace note, a bit of appoggiatura with which to decorate or even authenticate one's discourse. To the simple soul, those *like*s are so many hard, gemlike rhinestones. But, as with most nonsensical things, opposite interpretations may apply just as well. Thus *like* may be a disavowal of responsibility: if you say "I was like minding my own business," the *like* may cover you if someone discovers that you weren't minding it. The awful, impersonal *hopefully* functions similarly: no one need assume the responsibility for that hope. Eventually, though, the *like* becomes a mere unthinking habit, a verbal rut.

Aside from being odious in itself, it may have contributed to the sad demise of *as*. How many, even expensively educated, speakers nowadays casually drop a "like I said" or "like he was crazy"? To be sure, it may be a case of the chicken and the egg, and *like* may have spread in the opposite direction. No matter: disease is disease, whether it spreads from right to left or from left to wrong. Either way, the entrenchment of that unlikable *like* would have been impossible without mental—or, rather, mindless—inertia.

This sluggishness begets many monsters. Perhaps the most obvious one is faulty analogy, which I take to be the cause of many, if not most, grammatical errors. Consider the case of the gratuitous or galloping *of* that has taken to cropping up where it has no business. Only a few years ago nobody said "It's not that big of a deal" or "Get off of my back!" Those *of*s are logically off-limits (soon, no doubt, to become "off of limits"), but logic has long since overtaken hen's teeth in rarity. This *of* sneaked (or, nowadays, *snuck*—yuck!) in by faulty analogy—just like *sung* for *sang*, for instance. Surely if you say "He is not much of an actor," you would also say "He is not that big of a star," right? If "you won't get anything out of me" is correct, then so must be "you won't get a dollar off of me."

It is also a question of another principle as obsolescent as logic: manners. To the question "Who cares how you say it as long as you are understood; isn't 'like I said' just as clear as 'as I said'?" the answer is, "Yes, but rather more distasteful." You can blow your nose as efficiently with your fingers as with a tissue or handkerchief, but isn't the former disgusting? In the vanished days when *elitism* was not a dirty word, bad grammar was much the same as bad manners: an offense against civility. The aristocracy could speak as badly as the lower classes, mind you; it is as easy to forget your education as not to receive it. Correct speakers, like famous writers, come from all walks of life, tree-lined or cobble-stoned. Classiness is classless.

The quantity and quality of education is, of course, the root problem. It is also what makes the future loom blacker and blacker. And in case you think there is only one kind of black, please refer to the art (art?) of Ad Reinhardt, where you'll find a huge selection of blacks. Whom are the young to learn English from? Their parents don't know it; their teachers don't know it or abhor it for reasons of political correctness (though in their own writing, they still practice it to the best of their abilities); ergo, good English may be just one gasp less dead than a doornail. Indeed, I may be parading my outmodedness: "good English"—what kind of a dinosaur is that? "Good English" is a monistic notion; today, all good things are multi-, or at least bi-.

Can there be an end to poor education? Hardly. It is self-perpetuating. If A has not taught B properly, how properly will B, when it is his turn, teach C? And should you aver that things must eventually bottom out, leaving them nowhere to go but up, let me refer you to that Horváth motto again: dumbness is bottomless, the perfect image of infinity. The only thing that could, in theory, reverse the process is a cataclysm. But in these postmodernist days, when brinkmanship has yielded to abyssmanship—or, rather, abysspersonship—we have learned to live with cataclysms. "The Rector's pallid neighbour at The Firs,/ Death, did not flurry the parishioners," begins Robert Graves's delightful "The Villagers and Death." That was some time ago; in today's global village, Megadeath can move right in without a cry of "There goes the neighborhood!" Or do you think that Rwanda, Bosnia, or Northern Ireland can have a sobering effect, bring about some sort of reform? Only near-total global destruction might make a difference, but some cures are worse than the disease.

In our schools, the slippery slope was renamed the Road to Eldorado: the diploma as a guarantee of well-paid jobs. What matters is not how you get there; just getting there is enough. And *there,* of course, is not an education; it is material success. How did things come to this pass? Read the following essays of this book, then apply whatever common sense you've got. Finally, though, etiology is immaterial; materialism is in, and there is no panacea—not so much as a nostrum.

Examples are close to hand, in whichever direction you stretch it. Take the *New York Times,* which is now so full of bad English that, if you have a sensitive stomach, it is unsafe to read at breakfast. The paper used to have Theodore Bernstein to teach it linguistic manners, but that worthy died and was, significantly, never replaced. I cannot give you a comprehensive overview of the situation; a few salient examples will have to suffice. Let's start with the caption under the picture of an East Village Indian restaurant whose effluvia polluted the air of the block. According to that caption, the desideratum was "a more higher awning." That, you might rebut, was a mere caption writer, captiously adduced as evidence. But things are unwell across the board, as some of the most distinguished *Times* writers ride, or write, roughshod over the language.

Take the case of *who* and *whom.* In the old days, some flounderers wrote *who* for *whom.* That was a mistake, and when it got out of hand, the sachems came up with a directive: abandon all *whom*s! The terminal M was terminated. Not a happy state of affairs, but not quite the worst, either. When the *Times,* rightly but vainly, readmitted *whom,* we got both the old error and an uglier new one: *whom* for *who*. *Who* for *whom* is a vulgar misdemeanor, like spitting on the sidewalk. *Whom* for *who* is like eating with your hands at a posh dinner party. And it glares at us from every section of the paper. Most strikingly perhaps in such an example as this, from the July 16, 1995, *Book Review*. Suzanne Berne, identified as a teacher of writing at Harvard University, writes (and, presumably, teaches), "Mr. Picano seems determined to tweak the AIDS-era gay generation (whom Roger suspects would accuse him of 'a serious lack of seriousness'). . . ." I doubt whether a generation, gay or straight, is a *who* rather than a *that* or *which*, but it surely isn't, in this construction, a *whom*.

This *whom* may be simple incompetence or what Fowler called a genteelism, a term that justly made it into our dictionaries. (You remember dictionaries? They are those books now consulted about as often as Migne's *Patrologia*. Quite right, too; because if you happen to consult them, they are only going to endorse whatever the vox populi ever uttered. This is what is called descriptive linguistics, although prescriptions are needed from linguists as much as from physicians.) People assume that *whom* is a form of gentility, like *bosom* for *breast, expectorate* for *spit,* or *ecdysiast* for what the *American Heritage Dictionary* defines as "striptease artist," a genteelism if ever there was one.

Still, distinguishing between *who* and *whom* requires a certain linguistic prowess; logic alone will not suffice. There are, however, other areas of language where logic—actually nothing more than common sense— will do the trick. Yet here, too, people are losing the ability to cope. Let me demonstrate.

Time was when people would say, "She wants to eat her cake and have it too." Nowadays, this has been turned on its head, and you will hear even educated speakers say, "She wants to have her cake and eat it too." The person who esuriently gobbled down her cake, then absurdly still wanted to have it, was a fine example of human folly. This made perfect sense as a warning: you cannot have what you have already eaten. But "She wants to have her cake and eat it too" is not hortatory, does not convey the intended impossibility. You can, after all, *have* a cake in your fridge, and enjoy the knowledge of possession; when the appropriate time comes, you take it out and *eat* it with equal satisfaction. Simple, and in no sense greedy or unrealizable.

If you want a plainer example of this illogic, take the widespread "I could care less," which has all but replaced the correct "I couldn't care less." The latter, denying the existence of any way of caring less, is the ne plus ultra of not caring. But "I could care less" means at a minimum that something is not all that important, and at a maximum that it is pretty important, because you could with a little effort find something else less important. Illogic is everywhere: the very concept *multiculturalism* is illogical: can you, for instance, be a multimillionaire before you have been a millionaire?

But let's explore this lack of logic where it might be most important—in education. Take the now prevalent notion that separate classes for bright and backward students are a form of elitism, and hence intolerable. The democratic way is to lump all students together, thereby not really helping the uneducable, while boring the educable out of their skulls, and making them equally uneducated in the end. Or how about the noble notion of bilingual education? The idea is that it is unfair to the poor darlings who have been talking, say, Spanish or some form of black English at home and in the streets to be taught in Standard English—a foreign language to them—in school. Where, if not in school, are they to learn Standard English then? At home and in the streets?

I am reminded of a television debate from California, quite a few years ago, about bilingual education. An educated, well-spoken Anglo woman was arguing against bilingualism, calling it divisive, which she pronounced correctly, with a diphthong in the middle. A Hispanic woman, arguing for bilingualism, did not consider it divisive, which she mispronounced as "divizzive." I don't remember the result—if any—of the discussion; I do, however, recall that the Anglo woman was soon saying "divizzive" as well. I don't think it was a case of Gresham's law kicking in, or of the bad example rubbing off; rather, it was a pitiful attempt at political correctness, at not making the poor Hispanic woman feel bad. (This was in those long-ago days when ignorance could still make someone feel embarrassment.) The Anglo woman most likely went back to the correct pronunciation after the show, but thousands of innocent victims were surely turned on to saying "divizzive."

Gestures of appeasement are usually paid for dearly, and not just by the weak-kneed compromiser, but also by anyone who would hold out against stultification. Yet there is capitulation on all sides, perhaps even in this book, which is supposed to oppose it. Thus we have Anthony DeCurtis writing here a highly literate and, from his point of view, closely argued essay in defense of rock and roll, which I consider a vast mistake. Yet I do not think that Mr. DeCurtis is one of those intellectual snobs who defend rock and roll for dishonest reasons. But I do think that his "defense of popular culture" is to some extent a matter of class—an unpopular term, which I am using, be it understood, descriptively rather than pejoratively. He tells us that he "grew up in a working-class . . . family—neither of my parents graduated from high school." If he had been of solid middle-class stock, he would most likely have found his way to opera early on. Instead, he depended on the radio, which broadcast opera on Saturday afternoons, and pop the rest of the time. And pop meant rock. Very few of us outgrow our early habits—another reason for not expecting much from the future, which will be formed by the dismal present.

"What is the point," Mr. DeCurtis asks, "of pitting one type of music, or one work of art. . .against another, as if in a popularity contest?" I agree with him: none. Of course, if the two things compared were both works of art, there would be a point, the very point on which all criticism—that now debased and dying art form—is founded. One does compare Maya Angelou and June Jordan with Elizabeth Bishop and John Crowe Ransom, and finds the former pair sadly wanting—easily demonstrable to anyone with half a brain and no political correctness or reverse racial prejudice. Similarly, one can compare Verdi and Bartók with Busoni and Douglas Moore, and find the former two superior. But how do you compare rock and roll and rap with classical music? That they are not comparable should be obvious to anyone who, unlike Mr. DeCurtis, does not write books and articles on rock and roll. Where, I ask you, is the popular music of 1900 a mere century later? Unknown, except by a few specialists. But Bach and Mozart, like Schubert and Berlioz, are with us after a much longer time, and show no sign of fading—on the contrary. Art and ephemera are indeed not comparable.

I remember interviewing on television Galt MacDermott, the composer of *Hair,* the first wildly successful rock musical, at the time of his hit. "Rock," he said, "is a fad, like other popular music; after a few years, it will be gone." Alas, he was wrong: MacDermott is gone; rock is still noisily with us. But that is precisely part of the dumbing down: rock and roll can be dislodged only by something worse, and something worse will be hard to find. Rap would qualify, only it will take an even more dumbed-down world than today's to mistake something that isn't any kind of music for music. But never fear: we'll get there. If by then rap is gone, it will be something equally outlandish.

To me, the most interesting part of Mr. DeCurtis's argument is his view that rejection of rock and roll is a betrayal of "very traditional notions of . . . intellectual life." It would take more space than I have to demonstrate musically that rock is to serious music what toe jam is to Dundee marmalade. Verbally, however, the proof is easier than pie. Look at any rock lyric you wish, and set it alongside a lyric by Cole Porter, Larry Hart, or Stephen Sondheim—never mind an operatic libretto by Boito, Hofmannsthal, or one of Benjamin Britten's librettists. The difference will hit you in the face stronger than Muhammad Ali or Mike Tyson could. And it's no use arguing that rock lyrics serve a different purpose, which is incontestable: they are near-meaningless noise set to meaningless noise for popular delectation.

Other essayists here have pointed out the setbacks endured by the intellect in their respective disciplines, and intellect has a great deal to do with the advancement of culture; talent can go only so far. To be sure, there exists also the danger of overcerebration, or of the mental hardening that rigid political or religious ideologies can bring about. That is why I take issue with David Klinghoffer's chapter in this book: I do not think that the return to stricter, more orthodox forms of religion is a good thing for our or any culture: it impedes the free play of thought that Matthew Arnold considered essential to cultural progress. There is, to my view, very little difference between the hardening of the arteries of such established religions as Catholicism and Judaism, and the rise of the even worse fanaticism of fringe cults, whether they are the Branch Davidians or the National Rifle Association.

But gun control, too, presupposes intelligence and intellectual courage, not likely to be found in elected officials more eager for reelection than for laws that would save more lives than a cure for AIDS. That is one of the dispiriting things about our society: no sooner have the forces of enlightenment made abortion legal, and so struck out on a path toward protecting this overcrowded planet from self-destruction, than the shock troops of reaction and religion strike back with anything from murder at abortion clinics to compulsory prayer in school. Thus, too, there are laws to make it hard to try out not fully proven but potentially life-saving drugs, whereas the opium of the masses, as prescribed by the religious right, is ready to return us to the Dark Ages. And how grimly, clenched-toothedly fanatical are these legions: between them on the right and the bleeding-heart liberals on the left, the middle way may very well be lost.

I also disagree with Joseph Epstein about the discontinuation of the National Endowment for the Arts. Any support, even to the wrong artists, is better than none; at least it stirs up controversy, and makes an inert public more aware that the arts exist and matter. Of course, if the NEA were in the right hands—neither dumbed down into stodginess nor dumbed up into trendiness—that would be the true solution; but that, given our bureaucracies, is too much to hope for. Still, the odd, not to say bizarre, awards to a Mapplethorpe or a Karen Finley do not take away from some other, more judicious grants. Compared to the Pavlovian political correctness of the MacArthur Foundation, for instance, the NEA actually stacks up fairly well.

Culture wars, however, are unlikely to dislodge the popular preoccupation with its true educator, television; its true religion, sports; and its true passion, the computer. The talk show, the game, and the Internet, these constitute the new trivium, and also the new triviality. They need one another, like all good trinities: talk is really talk only on TV or the Net; a sport is best when interpreted for you by the sportscaster; your relationships with others who have bitten into the Apple Notebook are virtually real, and really virtuous. Most pitiful to me is the adulation harvested by a self-enamored, infantile buffoon such as David Letterman; or, at the "educational" end of the TV spectrum, the sensitively probing Charlie Rose, who asks the questions prepared by his assistants with the same soulful oiliness with which Barbara Walters inquires into Barbra Streisand's political future and sexual present.

Television is particularly noxious with the role models it provides in its newscasters, sportscasters, and intellectual flycasters who parade themselves as anything from news analysts to film critics, like those two pundits who think with their fingers, and can best be described as Thumb and Thumber. Just now I heard on NBC about a friend of O.J.'s who "followed he and Nicole" somewhere or other, the reporter contributing to the day's most widespread grammatical error with his orotund, newscasterly authority. God forbid that there should be a foreign name in the news. Confronted with the vocable "Kafelnikov," the name of a Russian tennis ace and not that hard to pronounce, the CBS sportscaster tried three times, failed thrice, and finally gave up. Or take the name of the Bosnian town of Srebrenica, which, of the twenty or so mouths I have heard grappling with it from the corridors of the White House to the halls of *Nightline,* not one has yet mastered. In the old days, the networks had experts whose job it was to establish pronunciations. These experts were not always right, but at least they were not always wrong. So our dumbest medium gets dumbed down further.

Or consider what happened when that, to Judge Ito's and my minds, dullest sport, baseball, temporarily closed shop because of the competing greeds of the players and owners. The national pastime turned into a national tragedy. Suppose now that football and basketball were to follow suit. I imagine there would be mass suicides, dejected hordes wandering the streets, a dramatic increase in every sort of crime, and countless oversized, overweight, and overpaid men screaming bloody murder. The one consolation left would be that the fourth-most-popular spectator sport, O.J.-watching, is guaranteed to go on forever. If at least we could learn from our pruriently voyeuristic participation that trial by jury is an outmoded farce, that would be something. Failing that, we could perhaps get rid of the TV camera in the courtroom, thereby greatly expediting judgment, and cutting down the cost to the taxpayers.

And, speaking of a dramatic increase in crime, I should perhaps, as a drama critic, give you an account of what goes, or dumbs, down in our theaters. I could tell of the depredations of commercialism (hardly any dramas anymore, except about AIDS; otherwise, only floundering musicals and witless farces), of multiculturalism (countless pieces by members of minorities—preferably female, black, lesbian, and white-hating—which is what gets the needed subsidies), of color-blind casting (e.g., a Shakespeare history play wherein the king is black, the queen white, the older prince Hispanic, and the younger Asian-American), of economic pressure combining with self-indulgence (innumerable one-man or one-woman shows by all sorts of self-anointed artists relating the abysmally boring stories of their lives), of bursts of conspicuous spending (mindless musicals bedizened with billion-dollar finery). But my weekly theater and biweekly film columns have, in these areas, bereft me of breath.

It is hard—almost impossible—to be a drama or film *critic* in this society. Most of the reviewers are either unreconstructed fans or upward-failing reporters, prepared to like everything they see. This, either out of dumb conviction, or out of fear of losing their jobs. No reviewer was ever fired for liking too many things; the opposite would be harder to affirm. In general, media criticism is supposed to represent the views and tastes of the common man, sometimes referred to by the euphemistic honorific "Reader." I myself would sooner represent the views and tastes of a one-eyed camel; at least it carries its water in the hump, not on the brain. The idea of the critic as teacher has become almost as obsolete as that of the teacher as teacher.

I remember the poet James Dickey lamenting to me that his grandchildren might no longer be able to get up of a South Carolina morning to be greeted by a concert of songbirds sweetening the summer air. In worrying about his grandchildren, he may have been a bit premature; but what about the grandchildren's grandchildren, in this ecological disaster area in which we live? And please don't call this crying wolf: that great-hearted predator will, by then, be likewise extinct. "At the speed of ten machines," wrote the Peruvian poet César Vallejo, "misery grows":

> crece el mal por razones que ignoramos
> y es una inundación con propios líquidos,
> con propio barro y propia nube sólida! . . .

Yes, "evil grows for reasons we know not/ and is a flood with its own liquids,/its own mud and own solid cloud!" But, right as Vallejo is otherwise, is it a solid cloud? Or is it, in fact, a soft, mushy one, a cloud of unknowing?

Will any of this—can any of this—get better? Not unless the cult of excellence, so ably defended by William A. Henry III in his book *In Defense of Elitism* (his sudden, pre-publication death buried the book along with him: why push something whose author can't make personal appearances?), takes over in the land or hell freezes over—whichever comes first. To expect things to improve is like asking for the return of the five-cent beer. Material inflation brings spiritual deflation. Never again can we with impunity make a mythological allusion, use a phrase in a dead language (such as Greek, Latin, or any other that isn't English), or refer to some famous historical event or literary character—if, that is, we expect to be understood by more than a handful of Luddites and desperadoes.

I have this vision of today's citizen trapped between a television screen and a computer screen. He or she is sitting on a revolving stool, and can move only from facing the one to facing the other. The screens are really reflecting mirrors in which the luckless citizen can watch him- or herself recede and diminish into infinity. The infinity of stupidity, of course.

PART ONE

Education

GILBERT T. SEWALL

The Postmodern Schoolhouse

Gilbert T. Sewall is director of the American Textbook Council, a research organization that conducts independent reviews and studies of schoolbooks in history, civics, and the humanities. A former instructor at Phillips Academy, Andover, and an education editor at *Newsweek* magazine, he is the author of *Necessary Lessons: Decline and Renewal in American Schools* and co-author of *After Hiroshima: The USA Since 1945*. His articles have appeared in *Fortune*, the *New York Times*, the *Wall Street Journal*, and many other publications.

The appearance in 1994 of a proposal for national standards for the teaching of American and world history is the public madeleine Gilbert Sewall dips in his tea for our contemplation. Funded jointly by the U.S. Department of Education and the National Endowment for the Humanities, their release provoked a widespread storm of reaction, culminating in their being voted against in Congress. Their inclusion of virtually every current interest group's favorite theme or personage from the past at the expense of the careful consensus of historians makes of history the equivalent of a national poll.

Equally troubling for Sewall is the supersession of the teaching of citizenship and the means to foster it by a train of lesson plans emphasizing self-esteem, therapy, sexual self-control, and the understanding of alternative lifestyles. Fueled on one side by those who assert the so-called social construction of reality and, on the other, by threatened defenders of tradition and continuity, the debate—and the downward pressure it has induced at the classroom level—goes on.

A GROWING NUMBER OF parents face a world outside their front doors—or in their living rooms, on TV—that they don't like. These parents go to the mall. They see blank-faced thirteen-year-old girls, dressed like hookers, and aggressive boys, Tupac Shakurs and Kurt Cobains in training, children who take gentleness and politeness to be signs of weakness. They understand how these feckless, cynical children have come to be, for news of family breakdown, crime, and general anomie has not escaped them. They do not understand, however, why many or most public schools—not only in inner cities—have responded to failing social habits by debasing the curriculum and installing misguided therapeutic programs.

Even in the toniest suburbs, where twelve-year-olds wear Yale and Stanford sweatshirts, parents encounter a disturbing situation: schools where academic programs are flaccid, where moral education is a hodgepodge of relativism and radical individualism. Sometimes, parents discover, schools are places where not much is going on, where students don't do much work, especially homework, where grades are inflated, and where a laissez-faire attitude toward dress and courtesy is expected. Principals, superintendents, and school boards try to avoid the clashing mores and cultural controversies that swirl around them. There are few places where faculty members can really "draw the line." The fear of litigation, not principle, is an animating condition of the system.

"The vision for schools is not hard to imagine except among the culturally sensitive," Albert Shanker of the American Federation of Teachers said to a symposium of the nation's leading educators in 1993. "Parents want their children to learn to read and compute. To go to school in safe, friendly places." A naive observer would imagine that such a statement, which cuts dually on the wise and the trite, would elicit universal enthusiasm among educators. It does not. Some educators press for new political and psychological programs to advance group consciousness, critical thinking, empowerment, and feeling good about oneself. Multiculturalism (also known as "inclusion" and "diversity") and self-esteem education have been the two most potent curriculum forces of the last decade. Both movements are fundamentally hostile to qualitative distinctions of form, idea, culture, and personality.

On the other hand, parents of all backgrounds now recoil when they hear clenched-fist rhetoric about schools. "Black children have been brainwashed since they started school in America to celebrate white heroes, concepts, and values," said Mabel Lake Murray of the National Alliance of Black School Educators to *Newsweek,* supporting the controversial 1994 history standards developed for the federal government. "What needs to happen now is a reverse brainwashing." In the fields of history and English, bitter controversies over subject content reflect larger and unresolved cultural battles involving civic education and common language. What the schools should do, what they should teach, and how they should do it are questions more puzzling than ever.

New lessons in social studies, values, and sexuality have incited parental concern about what schools now have to say about the world, the nation, and the individual. Three recent curriculum controversies—over the content of nationally developed standards in history, over sex education in Minnesota, and over multiculturalism/gay advocacy in New York City—illustrate how school planners disturb and alienate tradition-minded parents. They illustrate the sharp, evidently widening gulf of vision between the voting public and "culturally sensitive" curriculum officials in charge of the standards, lesson "frameworks," and textbooks that teachers and students use.

The proposed history standards that the National Alliance of Black School Educators and the nation's leading education associations endorsed had been commissioned in 1991 with great fanfare, part of a bipartisan education reform program, funded by the U.S. Department of Education and the National Endowment for the Humanities. When they were released three years later by the UCLA-based Center for History in the Schools, these proposed standards for United States and world history provoked fierce public opposition. This antagonism culminated in a January 1995 Senate resolution condemning them, surprising the academics and education associations that had created and reviewed the standards in draft.

What the public and elected officials didn't like about these new standards was their failure to affirm or celebrate the nation or the Western tradition. Just the reverse. Like a muffled drum through the U.S. history standards, African Americans, Native Americans, Hispanic Americans, Asian Americans, gay Americans, and women face and overcome centuries of oppression, neglect, and adversity. Students meet Speckled Snake and Dolores Huerta, Mahmud al-Kati and Madonna. These people were, according to the drift of the curriculum, the real American heroes. They and others replaced such white patriarchs as Alexander Graham Bell, Thomas Edison, Jonas Salk, and Albert Einstein. The defining reform institutions of the future? Political phalanxes like La Raza Unida and the National Organization of Women.

The standards reinvented the European discovery of the New World, changing a once triumphal Columbian conquest into a three-way "encounter" of Europeans, Africans, and Native Americans. From the beginning, disease-carrying Europeans encounter and enslave innocent people of color. Older paradigms of federalism, industrialism, and expansionism were minimized, along with heroic figures and their achievements. Hamilton and Jefferson, the Erie Canal, Gettysburg, and Promontory Point did not exactly vanish, but they were not much savored either. Teachers and students inherited a solemn, often bitter chronicle of unfulfilled national promise. Historical sufferers and victim groups receive belated recognition and redress. Participation in history becomes an empathetic act. By sharing the pain of exploited groups and learning the gloomy "truth" of the U.S. past, students presumably learn to become more virtuous and sensitive.

The world history standards pushed Western civilization to the side, straining throughout for equivalence of cultures. "Drawing on archaeological evidence for the growth of Jenné-jeno, interpret the commercial importance of this city in West African history," states one suggested activity. *"How did the commercial importance of Jenné-jeno in this era compare with that of contemporary western European commercial centers such as early Venice?"* The cultural achievements of Classical Greece, the Abbasid Caliphate "as a center of cultural innovation and hub of interregional trade in the 8th–10th centuries," and "the civilization of Kush" receive

equal weight in the standards. The miracles of Western science and public health are sidelined in favor of recherché topics interesting only to
university specialists. In order to demonstrate historical understanding,
eighth-graders could "create a summary evaluation of the Zagwe dynasty
of Ethiopia from the view of an Egyptian Coptic Christian" and ask
"How would a Muslim from Adal have evaluated the Zagwe history?"

Ancient Rome, Judeo-Christian theology, the Enlightenment, and
the Industrial Revolution all suffered from inattention, as new attention
was paid to Gupta India, Coptic Ethiopia, and Bantu culture. Old military heroes like Hannibal and Wellington disappear from the historical
scene. Now Julius Caesar and Marcus Aurelius, Augustine and Thomas
Aquinas, Martin Luther and John Calvin, Catherine the Great and Louis
XIV, Charles Darwin and Sigmund Freud play supporting roles, and are
no longer considered dominating figures of their respective historical
ages.

What do these world history standards stress about the modern
world? Economic imperialism, slavery and forced labor, pathogens, cultural dislocation, and raw deals for aborigines everywhere. Compare
"the consequences of encounters between intrusive European migrants
and indigenous peoples in such regions as the United States, Canada,
South Africa, Australia, and Siberia," suggests one standard on the "era
of Western military and economic domination, 1850–1914," an insinua-
tive spin sure to surprise millions of Americans whose forebears passed
through Ellis Island, settled the middle plains, and helped build an
American commonwealth.

But the problem is not only one of civic interpretation. With greater
alarm, perhaps, discerning parents are also beginning to notice that
non-academic courses focusing on personal behavior and social ailments
are replacing academic courses in the zero-sum school day. An affective
"curriculum of caring," especially popular at the elementary level, rea-
ligns school programs to try to improve student mental health, self-
esteem, sexual experience, and gender sensitivity. By many parents'
lights, these "proactive" programs reflect a misguided or repellent campaign by adults to promote open views of sexuality and self through
public education.

Therapeutic and problem-solving frameworks, syllabuses, and lesson
plans now circulate statewide and nationally, intending to "treat" well-
televised social disorders. One of these is "Girls and Boys Getting Along:
Teaching Sexual Harassment Prevention in the Elementary Classroom,
Grades K–6 Curricula," developed in 1993 by the Minnesota Department
of Education through a Title IV federal "sex desegregation" grant, later
withdrawn for "revision" after statewide dispute over its contents. From
the beginning it is evident this guide is a "psychologically correct" product:

Respect means treating ourselves and others around you [sic] as special people. Respect means treating their ideas and feelings, their bodies and clothing and trees, plants, animals, water and the whole Earth with care. We need to respect others with our actions and with our words. So I always say that respect is a way for us to say to ourselves and others: WE CARE.

But caring in this case is "Dealing with indicators of sexual harassment/sexual abuse," the guide announces, warning up front, "As always, during and after use of the curriculum, observe any change in student grades or attendance, expressions of anger, depression, bullying or acting out sexually. Such change may be an indication of possible sexual harassment or sexual abuse." This guide warns children to be on the lookout for "inappropriate" adult touching. It also advises teachers to be alert to signs that it might be going on. In the K–3 curriculum, students are introduced to the concepts of respect, dignity, and equality, as embodied by three animal characters, to be acted out by teachers: Respect the Turtle, Dignity the Snail, and Equality the Frog. The snail says "Dignity means we all are important" and the Frog says "Equality means we all deserve the same rights." Respect the Turtle says:

We all have special private places. It is important that we do not say mean words or swear words about each other's private places. A boy's body is different from a girl's body, isn't it? A boy has a penis, scrotum and testicles, and that's what makes him a boy. A girl has a vagina and vulva—that's what makes her a girl. Our breasts and buttocks (pat your backside) are our private places too, and if we respect one another we don't touch the boys and girls around us on their special private places.

That leads to the larger lesson: "Sexual harassment is unwanted sexual words or actions and put-downs that make fun of you for being a girl or a boy." At the end of each lesson, through all grades, there is a benediction, when children in unison repeat the pledge:

> Sexual harassment is a put-down,
> And put-downs are not OK.
> I pledge to do my best to stop sexual harassment,
> I will show RESPECT by caring for myself and others;
> I have DIGNITY, and will give it to others;
> I will work for EQUALITY, and treat everyone fairly.
> I am special, you are special, and we are all equal.

"Girls and Boys Getting Along" continues:

If you overhear a child saying to another of the opposite gender, "I have a penis and you don't," this can usually be handled by the teacher responding "That's right (child's name). That's what makes you a boy" and moving on to the teaching of the day rather than thinking that this age-appropriate comment is sexual harassment. If the same comment is made to another boy and/or is done in a very public put-down way, these same words can be hurtful and harmful and are likely to have crossed the line into sexual harassment.

Girl-against-boy "harassment" gets its due:

A group of girls are playing jump rope on the playground. Ramon is great at jumping rope and wants to play too. The girls, however, won't let Ramon join in. "This is for girls only," they say, "go find some boys to play with." Ramon feels bad because he wants to play jump rope; but he also wants to play with one of his best friends from his neighborhood, Maria.

The guide goes on to note, apropos of discussion questions, "If the students think Ramon is a 'sissy' or a 'fag' because he wants to jump rope with the girls, the teacher should try to address homophobia and/or that these words are not respectful." Would a teacher be willing to admit, in the same way that a boy has a penis, "Yes (child's name) you're right. Ramon is a homosexual"? Such lessons are a minefield for misunderstanding, confusion, and student trauma.

An appendix includes examples of "sexual harassment behaviors reported in elementary school." These range from the childish to the monstrous, namely, " 'spiking' (pulling down someone's pants), verbal comments about body parts, sexual profanity, sexual name calling (pussy, cunt, bitch), gestures with hands and body, 'flip up day' (boys flip up girls' dresses/skirts), 'grab the girls' private parts week,' inappropriate touching, 'snuggies' (pulling underwear up at the waist so it goes between buttocks), exposing genitals, rape, assault, requests for sex, threats with toy knives, pornography." This list, from verbal taunts to criminal acts, is more than disturbing. Who are these kids who are raping and attacking other kids? In second or sixth grade? Is a curriculum like "Girls and Boys Getting Along" going to make them mend their ways or only fuel their terrible anger and violence?

There is more in the curriculum that is sure to offend traditional parents who feel that it is wrongheaded for educators to dwell on sordid topics instead of nourishing innocence and play. Finally, unbelievably, in the midst of one K–3 lesson, with no explanation given, is the following essay or poem, entitled "Pain . . . My Witness," evidently written by a victim and addressed to an abuser, possibly to be read to a class of eight-year-olds:

> I have a witness to all the things
> you did to me. Pain. I did not
> feel it then, but now I can.
> Now I do. Everywhere I am turned
> in my life, the memories
> are there. Pain is there. You are
> there. I could not stop you then.
> I can now. I do. No more are you

allowed to hurt me. Never again
will I be a silent partner to your
disgusting displays of affection.

You make me sick. What you
did to me was perverse. The things
you whispered in my ear—
twisted. Are you proud for what you did?

How could you get your pleasure
from a young child? A child is not
equipped to know or handle sexual
arousal. You, your kind, have no
right to the young, their minds, or
their bodies. I have faced you,
I have fought you, and
I have won.

                    Traci A. Barcus

Thank you to my family for being there when I needed them and to the
staff and group members of the Itasca Alliance for Sexual Assault.

Sometimes curriculum battles lead to local political blowouts. A third
example, coming again from the elementary level, was a dispute over
multiculturalism and sex education that surfaced in New York City during 1992. The *Children of the Rainbow* curriculum guide was designed to
teach six-year-olds tolerance and respect for minorities and alternative
families, including those headed by gay and lesbian couples. This curriculum came under massive political fire, led by an ad hoc coalition of
Roman Catholics and Christian fundamentalists. The resistance centered exclusively on the issue of homosexuality, considered in a few paragraphs, in a tome of over 400 pages. A sample: "Teachers of first graders
have an opportunity to give children a healthy sense of identity at an
early age. Classes should include references to lesbians/gay people in all
curricular areas and should avoid exclusionary practices by presuming a
person's sexual orientation, reinforcing stereotypes, or speaking of lesbi-
ans/gays as 'they' or 'other.' "

Lost in the politics, which included the firing of New York City
schools chancellor Joseph A. Fernandez, who supported the curriculum
and the distribution of condoms in schools: The topic of homosexuality
was peripheral in *Children of the Rainbow*, only one of many topics and
causes that New York education authorities consider an integral part of
sound multicultural education. The curriculum guidelines entertained
other subjects in much greater detail. *Children of the Rainbow* worried
over social injustices, hidden biases, and gender roles: "By the time children enter first grade, society (predominantly via family, television, and
books) has instilled in them many sexist ideas and mores. . . . Challeng-

ing sexist myths can begin on the first day of school." A cultural diversity checklist suggested that teachers abandon chalkboard arithmetic for counting with beans and stones. "Multicultural understanding will result when children compare and contrast the climates of their countries of origin," this heavy-handed guide for teachers of six-year-olds declared. If such understanding were so simple.

The examples could go on, endlessly. For parents who oppose condom distribution, in fact, who expect their children to learn how to read and write at school, not how to behave sexually, this sort of curriculum change is alarming and offensive. Parents generally seek schools that teach "values" and have a positive, friendly "affective component." They want schools to let children know the difference between right and wrong, good and evil, wholesome and lowdown. They think this can be done without resorting to slanted, politically loaded, inappropriate, or debased subject matter that children are very likely not ready to understand.

How did these contemporary curricula come to exist? The educational revolution of the 1960s encouraged and institutionalized the assertion of individual rights, the contraction of adult authority, the romantic idea of "creative disorder," sexual freedom, and more. It demoted patriotism, mocked decency, and rebeled against Apollonian ideals. It sought counterintuitive truths. The impact of the counterculture on ideals in character education was swift and profound. *Summerhill,* a book written in 1960 by the eccentric English progressive A. S. Neill, professed that every child had unique creative impulses to be nurtured, that children should be free from dictated information, imposed behavior, and enforced devotion to received morality.

Neill held with grim self-righteousness that for a child to accept a "ready-made code of morals is dangerous." For Neill, "the first thing a child should learn is to be a rebel." Neill turned out to be something of a nut and misanthrope, but more than thirty years after *Summerhill,* much of what he idealized remains a vision to "caring" reformers. Later came Paulo Friere's famous 1970 book, *Pedagogy of the Oppressed.* The writings of the Brazilian guru–educator remain canonical among progressive educators and graduate students in education schools across the country. Still virtually unknown to the public, Friere is arguably the most influential educational philosopher since John Dewey and one whose revolutionary spirit, especially in his original pedagogy of "critical thinking" as a means of liberating the "oppressed," including students oppressed by facts, prevails in the nation's research universities and education schools. Asserted one 1988 essay published by the Modern Language Association, rejecting the conservative insurgency represented by William J. Bennett and Allan Bloom in the late 1980s:

It remains now for those groups born of the strife of the sixties and seventies and working largely until now in relative isolation to begin to know themselves and one another as part of a remarkable coalition that has its roots and its future in movements that are not only national but global: movements of colonized peoples, feminists, and literacy workers, all committed to enlightened self-consciousness and radical social change.

This elaborate Friere-inspired tapestry espouses anti-colonialism, feminism, and New Age individualism. Multiculturalism, therapeutics, and perhaps armed resistance intersect. What exactly is going on here, Albert Shanker and many others might ask? What is this contemporary complex of attitudes and moral hypotheses that undergirds the changing curriculum? Why does it exert such authority in curriculum planning and theories of learning?

Take ten statements:

1. There are many interpretations of reality.
2. No single perspective on reality can claim to be the exclusive truth.
3. Every act of interpretation or judgment reflects the symbols and norms of one or more social groups.
4. The self is "socially constructed," constituted by its membership in particular groups whose interests may be in conflict with dominant social pressures.
5. Every judgment or expression reflects the interests not only of individuals but more crucially, of the social groups or interpretive communities.
6. High culture in particular represents the ideas and symbols that have allowed the dominant race, class, and gender to maintain hegemony over others.
7. Works reflecting the interests of the dominant class must be unmasked, and their hegemonic biases—patriarchy, racism, and imperialism—revealed.
8. At the same time, work by and for the oppressed must be retrieved and fully appreciated.
9. If these works do not meet traditional academic standards, then the standards should be changed.
10. Ideals of truth, objectivity, reason, argument, evidence, impartiality, et cetera—elements of a "regime of truth"—are themselves the instruments of oppression.

Sound familiar? These are among what Jerry L. Martin has identified as primary components of *postmodernism*, the ruling ideology and set of assumptions about knowledge that has for some time driven curriculum change in education schools and the humanities. Old-time English grammar and Euclidean geometry are not feel-good subjects. They smack of tradition, and they have standards that are easy to measure.

Facts, spelling, rules, all demand rote learning, to which many Friere-inspired "critical thinking" advocates are allergic. They have traded knowledge for forms of inquiry based on feeling, not fact, and on principles based on an intellectual hall of mirrors, stressing perspective, relativity, illusion, and the "social construction of knowledge."

For the last three decades, the nation's cultural and academic arbiters have resisted a vocabulary of excellence, at least of the kind familiar for two centuries in the liberal West. "Contemporary liberalism is so intellectually and psychologically invested in the doctrine of ever-expanding rights—the rights of privacy, the rights of children, the rights of criminals, the rights of pornographers, the rights of everyone to everything—that any suggestion of the baleful consequences of that doctrine appears to them as a threat to the liberal idea itself," a *New Republic* editorial puts the situation.

What many educators seek for a better future is a "curriculum of caring." From Philip Rieff to Christopher Lasch, a few—but only a few—social scientists have perceived the radical ideological ambitions of the therapeutic and postmodern clerisies at work in schools and other cultural institutions. Tomorrow's curriculum is now developed in large part by educators trained in psychology, the human potential movement, and health education, many of whom have limited personal respect for and knowledge of venerable cultural traditions, especially religious ones. Since these educators almost always assume that people who resist innovative curricula and textbook revision of the kind they advocate are benighted or reactionary, they make little effort to "hear" the voices of those who resist their own gospel.

Since the 1960s, much of what has passed for curriculum reform has unintentionally reflected vast cultural decline. Unable to enforce high standards, increasingly unsure of what they are, trendy educators have chosen to attend workshops in emotional literacy. They have dismissed the English language as "privileged discourse" and have sought to undermine its authority through aggressive bilingualism. They have disparaged and deconstructed classic readings of the West. "A good education would be devoted to encouraging and refining the beautiful," wrote Allan Bloom shortly before his death. "But a pathologically misguided moralism instead turns such longing into a sin against the high goal of making everyone feel good, of overcoming nature in the name of equality. Love of the beautiful may be the last and finest sacrifice to radical egalitarianism."

The conversation over values and standards continues. But sometimes it seems as though the combatants now speak whole different languages. Most custodians of cultural symbols in the universities, media, and entertainment world shrug. Respect for the diversity movement continues to anathematize "Western," that is, Anglo-European and Victorian, ideals of art, philosophy, religion, and public life. Meanwhile, seductive images with greater force in children's lives than any curriculum dance across video screens throughout the land. A large number of U.S. educators are abandoning a civics of the kind that the critic William A. Henry III identified as "respect and even deference for leadership and position; esteem for accomplishment, especially when achieved through long labor and rigorous education; reverence for heritage, particularly history, philosophy, and culture; commitment to rationalism and scientific investigation; upholding of objective standards; most important, the willingness to assert unyieldingly that one idea, contribution or attainment is better than another." Whether or not the nation can reclaim these values—whether or not the civilization *wants* to reclaim these values—is a question at the center of the 1990s culture wars and school controversies.

C Y N T H I A O Z I C K

The Question of Our Speech:
The Return to Aural Culture

Cynthia Ozick's most recent collection of essays, and her tenth book, is *Fame and Folly*, to be published in 1996. Her last novel was *The Messiah of Stockholm* (1987). Her first play, *The Shaw*—a dramatic bridge between the aural and the print culture?—is slated for production in New York in 1996 as well.

Ozick's unsentimental and powerful eulogy for the print culture and its slow passing was first published in the *Partisan Review,* twelve years before the even more ferociously accelerated process of the decline which prompted this book. In looking back at the first decade of our century, when Ozick's mother voyaged in a year from steerage to a linguistic accomplishment which would be astonishing in a ten-year-old schoolgirl in the 1990s, she seems to suggest how far we ourselves have traveled in the interval, sailing backwards as fast as we can. Her prescience here is alarming: Perhaps we no longer have the flippant consolation of *"Après moi, le déluge."* For here it is.

WHEN I WAS a thirteen-year-old New Yorker, a trio of women from the provinces took up, relentlessly and extravagantly, the question of my speech. Their names were Miss Evangeline Trolander, Mrs. Olive Birch Davis, and Mrs. Ruby S. Papp (pronounced *pop*). It was Mrs. Papp's specialty to explain how to "breathe from the diaphragm." She would place her fingers tip-to-tip on the unyielding hard shell of her midriff, hugely inhaling: how astonishing then to see how the mighty action of her lungs caused her fingertips to spring apart! This demonstration was for the repair of the New York voice. What the New York voice, situated notoriously "in the throat," required above everything was to descend, pumping air, to this nether site, so that "Young Lochinvar came out of the WEST" might come bellowing out of the pubescent breast.

The New York palate, meanwhile, was consonantally in neglect. *T*'s, *d*'s, and *l*'s were being beaten out against the teeth, European-fashion—this was called "dentalization"—while the homeless *r* and *n* went wandering in the perilous trough behind the front incisors. There were corrective exercises for these transgressions, the chief one being a liturgical recitation of "Tillie the Toiler took Tommy Tucker to tea," with the tongue anxiously flying up above the teeth to strike precisely on the lower ridge of the upper palate.

The diaphragm; the upper palate; and finally the arena in the cave of the mouth where the vowels were prepared. A New Yorker could not say a proper *a*, as in "paper"—this indispensable vibration was manufactured somewhere back near the nasal passage, whereas civility demanded the *a* to emerge frontally, directly from the lips' vestibule. The New York *i* was worst of all: how Mrs. Davis, Mrs. Papp, and Miss Trolander mimicked and ridiculed the New York *i*! "Oi loik oice cream," they mocked.

All these emendations, as it happened, were being applied to the entire population of a high school for girls in a modest Gothic pile on East Sixty-eighth Street in the 1940s, and no one who emerged from that pile after four years of daily speech training ever sounded the same again. On the eve of graduation, Mrs. Olive Birch Davis turned to Mrs. Ruby S. Papp and said: "Do you remember the *ugliness* of her *diction* when she came to us?" She meant me; I was about to deliver the Class Speech. I had not yet encountered Shaw's *Pygmalion,* and its popular recrudescence in the form of *My Fair Lady* was still to occur; all the same, that night, rehearsing for commencement, I caught in Mrs. Davis and Mrs. Pap something of Professor Higgins's victory, and in myself something of Eliza's humiliation.

Our teachers had, like young Lochinvar, come out of the West, but I had come out of the northeast Bronx. Called on to enunciate publicly for the first time, I responded with the diffidence of secret pleasure; I liked to read out loud, and thought myself not bad at it. Instead, I was marked down as a malfeasance in need of overhaul. The revisions and transformations that followed were not unlike an evangelical conversion. One had to be willing to be born again; one had to be willing to repudiate wholesale one's former defective self. It could not be accomplished without faith and shame: faith in what one might newly become, shame in the degrading process itself—the dedicated repetition of mantras. "Tillie the Toiler took Tommy Tucker to tea," "Oh! young LOCHinvar has come out of the WEST, Through all the wide BORDER HIS steed was the BEST." All the while pneumatically shooting out one's diaphragm, and keeping one's eye (never one's *oi*) peeled for the niggardly approval of Miss Evangeline Trolander.

In this way I was, at an early age, effectively made over. Like a multitude of other graduates of my high school, I now own a sort of robot's speech—it has no obvious native county. At least not to most ears, though a well-tutored listener will hear that the vowels hang on, and the cadence of every sentence has a certain laggardly northeast Bronx drag. Brooklyn, by contrast, is divided between very fast and very slow. Irish New York has its own sound, Italian New York another; and a refined ear can distinguish between Bronx and Brooklyn Irish and Bronx and

Brooklyn Jewish: four separate accents, with the differences to be found not simply in vowels and consonants, but in speed and inflection. Nor is it so much a matter of ancestry as of neighborhood. If, instead of clinging to the green-fronded edge of Pelham Bay Park, my family had settled three miles west, in a denser "section" called Pelham Parkway, I would have spoken Bronx Jewish. Encountering City Island, Bronx Jewish said Ciddy Oilen. In Pelham Bay, where Bronx Irish was almost exclusively spoken in those days, it was Ciddy Allen. When Terence Cooke became Cardinal of New York, my heart leaped up: Throggs Neck! I had assimilated those sounds long ago on a pebbly beach. No one had ever put the Cardinal into the wringer of speech repair. I knew him through and through. He was my childhood's brother, and restored my orphaned ear.

Effectively made over: these noises that come out of me are not an overlay. They do not vanish during the free play of dreams or screams. I do not, cannot, "revert." This may be because Trolander, Davis, and Papp caught me early; or because I was so passionate a devotee of their dogma.

Years later I tried to figure it all out. What did these women have up their sleeves? An aesthetic ideal, perhaps: Standard American English. But behind the ideal—and Trolander, Davis, andPapp were the strictest and most indefatigable idealists—there must have been an ideology; and behind the ideology, whatever form it might take, a repugnance. The speech of New York streets and households soiled them: you could see it in their proud pained meticulous frowns. They were intent on our elevation. Though they were dead set on annihilating Yiddish-derived "dentalization," they could not be said to be anti-Semites, since they were just as set on erasing the tumbling consonants of Virginia Greene's Alexander Avenue Irish Bronx; and besides, in our different styles, we *all* dentalized. Was it, then, the Melting Pot that inspired Trolander, Davis, and Papp? But not one of us was an "immigrant"; we were all fully Americanized, and our parents before us, except for the handful of foreign-born "German refugees." These were marched off to a special Speech Clinic for segregated training; their *r*'s drew Mrs. Davis's eyes toward heaven, and I privately recognized that the refugees were almost all of them hopeless cases. A girl named Hedwig said she *didn't care*, which made me conclude that she was frivolous, trivialized, not serious; wasn't it ignominious enough (like a kind of cheese) to be called "Hedwig"?

Only the refugees were bona fide foreigners. The rest of us were garden-variety subway-riding New Yorkers. Trolander, Davis, and Papp saw us nevertheless as tainted with foreignness, and it was the remnants of that foreignness they meant to wipe away: the last stages of the great turn-of-the-century alien flood. Or perhaps they intended that, like Shaw's Eliza, we should have the wherewithal to rise to a higher station. Yet, looking back on their dress and manner, I do not think Trolander,

Davis, and Papp at all sought out or even understood "class"; they were reliably American, and class was nothing they were capable of believing in.

What, then, did these ferrywomen imagine we would find on the farther shore, once we left behind, through artifice and practice, our native speech? Was it a kind of "manners," was it what they might have called "breeding"? They thought of themselves as democratic noble-women (nor did they suppose this to be a contradiction in terms), and they expected of us, if not the same, then at least a recognition of the category. They trusted in the power of models. They gave us the astonishing maneuvers of their teeth, their tongues, their lungs, and drilled us in imitation of those maneuvers. In the process, they managed—this was their highest feat—to break down embarrassment, to deny the shaming theatricality of the ludicrous. We lost every delicacy and dignity in acting like freaks or fools while trying out the new accent. Contrived consonants began freely to address feigned vowels: a world of parroting and parody. And what came of it all?

What came of it was that they caused us—and here was a category *they* had no recognition of—they caused us to exchange one regionalism for another. New York gave way to Midwest. We were cured of Atlantic Sea-board, a disease that encompassed north, middle, and south; and yet only the middle, and of that middle only New York, was considered to be on the critical list. It was New York that carried the hottest and sickest inflammation. In no other hollow of the country was such an effort mounted, on such a scale, to eliminate regionalism. The South might have specialized in Elocution, but the South was not ashamed of its idiosyncratic vowels; neither was New England; and no one sent missionaries.

Of course this was exactly what our democratic noblewomen were: missionaries. They restored, if not our souls, then surely and emphatically our *r*'s—those *r*'s that are missing in the end syllables of New York-ers, who call themselves Noo Yawkizz and nowadays worry about mug-gizz. From Boston to New York to Atlanta, the Easterner is an Eastinna, his mother is a mutha, his father a fahtha, and the most difficult stretch of anything is the hahd paht; and so fawth. But only in New York is the absent *r*—i.e., the absent *aw*—an offense to good manniz. To be sure, our missionaries did not dream that they imposed a parochialism of their own. And perhaps they were right not to dream it, since by the forties of this century the radio was having its leveling effect, and Midwest speech, colonizing by means of "announcers," had ascended to the rank of stan-dard speech.

Still, only forty years earlier, Henry James, visiting from England after a considerable period away, was freshly noticing and acidly deploring the pervasively conquering *r:*

. . . the letter, I grant, gets terribly little rest among those great masses of our population that strike us, in the boundless West especially, as, under some strange impulse received toward consonantal recovery of balance, making it present even in words from which it is absent, bringing it in everywhere as with the small vulgar effect of a sort of morose grinding of the back teeth. There are, you see, sounds of a mysterious intrinsic meanness, and there are sounds of a mysterious intrinsic frankness and sweetness; and I think the recurrent note I have indicated—fatherr and motherr and otherr, waterr and matterr and scatterr, harrd and barrd, parrt, starrt, and (dreadful to say) arrt (the repetition it is that drives home the ugliness), are signal specimens of what becomes of a custom of utterance out of which the principle of taste has dropped.

In 1905, to drop the *r* was to drop, for the cultivated ear, a principle of taste; but for our democratic noblewomen four decades on, exactly the reverse was true. James's New York/Boston expectations, reinforced by southern England, assumed that Eastern American speech, tied as it was to the cultural reign of London, had a right to rule and to rule out. The history and sociolinguistics governing this reversal is less pressing to examine than the question of "standard speech" itself. James thought that "the voice *plus* the way it is employed" determined "positively the history of the national character, almost the history of the people." His views on all this, his alarms and anxieties, he compressed into a fluid little talk ("The Question of Our Speech") he gave at the Bryn Mawr College commencement of June 8, 1905—exactly one year and two days before my mother, nine years old, having passed through Castle Garden, stood on the corner of Battery Park, waiting to board the horsecar for Madison Street on the Lower East Side.

James was in great fear of the child waiting for the horsecar. "Keep in sight," he warned, "the so interesting historical truth that no language, so far back as our acquaintance with history goes, has known any such ordeal, any such stress or strain, as was to await the English in this huge new community it was to help, at first, to father and mother. It came *over*, as the phrase is, came over originally without fear and without guile— but to find itself transplanted to spaces it had never dreamed, in its comparative humility, of covering, to conditions it had never dreamed, in its comparative innocence, of meeting." He spoke of English as an "unfriended heroine," "our transported medium, our unrescued Andromeda, our medium of utterance, . . . disjoined from all the associations, the other presences, that had attended her, that had watched for her and with her, that had helped to form her manners and her voice, her taste and her genius."

And if English, orphaned as it was and cut off from its "ancestral circle," did not have enough to contend with in its own immigrant situation, arriving "without fear and without guile" only to be ambushed by "a social and political order that was both without previous precedent and example and incalculably expansive," including also the expansiveness of a diligent public school network and "the mighty maniac" of journalism—if all this was not threatening enough, there was the special danger my nine-year-old mother posed. She represented an unstable new ingredient. She represented violation, a kind of linguistic Armageddon. She stood for disorder and promiscuity. "I am perfectly aware," James said at Bryn Mawr,

that the common school and the newspaper are influences that shall often have been named to you, exactly, as favorable, as positively and actively contributive, to the prosperity of our idiom; the answer to which is that the matter depends, distinctively, on what is meant by prosperity. It is prosperity, of a sort, that a hundred million people, a few years hence, will be unanimously, loudly—above all loudly, I think!—speaking it, and that, moreover, many of these millions will have been artfully wooed and weaned from the Dutch, from the Spanish, from the German, from the Italian, from the Norse, from the Finnish, from the Yiddish even, strange to say, and (stranger still to say), even from the English, for the sweet sake, or the sublime consciousness, as we may perhaps put it, of speaking, of talking, for the first time in their lives, *really* at their ease. There are many things our now so profusely important and, as is claimed, quickly assimilated foreign brothers and sisters may do at their ease in this country, and at two minutes' notice, and without asking any one else's leave or taking any circumstance whatever into account—any save an infinite uplifting sense of freedom and facility; but the thing they may best do is play, to their heart's content, with the English language, or, in other words, dump their mountain of promiscuous material into the foundation of the American.

"All the while we sleep," he continued, "the vast contingent of aliens whom we make welcome, and whose main contention, as I say, is that, from the moment of their arrival, they have just as much property in our speech as we have, and just as good a right to do what they choose with it . . . all the while we sleep the innumerable aliens are sitting up (*they* don't sleep!) to work their will on their new inheritance." And he compared the immigrants' use of English to oilcloth—"highly convenient . . . durable, tough, cheap."

James's thesis in his address to his audience of young aristocrats was not precisely focused. On the one hand, in describing the depredations of the innumerable sleepless aliens, in protesting "the common schools and the 'daily paper,' " he appeared to admit defeat—"the forces of looseness are in possession of the field." Yet in asking the graduates to see to the perfection of their own speech, he had, he confessed, no models to offer them. Imitate, he advised—but whom? Parents and teachers were themselves not watchful. "I am at a loss to name you particular and unmistakable, edifying and illuminating groups or classes," he said, and recommended, in the most general way, the hope of "encountering, blessedly, here and there, articulate individuals, torchbearers, as we may rightly describe them, guardians of the sacred flame."

As it turned out, James not only had no solution; he had not even put the right question. These young women of good family whom he was exhorting to excellence were well situated in society to do exactly what James had described the immigrants as doing: speaking *"really* at their ease," playing, "to their heart's content, with the English language" in "an infinite uplifting sense of freedom and facility." Whereas the "aliens," hard-pressed by the scramblings of poverty and cultural confusions, had no notion at all of linguistic "freedom and facility," took no witting license with the English tongue, and felt no remotest ownership in the language they hoped merely to earn their wretched bread by. If they did not sleep, it was because of long hours in the sweatshops and similar places of employment; they were no more in a position to "play" with English than they were to acquire bona fide *Mayflower* ancestry. Ease, content, facility—these were not the lot of the unsleeping aliens.

To the young people of Bryn Mawr James could offer nothing more sanguine, nothing less gossamer, than the merest metaphor—"guardians of the sacred flame." Whom then should they imitate but himself, the most "articulate individual" of them all? We have no record of the graduates' response to James's extravagant "later style" as profusely exhibited in this address: whatever it was, they could not have accepted it for standard American. James's English had become, by this time, an invention of his own fashioning, so shaded, so leafy, so imbricated, so brachiate, so filigreed, as to cast a thousand momentary ornamental obscurities, like the effect of the drill-holes in the spiraled stone hair of an imperial Roman portrait bust. He was the most eminent torchbearer in sight, the purest of all possible guardians of the flame—but a model he could not have been for anyone's everyday speech, no more than the Romans talked like the *Odes* of Horace. Not that he failed to recognize the exigencies of an active language, "a living organism, fed by the very breath of those who employ it, whoever these may happen to be," a language able "to respond, from its core, to the constant appeal of time, perpetually demanding new tricks, new experiments, new amusements." He saw American English as the flexible servant "of those who carry it with them, on their long road, as their specific experience grows larger and more complex, and who need it to help them to meet this expansion." And at the same time he excluded from these widened possibilities its slangy young native speakers and the very immigrants whose educated children would enrich and reanimate the American language (eight decades later we may judge how vividly), as well as master and augment its literature.

Its literature. It is striking beyond anything that James left out, in the course of this lecture, any reference to reading. Certainly it was not overtly his subject. He was concerned with enunciation and with idiom, with syllables, with vowels and consonants, with tone and inflection, with *sound*—but he linked the American voice to such "underlying things" as "proprieties and values, perfect possessions of the educated spirit, clear humanities," as well as "the imparting of a coherent culture." Implicit was his conviction that speech affects literature, as, in the case of native speakers, it inevitably does: naturalism in the dialogue of a novel, say, is itself always a kind of dialect of a particular place and time. But in a newly roiling society of immigrant speakers, James could not see ahead (and why should he have seen ahead? Castle Garden was unprecedented in all of human history) to the idea that a national literature can create a national speech. The immigrants who learned to read learned to speak. Those who only learned to speak did not, in effect, learn to speak.

In supposing the overriding opposite—that quality of speech creates culture, rather than culture quality of speech—James in "The Question of Our Speech" slighted the one formulation most pertinent to his complaints: the uses of literature. Pressing for "civility of utterance," warning against "influences round about us that make for . . . the confused, the ugly, the flat, the thin, the mean, the helpless, that reduce articulation to an easy and ignoble minimum, and so keep it as little distinct as possible from the grunting, the squealing, the barking or roaring of animals," James thought it overwhelmingly an issue of the imitation of oral models, an issue of "the influence of *observation,*" above all an issue of manners—"for that," he insisted, "is indissolubly involved." How like Mrs. Olive Birch Davis he is when, at Bryn Mawr, he hopes to inflame his listeners to aspiration! "At first dimly, but then more and more distinctly, you will find yourselves noting, comparing, preferring, at last positively emulating and imitating." Bryn Mawr, of course, was the knowing occasion, not the guilty target, of this admonition—he was speaking of the young voices he had been hearing in the street and in the parlors of friends, and he ended with a sacred charge for the graduates themselves: "you may, sounding the clearer note of intercourse as only women can, become yourselves models and missionaries [*sic*], perhaps even a little martyrs, of the good cause."

But why did he address himself to this thesis exclusively in America? Could he not, even more emphatically, have made the same declarations, uttered the same dooms, in his adopted England? No doubt it would not have been seemly; no doubt he would have condemned any appearance of ingratitude toward his welcoming hosts. All true, but this was hardly the reason the lecture at Bryn Mawr would not have done for Girton College. In Britain, regionalisms are the soul of ordinary English speech, and in James's time more than in our own. Even now one can move from hamlet to hamlet and hear the vowels chime charmingly with a different tone in each village. Hull, England, is a city farther from London in speech—though in distance only 140 miles to the north—

than Hull, Massachusetts, is from San Francisco, 3,000 miles to the west. Of England, it is clear, James had only the expectations of class, and a single class set the standard for cultivated speech. Back home in America, diversity was without enchantment, and James demanded a uniform sound. He would not have dreamed of requiring a uniform British sound: English diversity was *English* diversity, earned, native, beaten out over generations of the "ancestral circle"—while American diversity meant a proliferating concatenation of the innumerable sleepless aliens and the half-educated slangy young. With regard to England, James knew whence the standard derived. It was a quality—an emanation, even—of those who, for generations, had been privileged in their education. As Virginia Woolf acknowledged in connection with another complaint, the standard was Oxbridge. To raise the question of "our" speech in England would have been a superfluity: both the question and the answer were self-evident. In England the question, if anyone bothered to put it at all, was: Who sets the standard? And the answer, if anyone bothered to give it at all, was: Those who have been through the great public schools, those who have been through either of the great pair of ancient universities—in short, those who run things.

This was perhaps what led James, in his American reflections, to trip over the issues, and to miss getting at the better question, the right and pertinent question: *the* question, in fact, concerning American speech. In Britain, and in the smaller America of his boyhood that strained to be a mirror of the cousinly English culture, it remained to the point to ask who sets the standard. And the rejoinder was simple enough: the people at the top. To risk the identical question in the America of 1905, with my mother about to emerge from Castle Garden to stand waiting for the horsecar on the corner of Battery Park, was unavoidably to hurtle to the very answer James most dreaded and then desperately conceded: the people at the bottom.

The right and pertinent question for America was something else. If, in politics, America's Enlightenment cry before the world was to be "a nation of laws, not of men," then it was natural for culture to apply in its own jurisdiction the same measure: unassailable institutions are preferable to models or heroes. To look for aristocratic models for common speech in the America of 1905 was to end exactly where James *did* end: "I am at a loss to name you particular and unmistakably edifying and illuminating groups or classes." It could not be done. As long as James believed—together with Trolander, Davis, and Papp, his immediate though paradoxical heirs: paradoxical because their ideal was democratic and his was the people-at-the-top—as long as he believed in the premise of "edifying and illuminating" models, his analysis could go nowhere. Or, rather, it could go only into the rhapsody of vaporous hope that is the conclusion of "The Question of Our Speech"—"become yourselves models and missionaries, perhaps even a little martyrs, of the good cause." Holy and resplendent words I recognize on the instant, having learned them—especially the injunction to martyrdom—at the feet of Trolander, Davis, and Papp.

No, it was the wrong question for America, this emphasis on *who;* the wrong note for a campus (however homogeneous, however elite) just outside Philadelphia, that Enlightenment citadel, whose cracked though mighty Bell was engraved with a rendering of the majestic Hebrew word *dror:* a word my nine-year-old mother, on her way to Madison Street, would have been able to read in the original, though presumably James could not—a deprivation of literacy my mother might have marked him down for. "All life," James asserted on that brilliant June day (my mother's life was that day still under the yoke of the Czar; the Kishinev pogrom, with its massacre and its maimings, had occurred only two years earlier), "all life comes back to the question of our speech, the medium through which we communicate with each other; for all life comes back to the question of our relations with each other." And: "A care for tone is part of a care for many things besides; for the fact, for the value, of good breeding, above all, as to which tone unites with various other personal, social signs to bear testimony. The idea of good breeding . . . is one of the most precious conquests of civilization, the very core of our social heritage."

Speech, then, was *who;* it was breeding; it was "relations"; it was manners; and manners, in this view, make culture. As a novelist, and particularly as a celebrated practitioner of "the novel of manners" (though to reduce James merely to this is to diminish him radically as a recorder of evil and to silence his full moral genius), it was requisite, it was the soul of vitality itself, for James to analyze in the mode of *who.* But for a social theorist—and in his lecture social theory was what James was pressing toward—it was a failing and an error. The absence of models was not simply an embarrassment; it should have been a hint. It should have hinted at the necessary relinquishment of *who* in favor of *what:* not who appoints the national speech, but what creates the standard.

If, still sticking to his formulation, James had dared to give his private answer, he might have announced: "Young women, I, Henry James, am that august Who who fixes the firmament of our national speech. Follow me, and you follow excellence." But how had this vast substantial Who that was Henry James come to be fashioned? It was no Who *he* followed. It was instead a great cumulative corporeal What, the voluminous and manifold heritage of Literature he had been saturated in since childhood. In short, he *read:* he was a reader, he had always read, reading was not so much his passion or his possession as it was his bread, and not so much his bread as it was the primordial fountain of his life. Ludicrous it is to say of Henry James that he read, he was a reader! As much say of

Vesuvius that it erupted, or of Olympus that it kept the gods. But reading—just that, *what is read*—is the whole, the intricate, secret of his exemplum.

The vulgarity of the low press James could see for himself. On the other hand, he had never set foot in an American public school (his education was, to say the least, Americanly untypical), and he had no inkling of any representative curriculum. Nevertheless it was this public but meticulous curriculum that was to set the standard; and it was a curriculum not far different from what James might have found for himself, exploring on his own among his father's shelves.

A year or so after my mother stepped off the horsecar into Madison Street, she was given Sir Walter Scott's "The Lady of the Lake" to read as a school assignment. She never forgot it. She spoke of it all her life. Mastering it was the triumph of her childhood, and though, like every little girl of her generation, she read *Pollyanna,* and in the last months of her eighty-third year every word of Willa Cather, it was "The Lady of the Lake" that enduringly typified achievement, education, culture.

Some seventy-odd years after my mother studied it at P.S. 131 on the Lower East Side, I open "The Lady of the Lake" and take in lines I have never looked on before:

> Not thus, in ancient days of Caledon,
> > Was thy voice mute amid the festal crowd,
> When lay of hopeless love, or glory won,
> > Aroused the fearful, or subdued the proud.
> At each according pause was heard aloud
> > Thine ardent symphony sublime and high!
> Fair dames and crested chiefs attention bowed;
> > For still the burden of thy minstrelsy
> Was Knighthood's dauntless deed, and Beauty's matchless eye.
>
> O wake once more! how rude soe'er the hand
> > That ventures o'er thy magic maze to stray;
> O wake once more! though scarce my skill command
> > Some feeble echoing of thine earlier lay;
> Though harsh and faint, and soon to die away,
> > And all unworthy of thy nobler strain,
> Yet if one heart throb higher at its sway,
> > The wizard note has not been touched in vain.
> Then silent be no more! Enchantress, wake again!

My mother was an immigrant child, the poorest of the poor. She had come in steerage; she knew not a word of English when she stepped off the horsecar into Madison Street; she was one of the innumerable unsleeping aliens. Her teachers were the entirely ordinary daughters of the Irish immigration (as my own teachers still were, a generation on), and had no special genius, and assuredly no special training (a certain Miss Walsh was in fact ferociously hostile), for the initiation of a Russian Jewish child into the astoundingly distant and incomprehensible premises of such poetry. And yet it was accomplished, and within the briefest period after the voyage in steerage.

What was accomplished was not merely that my mother "learned" this sort of poetry—i.e., could read and understand it. She learned what it represented in the widest sense—not only the legendary heritage implicit in each and every word and phrase (to a child from Hlusk, where the wooden sidewalks sank into mud and the peasants carried water buckets dangling from shoulder yokes, what was "minstrelsy," what was "Knighthood's dauntless deed," what on earth was a "wizard note"?), but what it represented in the American social and tribal code. The quickest means of stitching all this down is to say that what "The Lady of the Lake" stood for, in the robes and tapestries of its particular English, was the received tradition exemplified by Bryn Mawr in 1905, including James's presence there as commencement speaker.

The American standard derived from an American institution: the public school, free, democratic, open, urgent, pressing on the young a program of reading not so much for its "literary value," though this counted too, as for the stamp of Heritage. All this James overlooked. He had no firsthand sense of it. He was himself the grandson of an ambitiously money-making Irish immigrant; but his father, arranging his affluent life as a metaphysician, had separated himself from public institutions—from any practical idea, in fact, of institutions *per se*—and dunked his numerous children in and out of school on two continents, like a nomad in search of the wettest oasis of all. It was hardly a wonder that James, raised in a self-enclosed clan, asserted the ascendancy of manners over institutions, or that he ascribed to personal speech "positively the history of the national character, almost the history of the people," or that he spoke of the "ancestral circle" as if kinship were the only means to transmit that national character and history.

It was as if James, who could imagine nearly everything, had in this instance neglected imagination itself: kinship as construct and covenant, kinship imagined—and what are institutions if not invented kinship circles: society as contract? In the self-generating Enlightenment society of the American founding philosophers, it was uniquely the power of institutions to imagine, to create, kinship and community. The Constitution, itself a kind of covenant or imaginatively established "ancestral circle," created peoplehood out of an idea, and the public schools, begotten and proliferated by that idea, implemented the Constitution; and more than the Constitution. They implemented and transmitted the old cultural mesh. Where there was so much diversity, the institution substituted for the clan, and discovered—through a kind of civic magnetism—that it could transmit, almost as effectively as the kinship clan itself, "the very core of our social heritage."

To name all this the principle of the Melting Pot is not quite right, and overwhelmingly insufficient. The Melting Pot called for imitation. Imagination, which is at the heart of institutionalized covenants, promotes what is intrinsic. I find on my shelves two old textbooks used widely in the "common schools" James deplored. The first is *A Practical English Grammar*, dated 1880, the work of one Albert N. Raub, A.M., Ph.D. ("Author of 'Raub's Readers,' 'Raub's Arithmetics,' 'Plain Educational Talks, Etc.' "). It is a relentless volume, thorough, determined, with no loopholes; every permutation of the language is scrutinized, analyzed, accounted for. It is also a commonplace book replete with morally instructive quotations, some splendidly familiar. Each explanatory chapter is followed by "Remarks," "Cautions," and "Exercises," and every Exercise includes a high-minded hoard of literary Remarks and Cautions. For instance, under Personal Pronouns:

> Though the mills of God grind slowly,
>   yet they grind exceedingly small;
> Though with patience He stands waiting,
>   with exactness grinds He all.

> This above all, to thine own self be true,
> And it must follow, as the night the day,
> Thou canst not then be false to any man.

> These are thy glorious works, Parent of good,
>   Almighty! Thine this universal frame.

> Alas! they had been friends in youth,
> But whispering tongues can poison truth;
> And constancy lives in realms above,
>   And life is thorny, and youth is vain;
> And to be worth with one we love
>   Doth work like madness on the brain.

So much for Longfellow, Shakespeare, Milton, and Coleridge. But also Addison, Cowper, Pope, Ossian, Scott, Ruskin, Thomson, Wordsworth, Trollope, Gray, Byron, Whittier, Lowell, Holmes, Moore, Collins, Hood, Goldsmith, Bryant, Dickens, Bacon, Franklin, Locke, the Bible—these appear throughout, in the form of addenda to Participles, Parsing, Irregular Verbs, and the rule of the Nominative Independent; in addition, a handful of lost presences: Bushnell, H. Wise, Wayland, Dwight, Blair, Mrs. Welby (nearly the only woman in the lot), and Anon. The *content* of this volume is not its subject matter, neither its syntactic lesson nor its poetic maxims. It is the voice of a language; rather, of language itself, language as texture, gesture, innateness. To read from beginning to end of a schoolbook of this sort is to recognize at once that James had it backwards and upside down: it is not that manners lead culture; it is culture that leads manners. What shapes culture—this is not a tautology or a redundancy—is culture. "Who makes the country?" was the latent question James was prodding and poking, all gingerly; and it was the wrong—because unanswerable—one. "What kind of country shall we have?" was Albert N. Raub's question, and it *was* answerable. The answer lay in the reading given to the children in the schoolhouses: the institutionalization, so to say, of our common speech at its noblest.

My second text is even more striking: *The Etymological Reader*, edited by Epes Sargent and Amasa May, dated 1872. "We here offer to the schools of the United States," begins the Preface, "the first systematic attempt to associate the study of etymology with exercises in reading." What follows is a blitz of "vocabulary," Latin roots, Saxon roots, prefixes, and suffixes, but these quickly subside, and nine tenths of this inventive book is an anthology engaging in its richness, range, and ambition. "Lochinvar" is here; so are the Declaration of Independence and selections from Shakespeare; so is Shelley's "To a Skylark"; so is the whole "Star-Spangled Banner." But also: "Description of a Bee Hunt," "Creation a Continuous Work," "The Sahara," "Anglo-Saxon and Norman French," "Conversation," "Progress of Civilization," "Effects of Machinery," "On the Choice of Books," "Our Indebtedness to the Greeks," "Animal Heat," "Corruptions of Language," "Jerusalem from the Mount of Olives," "On the Act of Habeas Corpus," "Individual Character," "Going Up in a Balloon," and dozens of other essays. Among the writers: Dickens, Macaulay, Wordsworth, Irving, Mark Twain, Emerson, Channing, John Stuart Mill, Carlyle, De Quincey, Tennyson, Mirabeau, and so on and so on.

It would be foolish to consider *The Etymological Reader* merely charming, a period piece, "Americana"—it is too immediately useful, too uncompromising, and, for the most part, too enduring to be dismissed with condescension.

It was one of those heads which Guido has often painted—mild, pale, penetrating, free from all commonplace ideas of fat, contented ignorance, looking downward upon the earth; it looked forward, but looked as if it looked at something beyond this world. How one of his order came by it, Heaven above, who let it fall upon a monk's shoulders, best knows; but it would have suited a Brahmin, and had I met it upon the plains of Hindostan, I had reverenced it.

To come upon Sterne, just like this, all of a sudden, for the first time, pressed between Southey's sigh ("How beautiful is night!") and Byron's "And the might of the Gentile, unsmote by the sword,/Hath melted like snow in the glance of the Lord"—to come upon Sterne, just like that, is to come upon an unexpected human fact. Such textbooks filled vessels more fundamental than the Melting Pot—blood vessels, one might venture. Virtuous, elevated, striving and stirring, the best that has been thought and said: thus the voice of the common schools. A fraction of their offerings had a heroic, or monumental, quality, on the style perhaps of George Washington's head. They stood for the power of civics. But the rest were the purest belles-lettres: and it was belles-lettres that were expected to be the fountainhead of American civilization, including civility. Belles-lettres provided style, vocabulary, speech itself; and also the themes of Victorian seriousness: conscience and work. Elevated literature was the model for an educated tongue. Sentences, like conscience and work, were demanding.

What did these demanding sentences do in and for society? First, they demanded to be studied. Second, they demanded sharpness and cadence in writing. They promoted, in short, literacy—and not merely literacy, but a vigorous and manifold recognition of literature as a *force*. They promoted an educated class. Not a hereditarily educated class, but one that had been introduced to the initiating and shaping texts early in life, almost like the hereditarily educated class itself.

All that, we know, is gone. Where once the *Odyssey* was read in the schools, in a jeweled and mandarin translation, Holden Caulfield takes his stand. He is winning and truthful, but he is not demanding. His sentences reach no higher than his gaze. The idea of belles-lettres, when we knock our unaccustomed knees against it, looks archaic and bizarre: rusted away, like an old car chassis. The content of belles-lettres is the property of a segregated caste or the dissipated recollections of the very old.

Belles-lettres in the schools fashioned both speech and the art of punctuation—the sound and the look of nuance. Who spoke well pointed well; who pointed well spoke well. One was the skill of the other. No one now punctuates for nuance—or, rather, whoever punctuates for nuance is "corrected." Copy editors do not know the whole stippled range of the colon or the semicolon, do not know that "O" is not "oh," do not know that not all juxtaposed adjectives are coordinate adjectives; and so forth. The degeneration of punctuation and word-by-word literacy is pandemic among English speakers: this includes most poets and novelists. To glimpse a typical original manuscript undoctored by a copy editor is to suffer a shock at the sight of ignorant imprecision; and to examine a densely literate manuscript after it has passed through the leveling hands of a copy editor is again to suffer a shock at the sight of ignorant imprecision.

In 1930 none of this was so. The relentlessly gradual return of aural culture, beginning with the telephone (a farewell to letter-writing), the radio, the motion picture, and the phonograph, speeded up by the television set, the tape recorder, and lately the video recorder, has by now, after half a century's worth of technology, restored us to the pre-literate status of face-to-face speech. And mass literacy itself is the fixity of no more than a century, starting with the advancing reforms following the industrial revolution—reforms introducing, in England, the notion of severely limited leisure to the classes that formerly had labored with no leisure at all. Into that small new recreational space fell what we now call the "nineteenth-century novel," in both its supreme and its lesser versions. The act of reading—the *work*, in fact, of the act of reading— appeared to complicate and intensify the most ordinary intelligence. The silent physiological translation of letters into sounds, the leaping eye encoding, the transmigration of blotches on a page into the story of, say, Dorothea Brooke, must surely count among the most intricate of biological and transcendent designs. In 1930 the so-called shopgirl, with her pulp romance, is habitually engaged in this electrifying webwork of eye and mind. In 1980 she reverts, via electronics, to the simple speaking face. And then it is all over, by and large, for mass literacy. High literacy has been the province of an elite class since Sumer; there is nothing novel in having a caste of princely readers. But the culture of mass literacy, in its narrow period from 1830 to 1930, was something else: Gutenberg's revolution did not take effect in a popular sense—did not properly begin—until the rise of the middle class at the time, approximately, of the English Reform Act of 1832. Addison's *Spectator,* with its Latin epigraphs, was read by gentlemen, but Dickens was read by nearly everyone. The almost universal habit of reading for recreation or excitement conferred the greatest complexity on the greatest number, and the thinnest sliver of history expressed it: no more than a single century. It flashed by between aural culture and aural culture, no longer-lived than a lightning bug. The world of the VCR is closer to the pre-literate society of traveling mummers than it is to that of the young Scott Fitzgerald's readership in 1920.

When James read out "The Question of Our Speech" in 1905, the era of print supremacy was still in force, unquestioned; the typewriter and the electric light had arrived to strengthen it, and the telephone was greeted only as a convenience, not a substitute. The telephone was particularly welcome—not much was lost that ought not to have been lost in the omission of letters agreeing to meet the 8:42 on Tuesday night on the east platform. Since then, the telephone has abetted more serious losses: exchanges between artists and thinkers; documents of family and business relations; quarrels and cabals among politicians; everything that in the past tended to be preserved for biographers and cultural historians. The advent of the computer used as word processor similarly points toward the wiping out of any *progressive* record of thought; the grain of a life can lie in the illumination of the crossed-out word.

But James, in the remoteness of post-Victorian technology, spoke unshadowed by these threatened disintegrations among the community of the literate; he spoke in the very interior of what seemed then to be a permanently post-aural culture. He read from a manuscript; later that year, Houghton, Mifflin published it together with another lecture, this one far more famous, "The Lesson of Balzac." We cannot hear his voice on a phonograph record, as we can hear his fellow self-exile T. S. Eliot's; and this, it might be said, is another kind of loss. If we cherish photographs of Henry James's extraordinarily striking head with its lantern eyes, we can regret the loss of a filmed interview of the kind that nowadays captures and delivers into the future Norman Mailer and John Updike. The return to an aural culture is, obviously, not *all* a question of loss; only of the most significant loss of all: the widespread nurture by portable print; print as water, and sometimes wine. It was, in its small heyday (we must now begin to say *was*), the most glorious work of the eye-linked brain.

And in the heyday of that glorious work, James made a false analysis. In asking for living models, his analysis belonged to the old aural culture, and he did not imagine its risks. In the old aural culture, speech *was* manner, manner *was* manners, manners *did* teach the tone of the civilized world. In the new aural culture, speech remains manner, manner becomes manners, manners go on teaching the tone of the world. The difference is that the new aural culture, based, as James urged, on emulation, is governed from below. Emulation as a principle cannot control its sources. To seize on only two blatancies: the guerrilla toy of the urban underclass, the huge and hugely loud portable radio—the "ghetto blaster"—is adopted by affluent middle-class white adolescents; so is the locution "Hey, man," which now crosses both class and gender. James worried about the replacement in America of "Yes" by "Yeah" (and further by the comedic "Yep"), but its source was the drawl endemic to the gilt-and-plush parlors of the upper middle class. "Yeah" did not come out of the street; it went into the street. But it is also fairly certain that the "Yeah"-sayers, whatever their place in society, could not have been strong readers, even given the fissure that lies between reading and the style of one's talk. The more attached one is to the community of readers, the narrower the fissure. In a society where belles-lettres are central to education of the young, what controls speech is the degree of absorption in print. Reading governs speech, governs tone, governs manner and manners and civilization. "It is easier to overlook any question of speech than to trouble about it," James complained, "but then it is also easier to snort or neigh, to growl or 'meaow,' than to articulate and intonate."

And yet he overlooked the primacy of the high act of reading. No one who, in the age of conscience and work, submitted to "The Lady of the Lake," or parsed under the aegis of Albert N. Raub, or sent down a bucket into *The Etymological Reader*, was likely to snort or neigh or emit the cry of the tabby. Agreed, it was a more publicly formal and socially encrusted age than ours, and James was more publicly formal and socially encrusted than many of his contemporaries: he was an old-fashioned gentleman. He had come of age during the Civil War. His clothes were laid out by a manservant. His standard was uncompromising. All the same, he missed how and where his own standard ruled. He failed to discover it in the schoolhouses, to which it had migrated after the attenuation of the old aural culture. To be sure, the school texts, however aspiring, could not promise to the children of the poor, or to the children of the immigrants, or to the children of working men, any hope of a manservant; but they *did* promise a habit of speech, more mobilizing and organizing, even, than a valet. The key to American speech was under James's nose. It was at that very moment being turned in a thousand locks. It was opening gate after gate. Those who could read according to an elevated standard could write sufficiently accomplished sentences, and those who could write such sentences could "articulate and intonate."

"Read, read! Read yourself through all the stages of the masters of the language," James might have exhorted the graduates. Instead, he told them to seek "contact and communication, a beneficent contagion," in order to "bring about the happy state—the state of sensibility to tone." It offended him, he confessed, that there were "forces assembled to make you believe that no form of speech is provably better than another." Forty years on, Trolander, Davis, and Papp set their own formidable forces against the forces of relativism in enunciation. Like James, they were zealous to impose their own parochialisms. James did not pronounce the *r* in "mother"; it was, therefore, vulgar to let it be heard. Our Midwestern teachers *did* pronounce the *r;* it was, therefore, vulgar *not* to let it be heard. How, then, one concludes, *is* any form of speech "provably better than another"? In a relativist era, the forces representing relativism in enunciation have for the moment won the argument, it seems; yet James has had his way all the same. With the exception of the South and parts of the East Coast, there is very nearly a uniform *vox Americana.* And we have everywhere a uniform "tone." It is in the streets and in the supermarkets, on the radio and on television; and it is low, low, low. In music, in speech, in manner, the upper has learned to imitate the lower. Cheapened imprecise speech is the triumph of James's tribute to emulation; it is the only possible legacy that could have come of the principle of emulation.

Then why did James plead for vocal imitation instead of reading? He lived in a sea of reading, at the highest tide of literacy, in the time of the crashing of its billows. He did not dream that the sea would shrink, that it was impermanent, that we would return, through the most refined technologies, to the aural culture. He had had his own dealings with a continuing branch of the aural culture—the theater. He had written for it as if for a body of accomplished readers, and it turned on him with contempt. "Forget not," he warned in the wake of his humiliation as a playwright, "that you write for the stupid—that is, your maximum of refinement must meet the minimum of intelligence of the audience—the intelligence, in other words, of the biggest ass it may conceivably contain. It is a most unholy trade!" He was judging, in this outcry, all those forms that arrange for the verbal to bypass the eye and enter solely through the ear. The ear is, for subtlety of interpretation, a coarser organ than the eye; it follows that nearly all verbal culture designed for the ear is broader, brighter, larger, louder, simpler, less intimate, more insistent—more *theatrical*—than any page of any book.

For the population in general, the unholy trades—they are now tremendously in the plural, having proliferated—have rendered reading nearly obsolete, except as a source of data and as a means of record-keeping—"warehousing information." For this the computer is an admittedly startling advance over Pharaoh's indefatigably meticulous scribes, notwithstanding the lofty liturgical poetry that adorned the ancient records, offering a tendril of beauty among the granary lists. Pragmatic reading cannot die, of course, but as the experience that feeds *Homo ridens,* reading is already close to moribund. In the new aural culture of America, intellectuals habitually define "film" as "art" in the most solemn sense, as a counterpart of the literary novel, and ridicule survivors of the age of "movies" as naïfs incapable of making the transition from an old form of popular entertainment to a new form of serious expression meriting a sober equation with written art—as if the issue had anything to do with what is inherently complex in the medium, rather than with what is inherently complex in the recipient of the medium. Undoubtedly any movie is more "complicated" than any book; and also more limited by the apparatus of the "real." As James noted, the maker of aural culture brings to his medium a "maximum of refinement"—i.e., he does the best he can with what he has to work with; sometimes he is even Shakespeare. But the job of sitting in a theater or in a movie house or at home in front of a television set is not so reciprocally complex as the wheels-within-wheels job of reading almost anything at all (including the comics). Reading is an act of imaginative conversion. That specks on a paper can turn into tale or philosophy is as deep a marvel as alchemy or wizardry. A secret brush construes phantom portraits. In the proscenium or the VCR everything is imagined *for* one: there is nothing to do but see and hear, and what's there is what is literally there. When film is "poetic," it is almost never because of language, but rather because of the resemblance to paintings or engravings—one thinks of the knight on a horse in a field of flowers in Bergman's *The Virgin Spring*. Where film is most art, it is least a novelty.

The new aural culture is prone to appliance-novelty—a while ago who could have predicted the video recorder or the hand-held miniature television set, and who now knows what variations and inventions lie ahead? At the same time there is a rigidity to the products of the aural culture—like those static Egyptian sculptures, stylistically unaltered for three millennia, that are brilliantly executed but limited in imaginative intent.

In the new aural culture there is no prevalent belles-lettres curriculum to stimulate novel imaginative intent, that "wizard note" of the awakened Enchantress; what there is is replication—not a reverberation or an echo, but a copy. The Back to Basics movement in education, which on the surface looks as if it is calling for revivification of a belles-lettres syllabus, is not so much reactionary as lost in literalism, or *trompe l'oeil:* another example of the replication impulse of the new aural culture, the culture of theater. Only in a *trompe l'oeil* society would it occur to anyone to "bring back the old values" through bringing back the McGuffey Reader—a scenic designer's idea, and still another instance of the muddle encouraged by the notion of "emulation." The celebration of the McGuffey Reader can happen only in an atmosphere where "film," a copyist's medium, is taken as seriously as a book.

A book is not a "medium" at all; it is far spookier than that, one of the few things-in-themselves that we can be sure of, a Platonic form that can inhabit a virtual infinity of experimental incarnations: any idea, any story, any body of poetry, any incantation, in any language. Above all, a book is the riverbank for the river of language. Language without the riverbank is only television talk—a free fall, a loose splash, a spill. And that is what an aural society, following a time of complex literacy, finally admits to: spill and more spill. James had nothing to complain of: he flourished in a period when whoever read well could speak well; the rest was provincialism—or call it, in kindness, regional exclusiveness. Still, the river of language—to cling to the old metaphor—ran most forcefully when confined to the banks that governed its course. But we who come after the hundred-year hegemony of the ordinary reader, we who see around us, in all these heaps of appliances (each one a plausible "electronic miracle"), the dying heaves of the caste-free passion for letters, should know how profoundly—and possibly how irreversibly—the mummers have claimed us.

HEATHER MACDONALD

Writing Down Together

Heather MacDonald is a contributing editor to *City Journal*, the quarterly published by the Manhattan Institute. She is a journalist with a degree in jurisprudence whose cultural, social, and political criticism has been published in the *New York Times*, the *Wall Street Journal*, and the *New Republic* where her politely scathing discussion of "diversity training" first brought her acuity and analytic force to the attention of this book's editors. An earlier version of this essay was published in the summer 1995 issue of *Public Interest.*

Who could have imagined that an examination of current pedagogical practice in the teaching of writing expository prose would yield so ample a crop of issues central to the theme of a dumbed-down educational system? (Perhaps only the perturbed parents of children currently exposed to these self-serving innovations.) Ms. Mac-Donald's steely assessment uncovers the dismantling of form in favor of unexamined content, the cultivation of self-esteem over simple competence, and an educational program which has appropriated syntax, diction, and literacy itself for political purposes, while dissolving, in a wash of multicultural good feeling, the notion of the first-person singular, and its custody of the unique, subjective, and differentiated self.

    Ms. MacDonald's rigorous review of these methods steadily advocates excellence, but stops short of an intransigent purism: while disapproving deeply of the fracturing of culture, she cheerfully defends the split infinitive.

AMERICAN EMPLOYERS regard the nation's educational system as an irrelevance, according to a Census Bureau survey released in February 1995. Businesses ignore a prospective employee's educational credentials in favor of his work history and attitude. Although the Census researchers did not venture any hypotheses for this strange behavior, anyone familiar with the current state of academia could have provided explanations aplenty.

    One overlooked corner of the academic madhouse bears in particular on graduates' job-readiness: the teaching of writing. In the field of writing, today's education is not just an irrelevance, it is positively detrimental to a student's development. For years, composition teachers have absorbed the worst strains in both popular and academic culture. The result is an indigestible stew of sixties liberationist zeal, seventies deconstructivist nihilism, and eighties multicultural proselytizing. The only thing that composition teachers are *not* talking and writing about these days is how to teach students to compose clear, logical prose.

Predictably, the corruption of writing pedagogy began in the sixties. In 1966, the Carnegie Endowment funded a conference of American and British writing teachers at Dartmouth College. The event was organized by the Modern Language Association and the National Conference of Teachers of English. The Dartmouth Conference was the Woodstock of the composition professions: it liberated teachers from the dull routine of teaching grammar and logic.

Dartmouth rejected what was called a "transmission" model of English in favor of a "growth" model. In transmission mode, teachers pass along composition skills and literary knowledge. In growth mode, according to Joseph Harris, professor of English at the University of Pittsburgh, they focus on students' "experience of language in all its forms"—including ungrammatical ones. A big problem with the transmission model of English is that it implies that teachers actually *know* more than their students do. In the growth model, however, the teacher is not an authority figure; rather, he is a supportive, nurturing friend, who works with, rather than challenges, what a student has to say. Dartmouth proponents claimed that improvement in students' linguistic skills need not come through direct training in grammar and style, but rather would flower incidentally, as students experimented with personal and expressive forms of talk and writing.

The Dartmouth Conference and subsequent writing pedagogy reflected the political culture of the time. It was anti-authoritarian and liberationist; it celebrated inarticulateness and error as proof of authenticity. But it was also a response to the looming problem of race. The City University of New York began the nation's first academic affirmative-action program in 1966; other schools would soon follow suit. The movement to legitimate black English began at that time. Confronted with a barrage of students who had no experience in formal grammar or written language, it was highly convenient for professors to learn that students' natural way of speaking and writing should be preserved, not corrected.

There is a final ideological strand in composition pedagogy that has its roots in the late 1960s: Marxism. Teachers on the radical left began arguing that the demand for literacy oppresses the masses. Writing in *Radical Teacher,* MIT humanities professor Wayne O'Neil explains that "it has become important for the ruling class to exclude the potentially radicalizing elements of higher education from the colleges. Thus everywhere along the scale of education there is a relentless march toward the basics." James Sledd, emeritus professor of English at the University of Texas at Austin, wrote in *College English* that Standard English is "essentially an instrument of domination," and that coercing students to speak properly conditions them to accept the coercion of capitalism. Richard

Ohmann, humanities professor at Wesleyan University, has pronounced the "decline of literacy . . . a fiction, if not a hoax."

The Dartmouth Conference gave rise to what became known as the process school of composition. Peter Elbow of Evergreen State College in Washington is its most influential practitioner. Not all of Elbow's ideas are bad. He emphasizes that writing is a continuous process, composed mostly of rewriting. He encourages students to think of their essays in terms of multiple drafts, rather than as a single-shot effort. He has vigorously promoted "free writing," a warm-up exercise in which the author writes continuously for a fixed period of time, uninhibited by grammar, punctuation, or logic.

But the drawbacks of the process school cancel its contributions. In elevating process, it has driven out standards. Rather than judging a piece of student writing by an objective standard of coherence and correctness, teachers are supposed to evaluate how much the student has grown over the course of a semester. The hottest trend in grading—portfolio assessment—emerges from the process school. Peter Elbow created the method after he saw the "harmful effects of writing proficiency exams." Among the most harmful of those effects is undoubtedly the assault on self-esteem from a poor grade. In portfolio assessment, students' evaluations are based on drafts of papers, diary entries, letters, and other informal assignments compiled over the course of a semester, rather than on the freestanding merit of a paper or exam. Often the student "collaborates" with the teacher in assigning a grade to the portfolio. Portfolio assessment allows for the radical reduction of standards, imports greater subjectivity into grading, and is extremely time-consuming.

For the process school, politics determines pedagogy. Elbow added an additional week of free writing to the start of his courses at Evergreen State College when he saw how useful the practice was to "building community" in the classroom, among other benefits. Elbow rails against grading, because it interferes with his ability to connect meaningfully with his students. "Good writing teachers like students writing," he explains, and "it's hard to like something if we know we have to give it a D."

In keeping with the anti-authoritarian commitment of process practitioners, students in a process classroom teach each other. Students form small groups—one earth-mother teacher at City College calls it "making hoops"—to read aloud and comment on each other's writing, while the teacher surveys the scene benignly. The students may be admonished to say two good, as well as two critical, things about each other's essays—a diplomatic task that would tax F. R. Leavis. Many of the groups I have observed quickly turned their attention to more compelling matters, like last weekend's parties or the newest sneakers. And no wonder, given the abysmal prose they are supposed to discuss. The following two paragraphs are from a student's answer to CUNY's writing proficiency exam. The question was: "Do you think the personal life of a political candidate . . . should be considered a factor in determining his or her ability to do the job?"

We are living in a world that's getting worse everyday. And what we are doing nothing, just complaining about the other person life. We should stop because if we don't stop by looking on every candidate lifestyle and focus more on how, we could make it better. We all gonna die of, hungry, because we wouldn't have nothing to eat and no place to life.

People tends to make mistake in life. We all are humans. That's why we should never judge a person for the cover of a book. People change in life, most of them tends to learn from their mistake. We live in a world that we should learn to forgive and forget everyone mistake and move forward.

While peer teaching may have a value for more experienced student-writers, for the incompetent—which includes not just remedial students but increasingly all incoming students—it is an egregious case of the blind leading the blind. The following paragraph was written by a non-remedial student:

Peer critiquing is very helpful in writing a well develope essay. It points out mistakes you missed. Peer critiquing give the writer more idea's to add to the piece of work. This is also a way for you peer to ask what your writing about. Peer critiquing also helps you the writer to understand more about you own work.

Despite such positive reviews, peer teaching ignores the reason students are in remedial classes in the first place and violates the time-honored principle that one learns to write by reading good, not awful, writing.

The process school's determination to break down hierarchy extends beyond the teacher-student divide. A pioneering freshmancomposition course at City College combines students who failed the CUNY writing entrance exam with those who passed. Says Acting Provost Mike Aarons: "The idea behind the program [which is being replicated in other areas of the college] is that the more successful students help the less successful."

Aarons might have added that another idea behind such programs is radical egalitarianism. Individual effort must go to raising the collectivity, not to raising oneself above the collectivity; individual success betrays the good of the whole. The course received a grant from the Fund for the Improvement of Post-Secondary Education—apparently the federal government likes the idea of fighting elitism as well.

In a process classroom, content eclipses form. The college essay and an eighteen-year-old's personality become one and the same. Effie Cochran, an English as a Second Language professor at Baruch College,

stated: "Here I am—teacher-confessor. All these [gay] people are coming out to me through autobiographical reports who wouldn't come out
to a priest." One process professor recommends that the profession "pay
more attention to the experience of psychotherapists regarding role-
modelling, sexual tension, and transference."

Students who have been told in their writing class to let their deepest
selves loose on the page and not worry about syntax, logic, or form have
trouble adjusting to their other classes. A student at St. Anselm College
complained to her writing teacher that her humanities professor had
prevented her from developing her ideas on Homer, Cicero, and the
Hebrew prophets. His sin? He had insisted on numerous references to
the text and correct English prose. "In humanities," she whined, "I have
to remember a certain format and I have to back up every general statement with specific examples. Oh, and that word, 'I,' I just used. You
would never see that word in one of my Humanities papers." In process
school jargon, the poor humanities student has been denied "access to a
personal language."

With its emphasis on personal experience and expression, the process school forgets that the ultimate task of college writing is to teach
students how to think. In the personal essay, assertions need not be
backed up by anything more than the author's sincerity. According to
Rolf Norgaard of the University of Colorado, evaluation then becomes a
judgment upon students' lives, their personalities, their souls. But how
can you tell a student, he asks, that her experiences or family life were
not terribly original or striking?

The process school of writing has spread well beyond college campuses. Washington Irving Elementary School in Chicago introduced
process methods six years ago in the hope of improving students' cata-
strophic performance in reading and writing. Teachers tossed out their
red pencils and workbooks; from then on, students would simply write,
unfettered by such enthusiasm-crushing methods as rote learning. Students worked in groups; grades were out—cooperation was in.

The initial response was euphoric—and short-lived. Student groups
rarely completed their assignments. They made little progress in mechanics. Some teachers started giving grades and teaching the basics
again. But when they handed out "incompletes" and tried to hold students to higher standards, they caught heat from both parents and the
principal, who told them that their expectations were too high. *Lesson:*
once out of the bottle, the process genie is hard to get back in.

In the early eighties, a few process teachers started to sense that
something was deeply wrong. While they had been unleashing an orgy of
self-expression in their classes, across the hall in the literature department, the hippest teachers were preaching that there was no self—that
the self was a fiction, a mere product of language. The process theorists,

in other words, stumbled across deconstruction. In the seventies and eighties, this was not difficult to do, since just about every field in the humanities during that period scrambled to parrot the impenetrable prose of Derrida, de Man, and Lacar.

What an embarrassment for the poor process teachers! Deconstruction declared the self dead, and they had been assiduously cultivating it. And what to do about their favorite genre, the personal essay, which seems to presuppose a writing subject, a concept anathema to the deconstructionists?

The solution to this dilemma demonstrates the resourcefulness of college professors today. While some process advocates, such as Elbow, have continued their former ways unchanged, many others have simply grafted deconstructive rhetoric onto a process methodology. The result is pedagogical chaos. Students are still writing personal essays, but they are deconstructing them at the same time. Such writing assignments are designed with one sole purpose: to make the professor feel that he is at the critical cutting edge; they have nothing to do with teaching writing.

Witness the rhetorical sleight-of-hand of Joel Haefner, professor at Illinois State University. Haefner manages to demonstrate disdain for process pedagogy, while nevertheless preserving it. "Calls to revive the personal essay," he writes in *College English,* "carry a hidden agenda and rest on the shibboleth of individualism, and concomitantly, the ideology of American democracy. . . . As we interrogate our assumption about the essay genre and its role in a 'democratic' and 'individualistic' pedagogy, we will find, I think, that it makes more sense to see the essay as a cultural product, as a special kind of collective discourse. Hence there is still a place for the 'personal' essay in a collaborative pedagogy."

This tortured reasoning may preserve Haefner's credibility with the post-structuralists, but its practical result must tie students up in knots. Here are some of Haefner's deconstructive writing projects that are intended to "critique the fiction of a singular author": Writing groups create a personal essay that purports to be the work of a single author; individual students write a personal essay using "we"; teams rewrite a personal essay from other singular viewpoints; and—this is perhaps the most "innovative"—students are encouraged not to create a unified, coherent first-person singular voice, but rather a mix of "I" speakers.

This borders on pedagogical malpractice. Here are students who are unable to write a coherent paragraph, and they are being encouraged to cultivate an incoherent writing voice.

But academia can be cruel. No sooner did writing teachers master deconstructive jargon than a new improved version came along. After years on the top of the charts, deconstruction has been pushed aside by multiculturalism. Multiculturalism is both the direct offspring of deconstruction and its nemesis. The current obsession with racial, sexual, and ethnic difference grew directly out of deconstruction's obsession with so-called linguistic difference. But whereas deconstruction was a mandarin pursuit that had only contempt for political engagement, multiculturalism asserts the centrality of politics to every human endeavor.

For would-be composition theorists, the most important consequence of multiculturalism has been the reemergence of the self as the central focus of concern. But the new multicultural self is defined exclusively by racial, sexual, and ethnic identity. The multicultural writing classroom is a workshop on racial and sexual oppression. Rather than studying possessive pronouns, students are learning how the language silences women and blacks.

As Richard Bernstein described in *Dictatorship of Virtue,* the University of Texas at Austin exploded in controversy in 1990 over a proposed writing course called "Writing About Difference." The course text was *Racism and Sexism: An Integrated Study,* by Paula Rothenberg, a national leader in the movement to inject race and gender into every aspect of the curriculum. "One assumption of this book," writes Rothenberg, "is that racism and sexism pervade American culture, that they are learned at an early age and reinforced throughout life by a variety of institutions and experiences that are part of growing up and living in the United States." Students in the new writing course would use the text's readings to explore their own roles as oppressors or oppressed.

In a rare victory for common sense, the course was canceled after a bitter fight. Most colleges have not been so lucky, however.

Effie Cochran of Baruch College assigns her remedial writing students role-playing exercises so the women can vent their anger at the discrimination they suffer in and out of school. Whether these performances improve students' writing skills is anyone's guess.

The personal essay remains a cornerstone for the multicultural classroom; it is an especial favorite of feminists. But it has been supplemented by the "ethnography." David Bleich's students at the University of Rochester conduct self-reflexive ethnographies on social relations in the classroom, observing how their gender, race, and class allegedly determine their response to literary works. The most frequently assigned topic for student ethnographies, however, is popular culture—in other words, describe and respond to your favorite rock video.

Every writing theory of the past thirty years has come up with reasons why it's not necessary to teach grammar and style. For the multiculturalists, the main reason is that grammatical errors signify that the author is politically engaged. According to Min-Zhan Lu of Drake University, the "individual consciousness is necessarily heterogeneous, contradictory, and in process. The writer writes at the site of conflict."

It is the goal of current writing theory to accentuate that conflict. Today's theorists berate former City College professor Mina Shaughnessy, whose book *Errors and Expectations* heralded the remedial writing movement, for trying to introduce her students—however gently—to academic prose. Min-Zhan Lu writes: "We need to contest teaching methods which offer to 'cure' all signs of conflict and struggle which the dominant conservative ideology of the 1990s seeks to contain."

There is a basic law at work in current composition theory: as students' writing gets worse, the critical vocabulary used to assess it grows ever more pompous. James Zebrowski of Syracuse University claims that doing ethnographies makes students "constructors of knowledge." John Trimbur of Worcester Polytechnic Institute describes what he calls "post-process, post-cognitivist theory": it "represents literacy as an ideological arena and composing as a cultural activity by which writers position and reposition themselves in relation to their own and others' subjectivities, discourses, practices, and institutions." According to Trimbur, "literacy crises result not from declining skills but from the contention of various interested representations of literacy." In other words, students who can't read and write are simply offering up another version of literacy, which the oppressive conservative ideology refuses to recognize. Such double-talk harks back to the sixties, when open-admissions students were described as coming from a culture where "orality" was dominant.

The bottom line in regard to all this nonsense is drastically lowered expectations of student skills. Marilyn Sternglass, a composition theorist at City College, argues that students should be able to pick up the topics for CUNY's writing proficiency exam before the exam is administered, because "responding to the questions cold makes too many demands on students. If they concentrate on content, their mechanics will suffer; if they concentrate on mechanics, they lose their train of thought." It never occurs to her that such a zero-sum trade-off indicates precisely what the test is supposed to measure: the inability to write.

Professors are expending vast amounts of energy making excuses for their students. At a 1994 composition conference at the CUNY Graduate Center, Geraldine de Luca, director of freshman English at Brooklyn College, railed against grammatical rules. Though teaching rules in response to individual students' questions, she said, can be "empowering, the rules have a way of taking over. And some teachers think that's fine: 'It's about time they learned grammar,' they say. 'I knew this stuff when I was in the fifth grade.' But in what time, in what community, in what country?" asked de Luca melodramatically. "Even the concept of error," she concluded, "is beginning to feel repugnant to me."

Professors who exempt students from the very standards that governed them when they were in school feel compassionate, noble, and powerful. But professors' power is limited to their world. Though they may be willing to overlook spelling, punctuation, and grammatical errors in favor of a "holistic" approach to student writing, employers are clearly not as generous, as the Census survey suggests. De Luca's response to the demands of the world outside the academy shows just how out of touch professors can be. "When we talk about the real world," she says, "we have to consider how much our students' self-esteem and spirit will be needed for them to succeed in their lives. Their inner world, their ability—or inability—to imagine, to enjoy the play of ideas in their own mind, will be as much a part of their reality as the world of work."

This statement is ludicrous for two reasons: First, however much a person may be enjoying the play of ideas in his own mind, that counts for nothing if he is unable to get a job. It also counts for nothing in *getting* a job. More important, the premise that self-esteem is built up through a dispensation from rules and judgment is deeply flawed. In *Death of the American University,* a chronicle of open admissions at City College, classics professor Louis Heller describes a different formula for self-esteem. Decades ago, he writes, "there was genuine hunger, and deprivation, and discrimination too, but when a child received a failing mark, no militant parent group assailed the teacher. Instead parent and child agonized over the subject, placing the responsibility squarely on the child who was given to know that *he* had to measure up to par, not that he was the victim of society, a wicked school system, teachers who didn't understand him, or any of the other pseudosociological nonsense now handed out."

Heller's view lost out a long time ago, of course. Today, at CUNY and elsewhere, there is a growing movement to abolish the distinction between remedial writing and reading courses and regular freshman courses, on the ground that placing students in remedial courses injures their self-esteem. Remedial writing courses at Baruch College and elsewhere are now known as "English as a Second Dialect" or ESD courses. Proudly displaying their knowledge of Foucault, composition theorists argue that the category "remedial education" is merely an artificial construct imposed by the ruling classes on the oppressed. Marilyn Sternglass of City College quickly corrected me when I asked about students who needed remedial work: "They are 'judged' to need remedial classes," she retorted haughtily. An influential report at CUNY argued that Latinos shouldn't be kept from upper-level courses, no matter what their skills, because holding them back for remediation sends the message that they are deficient in skills. One might respond, well, yes, it does, because they are.

Students' serious writing and reasoning problems originate outside the college and high school writing classroom, in homes without books, and in elementary education almost devoid of reading. But pretending that everything is rosy won't make it so. Instead of coming up with fancy theories to legitimate the abysmal status quo, writing teachers should be proclaiming from the rooftops that we are in danger of becoming a society of functional illiterates.

S T E V E N   G O L D B E R G

The Erosion of the Social Sciences

Steven Goldberg is chairman of the Department of Sociology of City College, City University of New York. His academic and scientific articles are devoted to the analysis of logical and empirical aspects of social issues—like those addressed in this essay—which frequently send him into those battlefields where no prisoners are taken and from which few return. Recent books include *Why Men Rule* (1993) and *When Wish Replaces Thought* (1991).

Goldberg looks in this piece toward a curious convergence: the marketing spirit; a softening of his own academic discipline; and an almost universal failure to share his own ebullient conviction that the greatest possible pleasure lies in pursuing the truth. No particular piece of human folly or wrongdoing in recent decades surprises Goldberg as much as the deluge of curious explanations for it. Unlike some of the contributors to this book, he still defends the sixties. He feels that where wrongheadedness prevailed in that decade, at least its mistakes were generous ones, but that wrongheadedness in the nineties produces little but profiteering and self-promotion.

He is confident that critics of the invasion of the social sciences by ideology are unlikely to be boiled in oil these days, since the practice is condemned as ecologically unsound anyway.

*T*HERE WAS A TIME when you could assume that an intelligent person looking for the truth was guided by the most basic of scientific intuitions: nature will give you a lift only if you're going her way. The fallaciousness of the *ad hominem* argument and the argument from consequence, for example, was so obvious that the anticipation of the embarrassment you would feel if you invoked such arguments was sufficient to preclude your doing so.

In social science today we can no longer make this assumption. Even if we continue to assume that we are dealing with intelligent people, we find no way to maintain the belief that such people act on an impulse to find the truth. Instead, we find large and increasing numbers of ideologues who act not as if nature is something to be discovered no matter what she should turn out to be, but rather as if she is a handmaiden whose purpose is to satisfy one's psychological and ideological needs. Lacking the rudimentary scientific impulse of self-refutation (i.e., if you are happy with the conclusions reached by your research, double-check and triple-check those conclusions), the ideologue assesses truth not by its concordance with reality, but by its concordance with psychological and ideological needs. Whether incompetence or deceitfulness is to blame is neither here nor there; the work itself is effectively both incompetent *and* deceitful. And once the desire for truth is not the only permissible impulse, one is no longer playing the same game we are.

So, for example, a certain sociologist, on learning that I had once written a book titled *The Inevitability of Patriarchy,* told me that she would never read such a book because "it was obvious that it was written by a reactionary" and asked whether I would read a book titled *The Inevitability of Matriarchy.*

Here, in bold relief, we see the attitude that has come to infuse much of the social sciences. My answer, of course, was, "Would I read it? Lady, I'd have been parked on the steps outside the bookstore waiting for the first delivery." The first responsibility, and, it used to be assumed, the first impulse, of one who presents an explanation of an empirical reality is to address criticism, and if the criticism is correct, to correct or surrender the explanation.

Were this all encapsulated in the world of the social scientist it would perhaps not matter much. If one has faith, as I do, that truth always wins in the long run—that the emotions that wrap themselves around the nucleus of an incorrect theoretical explanation or empirical claim always sooner or later attach themselves to something else—then one could be sanguine. The cost in wasted resources would be lamentable, but the intellectual miscreants would, in the long run, be hurting only themselves as they became another failed attempt in our evolution toward truth.

But in the social sciences, discussion is not encapsulated. People do not sit around the dinner table discussing Higgs fields or heat transfer or Sanskrit verbs (at least they don't in my neighborhood). But they do discuss, indeed argue about, men and women and the death penalty and health care and homosexuality and values and race and abortion and test scores and crime and, in short, most of the empirical realities studied by the social scientist.

And what do they get from far too many social science courses relevant to the issues they discuss? At *best,* when they are not given outright misinformation and fallacy, they get a haggis of overwritten nonsense that is restatement of the trivial and the obvious. The following comes from one of the *better* books occasionally assigned in women's studies courses, a biography of a scientist:

We need a language that enables us to perceptually and conceptually negotiate our way between sameness and opposition, that permits the recognition of kinship in difference and difference among kin; a language that encodes respect for difference, particularity, alterity without repudiating the underlying affinity that is the first prerequisite for knowledge.

A nice exercise for a freshman composition student would be to analyze a sentence comparable to this and to decide whether that which it attempts to make profound is true and trivial or false and misleading. Of course the student would have to be warned against being fooled, as the authors of many sentences like these have been, into thinking that foolishness is any less foolish because it is "supported" by a plethora of footnotes even dopier than the text that is being supported.

2

The term "social science" was never meant to imply that the empiricist can control the experimental environment to the extent that the physicist can. Everyone understands that practical problems, such as the self-fulfilling prophecy, raise difficulties that the physicist can, most of the time, avoid—as does the fact that 250 million people get very grouchy if you try to tell them what to do. Until recently, everyone *also* understood that the social sciences were, as Ernest Nagel so beautifully explained in his *The Structure of Science*, "scientific" in principle: they are bound by precisely the same constraints—the same logic, the same rules of evidence, and the same methods of validation—as are the hard sciences.

Then, at the height of the politicalization of the sixties, increasing numbers of sociologists began espousing the view that objectivity in the social sciences was a myth. And, since objectivity was a myth, the social sciences were not accountable to the logic of science and could, in effect, drop the "science" from social science and incorporate ideological dispositions into the "social." The belief that there could be no "value-free sociology" became an excuse to infuse theoretical framework with political wish.

This view was not *totally* without salutary effect. It did expose those social scientists whose work represented nothing more than pimping for the interests that sponsored them.

But this view tremendously exacerbated the very problem it claimed to ameliorate. Scientific logic is infinitely our greatest defense against the bias of individual wish and ideology. It requires the scientist to do everything possible to refute his conclusions. To be sure, the scientist is human, and occasionally a psychic need or ideological impulse trumps his knowledge that, in science, an ability to resist the demands of such need or impulse is what separates the grown-ups from the children. However, the *other* scientists who assess his conclusions manifest a ruthlessness—a ruthlessness encouraged by science itself—in attempting to expose any fallacy and error. If wish or ideology has introduced fallacy or error into the conclusions, they will be found and exposed. (If there is no fallacy or error, it does not matter how biased or ideological the scientist might be; the world is round even if it is Hitler making the claim. To argue otherwise, as do those who see social science as a "myth," is to attempt to make a virtue out of the *ad hominem* fallacy.)

The new sociological view was a woefully simplistic version of a then-current view of science proposed by Thomas Kuhn. Many social scientists represented Kuhn as believing that science did not progress primarily by a step-by-step process of failed experiment and better explanation of the empirical reality being addressed, but by "revolutions" that took place when a great scientist ignored cultural constraint and myopia induced by the contemporary view of things. There is a relationship between Kuhn's claims and this view, but the quantitative chasm between the two is such that it is like the difference between a claim that Mars plays the gravitational role we observe and the view that Mars is virtually the *only* thing that plays such a role.

Nearly all scientists correctly believe that Kuhn overemphasizes the discreteness—the detachment of the great discovery from the work that preceded it—of scientific progress. (Even Newton, a scientific revolutionary if ever there were one, subscribed to the view that he was "standing on the shoulders of Giants.") Nearly all science consists of an empirical finding's, or, especially, an empirical anomaly's, determining the next theoretical step and the next empirical investigation. But most would also agree that there have been times when a dramatic "paradigm switch" deserves close inspection in order to see whether cultural cognitive and perceptual limitations had previously forestalled scientific discovery. (Clearly, Kuhn's approach, even if it is not the best description of most science, is valuable in helping us to understand the—perhaps rare—situation in which Discovery C, which in retrospect seems virtually entailed in Discoveries A and B, was not recognized for two centuries after A and B.)

The social science misrepresentation of Kuhn consists of equating Kuhn's emphasis on exceedingly subtle distortions of cognition and perception with the sort of heavy-handed scientific detours generated by, for example, Lysenkoism, and concluding that science is little more than the handmaiden of the ruling class (a view that, in addition, appeals to a great many non-academics grateful for a seeming justification for equating ideology with truth). The "methodology" for such courses consists of unending discussions of "paradigms," discussions found irresistibly enticing to the third-rate. In Kuhn's work, "paradigm" simply refers to sets of codifying assumptions somewhat too general to provide clear empirical anchorage; in a great many social science works (and, incidentally, even in works by the—admittedly uninfluential—"feminist science" adherents in the hard sciences) the term provides subject matter for people who do not ever actually *do* any real science (social or hard). As was the case with the authors who confuse an excess of footnotes in support of foolishness with serious scholarship, the paradigm people have somehow learned the form, but not the process.

Similarly, some sociologists have taken Émile Durkheim's ultimately sensible "social fact" and have used it to justify denials of truth. Durkheim had simply made the point that if, for example, the culture of a primitive people sees the earth as flat, you must see the world through the eyes of one who bases many of his conclusions about the world on this belief. Durkheim didn't mean that the earth *really* is flat. But a number of politically motivated sociologists have, in effect, used the concept of a social fact to make claims about how society works that are equivalent to saying that the earth *really* is flat. These sociologists will occasionally, when under pressure, give lip service to the difference between a "fact" and a "social fact" (which *is* a fact, but simply a fact describing what a people believe, with no implication that the belief is correct or incorrect). However, their actual work conflates the two.

The reason for a social scientist's presenting Kuhn's and Durkheim's work in this way soon became obvious. If science is nothing more than a Lysenkoan rationalization for ideological belief, then *every* scientific claim is as valid as every other. And if *every* scientific claim is as valid as every other, then each person can believe whatever he wants. In other words, the very purpose of science, the separation of the true from the non-true—and the limitations on belief that this entails—is jettisoned.

3

The reader may well think that I am exaggerating the degree to which ideology has invaded the social sciences. And the reader would certainly be right to point out that there are exceptions: There are individuals who maintain scientific standards (though it tells us *something* that in the social sciences today one must be an exception to exhibit the standards that are the minimal expectation of the physical scientist). Likewise, there are areas of the social sciences that are relatively free of ideology (i.e., statistical demography, immigration, neuropsychology, etc.), though precious few in sociology.

And, to be sure, there are college courses, even in sociology, that are removed from the issues that ideology infects. But not many. And, tobe sure, when all this is stated this bluntly, no social scientist acknowledges that any of this describes him. But this is rarely stated bluntly, so a hundred like-minded sociologists and anthropologists never need face the softness of the evidence for their beliefs. (Indeed, addressing these people directly does little good. In one-on-one debates—which they avoid with all the alacrity their error and illogic would advise—they will acknowledge the softness of their arguments; they have no choice. But as

soon as they rejoin those who share their biases, they effectively forget
that their arguments are worthless. Much more successful is debating
these people before an audience not already sharing their—or any—
biases. No one likes looking stupid.)

But these *are* the exceptions. Let me give you an example—by no
means atypical—of the current standard.

In the late seventies, I noticed that a number of texts in introductory
sociology and in the family began their chapters on sex roles with the
claim that Margaret Mead had found that the Tchambuli of New Guinea
reversed sex roles.

Now, it is true that—writing at a time (1935) that unquestioningly
accepted the view that nearly all male-female differences were rooted in
physiology—Mead did, understandably if wrongly, tend to exaggerate
the malleability of sex roles in an attempt to balance things. As the
female sociologist Jesse Bernard pointed out, a lot of Mead consisted of
talk about effete male headhunters and husky women at their looms,
descriptions that intimated a lot less role malleability if one ignored the
adjectives.

Nonetheless, Mead never claimed that sex roles were reversed (i.e.,
that the Tchambuli failed to exhibit patriarchy, male attainment of status, or male dominance in male-female relationships and encounters).
When harshly criticized in the anthropological journals for even her
lesser exaggeration of malleability, Mead wrote:

Nowhere do I suggest that I have found any material which disproves the existence of sex differences. . . . This study was not concerned with whether there are
or are not actual and universal differences between the sexes, either quantitative
or qualitative.

Moreover, in reviewing the first edition of my book *Why Men Rule*,
Mead found my evidence "accurate" and "persuasive" and added:

It is true . . . that all the claims so glibly made about societies ruled by women are
nonsense. We have no reason to believe that they ever existed . . . men everywhere have been in charge of running the show . . . men have been the leaders in
public affairs and the final authorities at home.

From the time she published her work on the Tchambuli, sixty years
ago, until her death, Mead reiterated the point time and again. To no
avail.

To quantify my impression that a great many introductory sociology
texts began their chapters on sex roles with the claim that Mead had
demonstrated the possibility of sex-role reversal, I went to Barnes &
Noble and looked at the sex-role chapters of nearly forty introductory
texts. I found that over 90 percent of these texts did, in fact, make this
claim.

I pointed out this misrepresentation in a letter published (in 1979) by *Contemporary Sociology,* the book-review journal of the American Sociological Association and a publication read by virtually everyone who publishes in mainstream sociology. Similar trips to Barnes & Noble a decade later demonstrated that—as I was pretty certain would be the case—the letter had had no effect whatever.

It is difficult to say precisely which form of dishonesty is manifested in the continuing misrepresentation of the evidence. It is a traditional—if unacknowledged—practice of introductory textbook authors to crib wildly from other texts. One is reminded of the claim of Kurt Vonnegut, Jr. (I believe), that the easiest thing in the world is to publish the best dictionary: simply copy the previously best dictionary and correct one error. Thus, some of the authors undoubtedly know nothing whatever about Mead's claim, universal sex-role differences, sex roles in general, men, or women. (Writing an introductory text is—I imagine—an unbelievably boring task. No one is interested in "sociology" in the sense that the introductory textbook requires; writing the chapter on formal organizations strikes me as equivalent to—to use my friend Faith Scheer's phrase—"catching darts for a hobby"; other people find formal organizations spellbinding and have no interest in the things that fascinate me.)

However, it is undoubtedly the case that many of these authors knew perfectly well that Mead's work does not support the claim of male-female behavioral reversibility. They assert away the possibility of universality because universality suggests the possibility of physiological constraints to which the social must conform. They do this in part because sociologists believe that they have a vested interest in purely social explanations and in part because they don't know any biology (in this case, neuroendocrinology). But mostly they do it because they fear what they see as the implications of an acknowledgment that (hereditary) physiological differences have something to do with the differences between men and women.

More generally, the Left, having been far more influenced by empiricism (as I have been) than has been the Right and feeling that the fact that values are anchored only in the subjective renders any argument for values impotent, is moved to invoke empirical facts as if facts can somehow support values. Dubious "facts" are made up to camouflage the inherently arbitrary nature of values. Thus, for example, it is incorrectly asserted that it has been demonstrated that the death penalty doesn't deter, rather than that (as the Left believes) the death penalty is morally wrong, whether it deters or not.

(It should not be necessary to add that none of this implies that moral values themselves cannot be studied as empirical phenomena. The hypothesis "A society that is in a period of strong initial economic development will see premarital intercourse as morally wrong" is clearly a scientific hypothesis, whether correct or not being another question. But, according to the strict empiricist, the moral claim that "premarital intercourse is morally wrong" is not a scientific hypothesis.)

On a practical level, the contamination of the social sciences is the result of contributions by virtually all members of the academy. Those who are most capable of fighting it, the most talented, are not willing to give up their serious work to attend endless campus committee meetings and professional conventions where the ideologues rule. To be quite blunt, people who are doing serious research and teaching do not have the time to battle ideology on all the various levels. This enables the second- and third-rate to dominate the deanships, committee chairman-ships, and—especially—positions of leadership in the professional asso-ciations that transmit the contamination and guarantee its survival and, perhaps, dominance. The deans and other administrators act not merely out of philosophical agreement with the nonsensical, but for the spoils accruing to those who cater to adolescent wishes: you get more students to register for "Racism and Homophobia in a Patriarchal System" than for "Social Theory from Plato to Weber."

The contamination has been entirely unalloyed at the level of the professional association. One need merely skim the publications of the Modern Language Association or American Anthropological Associa-tion, or the papers that these feature in their annual meetings, to see that they engender the purest form of the victory of wish and ideology over the willingness to take truth as it comes. (While the unbelievably narcis-sistic excrescences of "postmodernism" that have destroyed so much of the study of literature in this country do not play a major role in the social sciences—which seem to prefer ideology to mental masturba-tion—we do occasionally encounter titles like "S[t]imulate Me: A Loose Manifesto.")

4

While the infection of the social sciences by ideology is primarily an infection from the Left, the Right has also done its part to prepare the stage for an attack on objectivity.

This is seen most clearly in the conservative attack on the tenet known as "cultural relativity." "Cultural relativity" is the principle that any judgment of the moral status of a society—any comparison of societies that finds one society morally superior to the other—is by its nature invalid.

Epistemologically, "cultural relativism" is simply the social version of the empiricism that—while traceable to early influences such as the work of Roger Bacon and David Hume—blossomed in this century. This development—associated with Bertrand Russell, the Vienna Circle, and the like—had as its primary target nineteenth-century "theories" that explained everything (i.e., with "explanations" logically analogous to "the Forever Is Eternally Unfolding"). Empiricism dismisses hypotheses that cannot, even in principle, be refuted by sense data (i.e., *whatever* is discovered was confirmatory; how would we know if "the Forever *Isn't* Eternally Unfolding"?). Empiricism is the principle that says, "if you couldn't lose, you can't win."

To be sure, there are arguments about the ultimate validity of empiricism. (A) Empiricism itself rests on an unverifiable assumption; (B) acceptance of pure empiricism raises doubts about those aspects of the generalized Darwinian theory of evolution that can validly be summarized as "survival of the fittest." (Since whatever survives is declared the "fit," some feel that it is not clear how, even in principle, this could be refuted. As opposed to "survival of the biggest"—which is, of course, incorrect—"survival of the fittest" "succeeds" no matter what empirically happens: if dachshunds survive and dinosaurs don't, then they are deemed to have been fit; if dinosaurs survive and dachshunds don't, then *they* are deemed to have been fit.) My point here is not to take sides on the argument about the validity of empiricism or that concerning evolutionary theory, but merely to acknowledge that objections to empiricism have been raised.

Nonetheless, while many raise such questions about the demarcation line of the "empirical" and the "non-empirical," the basic empiricist distinction is accepted nearly all the time by nearly all scientists. And nearly all of *these* scientists accept the conclusion that moral issues fall outside the perimeter that defines the area that can be meaningfully studied by science. (After all, whatever the basic unverifiable aspects of empiricism, it does result in something *more* than tautological truth: testable prediction.) Moral questions, according to the empiricist, cannot be answered by scientific means nor can a scientific finding ever entail a particular moral (or political) view. As the philosopher says, "is cannot generate ought."

Even that small minority that does not accept the separation of science and morality does not argue that a scientific conclusion can be refuted by invocation of the social *consequences* of a belief in the conclusion. It has been recognized for millennia that an appeal to consequence is a fallacy.

But it is precisely this fallacy on which the conservative view of "cultural relativism" rests. The conservative view rests on a fear (often unarticulated) of (what the conservative sees as) the consequences of a belief in "cultural relativity." This conservative view of the individual and social consequences of "cultural relativism" (*and* empiricism, *and* the objectification inherent in modern life in general) is, in my opinion, terrifyingly correct, but irrelevant to the truth of the claims themselves.

Thus, the conservative claim that "cultural relativism" represents a nihilism of sorts is quite likely accurate in its portrayal of modern society and modern society's tendency to make impotent the values whose former power gave cultures their strength by binding the members of their societies. But it is a nihilism that represents not the betrayal of rationality and scientific progress (as conservatives often imply), but the highest achievement of these. Indeed, one might well argue that this objectification, so great a victory in terms of the achievement of knowledge, represents modernization's inevitably containing the seeds of its own destruction.

"Cultural relativism" is the quintessentially objective epistemological perspective and heuristic lens for the study of society. It objectifies to the point that nothing is left but the objective. Which is just what objectification is supposed to do, just what the modern world does, and just what the conservative dreads.

Objectification of this sort is the path to scientific truth. Whatever role the logically and empirically indefensible passions may play in scientific creation and discovery (and our response to these), passion can never play any legitimate role in the validation or refutation of any scientific hypothesis. For finding out about the way the world is, nothing in human history approaches science. The objectification of which science is a manifestation is so powerful a tool for the discovery of a claim's accord with nature—and for attainment of any physical goal—that the leaders of every nation in the world have been forced to accept it.

But, as conservatives so correctly intuit, objectification undercuts the values that bind us into one group or another. The very value of a value is its ability to inculcate an adherence to—to have us attach emotion to—a belief that imposes a feeling of truthfulness to that which can't be justified as being an issue of truth. These values bind the members of a group, save them from loneliness and extinction, and give their lives meaning. (It is not coincidental that the word "religion"—which represents the purest form of social values—is likely derived from the Latin for "binding together.")

Values win many a battle on the individual level, but over time they lose their power. Institutions that were so much a part of life that they were a part of oneself become objects to view as the biologist views a specimen. At the very least, the "unspeakable"—an irresistible prey for anyone with even a bit of the modern mind—becomes exposed and spoken about to death. From science to Oprah, the very process of objectification—not any "attack on specific values"—corrodes the values that make us what we are as a society. When Oprah has a family on her show it, by its nature, makes "the family" something studied from a distance rather than a part of the you that is part of it.

This, incidentally, was the insight captured by those who opposed teaching sex education in schools. While these opponents argued so badly that it often seemed they favored pregnant thirteen-year-olds and syphilis, their real insight, and motivation, was the understanding that discussion of premarital sex—no matter how scientific and academic—removes the sanction of unspeakability and is likely to increase the frequency of premarital sex. (One can acknowledge this and then may still favor education over ignorance even if education increases frequency. Or one may favor keeping sex education out of the schools precisely to prevent the increase in premarital sex. One's position here is irrelevant to the point I make.)

None of this matters when assessing a claim to truth. The correctness of the conservative view of social consequences does nothing whatever to cast doubt on the epistemological validity of the tenet of "cultural relativism." Truth has nothing to do with consequence. Even if our learning that the earth is round led to human extinction, that would not make the earth flat.

Nonetheless, the primary attack on objectivity comes from what is usually called the Left, an appellation that is, I think, a bit unfair to what used to be called the Left.

The Left of the 1930s *thought* a lot. Depending on one's politics, they either saw the economic truths at the core of social life or began with bizarre assumptions about the malleability of human nature and exaggerated ideas about the centrality of the economic. But even those with the latter view will grant that the Left of the 1930s exhibited a rigor that is desirable in any intellectual enterprise. (Indeed, conservatives virtually *have* to agree; many of these sorts of Marxists became neoconservatives later in life.)

The current set of widely shared ideological beliefs of the Left is not comparable to the tenets of the Left of the 1930s or even the 1960s. There is no powerfully reasoned theoretical underpinning, only a series of mushy and unreasoned beliefs in dubious or undemonstrated empirical "facts" (e.g., physiology is unimportant to male-female differences, homosexuality in no way reflects pathology, group differences are socially caused, and the like). The beliefs, rather than being examined or analyzed, quickly become concretized in a set of attitudes that bind the group. Group pressure is then substituted for individual thought, the attitudes go unexamined, and we are left with something that may fairly be subsumed under the term "political correctness."

Someone once complimented Freud on his courage in speaking about the unspeakable. Freud responded that no great courage was needed—at worst people would stop speaking to you that you don't particularly want to speak to anyway. Now, five hundred years ago they boiled you in oil. BOILED YOU IN OIL. *That* took courage.

They no longer boil you in oil, and a professor whose specialty is one of the currently sensitive areas, who is willing to dedicate his career to opposing the accepted views, who has the personality to ignore violent criticism as long as it is stupid criticism, and who has tenure can do so, at least at the serious universities (though perhaps not in the study of literature, where postmodernism has, at some universities, entirely driven out serious scholarship while draining the process of reading of all enjoyment). At the serious universities there remains sufficient residue of the respect for truth that the powerful argument can still be manifested in tenure and promotion.

This is not to say that there is no price extracted. I have had, lest I appear paranoid, to refrain from publicly enumerating dozens of experiences comparable to that of the head of a leading sociological group threatening an editor of a leading journal that the response to his publishing an article of mine would prove costly. (Fortunately, in this case, but not in many others, the editor showed courage and integrity.) I might mention, however, that for as long as my work on male-female psychophysiological differentiation has appeared in books, bookstores and editors have wondered why a store is out of one of my books while the computer claims that a number of copies are left. The answer, verified on numerous occasions, is that a book buyer who dislikes what (the book buyer believes) I say moves the copies of my book from the appropriate section of the bookstore to the section on, say, Tahitian ornithology, placing the books spine-in, lest there be *any* possibility that it catch an interested person's eye.

Such is merely humorous. A more serious problem is the effect the ideological view has on professors whose work only occasionally touches on the relevant areas—the teacher of an introductory biology class, for example, who feels the need to underplay, or leave unmentioned, the volumes of work on the physiology of sex differences. (Why walk on a battlefield that can be easily avoided?)

Most destructive is the professor of introductory sociology or psychology who—knowingly or unknowingly—teaches students "truths" that are either unknown or untrue. There are now hundreds of thousands of students who have been force-fed ideology rather than been taught that which is most reasonably believed to be true.

The students do not necessarily *believe* what they have been taught. When teaching conflicts too strongly with reasonable intuition, the students will parrot the nonsense they know the professor wants to hear and will, quite wisely, continue to believe what they observe.

So, for example: A student in an introductory sociology course of mine, repeating what he had been taught in another introductory course taken by most of my students, mentioned that he had been taught—and had written on a test—that there was no reason why the male makes the first overt sexual move in a dating relationship.

I asked the class whether it agreed with this and something like sixty of sixty-two students agreed. I then asked the students to write on pieces of paper (anonymously, of course) the sex of the person who *actually* had made the first overt sexual move in their last relationship. Virtually all acknowledged that it was the male. It is, in principle, logically possible that this fact is owing only to socialization—and not at all to male-female physiological differences—but it is clear that many professors of sociology do not want to have to deal with the possibility that physiology plays a crucial causal role. So they simply leave this possibility unexplored.

In this case it is likely that the students at least suspected that experience represented an underlying truth more than did the claims of aprofessor. If so, the result is simply an accelerating tendency of students to believe that what they are being taught is nonsense, a terrible trend, of course, but better than students' actually believing that which they are being taught. (I suspect that the same thing is true of textbooks; the student who sees pictures of equal numbers of female construction workers knows perfectly well that most construction workers are male and concludes that textbooks just make it up as they go along. Students are sufficiently wise to reject the textbook's assumption that all social realities are manifestations of socialization; they know that socialization often conforms to realities that "precede" society; an adult male's ability to grow a mustache is not *caused* by our telling little girls that facial hair is unfeminine.)

In other cases, the student's inherent common sense is not sufficient to act as counterpoise to ideology. When deep causal explanations of behavior are at issue, intuition is not much help. Thus, when the student is told that the death penalty does not deter—a claim told to virtually every introductory sociology student—he has no way of knowing that this issue is excruciatingly complex and that no one yet knows whether the death penalty deters or not.

When I was a graduate student, there was a great fashion among young sociology instructors for giving their students the "Common Sense Sociology Test." This test, which is to this day updated and published in the best-selling textbook, presents fifteen true-false questions. Each question is meant to elicit the incorrect answer from the first-day, freshman student, thereby showing the student how seriously he needed an infusion of sociology to repair his twisted view of the world.

I remember that, even when I first saw the test, something about it bothered me. I was not teaching at the time, so it was not until a few years ago (when I saw the textbook version) that I realized how duplicitous was the test.

Some of the "correct" answers given by the test are simply incorrect. More wives *are* murdered by husbands than vice versa. But the more interesting duplicities are of this type:

Q. True or false: The income gap between male and female workers has narrowed in recent years.

Answer according to the test: The income gap between male and female workers has widened rather than narrowed; women hold few high-paying positions and the average white woman earns less than the average black man.

Now, the answer as given simply *asserts* that the gap has widened. Even in its own terms, the test must at least claim—in the clause after the semicolon—that women now hold *fewer* high-paying positions than previously. But let us be generous and assume that the answer means the only thing that it could mean if it is to be even duplicitously correct: The very factors that have made male and female salaries for the same position much more nearly equal in the past twenty-five years have brought into the marketplace millions of women who had not worked before. Obviously these women were going to begin with entry-level salaries, and this widens the gap between the average pay of male and female.

Remembering that this test is aimed at the first-day student, it is easy to see what is duplicitous about it. The student quite understandably thinks that the question refers to men and women applying for, or serving in, the *same* position. And when the student answers "true," his answer reflects the *correct* belief that male and female salaries for the same position are much closer than they were twenty-five years ago. Indeed, only if this were *not* true would the test successfully elicit the slap-on-the-forehead response from the student that it wishes.

Similarly, another question asks:

Q. True or false: People who are regular Christian churchgoers are less likely to be prejudiced against other races than people who do not attend church.

Answer according to the test: Regular churchgoers are not less prejudiced than non-churchgoers; in fact, they tend to be more prejudiced.

This question and the answer *seem* to address the effect of religion (or at least of churchgoing) on prejudice. In fact, the answer merely reflects the fact that disproportionate numbers of Protestant churchgoers come from groups tending, for reasons having nothing to do with Christianity or churchgoing, to be more prejudiced (rural southern Fundamentalists as opposed to urban non-believers, for example). Justification of the test's answer and refutation of the student's belief that churchgoers are less prejudiced would require that, for example, the degree of prejudice of rural southern Fundamentalist churchgoers be compared with the degree of prejudice of otherwise equivalent rural southern non-churchgoers. This was not the research on which the test was based, so its conclusion was analogous to one that concluded from the fact that Japanese churchgoers are shorter than Canadian non-churchgoers that going to church makes you short.

Of the fifteen questions, only one clearly is successful in unduplicitously eliciting the incorrect answer, and surprise, from the student. This is the question from which the students are surprised to learn that revolutions are more likely to come during times of economic improvement than in the worst of times. (The entire test, test answers, and analysis of each test question and answer appear, as do essays on the death penalty and other empirical issues mentioned in this essay, in my book *When Wish Replaces Thought.*

5

Dead white males didn't invent the rules of science; they discovered them. These rules enable science, and science alone, to make prediction.

And prediction is only evidence acknowledged by science to demonstrate that one is on the trail of the truth. One may, of course, invoke anything one wishes in attempting to come up with a successful scientific claim. If a dose of intuitional astrological foot fetishism helps one to come up with an empirical claim, fine. But the claim gains no scientific *validity* until it can successfully make a prediction that does not require allegiance to—or use of the specialized concepts and vocabulary of—intuitional astrological foot fetishism.

Prediction is the determinant of scientific truth and—many believe—the determinant of *anything* (other than logical and mathematical truth) that can coherently be termed "truth." Prediction plays this role because science holds that "truth" can meaningfully be defined only as the concordance of a claim (a description, hypothesis, theory, or explanation) with nature ("reality"). And only a claim's ability to predict can give us reason to believe that we are nearing truth—as opposed to merely experiencing a powerful, but quite possibly deceptive, *feeling* that we are nearing truth.

To be sure, there are those who apply the word "truth" to beliefs and moral values, concepts that are not, even in principle, capable of giving us reason to believe that they are more than arbitrary preferences based on subjective feelings. Such people tend to gravitate to empirical areas relevant to social issues: male-female differences, homosexuality, the death penalty, abortion, and the like. This, in addition to the fact that the less-controversial questions addressed by the physical scientists tend to attract smarter people, accounts for the fact that so many who write on empirical social questions are so willing to subordinate even elementary constraints of logic to ideological desire.

Science can, of course, address such empirical issues as "which social and economic factors increase the likelihood that religious beliefs will be entwined with moral beliefs." It can consider such empirical claims *about* morality as, say, "societies in a stage of strong economic birth tend to see premarital sex as wrong" and, if such claims are true, it can explain the realities.

But science cannot make coherent the question of whether or not there is a God and it cannot tell us whether it is better to favor sexual freedom or economic growth. Science cannot, in other words, conceive of any system of thought that can validate issues for which there is no possibility of test even in principle. Science doesn't know good from bad or right from wrong. The closest it gets to an objective moral claim is a belief that survival is good. And that's not very close in a universe that we have no reason to believe is in the slightest concerned with our survival.

Science does not care whether a claim is made by a man or a woman; a black, a yellow, a white, or a goldfish; a Nobel laureate, a plumber, or a clerk in a patent office. While the non-scientist part of any person worthy of being called "human" cares about the uses to which new knowledge will be put, such issues are as irrelevant to one's being a "scientist" as to one's being a football player. The only goal of science is the diminution of the distance between present knowledge and truth. To the scientist, the willingness to validate an empirical claim on the basis of bias, prejudice, or emotional and political need—or to reject a claim on the basis of the motivations of the claimant or the putative consequences of acceptance of the claim—represents an infantile narcissism; to the intelligent believer, these represents a lack of faith and a blasphemous conviction that one knows better than God does.

In truth, the scientist cares more about hunting down the prey than tasting it. The finding is more fun than is the found. The pull of the hunt for undiscovered truths is so great that there is the ever-present threat that the cracks in a "truth" on which one already stands will be overlooked. That is why science systematically attempts to eliminate all illegitimate reasons for holding to a truth. This process comes with only a partial warranty, so there is always the possibility of error. Some of these errors have, when exposed, launched the highest flights of intelligence and imagination. But even at worst, science protects itself far, far better than does any other sort of investigation.

It takes time. But the power of the truthful explanation is always too much for an argument forced to invoke untruths. This is not an exception to the Conservation of Passion; it's just that the issues to which people attach emotions change, and when they do, the fatal inadequacy of the bad explanations is exposed.

There will always be many who believe that science defines its own victory and that there are alternative routes to truth. But the claimed alternative routes to truth give us no prediction, no reason to believe that they exhibit anything more than a feeling and an insupportable claim of truth, a claim whose validity is as dubious as its ability to soothe is obvious.

6

It is often claimed that the intellectual malfeasance described above is owing to misconceptions in the worldview and actions of the sixties. To a great extent this is correct. But to those of us who loved the sixties—who would trade five future years for one of those past years—such claims appear not as powerful, but merely as, well, adorable. The intellect is powerless against love and, of course, that's as it should be.

However, it is crucial to remember that, for some of us who loved the sixties, the primary attraction was a ruthless anti-authoritarianism that distrusted any claim that substituted arbitrary moral belief and social value for truth, something that all social systems—by the nature of social systems—must do. Social systems do this because their cultures need both an authority system and a system of values to give meaning in a universe that cares about nothing.

Thus, the authority system and the culture that it protects—*whatever* the nature of that culture—are by their nature opposed to truth. Membership in any society, indeed in any group, demands denial or suppression of some truths and a pretense that the arbitrary moral and normative choice is an empirical truth. It is because of this that truth is the enemy of culture.

Every society demands of its members the suppression of some truth in exchange for membership. For some of us from the sixties, society's coercive attempt to use social acceptance as leverage to force denial of truth is intolerable. Fortunately, there is a weapon—the only weapon—that no social system can countenance or counter: the willingness to give priority to the truth, *especially* those specific truths that one's own society would have one deny.

To be sure, it is the great glory of the modern democracy that free speech and a belief in freedom make all this less true of the modern democracy than of any other form of society. But for some of us from the sixties, even this is not enough.

And, to be sure, even we recognize that the greatest thing about truth is that it is true. But, unlike those, whether from the Right or Left, who battle for one sort of social system or another (and unlike those of the sixties who bestowed upon an especially jejune value system all the authority given to the worst dictatorships), we also feel that a close second is the fact that the truth and its handmaiden, education, are, by their nature, subversive. This is what, for so many of us from the sixties, makes the truth so much fun.

BRAD LEITHAUSER

The Saving Minutes

Brad Leithauser is a poet, novelist, critic, and anthologist (most recently of ghost stories), and introduced the collected criticism of Randall Jarrell. A new novel, *Friends of Freeland,* is forthcoming from Knopf. He teaches literature at Mount Holyoke and, although he has a degree from Harvard Law School, prefers to practice the even stricter rules of form and metric.

Leithauser, whose considerable literary production has just expanded to include theater reviewing, still worries about what, at the very least, a graduating English major ought to have under his belt, and believes that the memorization of poetry is intrinsic to its survival. Without the demand of that functional and fulfilling task, teachers of literature may find themselves inhabiting a world of ghosts, indeed, where critics become well-rewarded mediums, presiding over increasingly faint and spectral evocations of the texts which once lived with us as lively and essential beings. In chime with Cynthia Ozick, he fears the passing of the print culture, and like Sven Birkerts, he raises the question of whether the storage capacity of the computer may eclipse the humane task of memory itself.

Leithauser, in his essay, several times quotes Robert Frost, the last poet to read a real poem at the inauguration of an American president. But that was in another country, and besides, the poet is dead.

IT'S AN OBSERVATION so basic as to seem scarcely worth remarking: foreign languages are best acquired by the very young. Learn a language in your twenties, to say nothing of further along, and you'll never swim in its currents with a child's otter-like ease.

It's an observation, however, that assumes rich implications once you realize that, in a prosaic age, poetry itself is sometimes a foreign language. Its rhythms and vocabulary and conventions may be alien even to college English majors. And what our students fail to encounter in high school or college they aren't likely to meet elsewhere; we can make no blithe assumptions that poetry is something they will simply absorb— something "in the air." The air indeed throngs with voices, but most are radio and television signals, battling for market share.

Many of the forces that have distanced us from poetry exist outside the educational system. They are linked to social transformations so vast as to be—like the mathematics of the interior of a tornado—unreckonable. My concern here is narrower—I suppose you could call it curricular.

In the classroom, how do we best nurture a love of poetry? What do we do for students who feel unease, blended with an anticipatory wave of boredom, when confronted with anything written in verse?

Something has gone wrong, and any search for culprits will soon zero in on the growing role of criticism in the classroom. This is a process, admittedly, that has been going on for quite some time. In the fifties Randall Jarrell was already lamenting the arrival of what he called "the age of criticism." Or consider this lament: "Of course the multiplication of critical books and essays may create, and I have seen it create, a vicious taste for reading about works of art instead of reading the works themselves. . . ." It's from T. S. Eliot's "The Function of Criticism," written seventy years ago.

This taste can be particularly unfortunate—"vicious"—when fostered in students. If poetry is a foreign language for many of them, they need to learn it young—preferably in elementary school. It can't be put off the way many other literary disciplines can be. Poetry, it turns out, is both an exacting and an impatient taskmaster, since so much of what it teaches is not conceptual but instinctual, less an idea than a "feel."

How is this "feel" to be obtained? Ideally, there would be no call for anyone to set about acquiring it—its presence would be bred naturally. The enveloping culture would work, on any number of fronts, to instill an appreciation of the literary tradition. This was what Lafcadio Hearn envisaged when, writing a hundred years ago, he contemplated the "ghostly" and "pure" pre-Meiji Japan that predated the arrival of *gaijin* like himself. He saw himself as the memorialist of a vanishing world. Whether or not Hearn was romanticizing his adopted land—as he frequently did—his is one of the most touching visions I've met of a prelapsarian society where poetry really is the "living word," wholly integrated into the quotidian:

The toil of the fields and the labor of the streets are performed to the rhythm of chanted verse; and song would seem to be an expression of the life of the people in about the same sense that it is an expression of the life of cicadae. . . . But poems can be found upon almost any kind of domestic utensil,—for example upon braziers, iron kettles, vases, wooden trays, lacquer ware, porcelains, chopsticks of the finer sort,—even toothpicks! Poems are painted upon shop-signs, panels, screens, and fans. Poems are printed upon towels, draperies, curtains, kerchiefs, silk-linings, and women's crepe-silk underwear. Poems are stamped or worked upon letter-paper, envelopes, purses, mirror-cases, travelling-bags. Poems are inlaid upon enamelled ware, cut upon bronzes, graven upon metal pipes, embroidered upon tobacco-pouches.

Where does this leave us? In a world whose manufactured objects are stamped not with verses but with designer logos, how is poetry to be upheld? I suppose every poet and every teacher of poetry—both of which

I am—has different notions of where to start. My belief is that we ought to begin at the beginning—back in that misty, prehistoric realm before the arrival of the book, when any words worth keeping had to be kept in the head. There is no substitute for memorization.

Recitation Day in a one-room schoolhouse? Scuffling schoolchildren summoned to the front of the room to declaim Longfellow or Whittier or Bryant? As a curricular strategy, memorization may look hopelessly out-dated to both the old guard and the new. My own education, as an English major at Harvard, might be characterized as old guard—at least as it existed in 1975. It stressed facts. In my senior oral exams, I can remember being asked to define a fabliau, and getting it right, and being asked Shakespeare's birthdate and getting it wrong (off by two years). We were expected to have some rudimentary grasp of dates and vocabulary, and to be able to sketch the lines of influence from one generation to the next. The exams were all rather dispassionate and progressive. My trio of interrogators were not there to determine whether I had a "feel" for the material (an amorphous, unscientific presence that presumably could not be tested), but whether I had acquired a body of information. A certain amount of memorization was required to do well on such exams, but what the student needed to have by heart wasn't lines of verse so much as data.

Even this degree of memorization wasn't likely to find favor with a new guard for whom rote learning smacked of everything that was retro-grade and authoritarian. We retreated further from the principle that poetry was something to hold in the head. As a heuristic device, the forced memorization of poetry was doubly suspect, doubly conservative: by propelling students and teacher toward what was easily memoriza-ble—what was literally memorable—it was apt to lead, willy-nilly, toward an embrace of the traditional tools of meter and rhyme.

It may be, these days, that a classroom emphasis on memorization is likely to please nobody—for it's apt to put off, as well, the young people it seeks to benefit. As anyone with young children knows, memorization has become a discounted skill. The computer has radically altered the value placed on feats of memory. In a world in which a little diskette, purchaseable for thirty cents, can store *Hamlet* or an eight-hundred-page novel (its every preposition and punctuation mark firmly in place), *no-body's* memory looks all that prepossessing. Why should we struggle over a task that our machines can do so much better than we ever will? Mathe-matics teachers across the country complain of student resistance to memorizing times tables and simple formulae. To a generation for whom a computer seems as typical a companion as a pencil did to their predecessors, this business of "imitating" the computer by reiterating your times tables—or, for that matter, memorizing a poem—naturally feels artificial.

Which indeed it is. But so is playing Czerny's scales, hour by hour. Serious young pianists understand (it's one of their teachers' tasks to ensure that they do) that mastery of the free-ranging terrain of a Liszt impromptu or a Scriabin étude is only to be arrived at through the "merely mechanical." Only when we come to accept that the reading of a poem is no less a discipline than the reading of a sonata will the utility of memorization seem inescapable.

I've spoken very generally of a "feel for verse," but it's a phrase that, once we enter the domain of meter, can be honed to a nicety. I'd illustrate with four examples, all drawn from celebrated passages from Frost. The first is taken from perhaps his most famous lyric, "Stopping by Woods on a Snowy Evening":

> Whose woods these are I think I know.
> His house is in the village though.
> He will not see me stopping here
> To watch his woods fill up with snow.

This is iambic tetrameter of a special sort: you could say it is rare for being so unexceptional. Complete metrical regularity is almost unknown in English-language verse; most poems, however metronomic their feel, actually contain a few variations. But in every one of its sixteen lines this one is absolutely regular.

The second selection comes from "The Road Not Taken."

> I shall be telling this with a sigh
> Somewhere ages and ages hence:
> Two roads diverged in a wood, and I—
> I took the one less travelled by,
> And that has made all the difference.

This stanza, too, is iambic tetrameter, but with variations—an anapest instead of an iamb, a double trochee, and so forth. I've occasionally asked my students to convert this poem into perfectly regular meter while inflicting as little violence as possible. "I shall be telling this with a sigh" has become "And I shall tell this with a sigh" and "I shall have told this with a sigh. . . ." Needless to say, the resulting violence is great, despite the best intentions: with a few such seemingly trifling changes, Frost's poem is transmogrified.

My third selection is in iambic pentameter, and although not quite so uniform as "Stopping by Woods," the meter is strict:

> And further still at an unearthly height
> One luminary clock against the sky
> Proclaimed the time was neither wrong nor right.
> I have been one acquainted with the night.

My last example, also in pentameter, is set in loose rather than strict iambics, and the feel is altogether different:

> Once when the snow of the year was beginning to fall,
> We stopped by a mountain pasture to say, "Whose colt?"
> A little Morgan had one forefoot on the wall,
> The other curled at his breast. He dipped his head
> And snorted at us. And then he had to bolt.
> We heard the miniature thunder where he fled,
> And we saw him, or thought we saw him, dim and gray,
> Like a shadow against the curtain of falling flakes.

Four examples, then: two of iambic tetrameter, one strict and one loose, and two of iambic pentameter, one strict and one loose.

Frost once pointed out that English verse has but two basic meters, loose iambic and strict iambic. Over the centuries, at least until this century, the iambic line has preponderated to the point where other meters seem mere curiosities. To be sure, some of the most illustrious poems in the language are set in variant meters: "The Sick Rose," "Christabel," "The Destruction of Sennacherib," "The Raven," "Hiawatha," "The Forsaken Merman." But such poems, however memorable, represent a statistically insignificant series of forays.

As my four examples suggest, one could expand on Frost's pronouncement to say that, just as there are two basic meters in English (loose and strict iambic), there are two basic lengths (tetrameter and pentameter). In combination, they give us four forms: strict iambic tetrameter, loose iambic tetrameter, strict iambic pentameter, loose iambic pentameter. You might call these the four building blocks of English verse. Or you might otherwise call them a "feel for poetry."

And if our students have a "feel" for these four forms, we've done right by them. If they don't, we haven't. This sort of "feel" doesn't hinge on an ability to identify by name anapests and dactyls—though that's a useful and simple enough skill. It's an instinctive, visceral comprehension of how these four lines behave. It's a sense of music. It's a sense of balance—a sensitivity to aural symmetry and asymmetry. It's a heightened awareness of the metrical norm, so that any deviation is perceived immediately, unthinkingly, potently. It's a set of antennae, a forward-probing tendency to predict how the line is likely to go.

It is, in short, an intricate business. Each of the feet in an iambic line has its own characteristics. Working collaboratively, and for the most part intuitively, our poets over time have created in their audience a body of expectations. The first foot is apt to employ a metrical substitution; the second, the "sensitive foot," will do so sparingly; the likely substitution in the final foot is an amphibrach rather than a trochee; and so forth. Traditionally, feet have tended to cluster in certain patterns, caesuras to fall at certain junctures. And how do we absorb this tradition? Obviously, the poems we know best—the ones we have by heart—will contribute the most to the body of assumptions we bring to any new poem. It is on them we must chiefly depend if we're to be equal to the experience of reading a new poem—if we're to bring to it a bank of inner resources commensurate with the poem's potential wonders.

Given the dominance of the tetrameter and the pentameter, other lines are destined to be read against them, defined in terms of them. Hence, the iambic hexameter's vigor resides in its way of echoing the pentameter and then—with a little headlong push—spilling over the threshold the ear has prepared for it. Iambic trimeter, conversely, draws much of its potency from its feeling of incompleteness; it often comes across as a truncated tetrameter. Any undergraduate equipped with an instinct for the four metrical building blocks stands prepared to read the corpus of English verse written over the last six hundred years, including free verse, which contains behind it (I draw on Eliot again) the "ghost of a meter"—that ghost being, almost inevitably, either the iambic tetrameter or the pentameter line.

How could a mere pair of meters manage, over so many generations, to accommodate so much of the pungency and variety and ferocious eccentricity of English poetry? The answer lies partly in the gulf separating the two lines. A mere foot distinguishes them, a simple *da dum*, and yet its effect is transfiguring. Neatly symmetrical, the tetrameter naturally divides into a line with two beats on a side. In its "fourness," it has atmospheric ties to music—to 4/4 time, to the 4's, 8's, 12's, 16's of musical measures. The pentameter, on the other hand, will *not* be made symmetrical. You can break it in two—five syllables to a side—but you wind up with a "bigger half" and a "smaller half" of three stresses and two. Nor will it split cleanly into smaller components—into equal thirds, or fourths. It is a singular creature—at once stately and spacious, uneven and restless.

The two lines are sufficiently disjoined that certain poets, not feeling at home in both, have chosen to inhabit one or the other almost exclusively. Both Housman and Dickinson virtually vanish once we remove the tetrameter line from their repertoire. Pope and Byron are reduced to mere husks if we disallow them their pentameter. For each of these meters, what better testament to their amplitude could there be than this: that rich, ranging literary careers have been created almost entirely within their borders?

Just as the child is father to the man, the student is father to the critic. Any recommendation for how poetry ought to be taught in high schools and colleges is ultimately a prescription for a particular brand of criticism. My own plea is for a criticism attuned to how the past operates, metrically, on the present. Although there are a handful of highly gifted poetry critics on the scene today, at times we seem overrun with, on the one hand, poet-critics convinced that poetry truly began after the Second World War and, on the other, academic critics who sense that English-language poetry was meant to terminate with the haunting, witty, cracked, elegiac voice of T. S. Eliot, who was last meaningfully heard from during the Second World War. For this latter group of critics, the presence of a contemporary poetry scene that has some appearance of being ambitious and forward-looking is a sign of naïveté or unseemliness. They ask, in effect, Why doesn't poetry have the good taste to die?

A firm grounding in metrics might act as a curative, encouraging a criticism that would pay less attention than is customary to the what-is-said and more to the manner-of-its-saying, less to poetry's content and more to its music. Housman perhaps overstated the case when he argued that "Poetry is not the thing said but a way of saying it" and "Meaning is of the intellect, poetry is not"—but not by much. It would be hard to name a modern poet further removed from Housman than Pound, but the latter offered something quite similar when defining poetry as "a composition of words set to music." While some great poems do manage to encapsulate notable or novel ideas, there are legions of others, equally great, whose sentiments are commonplace. What unites the two is their musical achievement. Deathless poets may or may not be original thinkers; but they must be gifted musicians.

Why does so much poetry criticism favor content over manner? Three reasons leap to mind. First, it's simpler to review content; the music of poetry is an elusive business, not easily captured or condensed in a brief review. Second, in a hectic, accelerated age we're accustomed to reading for information rather than style; we bring to the reading of verse the habits we've developed with newspapers and magazines. Third, to review for content is safer, since nothing is more tedious, in the wrong hands, than a discussion of the technical aspects of verse. Anybody whose classroom experience includes a wooden analysis of prosody, the blackboard a blizzard of scansion marks, knows how deadly the subject can be. For the teacher, it's a vexing paradox: the closer we approach the musical heart of verse, the greater our risk of becoming stupefyingly dull.

A continual stress on poetry's music has another, collateral virtue: it fosters humility, it tempers the critic's urge to explain what the poet "really meant." Lessons in humility are no doubt beneficial for anyone who writes criticism, but perhaps especially so for those who are not themselves creative artists. No poet-critic or novelist-critic ever seems to claim what the pure critic-critic will sometimes argue: that criticism is an art form equivalent to poetry or fiction. To the contrary: the creative artist is apt to be dismissive, even sheepish about his critical forays. Think of W. H. Auden, who once noted, "All the poems I have written were written for love," while all the criticism was written "because I needed the money." Or E. M. Forster, who called his one extended venture into criticism, the lectures that appeared as *Aspects of the Novel*, "backwaters and shallows." Or John Updike, who—likewise turning to marine imagery—observed that "Writing criticism is to writing fiction and poetry as hugging the shore is to sailing in the open sea."

The apologetic tone of these remarks reminds us that criticism is one of those jobs that wouldn't exist in an ideal world, where excellence would speak with an urgent, cogent voice, and all the rest, being nothing but the rest, would have its fleeting say and expire. The poet-critic, like the drug counselor, or the insect exterminator, or the head of a Department of Corrections, seeks to create a world that would have no place for him.

Although banished from the ideal world, the critic faces necessary, fundamental tasks in the untidy world we actually live in. Naturally these will change as the age changes—sometimes quite quickly and dramatically, as we can see if we approach our nation's poetry over quarter-century intervals. In the year 1900, as a new century dawned, what was the American poetry critic's primary task? If he or she realized that Edwin Arlington Robinson, whose first volume had emerged a few years before, represented something novel and durable, so much the better. But surely the age called chiefly not for praise but for tempered skepticism. Some beautiful American verse had flowered in the nineteenth century, but by the year 1900 most of it had passed, and the critic who pointed out that things had settled into a trough—that it was a time to eschew false gods and to simply watch and wait—was the most valuable messenger around.

By 1925, odd new wonderful things were happening: Moore, Eliot, Pound, Stevens, Ransom, Cummings. . . . Theirs was a movement which, in its boldness and queerness, was destined to face stiff resistance, and the prime task for the critic was surely to solicit on behalf of the modernist movement, to bring illumination to bear against animus.

And the great challenge facing the critic in 1950? A more difficult question, clearly, but perhaps the era's most noteworthy development was the emergence of various formal poets who, while steeped in what by then had established itself as the modernist tradition, had chosen to work in verse that was by comparison more systematic, more easily scannable, less allusive, less fragmentary. I'm thinking of Richard Wilbur, whose first book had been published in 1947; of Robert Lowell, whose

Lord Weary's Castle had appeared the same year; of Elizabeth Bishop, whose second book was about to emerge. Actually, the 1950 example need hardly be treated as a hypothetical, since there was on the scene a daring and resourceful and often clairvoyant critic—Randall Jarrell—who explicitly set out to assess our poetry near the mid-century mark. In his assessments, the poets I've mentioned—particularly Lowell and Bishop—figured prominently.

And what of the critic in 1975? A kind of optical farsightedness comes into play: the nearer things stand, the more jumbled they seem. Any list is apt to look idiosyncratic and partial, but *some* of the issues which the critic might have been expected to examine would include the rise of what was called (for lack of a happier term) confessional poetry, and the tragic, suicide-ridden lives of many associated with it; the resurgence of the long poem, as evidenced by Berryman's *Dream Songs* and the early stirrings of Merrill's *Sandover* trilogy; the influential presence in our midst of writers who originated elsewhere (Brodsky, Walcott, Heaney et al.); and the virtual absence of spirited but cool-headed, of passionate but respectful debate among poetry critics, all too often replaced by acrimonious exchanges between enemies or a soft-headed passing of valentines between friends.

And what of the critic of the year 2000? Or if that's an impossible stretch, what of the critic of the year 1996? The situation continues to diversify and ramify, but surely we could safely say that *a* central, and perhaps *the* central, issue of our time is the poet's relationship to the academy. I'm thinking not so much of the fact that most poets teach—itself no insignificant condition—but of the role the university plays in shaping our vision of both the current scene and the poetry of the past.

The poet's relationship to academia is different—both in degree and in kind—from the novelist's. Many fiction writers teach only occasionally, if at all. Anne Tyler, John Updike, Philip Roth, Thomas Pynchon, Cormac McCarthy—these are people who steer clear of the academy. On the other hand, virtually all successful poets hold academic positions. To some extent, there's no surprise in this: writers like Tyler and Updike and Roth and Pynchon and McCarthy can draw a profitable living from their books, whereas the typical poet's semiannual royalty check won't cover his postal bills.

Yet the poetry world has its share of writers who are not in the academy for the money—people of sufficient means or savvy to support themselves elsewhere. What lures them to the classroom? Perhaps a widespread perception that, in the current world, poetry as a living presence—something scrutinized and analyzed, pored over and argued over—is to be found almost exclusively there. How many twentieth-century American poets, good and great, could stay in print independent of classroom sales? While a few—Cummings, Millay—appear to have an outside reading public independent of their academic standing, they're a precious minority. Most poets have come to feel that their future depends not on word-of-mouth or bookstore sales, but on readings at educational institutions and appearances on course syllabi. The Tylers, Updikes, Roths, Pynchons, McCarthys may attract a large enough and appreciative enough public to view themselves as vitally present within society at large. The poet, on the other hand, must be either a one-in-a-million popular phenomenon or, more likely, an unsurpassed egotist to feel that the academy is extraneous to his life.

Having began with an educational question—the place of memorization in the curriculum—I wind up back in the academy. Clearly, all these issues are linked, even if their precise linkages are unclear: the decline of memorization; the teaching of poetry as a quasi-scientific discipline; the dominance of criticism that scants the importance of music; a conflicted sense on the part of most poets that the academy has its values twisted and yet is their primary home.

Maybe home is what you make it. Certainly the poet has an interest in seeing that the academy does right by poetry. The academy is unavoidably subject to aims and impulses that distort the nature of poetic achievement; the poet can serve as a "reality check."

For example, the teacher, like the critic, is drawn toward what needs explication, toward what (at the most basic level) will fill up a class hour. In its simplicity, its lucidity, its beautiful self-sufficiency, the small lapidary lyric by Herrick or Clare or Housman or Bogan provides the teacher with very little to do. Hence, the poems that tend to get taught, and also written about, are those that are "problematic." Built into the academic's job is a bias in favor of the obscure, the riddling, the incomplete. Inevitably, an era's poetic achievement will be skewed as a result.

Similarly, the teacher is drawn to taxonomy. Where the material is vast, and the number of weeks in a semester is small, one does what one can to lend things an overall coherence.Categories and classifications are applied; family trees are set up; the lineage of influence is traced. But coherence of this sort is always purchased at some cost. All literary categories wind up being procrustean, and poems that don't fit the framework naturally get shortchanged.

The teacher/critic is also under a strong temptation to yield to "democratizing" impulses. This was true long before "p.c." debates filled our faculty lounges. English departments tend, by their very natures, to uphold the notion that every age, region, social class, and so forth, must have its distinctive geniuses. Yet one of the most striking aspects of literary accomplishment is how weirdly irregular—"bunchy" —is talent's distribution. Suddenly will appear an influx of immensely gifted southern writers or Jewish writers or gay writers or what have you— and who's to say where the next renaissance will come? Yet academia, with its emphasis on coherent evolutions and proportional representation, has a way of smoothing out what is erratic, clustered, incongruous.

Finally, the teacher/critic (partly as a means of imposing order on a wayward mass of material, and partly I'm afraid as a means of concentrating on juicy biographical details) often focuses on the poet rather than the poem. Our obsession with the distinction between "major" and "minor" figures is one reflection of this. At times this distinction seems fully justified. Who would argue with the proposition that the major poets of the Romantic era—Wordsworth, Coleridge, Shelley, Keats, Byron—produced the bulk of what's best in their age? But in other times, such as our own, the distinction may be less helpful.

Ours is apparently an era not of great poets so much as of great poems. An era when, if we lack any single figure who throws a commanding shadow all the way across the continent, let alone across the Atlantic, we have a profusion of poets who sometimes compose beautiful objects. And of course in the end it is not poets that matter, whether of the major or minor variety, but poems. Hence, in an era like our own the critic faces a particularly taxing but rewarding job: the winnowing out, in the work of one poet after another, of the one or two little lyrics that call for preservation. The times call for a new Palgrave.

The hope is that what some anthologist selects will, like *The Golden Treasury*, prove imperishable. In the meantime, as we wait for that book's arrival, we might marvel at the littleness, the seeming frailty, of the goods involved. I suppose anyone who has published a volume of poetry has had an experience similar to my own on the day when I bid farewell to my first book, mailing off the final galleys to my editor. Proofreading one last time, I read the manuscript straight through, aloud. I was then twenty-eight, and I suppose you could say I was proceeding through my entire life's work. Well, the whole manuscript took me roughly an hour— roughly the time it would take to watch, say, two episodes of *Wheel of Fortune* or *The Bill Cosby Show*. I was chiefly struck neither by the virtues of the poems nor by their shortcomings, but by their simple brevity.

I had a similar, even more pointed experience a couple of years ago, when I wrote the introduction to a biography of the English poet Charlotte Mew. Hers was a tragic story, tinged with insanity and culminating in an especially gruesome suicide. I love Mew's poems, but in her fifty-eight years this odd, doomed, wonderful woman wrote very few of them. To my mind, there are five absolutely first-rank poems. To read them through is a matter of less than ten minutes!

Less than ten minutes in the reading, but how long in the writing? Well, when measured against the extended, anguished span of her fifty-eight years, you might say they took only a few minutes to write. How fleeting, after all, were those interludes when inspiration warmed her. And yet they make all the difference—these are the interludes that redeem her deepest disappointments, refute her grimmest self-appraisals, and rescue her life from the pitiful ranks of those unreckonable billions who, having passed their lives in anonymous sorrow, have now utterly vanished.

Those times when she was writing with the true fire inside her? They are the exonerating moments, the saving minutes of a life. It is to them that the critic's allegiance lies. His or her highest duty? To commemorate those instants when, with the lever of a fresh image or a felicitous phrase, a poet suddenly heaves aside mountains—mountains of confinement and tedium and sorrow—to disclose behind them a firmament sharp with stars.

D A V I D   R .   S L A V I T T

Circling the Squires

David Slavitt teaches writing at the University of Pennsylvania and does a little writing himself. He is the author of *The Cliff* (1994), a comic novel shamelessly revealing his utter ingratitude to the celebrated artists' colony in northern Italy which housed him for a month the previous year. At the last count, the list of his publications came to fifty books of fiction, poetry, and translations from the Latin. He studies classical languages in the early hours before sharpening his pen for the book and film reviews which display his taste for the antic and the unfashionable.

Insisting to a skeptical interlocutor that his tally of twenty out of twenty students in his expository writing class who were unable to place Lisbon in Portugal was absolutely correct, Slavitt went on to add ruefully that no doubt half of them had probably been there. . . . Our vastly expanding affluence, Slavitt implied, has not proved a path to excellence any more than the vast expansion of higher education after World War II, and the "jolly equality of the New Age classroom" may have served us ill indeed, as the possession of classical learning and high culture has become the privilege of even fewer than in those days when he was a student at Andover and Yale.

Slavitt does not object to being labeled an elitist, but does mind very much the standard repertoire of jokes about Philadelphia, a city he defends vehemently.

*J*UST BECAUSE people have been saying for generations that the good old days are gone and our present condition is worse than anything in memory doesn't mean it isn't true. During our lifetimes and those of our parents and grandparents, the culture changed drastically. The automobile, the airplane, radio, television, VCRs, CD players, virtual reality . . . these were all new things, most of which turned out to be mixed blessings.

I remember when LP records were released, right after World War II. I was ten or eleven years old and I assumed that classical music would now be available to everyone and that all the stupid pop music would just go away. (What did I know? I had also expected that, when the war was over, there wouldn't be any more news programs because there wouldn't be any more news. These dreary interruptions of our entertainment seemed a temporary inconvenience, like the rationing of shoes.)

Television has changed the world. My children grew up with television, which was the primary arena of their encounters with narrative.

(Even though I'm a writer and a snob. Unless you have servants, the TV keeps the kids quiet.)

Now, it's much worse. The kids I teach at Penn—an Ivy League university, if only just—had video games as their main entertainment. Donkey Kong and Super Mario Brothers. It comes as no surprise that the attention span of men and women of the middle class is not what it was. The editors of the *New York Times Magazine* have taken the deliberate step of reducing the demands they make upon their readers. One longish article is all this upscale group can take each week. The rest is shorter, punchier, with more pictures.

And this is a business. They're not wrong. *Time* is dumber than it was. And *Newsweek.*

Back when John Denson was the editor, I used to work at *Newsweek,* and they used to have, at the end of each critical piece, a "Summing Up." Its purpose, I suppose, was to inform those whose lips got tired as they slogged through the absurdly simple copy and needed a ping at the end. One wrote, in, I think, 12-point Bodoni Modern: Summing Up ↬ (adding this little dingbat thing), and then one had a line and a half— about fifty characters—in which to say something clever. Denson left and they gave up these summings up, but almost thirty years later, I still have nightmares in which I'm back there, and they're doing it again. And it's my job to reduce all experience to fifty characters of pith and vinegar.

But it isn't just a nightmare. *Time* is doing this now. They call it "The Bottom Line," because it's on the bottom line, I suppose. And they have a guy who gets up and goes to work every day at my awful oneiric occupation.

When I was at *Newsweek,* it wasn't a magazine that most of the people who worked there would have read voluntarily. I mean, when they taught me that I was supposed to write "Plato, the Greek philosopher, once said. . . ," it wasn't a joke. The identifying appositive had to be there. (I always tried to imagine someone out there slapping his forehead and thinking, *Oh, yeah, right,* that *Plato.*)

We had to write "In New York's Manhattan," to contradistinguish, I expect, from the town in Kansas.

I used to be ashamed of myself for doing things like that.

Some years later, at a poetry reading, I heard Ted Weiss, who teaches at Princeton, refer, quite reflexively and automatically, to "Racine, the great French tragedian," and I thought, Princeton has apparently gone to hell. Then, a couple of years ago, in an English class for upperclasspersons at Penn, I was astonished to discover that not a single student knew what country Lisbon is in. And these are Ivy League students. Penn plays games with Princeton.

Edmund Wilson went to Princeton. And Wilson, I remember, once wrote about the Lucepapers, saying that the country and the civilization they described wasn't one he lived in or even recognized. Wilson's idea was of a kind of educated squirearchy, gentlemen farmers with Horace or Virgil or Ovid tucked in the pockets of their bib overalls. A fantasy, maybe, except that there are people like Fred Chappell, the poet and novelist, who sometimes lead me to suppose that in the right hollow back in the North Carolina mountains, I just might find a few of them. Or could have done, a generation or two ago.

But more than technology besets us. The trouble, I think, is also social and—God help us!—sociological. Franklin Roosevelt's idea for the GI Bill was generous in intention, but the result was that our country declared itself to be middle class. At a stroke of the pen, we were going to be squirearchs, every man Jack and woman Jill of us.

A good idea, perhaps, but not necessarily God's idea.

Universal opportunity is all they had in mind, but the politics of the Vietnam War changed the terms of the game. Those who didn't get admitted to colleges were . . . cannon fodder. And even those who did were at risk. Grade-flation goes back to Vietnam, when the marks college professors gave out began to mean different things. A, B, and C were okay, but D could be, quite literally, Death.

Not surprisingly, going to college became a very popular thing to do. The French, I think, send 30-something percent of their young people to one form or another of higher education. We send 60-something per-cent. And we are not, by any reasonable measurement, twice as intelli-gent as the French.

Wilson once said to me—I knew him only slightly, but I remember this vividly—that the British experiment of universal free compulsory education was a great failure. They tried that in the 1870s, and the only result was that, in the 1890s, the yellow press was born. There are all kinds of people reading who shouldn't be. They weren't meant to do it. They don't like it. They think it's a nuisance and an imposition, and they're right. Paul Goodman, the liberal social thinker of the early sixties (you see, I can still drop those appositives), suggested in *Growing Up Absurd* that this tyranny of education wasn't such a kind idea maybe.

Universal *free* compulsory college education has never been seriously suggested. What we have is much more cruel. It is expensive and, by and large, irrelevant to the interests and aptitudes of the youngsters who are forced to endure the experience which impoverishes their parents and saddles them with an absurd debt with which to begin adult life.

I look out with some sympathy at all these nice incurious kids here at Penn, highlighting their way through a not very demanding set of books, in the hope of getting decent jobs in the middle class that they would have been able to get before World War II with a high school diploma. The Penn kids are being fooled, because there aren't any jobs out there after a B.A., which doesn't mean anything anymore anyway. They can't write, can't read very well, don't know any math, and have no idea where Lisbon is.

I am reminded by the foregoing that a young woman in one of my Penn classes referred recently in one of her papers to "World War 2," and one of the other students asked whether the usual practice wasn't to employ Roman numerals. When I agreed that he was correct, the young woman protested, "My computer doesn't *do* Roman numerals." (We laughed, of course, and she was embarrassed, and I tried to soften the blow a little by telling her about the chief executive officer of Prudential Bache who addressed his brokers and, obviously reading from a speech that someone else had prepared, discussed the general rise in the value of stocks that had been going on since "World War Eleven.")

The Penn kids are better off, at any rate, than those downtown at Temple, who pop out of a subway station on their way to class, investing almost as much money and even greater amounts of time and effort. They have what is virtually open admission there, and it can take a kid two years or more to find out that the likelihood of his actually graduating is nil, but he's wasted a lot of sweat and has had his hopes raised. Most of the vandalism at Temple is from graduates *manqués*, who spray-paint four-letter words on the buildings in a gesture of resentment that may be deplorable but is hardly mysterious.

If education were the issue here, the fact that smarter people have an easier time than dumb ones would be a reasonable peculiarity of the system, but all men are supposed to be equal, at least in civil rights, in economic opportunities, and in social ways.

I used to suggest to my friends that we could declare dyslexia to be a disease, and it would immediately follow that grades and SATs are not only elitist but even a violation of a young person's civil rights. I thought I was making a joke but, as so often happens, the reality is far beyond any feeble attempt at hyperbole or satire. There are, indeed, officers at various universities who counsel the dyslexic, the dysgraphic, and the dysnumeric in how to demand from their teachers extra time on exams, special note-taking aides, tutoring help, and other sorts of attention. (There is, at Boston University, an extra charge of $1,200 a semester for these services.)

Alternatively, my suggestion is to give every American citizen a Ph.D. at the age of eight. Then the only people who hang around in schools or colleges will be those who want to learn something. For those who like intellectual activity, the way some people enjoy spelunking or free-fall skydiving or snorkeling, purely as an entertainment, there will be a small, appropriate, and quite lively student body.

That's what we had, more or less, when Edmund Wilson was at Princeton. A college education wasn't expected, let alone required, as a condition of employment in any job more selective than, say, day laborer. Roosevelt's idea may have been to extend the benefits of higher education, but what he actually accomplished was to condemn large numbers of young men and women to slogging through a whole series of courses in which they have no interest and for which they have no talent.

But surely, you are thinking, there is benefit even to a second-rate college education. These students must be getting something out of it.

I'm not at all sure. Indeed, from my vantage point, as an adjunct to an English department, I think the opposite view is likelier—that the experience does actual harm. The teaching of English, surely, is a grotesquely Swiftian parody of what it should be. Every young child loves language, delights in puns and rhymes and the rhythms of speech. In other words, every five-year-old boy or girl is a natural reader of poetry. (Or, better yet, a natural listener to it.) Put that child through twelve years of primary and secondary schooling, and then ship him or her off to a university—even a good one—and that delight will be ruined, corrupted. The very look of a poem on a page will be enough to produce performance anxiety.

A group of graduate students at Penn expressed their fears about reading poetry. (Fears? What in God's name did they have in mind when they applied for admission as graduate students in English? What did they think goes on here?) In a department meeting, it was decided that an informal group should meet with these students to try to allay these fears and teach them how to go about approaching a poem.

I went to one of these sessions. A colleague of mine had brought along a sheaf of Xeroxed sonnets, from Wyatt to Marilyn Hacker, and his idea was that we'd read through these poems. I noticed that there was a sonnet of Wordsworth that I particularly dislike, and I undertook to mention that it wasn't necessary to like every poem. One could pick and choose. Some are better than others, and some speak to a given reader in ways that others don't. The object is to find poems one enjoys. . . .

A smart, sensible, even accomplished colleague of mine took it upon herself to correct me, saying that "it isn't our job in the English department to distinguish between good and bad poems."

A strange remark, I thought, but what was even stranger was the reaction of the group of graduate students. My attempts at reassurance had been utterly misplaced. I was telling them that poems were to enjoy, and they were here because they had forgotten how to enjoy them. I was telling them, in other words, that it was their fault, that they were somehow deficient. . . . And they didn't want to hear this.

If poems are not to be distinguished, good from bad, or enjoyable from boring, then no particular talent is required on the part of the writer or the reader either. It's much fairer, much more egalitarian. Writing jobs in universities can be apportioned by race and gender. Students' reading preferences can be accommodated, because if all literature is equal, there's no particular advantage in studying Spenser or Dryden, and one might just as well teach Kurt Vonnegut (who writes in short sentences and short chapters) or Toni Morrison (who is *relevant*).

If you figure, as I do, that the colleges are doing actual harm, are diminishing the aptitudes of their students, making them stupider than they were when they showed up as uneducated but only moderately turned-off freshpersons, then you must allow that the decisions of the magazine editors make sense. The *Time* and *Life* and *Fortune* Wilson didn't recognize as describing his country or his world are now marginal. Their thriving spawn are *Sports Illustrated, People,* and *Entertainment Weekly*—which is to say *Time* with all the hard parts left out. *Time* for dummies.

Worse yet, the *The New Yorker* now is a very slightly upscale version of *People* with its Richard Avedon photographs and its short, punchy pieces. (You get a high-toned Brit to vulgarize your book, and you can declare yourself to be grunge-chic.) *Esquire* and *Vanity Fair* are edited, apparently, for morons.

Luce, a child of missionaries, had a misguided but undeniably sincere notion of converting the heathen. *Time* was supposed to be an uplifting enterprise, and he spoke about it in those megalomaniac terms, referring to it, once, as "a weekly record of our civilization." (*Newsweek,* a frankly cynical knockoff, had fewer delusions and was, therefore, a slightly less unpleasant place to work.) But that general ambition for his readers would now be seen as elitist and intolerable. Editors now think of their strenuous exercises in pandering as egalitarian—if not Jacobin— political correctness. Besides, they can defend themselves and their enterprises on the ground that their very nature is generally ameliorative. It's print, right? And print is supposed to be good for us. It has an old-fashioned, almost Ralph Lauren claim of classiness that's built in. They can also, during their rare twinges of conscience, look at the deterioration of television and exonerate themselves because their own has been no more precipitous. Television used to be a middle-class medium, because television sets used to be expensive. As soon as the prices dropped so that all but the homeless could afford a set—and there were more houses in America with television than with indoor plumbing—the "Golden Age" of TV was over. The broadening of the market meant the end of *Playhouse 90* and *Omnibus,* a new era of *Beverly Hillbillies,* then a newer era of *Donahue, Oprah,* and *Sally Jessy,* and, with the technological improvement of cable, the present arrangement with MTV, the shopping networks, and porn channels. Meanwhile, PBS, grubbing endlessly for money because it's cultural and good for us, offers old movies and reruns of old Lawrence Welk shows.

The trouble with being educated is that it cuts you off from the great mass of people who, let us be frank and admit what is obvious, aren't. So, in a savagely egalitarian society, where is the place for a man or woman of some culture?

That was the question Wilson was both posing and dodging in his notion of the cultivated squires. He was a man of the Left, and didn't want to allow for an aristocracy, which is where elitism inevitably leads. A pure meritocracy seemed to him relatively ruthless, urban, and grubby, with all the worst aspects of the civil service and none of the openness of what he supposed America ought to be.

That kind of concern now seems to have disappeared. We used to care about the balance between liberty and equality, and we would rely on fraternity as the mortar that might hold those contrarieties together. The fraternity is forgotten, and in the name of equality, bright kids are being deprived of what they deserve in the way of opportunities. Those youngsters I see at Penn aren't dopes. They would have been in the fast track, a generation ago, would have been challenged and ridden a little, taught to proofread and to take responsibility for their work. Now, so that everyone may feel good, the students are lumped together, the bright and the normal and the "special." The smartest students are, not surprisingly, bored out of their minds. They stare out the window and wait for the slower kids to catch up, but that never happens. The college education that used to be a privilege has become a necessity and, because we Americans like to be nice people, we translate all necessities into entitlements. Now it's their right. And a teacher who gives a student a less desirable grade is, in this Doonesbury world, guilty of discrimination.

Wilson thought a great deal about the meaning of American culture. Or even the possibility of American culture. And he imagined, in an attractively vague and perhaps romantic way, a country gentleman with his library. Not a city figure, neither dilettante nor bohemian, but this squire of the country or village—Red Bank, New Jersey, say, or Talcotville, New York. Wilson, himself, for instance. He wasn't alone in this. The southern fugitives had the same general suspicion of city life as an inappropriate location for the important business of continuing the culture. New York is where you buy and sell things, but hardly a place to live.

Cleanth Brooks, one of my teachers at Yale, lived in a gorgeous saltbox farmhouse he'd moved to a nice hillside and had rebuilt, board by board. Red Warren lived in a converted barn in Fairfield, Connecticut, and he came up to New Haven one or two days a week in the fall. (He spent the spring, which is not Connecticut's best season, elsewhere, often in France.) The way these men lived suggested a good deal to me about what they thought the point was of the literary life. The general tone back then of a place like Yale was relatively gentlemanly, and if anybody had asked us what we were doing, we'd have been able to say that we were preparing to be the beneficiaries of enormous trust funds. A man of leisure should know how best to use his time interestingly and profitably. Most of us had no such prospects, but to live as if we did seemed a good idea. You don't have to be rich to live rich.

Wilson's Princeton and my Yale were delivering a quite different message from that of Columbia and Harvard, which are urban universities. At Columbia and Harvard and Penn, which are in great cities, the important pretense toward that countryman's poise and ease, that gentlemanly amateurishness, seemed silly, I guess. I went to graduate school at Columbia and I never quite got used to the place. The trouble with it was and is that Madison Avenue is just a quick cab ride downtown.

What happened to Yale after I left is another essay, another book even. The gentlemanly ease gave way to an aggressive and absurd combination of theoreticians and lunatics, some of whom had hidden agendas—Paul de Man, a Fascist collaborator, had reason to hope that the meaning of any text was indeterminate and that there was no close association between, let alone any responsibility on the part of, an author and what he'd written. Harold Bloom, who sees literature as a kind of arm wrestling, believes that a strong misreading is the equivalent of a new poem, which seems to me like saying that a violent crime is the equivalent of a new morality. Yale became a joke to those few people who had any sense of humor. Harvard, of course, had always been a joke.

What I'm getting at is that I never challenged the precariousness of Wilson's underlying belief about the interdependence of culture and civility because I had grown up with it and shared it. I was shocked, as a young man, to discover that someone could be smart as a whip and well schooled and a villain.

A villain, in its root meaning, is of course not merely a scoundrel or an evil or worthless person, but a peasant. Someone out there in the country who isn't a squire. The pursuit of culture has to be a pursuit, which means that there has to be leisure in which to do it and inclination. "Money, money is a man," says Pindar, and there is a gritty truth to that. We cannot decide as a society that culture is a good thing and that all the underprivileged should be enrolled in Reading Is Fun programs that will lead them to become scholars, judges, doctors, and statesmen in a generation or two. The Jews and the Italians and the Irish who actually worked hard and studied at places like CCNY to get ahead did so in the face of considerable discouragement from a society that wasn't very welcoming at all. Now many of the blacks and the Hispanics, who are having these cultural benefits rammed down their throats, are gagging and protesting. They resent White European Men's history, or culture, or language. They don't want the pictures of Washington and Jefferson and Lincoln on the walls of their classrooms. They invoke affirmative action and insist on Martin Luther King, Jr., Nelson Mandela, and Malcolm X.

Wilson's notion of the educated squire would seem to them an outrage and an affront, but I don't understand where else the process of cultivation is likely to lead. "Discrimination," every campus sloganeer tells us, is a bad thing, un-American, subversive, and elitist. But the whole point of a university education used to be to teach discrimination, to get students to discriminate between good art and bad, good writing and bad, sound science and bad. Plato, the Greek philosopher (yeah!), explained all this with admirable clarity. Readers of *Time* and *Newsweek* not only don't know what he said but have to be told who he was. And they are the aristocrats. The villains are the ones reading those dreadful newspapers about Bigfoot and JFK spotted together in the Himalayas where they consort with space aliens, just as Nostradamus predicted they would.

Just as Edmund Wilson predicted they would.

What do those tawdry papers have to do with us, though? The classy Brits who come over to save our dying papers and magazines imitate them. The *National Enquirer* and *The New Yorker* are less and less distinguishable. Both are going nuts about O.J., although *The New Yorker* still allows its writers to indulge from time to time in dependent clauses.

What's worse is that there is no longer any way to declare with assurance that anything—or anyone—is wrong. The notions of good and bad have themselves been dismissed as elitist and oppressive. The idea of a canon of important texts is old hat. Indeed, the text itself is more or less *vieux jeu.* According to "reception theory," a text means anything we want it to mean. In the jolly equality of the New Age classroom, learning displays itself at its casual best by deconstructing Madonna commercials (I am not being satirical, having sat through exactly this demonstration at Penn a couple of years ago).

An idea of excellence may require adjustment and fiddling. But to abandon the whole enterprise and say that any text is worth attention, that any level of performance can be interesting to the academic . . . that seems to me just nuts. Not surprisingly, book publishing attends to academic trends the way Willie Sutton attended to banks—produce what sells: to a semi-literate trade public, and to anti-literate campuses. The anthologies prepared for those general introductions to literature in cow colleges are a disgraceful series of political compromises. They would have to be, if a committee meets in which nobody can say that A, a white male, is simply a better poet than B, a blind, black, Hispanic-surnamed, lesbian, Marxist dwarf. "Better" is a word that will soon be as offensive as "water buffalo," which is the epithet that a Jewish kid yelled out at some black sorority girls at Penn who were making noise quite late at night. He was translating from the Hebrew—*Behemah*—and various committees were called into session to determine whether this was offensive and therefore prohibited speech. Academic freedom has become the freedom to be censored by deans and committees, but that's another story, just as sad, just as silly.

Another classroom moment: The same young woman who'd written "World War 2" went on to discuss the jokes in the Mel Brooks version of *To Be or Not to Be* about "Jews and Homosexuals." I asked her about the majuscule she had awarded the second noun. "Are they now an ethnic group?" I inquired.

"I discussed this for a long time with my roommate," she insisted. "And she's an English major!"

"And a lesbian?" I asked.

"No, but she's from San Francisco."

Listen, I sound like a mandarin. I admit that. But I'm a Jew who went to Andover and who was forced there to attend compulsory chapel services. And then to Yale. I had as keen a sense of "their" culture as anyone can. But my parents understood, and I came in time to agree with them, that it was "their" country we had come to, and that in order for me to get an education and acquire an idea of how to think and how to be, "their" culture was the only game in town. I didn't have to forget my own, or pledge allegiance to every single book and poem and play I read, but I ought to know what they were talking about. I could, later on, pick and choose—when I had the sophistication to know how to do so. Simply to reject everything that they had on offer would have been to deny my own interests and talents. No seventeen-year-old likes slogging through Cicero, but to beat them at their own game, I had to learn the discipline of the game. (And then, reading Freud and Marx and Proust, I came to learn how much of their game was mine, after all.)

What seems to have disappeared in just a generation or so is the willingness we used to have to defer judgment until we had enough experience and breadth of knowledge to make a judgment. The students, more socially ambitious than intellectually curious, feel put upon and won't abide what they believe to be the absurd and arbitrary demands of their instructors. The instructors have devised a way to pander to this classroom anarchy by incorporating it into their peculiar hermeneutic theories of literature—or else they have abandoned faith in the very idea of objective worth. They don't have the nerve to stand there at the front of the classroom and announce what is painfully obvious: "You're young, you're dumb, and you're wrong."

With their new tactfulness, they aren't doing the youngsters any great favor, either. I have in one of my classes at Penn a recent graduate of Phillips Academy who has no idea what a run-on sentence is (he writes them all the time) and who was not at all joking when he suggested, in a paper, that Laurence Olivier's *Hamlet* was "almost as good as the novel." Because he is black, nobody at Andover had the nerve to fail him—or to admit that they had failed him. Their bizarre assumption had to be either that he'd pick this stuff up later or, more probably, that he could perfectly well get along without it. (If this is what they were thinking, they were not altogether wrong for, obviously, the young man did get into Penn.)

The barbarians have come and have taken over. The few squires who are left, the inheritors of Jefferson's idea of the American gentleman that Edmund Wilson could still take seriously, can only circle their wagons, post sentries around the camp, and, by the light of the fire, read what Ovid wrote out in Tomis, in *Tristia* III, 14:

> By a guttering lamp I go over these pitiful pages
> looking for any solecisms or Pontine lapses.
>   The guards at the gates are supposed to fend off the raids
> of the Getic brutes on our outpost. I'm on guard as well,
>   alert to their subtle incursions, but weary, weary . . .
> It's not just a conceit: out here I am Rome.

PART TWO

Arts & Sciences

KEN KALFUS

Last Night at the Planetarium

Ken Kalfus's brief Op-Ed piece for the *New York Times,* and its fortuitous mention of
the insidious but vivid process of "dumbing down" in America, was the catalyst for
this book. A freelance science writer who is at present living in Moscow with his wife,
a correspondent for the *Philadelphia Inquirer,* and daughter, he is working on a novel
and, while surveying Russia, thinks things might even be worse at home.

In Kalfus's piece, it's immediately apparent that he's not just mourning the disappearance of a landmark familiar from his childhood, but that he is witnessing a
larger transformation. That haunting image of burnt-out lightbulbs in the defunct
exhibit of nearby stars is oddly emblematic of the themes of this book. We are forcibly
exposed here to more than a dimming down of the cosmos, to the rupture of a long
discourse with scientific knowledge, and to the by-now routine boutiquification of a
great museum. The substitution of science fiction for science, instant fun for deep
pleasure, is a phenomenon which becomes a symptom for a wider malaise. We have
replaced the childlike with the childish, we renovate without first carefully restoring
and maintaining, and perhaps, as we extend multiculturalism into dreams of extraterrestrial life, we'll even discover that space travel is narrowing.
    No warp drive is likely to rescue us as we cruise the gift shops and play with the
educational toys of the science museum: plans are at present well under way for
a bigger, better, and doubtless more profitable American Museum of Natural
History.

*A*s a child growing up in suburban Long Island at the dawn
of the space age, I was slow to learn that there were planetariums in the
world other than the Hayden Planetarium in New York. At the time I
barely recognized that there were cities in the world other than New
York, even though I knew the Mets and Yankees occasionally played away
games.
    If unaware of the existence of, say, St. Louis, except for the sanctuary
it gave Lou Brock, a child of the space age might at least apprehend that
there were other planets orbiting the same star as we did, other stars in
our galaxy, and other galaxies in the universe. At the Hayden Planetarium, a New Deal–era, Art Deco–furnished astronomy museum perfumed
(in my recollection) by the roasted chestnuts and pretzels visitors
brought in from the vendors on Central Park West, the breadth and
complexity of the universe and our trifling position within it were made
transparent. Through school field trips and family outings, and then

through solitary, studiously attentive visits on my own, I became as familiar with the Hayden as I was with my own backyard.

The museum's main attraction was the great insect-like, many-lensed Zeiss projector, which stood as a symbol for the planetarium itself. As portentous music thundered within the second-floor sky theater, the Zeiss cast the bloody colors of the gathering twilight on the inside of the building's 75-foot dome. Then the planets and brightest stars twinkled on, followed by a cascade of stars, their positions and appearances scrupulously rendered. This was the sky show, narrated by a member of the planetarium staff who, waving a flashlight, bounced a green arrow among the constellations and explained the basic principles governing the stars' motions across the sky. It was a magnificent performance, and I may be excused for believing that it could not be reproduced elsewhere.

The second of the planetarium's two large mechanical devices was an orrery, a clockwork apparatus that orbited model planets on concentric rails around an illuminated model sun suspended from the first-floor ceiling. Moving the solar system through its paces, with the earth spinning on its axis and orbiting the sun about every twenty minutes, the orrery demonstrated a fundamental experience of terrestrial life, the passing of the seasons. It also illustrated two other phenomena—the phases of the moon and the odd, back-and-forward passage of the planets among the stars of the zodiac—the observation of which has been intimately involved with the development of human civilization.

These days, the orrery no longer works, its intricate gearings gathering dust and grime. On a recent sentimental journey back to the Hayden, I could see the planets dead in their tracks above the *Star Trek* exhibition that was now the planetarium's temporary centerpiece—a homage to another component of a typical 1960s space-age childhood. At the exhibition's entrance, visitors posed for photographs in the starship *Enterprise*'s transporter room. In glass cases beyond it hung the uniforms and costumes worn by the *Enterprise* crew and the aliens they encountered. Another display housed a stuffed "tribble," one of the furred, explosively reproducing animals that once threatened to overcome the starship. Photographic stills highlighted favorite episodes, and in one hall a filmed documentary about the television series ran continuously.

Upstairs, a new Zeiss projector presented a filmed, simulated flight aboard a Federation starship to exotic deep-sky objects like the Orion Nebula, a fiction dependent on the chimera of faster-than-light interstellar travel. We were briefed by Vulcans and thrillingly flew through fourth-dimensional wormholes. The show's spectacular special effects guaranteed that the possibility of such travel would make a greater impact on visitors than the program's incidental lessons in astronomy. The Zeiss, an instrument advanced from the one I knew, was equipped to project an image of the sky as seen from any part of the world at any epoch; showing a *Star Trek* movie, it was being woefully underused.

The Hayden Planetarium's baleful confusion of science, fantasy, and pop culture reflects what's happening in many of the hundreds of planetarium domes that, it turns out, dot the entire American landscape, from its cities to its smallest, flyblown hamlets. (The traveling memorabilia show originated at the Smithsonian Institution; the film was produced by the Oregon Museum of Science and Industry in Portland, and was to have moved on to about a dozen institutions by the end of 1994.) In the sky theaters where the night sky was once reproduced with stunning clarity, lecturers no longer beckon us to step outside on dark, star-swept nights. The live programs have been replaced by canned, pseudo-scientific documentaries, most of them emphasizing space travel and extraterrestrial life, two staples of science fiction.

Planetariums have now followed their parent science museums in a cynical quest to make science "fun" for children and their parents, unwisely throwing themselves into competition with better-financed Hollywood studios that can bring to bear dazzling special effects surpassed only by the Pentagon. These institutions contribute to public attitudes about science (of which astronomy is only a single example) that trivialize and dissipate the scientific adventure.

While producing new, expensive, glossy entertainments, many science museums and planetariums have slighted science, if they haven't abandoned it altogether. Around the dome on the Hayden's second floor a ring of exhibits was once arrayed, detailing the inner workings of the universe. Today the universe, like every other public facility, is underfunded and carelessly maintained. As I left the theater where I had seen the sky show, my eyes adjusting to the sub-warp environment, I found that the simulation of a solar eclipse on the ceiling of the Hall of the Sun exhibit was no longer operating, cast by neglect into perpetual eclipse.

Also dark were the busts of Kepler and Copernicus and the sample spectroscope, the laser beam that was supposed to illuminate a line representing the distance between the sun and the earth, and several of the panels explaining the birth of the sun.

The interactive exhibit that was supposed to demonstrate why the sky is blue didn't interact. The refracting telescope trained on a photograph of deep-sky objects across the room refused to be focused. The exhibit that demonstrates the parallax effect was missing the lightbulbs meant to represent the nearby stars, making it incomprehensible (a few visitors stared into the case puzzled, convinced that astronomy is too difficult a subject after all). The device that computes your age on other planets and the scale that computes your weight on the moon also registered *Tilt!*

Those who defend the introduction of science fiction in our science museums often promise that it will interest children in science, so that they will go on to pursue "real" science, or at least put more effort into it at school. But when adults use science fiction to demonstrate that "science is fun," they imply that science taken straight is not fun and needs to be sugar-coated with fantasy. At the Hayden it can be dispensed with altogether. As anyone learns after a few years of being a kid, adults characteristically insist to children that pursuits like science, reading, and school are fun, while they display no interest in these subjects themselves.

The reason "real" science isn't fun is that it is usually depicted as a single body of knowledge, or basically a collection of facts. What devalues these facts is the popular belief that scientists are always replacing them with new ones. In our popular media the history of science is often portrayed as the rise and fall of dogma. In the long run, all these "facts" are equally valid and their proponents will eventually be vindicated. As everyone knows, they all laughed at Christopher Columbus, when he said the world was round. They all laughed, when Edison discovered sound.

There is too little in the schools—and virtually none at all in planetarium programs, in the mass media, or in the lyrics of Ira Gershwin—about science as a process, a means of comprehending nature using the tools of observation and reason. The establishment of the scientific process as the basis for society was the triumph of the Enlightenment, and since then its principles have remained intact. At times, usually when advances in technology have offered closer looks at natural phenomena, observation and reason have forced scientists to reconsider previously held theories. The embrace of new theories may have been bitter defeats for the old theories and their proponents, but they were victories for the scientific process.

Other means for comprehending the universe are of course available, such as those that employ the tools of faith and mysticism, and they have their uses. But when they become confusedwith science, they bring with them the brimstone whiff of the medieval.

A pungent example of this was offered recently by a planetarium sky show presented at the Maryland Science Center in Baltimore. After a propagandistic promotion for a human expedition to Mars and some typically overwhelming declarations about the vastness of space (accompanied by the now-familiar myriad of stars gracefully streaming toward us and then off the screen), the show concluded with the assertion that some unidentified "scientists think the only limits in the universe are those we place on our own imagination."

This is mysticism at the furthest, brain-dead limits of intellectual laziness, and not at all unusual in our public discourse. If science means anything at all, it is that the universe's size and complexity are finite, and that our imagination has nothing to do with it.

When science is devalued, other processes rush to take its place in public life. This allows some of religion's advocates to make the claim, for example, that faith-based descriptions of nature, such as creationism, deserve equal time with science-based theories in the public classroom. Others make claims for astrology and the occult, which for decades have outnumbered popular science titles in our bookstores. Most dangerously, the door has been opened today for mystical thinking about race and blood.

Science has always been the basis of the American experiment. The United States was founded by scientist-citizens like Jefferson and Franklin who quickly disseminated and applied the latest advances in agricultural knowledge, animal husbandry, and mechanics. At the same time, they turned recent European developments in political philosophy into a concrete American ideology. Well into the last century the idea that a democracy rested on the scientific knowledge of its citizens was kept alive by statesmen, educators, businessmen, and, especially, the magazine *Scientific American,* which was established in 1845 by the itinerant New England painter and self-taught inventor Rufus Porter.

When Mark Twain's Connecticut Yankee, a character possibly based on Porter, found himself in King Arthur's court, his practical knowledge of science made him a wizard even greater than Merlin. With native ingenuity and an awareness of scientific principles, he reinvented (or pre-invented) the telegraph, the revolver, and other nineteenth-century artifacts. But if he had been transported instead to the late twentieth century, would his wizardry have been any less remarkable? If a twentieth-century Connecticut suburbanite found himself in the Dark Ages, would he be able to reinvent anything more complicated than a gin and tonic? Less hyperbolically, can a conventionally educated adult American of the twentieth century claim to know more about science than a conventionally educated adult American of the nineteenth century?

Today the advance of science has outpaced the public understanding of it, yielding appliances whose functions obscure the scientific principles that inspirit them: televisions, microwave ovens, computers, vaccines. A product is understood to have come into its own when its consumers can use it without knowing how it works. It has exited the realm of science and entered that of technology.

In the big new science museums built in the last decade, technology has triumphed over science. I'm thinking in particular of the museum I now know best, the Franklin Institute's Futures Center in Philadelphia, where I lived until recently. A favorite destination of my out-of-town guests, the Futures Center was opened in 1990 in a wing adjacent to the Franklin Institute's old, somewhat musty science museum. In the Futures Center and in the other new museums, there are mock-ups of spaceships, models of microcomputers, videophones, and other products of the future, but little explanation of the science that makes them work.

The virtue of these new exhibits is supposed to lie in their "interactivity," one of the great hustles of the 1980s and 1990s. Press a button, and a light goes on to illuminate a panel about, say, microsurgery. Turn a crank and some plastic balls levitate in an upright plastic canister, God knows why. Kids punch the buttons of these exhibits with rising frustration as they discover that their effect is considerably less than that of the buttons on a television remote control. Then they rush off to the next set of buttons. These exhibits, as we have seen at the Hayden, tend to break down often. In this respect, they may predict the future very accurately.

Coming attractions of consumer goods have long been a mainstay of world's fairs, where they have served their corporate sponsors in promoting optimism about capitalism and our future prosperity. In the Futures Center, the future itself is a commodity, particularly a future in which technology dominates daily life. Much is made of the choices available to the individual, but they are mostly in regard to the kinds of technology we would prefer: shall it be nuclear power or solar energy? With kitchen appliances that talk and computers that help visitors design automobiles and clothing fashions on a video screen (from some very limited choices), we are presented with a vision of the twenty-first century as a kind of shopping mall. Meanwhile, to raise some of the $72 million it needed for the project, the Franklin Institute sold off its remaining research facilities, including its Antarctic substation.

To its credit, exhibits at the Futures Center warn of environmental problems, but amid the futuristic hucksterism they have the impact of the Surgeon General's warning on a pack of cigarettes. As they come to dominate our science museums, these exhibitions foretell our transformation from citizen-scientists into passive consumers of technology.

Some of the features of this metamorphosis can be seen in our popular culture and planetarium shows, as well as in our public policy debates about the direction of the space program. For the first visitors to the Hayden Planetarium in 1935, the sky was a palce to be contemplated from a dark field outside the city—an effect re-created by the planetariums of the era, which then invited the public to visit that dark field. (These were the days before suburban sprawl made dark fields inconveniently distant). The advent of space travel has now made the sky a destination for the selected and trained few and a vividly imagined one for the rest of us.

Many American planetariums indulge the fantasy, emphasizing space travel in their sky shows, eschewing science for the spectacular

3–2–1–*blast off!* of aerospace technology. A disproportionately large number of shows are dedicated to Mars, the planet that the space lobby in Washington has identified as the next destination for human space flight, to be followed eventually by human settlement. The arguments planetarium shows and other media employ in favor of such an expedition betray some revealing assumptions about how we have come to think of our place in the universe.

The grand prize of an expedition to Mars—what an article in *U.S. News and World Report* called "the overriding question driving this exploration"—would be the discovery of extraterrestrial life. This has become the bottom-line question for nearly all astronomical and space research. Unfortunately for Mars, the planet's tenuous atmosphere, extreme cold, and observed absence of life have persuaded mainstream scientific opinion that it's biologically dead; no evidence has been found to suggest that it was ever anything but. The Mars show at the Baltimore planetarium gamely promoted the possibility anyway, vaguely stating that even more unidentified "scientists still wonder about life on Mars . . . some believe Mars may have had life in the past."

In this instance, it is very easy to find these unidentified scientists; many of them work for NASA and aerospace companies that have a stake in the future exploration of Mars. They have led the campaign to drive public policy in favor of such exploration, frequently publishing articles in popular science magazines that exaggerate the possibilities of past, current, or future life on the planet. One of the space-propaganda market's high-tech catchwords is the verb "terraform," meaning to modify another planet's environment to make it more like Earth's, and it is usually employed in connection with making Mars more livable for human pioneers (of course, humans have shown greater promise of success in modifying *Earth*'s environment to make it more like the environment of, say, smog-shrouded Venus).

The Baltimore show, set in a future Martian settlement, envisions that all life-support supplies will someday be produced by the settlers themselves. It declares that "only luxuries" will be imported from Earth, modeling a Martian future along the same lines as America's past. According to this popular, space-age version of Manifest Destiny, the human race will explore and eventually colonize the solar system and the galaxy. This treacherous analogy, virtually a commonplace in our expectations of the future, minimizes the differences between seafaring and spacefaring, and between the fertile plains of the American continent and the airless, sterile, radiation- and crater-scarred surfaces of other planets.

The scientists campaigning for a $100-billion Mars mission bring to mind the grant-hungry scientists who in the 1980s lined up behind the most brazen science hoax since Piltdown Man, President Reagan's Strategic Defense Initiative. Sold to the public as a shield against Soviet missiles, "Star Wars" was scientifically infeasible—and was yet another Big Science project that drew its inspiration from Hollywood. While it is perfectly natural for cultural imperatives to drive science, we should guard against them *replacing* science, and bankrupting us in the process.

Human space flight has its charms, some of them scientific, but its drain on the NASA budget has severely curtailed more productive space exploration, especially exploration by robotic spacecraft like the Voyagers, Mariners, and Pioneers that revolutionized our knowledge of the solar system in the 1970s and 1980s. The federal government can spend only so much on basic research; what's lost in space doesn't reach more compelling science projects, such as the recently killed, distinctly less entertaining Superconducting Super Collider.

What would a human expedition to Mars provide that robotic probes could not? According to a recent show produced by the Franklin Institute's Fels Planetarium, the answer is . . . great TV. Borrowing real newscasters from the local public radio station, the Fels show simulated a twenty-first-century television newscast about the first human flight to Mars, aboard a spaceship named after the science fiction writer Arthur C. Clarke. The news team interviewed crew members and breezily narrated animated film clips about the flight.

The public's retreat from participation in science has never been starker. If once we could see the stars from our backyards, possibly gazing through a cheap telescope, now the universe is something to be observed on television. Our science fiction series have prepared us for this. Note that on the bridge of the *Enterprise* there are no windows. Comfortably settled in a souped-up La-Z-Boy, Captain Kirk watches the stars rush by on a large-screen TV.

The very popular film image of stars rushing by a spaceship in flight, or even swimming by in a leisurely fashion, obscures basic knowledge about the universe we live in: its size, the distances between stars, and the flat-out impossibility of closing the distances between them by traveling faster than light. Despite rhetorical allusions to the vastness of our universe, our popular culture shies away from accepting these constraints in its fictions because they're too scary: to comprehend the size of the universe is to comprehend our isolation within it.

If religion employs faith and the occult employs mysticism, then the favorite tool of science fiction is wishful thinking, particularly the wishful thought that we might someday travel faster than light. While wishful thinking makes for good space opera, should it be a factor in public science policy? Here before me is a recent space-travel-boosting issue of the popular science magazine *Discover* (published by a subsidiary of the people who urge us to wish upon a star, the Walt Disney Company). In it,

NASA administrator Daniel Goldin proposes establishing a lunar observatory, free of atmospheric distortion, to search for Earth-like planets outside our solar system. He suggests that the discovery of such planets "might inspire us to invent warp drive."

In fact, it would take more than inspiration to invent a faster-than-light "warp drive"; it would take a refutation of our understanding of the laws of physics. To talk of such a refutation, based on neither observation nor reason, is to degrade the means by which this understanding has been accomplished. When it's done by the chief of the National Aeronautics and Space Administration, it denigrates the entire scientific enterprise.

The trivialization of science in the popular media runs counter to another trend, the general improvement in American science writing. Today's best popularizers of science, Stephen Jay Gould, Chet Raymo, Oliver Sacks, and the late Lewis Thomas, far surpass the work of their predecessors in style and content, occasionally bridging the traditional abyss between science and literature. Today most big-city newspapers run their computer advertisements around at least one page of science news each week; these science articles are middling fair to good, often written by reporters with training in science journalism. *Scientific American,* despite some recent format changes that disturbed its readers nearly as much as other recent format changes disturbed readers of the *New Yorker,* continues to write of science as a process intrinsic to democracy. In our diverse society, you can always find what you need. Perhaps, as is often the case in American life, the efforts of the few will eventually make an impact on public consciousness.

A single idea commonly runs through the best science writing: that we live in the universe, a discovery first made by astronomers five hundred years ago. Before Copernicus, most theories and popular ideas of the universe conceived of the heavens as a place apart from the natural world, a residence of gods or a God hidden from human observation. Whether the constellations were the celestial remains of mythical heroes or the sky a transcendent realm whose glory lies behind an opaque, light-studded sphere, the universe was a place whose physical laws and texture of reality were distinctly apart from the terrestrial. The work of Copernicus and the first astronomers to use a telescope presented humankind with evidence that the planets were large, solid, non-incandescent worlds like our own, and that the stars were like the sun, and that the only thing that separated us from them were vast distances, which became even vaster as the tools of astronomy improved.

It was the work of the Hayden orrery and Zeiss projector to place us in this universe by demonstrating how the visible turnings of the night sky are caused by our residence upon a tilted, spinning, and orbiting planet. Simulations of space travel remove the universe from our normal experience; they make it a place we must travel to, aboard sophisticated conveyances. In the new *Star-Trek*ked planetarium and hyped-up technology museum, in our popular culture, and in our public discussion of science, the universe has receded from the naked eye and the questioning intellect.

Voodoo Science

Robert L. Park is professor of physics at the University of Maryland. This essay is expanded from an Op-Ed piece published in the *New York Times* (July 9, 1995).

Ten years ago the term *postmodern* seemed to couple a certain promise of liberation from the shackles of the past with a defiant challenge to doubters to prepare for a new era that would not hesitate to revalue—in the name of truth-seeking—all that was once held dear. Today it is widely ascribed to the words and deeds of a new breed of Levelers and Luddites who believe in the "social construction of reality" and who sniff out for destruction any hint of hierarchical value with all the joy and lust of a bloodhound. Orwell called it the fascism of the Left.

Most science fiction is about utopias descending into dystopias. Robert Park's essay describes no fictive world, but the postmodern world we currently spend our days in, a world that eagerly discredits centuries of technical and scientific achievement and seems hell-bent to return to a less complex time—when people died of toothache and sacrificed virgins for higher crop yield.

THE "UNABOMBER," who has been killing and maiming people—mostly academics—for two decades, explained in a letter to the *New York Times:* "We would not want anyone to think we have any desire to hurt professors who study archaeology, history, literature, or harmless stuff like that. The people we are out to get are the scientists and engineers. . . . We advocate eliminating industrial society."

But the Unabomber poses no more threat to "industrial society" than do random bolts of lightning. There is simply no way back. Earth cannot sustain its burgeoning population of five and a half billion people without modern agriculture, transportation, immunization, sewage treatment, etc. With no control on population growth, technology is in a desperate race just to keep even.

Nevertheless, growing numbers of people, in one way or another, share some of the Unabomber's romantic longing for a simpler world. Unable or unwilling to comprehend the technology on which they depend, they are deeply distrustful of the science behind it, and reject the Western scientific tradition that created it. It is a romantic rebellion, led not by the semi-literate yahoos of fundamentalist religion, who are the traditional foes of science, but by serious academics who regard themselves as intellectuals. They range from the hysterical environmentalist

Jeremy Rifkin, who sees disaster lurking behind all technological progress, to a University of Delaware philosophy professor, Sandra Harding,
who seems to believe that the laws of physics were constructed to maintain white male dominance.

An Afrocentric writer, Hunter Adams, contends that black Africans
were "the wellspring of creativity and knowledge on which the foundation of all science, technology and engineering rests." John Mack, a
professor of psychiatry at Harvard, responds to patients who believe they
have been abducted by aliens by agreeing with them. A physicist, John
Hagelin of Maharishi International University, claims that experts in
transcendental meditation can generate "consciousness fields" that induce tranquillity throughout society.

What these people share is a profound hostility to the reliance on
reason and evidence that is the basis of modern science. This anti-science
rebellion has spread though popular culture like a virus.

Science Friction

In the film *Jurassic Park,* the premise is that having gained control
over the genetic basis of life itself, scientists use their incredible power to
make an amusement park populated by flesh-eating dinosaurs! The fictional theme of arrogant scientists creating monsters they cannot control
is hardly new. Hubris, after all, was the downfall of poor Dr. Frankenstein. But the same theme is to be found in an exhibit at the Smithsonian
Institution's Museum of American History.

The "Science in American Life" exhibit at the Smithsonian was actually paid for with money provided by American chemists. Concerned that
people give little thought to the impact of science on their lives, the
American Chemical Society approached the Smithsonian in 1989 about
creating a permanent exhibit to remind people of how they benefit from
science. The chemists raised $5.3 million for the Smithsonian to develop
the exhibit.

Historians at the Smithsonian had their own ideas of what science
meant to American life. When I visited the exhibit shortly after it opened
in 1994, a middle-aged docent in a white lab coat explained: "In the
twenties we thought scientists were gods, now we know they're the source
of our biggest problems." That's not exactly what the chemists had in
mind. They envisioned something along the lines of the old DuPont
commercial "Better things for better living through chemistry"—what
they got was closer to Love Canal.

The first stop on a tour of the exhibit is a re-creation of the 1876
chemistry laboratory of Ira Remson at Johns Hopkins University. It's a
good place to start. In 1879, Constantine Fahlberg, a German scientist
working in Remson's lab, accidentally stumbled on saccharin while

studying the chemistry of coal tars. The discovery marked the beginning of the synthetics industry.

Life-size talking mannequins of Remson and Fahlberg stand in the laboratory among the beakers and test tubes. But they aren't discussing the wonders of coal-tar chemistry, they are engaged in a bitter debate over credit for saccharin's discovery. The point of this elaborate display is not that basic research produces unexpected practical benefits; rather it is that scientists, no less than others, are vulnerable to vanity and greed.

Nearby, an 1890 photograph is displayed showing Remson with his large group of graduate students. The caption asks, "What do the people in this group have in common?" The answer is they all have facial hair. And not only are they all men, they are all white men. In 1890, the same would have been true if they had been stockbrokers, or law students, or architects—or historians for that matter. But that's just the point. Scientists, the curators want us to know, suffer the same character flaws as the rest of society—and thus have no special claim to authority.

As you proceed from Remson's lab to the present, the exhibit is a catalogue of environmental horrors, weapons of mass destruction, and social injustice. Missing is any sort of balance: no hint of the millions of lives saved by the discovery of antibiotics; no mention of those spared from starvation by pesticides and fertilizers; no value assigned to improved working conditions and the leisure to indulge in whatever activities bring us personal satisfaction.

A visitor to the exhibit might come away convinced that science is a threat to life. But in the century covered by the exhibit, the life expectancy of Americans has more than doubled. It is science that made that possible. What century, you are left to wonder, would the Smithsonian historians prefer to have lived in?

In defending the exhibit, John Lankford, a historian at Kansas State University, explained that until recently the history of science was written by scientist-historians. Now, he proudly explained, science history is written by "non-practitioner historians"—unprejudiced, it appears, by any knowledge of their subject.

What Science?

Consider the proposed national standards for teaching U.S. history in grades 5–12, released in 1994. Dozens of historians labored for three years to produce this new curriculum without encountering a trace of science. Electricity, radio, jet travel, weather satellites, nuclear weapons, antibiotics, the Apollo moon landing, the eradication of smallpox, genetic engineering, and computers might as well have dropped from the sky.

Well, to be fair, a word search of the 250-page document did turn up the word "science" one time—in a list of professions from which women have been systematically excluded. A search for "scientific" turned up this gem: "The swordplay of the United States and the Soviet Union rightfully claims attention because it led to the Korean and Vietnam Wars, as well as the Berlin airlift, the Cuban missile crisis, American intervention in many parts of the world, a huge investment in scientific research and environmental damage that will take generations to rectify." So there you have it. Scientific research is just an expensive consequence of "swordplay," along with two wars and destruction of the environment. But the history standards' neglect of science seems benign compared to the Afrocentric curriculum finding its way into urban schools across the nation.

The Afrocentric curriculum is based on Hunter Adams's essay "African and African-American Contributions to Science and Technology," commissioned by the Portland, Oregon, public schools. This is feel-good history, meant to raise the self-esteem of black inner-city children. Adams attributes the discovery of flight, metallurgy, electricity, the theory of evolution, and modern cosmology to the ancient Africans.

Silly perhaps, but not particularly dangerous. But Adams also espouses the "melanist" claim that black Africans are imbued with special psychic powers: "The ancient Egyptians," he writes, "were known the world over as the masters of magic, precognition, psychokinesis, remote viewing and other underdeveloped human capabilities." Does anyone really believe that minorities will be helped by a belief in magic and psychics?

In an attempt to accommodate diversity, however, many educators treat all ideas as equally deserving of respect. All ideas, that is, except those of Western civilization. For these postmodernists there is no objective truth; one narrative account of the world is as good as another. "The task of the historian is not to discover ultimate truth," according to Kansas State University historian John Lankford, "but rather to construct a convincing explanation of selected aspects of human behavior."

It is as though beliefs are arranged on a shelf; everyone is expected to walk by and select one. It doesn't much matter which one, as long as you believe in something. Given such a choice, why would anyone pick something like science that requires you to do a lot of hard thinking—or, God forbid, learn mathematics?

"The meaning doesn't matter if it's only idle chatter of a transcendental kind"
Sir William Gilbert, Patience, Act I

Unfortunately, even a Ph.D. in physics is no inoculation against nuttiness. In the summer of 1993, an organization calling itself the Institute of Science, Technology and Public Policy, headed by Dr. John Hagelin, a Harvard-trained particle theorist, launched a $6-million experiment to reduce crime in Washington, D.C. Four thousand transcendental-meditation experts from eighty-two countries assembled in Washington for a seven-week period, during which they practiced meditating in unison to generate a powerful anti-violence field. The field, Hagelin predicted, would spread peace and tranquillity throughout the nation's capital and even make President Clinton more effective in running the nation.

And was it successful? Following a year-long analysis of crime reports, Dr. Hagelin proudly announced the results at a Washington press conference: violent crime, he said, decreased 18 percent during the period of the experiment. "Eighteen percent relative to what?" I asked. "Relative to what it would have been without the meditators meditating," he patiently explained. "And how could you know what the crime rate would have been?" I persisted. With just a trace of irritation, he explained that the expected crime rate was calculated by "scientific time-series analysis" carried out by the Institute of Science, Technology and Public Policy. The analysis took into account such variables as temperature, precipitation, the economy, and "geomagnetic field fluctuations."

But how did violent crime during those seven weeks compare with the crime rate in the seven weeks before the test, or the seven weeks after the test, or during the same seven weeks in previous years? Well, actually, the number of murders during the meditation period was higher than for any seven-week period before or since! True, but without the meditators, Hagelin solemnly explained, the toll would have been even higher. It's lucky the meditators were there just when they were most needed.

How are we to account for such widespread nuttiness? Is it indelibly coded into our DNA? Is there, so to speak, a "belief gene"? Perhaps. Without getting into questions of technical feasibility, imagine using DNA from a mosquito preserved in amber to clone one of our Stone Age ancestors instead of a tyrannosaur. Cro-Magnons lived in the Pleistocene era some 30,000 years before the dawn of civilization. Would a Cro-Magnon clone be a savage brute that could escape and terrorize society? I'm afraid "Pleistocene Park" wouldn't be that exciting: a Cro-Magnon reared today would be virtually indistinguishable physically and mentally from the rest of us.

Evolution is a slow business. We are pretty much unchanged from the savages that survived in the Pleistocene forests by eating grubs off rotten logs. It seems remarkable that creatures who evolved to find food and avoid predators should be capable of writing sonnets and doing integral calculus, but our genes were shaped before humans had any concept of natural law. Perhaps an acceptance of supernatural forces conferred some survival advantage on our Stone Age ancestors. But in a modern technological society, it carries serious risks.

It's the Pits

Aided by the silence of the scientific community, a resurgence of belief in magic and psychic phenomena has spread to all levels of society—even to the National Institutes of Health. A recent NIH report, *Alternative Medicine: Expanding Medical Horizons*, discusses various magical cures, ranging from "Lakota medicine wheels" to "mental healing at a distance," as though they deserve serious attention. It is surely the most credulous document ever offered in the name of medical science. Its release in the spring of 1995 at a Capitol Hill press conference was hosted by Senator Tom Harkin of Iowa. It was Harkin, three years before, who fathered legislation mandating creation of the Office of Alternative Medicine at NIH, to the dismay of most members of the medical community.

This was not the first time Congress had inserted itself into medical controversy. Remember laetrile, the toxic concoction of apricot pits that promised to cure cancer? The FDA sought to ban laetrile, but cancer patients, desperate for any straw, appealed to Congress. Congress directed the FDA to conduct clinical trials, and when the trials showed no efficacy, bills were introduced to force the FDA to release the drug anyway. Meanwhile, laetrile clinics sprang up across the border. Cancer patients traveled to Mexico in droves and gave grateful testimony to laetrile's life-saving powers. Until, one by one, they fell forever silent.

The FDA saw its responsibility in the laetrile case as the protection of an unsophisticated public from medical quackery. Now, it seems, the quacks have their own branch of NIH. It is not the federal funding that is so objectionable as the credibility that comes with it.

Ancient Cures

Nowhere is the desire to return to an earlier time more evident than in alternative medicine. Almost all the alternative therapies rely on some ancient "cure"—the older the better. We must assume that before the discovery of the circulatory system and the germ theory of infectious disease, before the discovery of genetics or vitamins, there was knowledge of cures that has since been forgotten.

Take "biofield therapeutics," or "touch therapy," for example. It is derived from the ancient practice of "laying on of hands." The earliest reference dates back thousands of years to the *Huang Ti Nei Ching Su Wen*, which translates something like "the emperor refuses to take any more medicine." If it's that old, the argument seems to be, there must be something to it. In its modern form, the hands do not even have to touch the patient. Close proximity will do just as well, since it's the patient's "aura" that the practitioner is manipulating; I've never seen one myself, but auras apparently stick out. The hands are used to scoop off the negative energy in the aura.

There may be risks involved; a patient in a midwestern hospital reportedly complained after a careless biofield practitioner working on a patient in the next bed inadvertently scooped some of the negative energy over onto him.

Or consider "homeopathic medicine." It began in 1786 when a German physician named Hahnemann, curious about how quinine cured malaria, decided to try a little quinine bark himself and found to his astonishment that he developed the chills and weakness characteristic of malaria. "Öha!" he exclaimed, "Gleiches heilt Gleiches"—"like cures like." This means that substances that cause certain symptoms when given to a healthy person can cure those same symptoms in someone who is sick. Sort of like bleeding, which was also practiced at the time. They both worked about equally well.

Hahnemann spent the remainder of his life, which was understandably brief, ingesting all sorts of natural substances to see what symptoms they caused and then prescribing these substances for people who already had the symptoms. He did encounter a problem; there were often unfortunate "side effects." That led Hahnemann to his second great discovery: if he diluted the substance enough, the side effects went away, which certainly sounds reasonable enough. But no matter how much it was diluted, the medicine was undiminished in its effectiveness! That I can believe as well.

Indeed, proponents of homeopathy contend the medicine retains its bioactivity even after it has been diluted until the probability of even a single molecule of the medicine remaining is essentially zero. The structure of the water, they explain, is altered by the medicine during the process of dilution, and it retains this structure even after none of the medicine remains. In short, the water "remembers." Conveniently, it only seems to remember the cure and not the side effects.

The first scientific attempt to examine mental healing was by Sir Francis Galton in 1872 in a paper titled "Statistical Inquiries into the Efficacy of Prayer." Figuring that heads of state and clerics were prayed for more frequently than anyone else, he looked for any indication of increased longevity among monarchs and bishops. He concluded there was no demonstrable effect, but Sir Francis may have been a little unclear about just what the common people were praying for.

Modern studies to assess the ability of humans to affect the physiological functions of living systems by mental means use bacteria, yeast, fungi, plants, protozoa, and insects as "targets." This certainly seems to rule out placebo effects, and informed consent does not appear to be an issue either.

The results of these studies have all been positive, according to *Alternative Medicine,* but the report raises serious ethical concerns. Is it possible to *harm* distant organisms by mental means? If further research were to establish such a possibility, it would amount to confirmation that it is possible to put a curse on your enemies, which is also ancient wisdom. That should take us back far enough to satisfy the most hopeless romantic.

How can the public be protected from fraudulent or misguided mental "healers"? "Perhaps," the report muses, "it is possible to establish a requirement akin to board certification of mental healers to ensure efficacy and protect consumers from worthless healers and predatory quacks." I, for one, certainly hope so.

An Orderly Universe

Where is the outcry? Why have the scientists themselves, who are forever bemoaning the general scientific illiteracy, been so timid about condemning this sort of nincompoopery? Alas, scientists, no less than others, are afraid of being cast as intolerant—even of being thought foolish.

The public needs to hear that we live in a universe governed by natural laws. It is much less important for people to know what those laws are than to be aware that they cannot be circumvented. But they can be understood and used to benefit humanity. Progress is never smooth. Each new application begets new problems.

But it is science that uncovers the problems, and it is to science that we turn to solve them. Not because scientists have any claim to greater intellect or virtue, but because science is the only means we have to sort out the truth from ideology or fraud or mere foolishness.

ANTHONY DECURTIS

I'll Take My Stand: A Defense of Popular Culture

Anthony DeCurtis is a correspondent for cable-television channel VH1 and a contributing editor of *Rolling Stone.* He is the editor of *Present Tense: Rock & Roll and Culture* and co-editor of *The Rolling Stone Illustrated History of Rock & Roll.* His essay accompanying the Eric Clapton retrospective album *Crossroads* won a Grammy, and he has twice received the ASCAP Deems Taylor Award for excellence in writing about music. He holds a Ph.D. in American literature.

Wondering whether the absence in a young college graduate of knowledge about early-twentieth-century French art music is comparable to his own forty-something shakiness on computer technology, Anthony DeCurtis takes a contrarian position on the central thesis of this collection, namely, that native intelligence and an open mind are insufficient tools for maintaining a culture of enduring value.

Is the current debate about I-know-more-than-you-do-and-therefore-you're-stupid? Surely this is valid criticism of much of the ink being spattered about (compare the so-called cultural-literacy industry). The deeper question may be whether there is intrinsically greater value in certain kinds of knowledge and, if that is so, how to explain why so few people believe in them anymore, much less put their beliefs into practice.

In the end, DeCurtis may be in agreement with Hannah Arendt, who noted a pernicious tendency of the rising middle class in the nineteenth century to "monopolize" (perhaps today "coopt" is the operative verb) high culture as a way of aggrandizing its need for class and status. Surely there is less need to own this cultural heritage than to internalize the value of experiencing it, thereby fostering it and enriching one's own life and the lives of others.

O NE RECENT EVENING a writer who occasionally freelanced for *Rolling Stone,* where I edited the record review section for five years, dropped by my apartment to listen to music. To say that techno—a hyperkinetic, electronic dance music that had become hugely popular in Europe and that was beginning to develop a following in the United States—was his specialty would be to vastly diminish the extent of his commitment to that genre and the ecstatic "rave" scene that surrounds it. He played some hard-to-find techno tracks for me, discussed them with insight and passion, explained the social ramifications of the music, and gave me some recommendations for future listening.

Because of his growing interest in ambient techno—a much slower and dreamier electronic music that ravers use to ease themselves down after their mad dancing—I put on some pieces by Erik Satie for him to hear. The idea was to connect Satie's notions about music that would mingle amiably with its environment and the intentionally atmospheric function of ambient techno. "Who is Erik Satie?" he asked.

I'll admit it: at first I was shocked. We'd touched on such a wide range of subjects that I assumed he'd be generally familiar with Satie, as I am; I just wasn't sure if he'd ever thought of him in this particular context. The evening had also included a viewing of *The Last Seduction* and a long talk about the history of film noir and the reasons for its current revival. We'd listened to Bob Dylan and Syd Barrett and rambled through a chat about the Beats and the intricacies of the most up-to-the-minute computer technology. How could this obviously intelligent, insatiably curious twenty-six-year-old product of a good university never have *heard* of Erik Satie?

For a moment, I found myself shedding my identity as an editor at a consumer magazine and reverting to my former role as a literature professor and, more or less by implication, ardent defender of academic "standards." What are they teaching these people nowadays?!?

That feeling, however, was quickly replaced by a more immediate delight. There was no question but that he would love Satie, and now I—while not an expert by the furthest stretch of the imagination—would have the pleasure of turning him on to that music. The antidote to my initial outrage seemed easy enough to achieve: I'll tell him, and then he'll know who Satie is. Somehow, that was a simple and fit end to a long evening of aesthetic exploration, sharing, and discovery.

Afterwards, at some remove from the actual event, I thought more seriously about whether or not my friend's ignorance of Satie constituted an indictment of our educational system—or even of him. I don't think it does at all—any more than I would like my ignorance of computer culture or the ramifications of techno to stand as an indictment of me. Somewhere my friend had learned how to be excited by knowledge and how to synthesize what he'd learned into fresh formulations. He'd learned how to listen, how to learn from someone else, and how to teach. His formal education must have played some role in all that, even if it wasn't an exclusive or even determinative one.

I also realized something else. Knowing about techno and not knowing much about classical music might be somebody else's very definition of dumbing down, but it certainly isn't mine. It's often struck me that many skeptics about popular culture succumb to one of its more obnoxious aspects—the reduction of complicated aesthetic issues to a hit parade—when setting forth what they think should or shouldn't be part of the curriculum or the canon, or even when just expressing their conviction about what is worth knowing. What is the point, though, of pitting one type of music, or one work of art, or one type of knowledge against another, as if in a popularity contest? That seems to me to betray even very traditional notions of the attitude an intellectual life should instill.

That type of thinking helps no one and really derives from issues that have little to do with aesthetic matters but everything to do with maintaining the cultural perquisites of class privilege. I remember feeling bifurcated in my intellectual passions when I was in college in the late 1960s and early 1970s. I'd loved rock and roll since I was a child, and in the mid-1960s I was delighted to find that, at least in the underground press, a serious, powerful brand of criticism was developing in response to the increased ambition evident in the music itself. That development paralleled my own burgeoning interest in literature; in fact, many early rock critics had been trained in the New Criticism that dominated university English departments in the 1950s and early 1960s. These writers approached the music *as* literature, concentrating on close readings and lyrical exegesis to the virtual exclusion of musical analysis.

In many ways, both the bohemian world of rock criticism and the erudite, upper-crust world of the literary Great Tradition and its students were equally foreign to me. I grew up in a working-class Italian family—neither of my parents graduated from high school—and, because of that, it's important to consider the different routes through which popular music and literature came into my life. Music, of course, was readily accessible to me through the media—I could hear it on the radio and, somewhat less frequently, watch performances of it on television. Singles were inexpensive and, once I reached the age of ten or so, I could buy them nearly as often as I would like.

Critical writing about the music was almost as easy to come by. Underground newspapers were inexpensive; some were given away free. Because my family lived in Greenwich Village—which in those days was as much an Italian neighborhood as a bohemian enclave—I had as much access to that type of publication as I could have wanted.

The social process of learning about literature, unfortunately, was far more complex and problematic, as it no doubt continues to be for people from backgrounds like mine. Within the family itself, things were fine. Education was regarded as an important route to a better life. My older brother and sister encouraged me to read; their schoolbooks and other reading material were readily available around the house. My father read three newspapers a day and argued loudly with what he read in the sports and political columns; that was its own encouragement and no small contributor to my eventual career in journalism.

But penetrating the mysteries of literature required teachers and a formal education primarily because access to the world of such "high art" was almost exclusively a function of class. To learn about Dion and the Belmonts all I had to do was flip my radio or television on. To learn about Shakespeare, I would have to reorient my entire life and challenge the full spectrum of social expectations for someone like me.

Fortunately, at the time, the City University of New York offered an excellent education for free—I never could have afforded to go away to school, nor did I have any of the social skills or emotional wherewithal to survive in such an environment, even if my family could somehow have come up with the money. As for my teachers' occasional condescension toward popular music, one of them as recently as a year ago wrote to the *New York Times* complaining about a critic's characterization of rap lyrics as "poetry"—who cared? I knew that Bob Dylan, Muddy Waters, and the Rolling Stones would always be as sustaining to me as any literature I would ever read—they still are—and I didn't need professors to tell me why, or why they shouldn't be.

Moreover, it simply didn't seem important whether my professors cared about popular music or not. Whenever our teachers attempted to reach across the then-much-brooded-upon generation gap by discussing popular music with us, my friends and I would laugh. As one exercise, the senior professor who taught my freshman honors seminar asked us to analyze the significance of *Abbey Road,* which had just come out, and I didn't even bother to write the paper. *He* was supposed to grade what I knew about the Beatles? Get real. (I did, however, write a term paper in that course on the Rolling Stones—this was 1970, after all. After giving me an A, the professor, unconsciously substituting his own criterion for mine, asked me if I thought it would be pleasant to sit down and have dinner with the band.)

I can now see that what I set out to get from my teachers was two things—one obvious, one subtle, a kind of cultural secret. The first was a literary and critical training that would enable me to do the work I wanted to go on to do—my ambition at the time was to become an English professor. For the second, I wanted to crack a social code, a way of speaking, dressing, acting, and even thinking that disguised my class origins and made me seem like the sort of person who *could* go on to become a professor.

It's not that I intended to adopt all the mannerisms I learned, but I needed to know where the points of differentiation were. It was "upward mobility time," as a friend later described it, and I needed people to point out to me, intentionally or not, where the ladder was, because I didn't have a clue. All I knew, after having watched any number of my incredibly savvy neighborhood friends slide down the societal chute to dead-end lives, was that it wasn't exclusively about intelligence or merit by a long shot.

A good deal has changed in the last quarter-century, but the lessons of those years about the profound degree to which knowledge—types of

knowledge, access to knowledge, validation of knowledge, uses of knowledge—functions in a social context, sometimes to very brutal ends, still
shape my vision of things. Class issues are rarely discussed in relation to
the subject of "dumbing down"—in fact, they're rarely discussed at all
without prompting absurd charges of "inciting class warfare"—but they
are crucial to it. A "pure" understanding of what it is essential to know
cannot be attained—it simply does not exist. As has always been true—
and, at least in this country, nearly always disguised—that question must
be answered from a position within the rapidly shifting dynamics of our
society.

If it was ever possible to establish a clear, pragmatic hierarchy among
types of knowledge—and I don't think it ever was—it's no longer possible now. There are too many things to know and too many ways of
knowing. A genuine education today must consist of providing people
with the skills to engage and enter the enormous number of worlds—
aesthetic, intellectual, technological, scientific—that will increasingly be
open to them. People must learn to converse across their differences, not
learn the same rigidly defined things.

Despite reactionary arguments to the contrary, it is not content—
opera as opposed to rock and roll, literature as opposed to film—but the
nature of the critical approach that determines whether or not a specific
discipline has been dumbed down. In the case of popular music, innumerable books, journal articles, newspapers, magazines, fanzines, documentaries, videos, and films address every issue of conceivable importance from every conceivable angle. Anyone who is interested enough to
inquire will discover a level of cultural debate that is every bit as sophisticated and rich as that addressing any other subject.

Which is not to say that far too much popular music—not to mention
much that is written or said about it—is not frighteningly stupid, and
perhaps even dangerous. The escalating and overwhelming commercial
imperatives of American culture dictate that only what is popular can
survive. And what is popular will sometimes prove to be what is pandering.

That will be true as long as economics drives culture to the extent
that we permit it to at this time, in this place. And that reality speaks to a
paradox that the cultural Right in our country has yet to sort out. I
debated Hilton Kramer at a college in Minnesota not too long ago, and
he was attacking the Corporation for Public Broadcasting and National
Public Radio, on the one hand, while espousing traditional American
free-market values, on the other. So who will pay for symphonies, museums, and opera? I asked. Rock and roll does not require government
grants, I pointed out; it does quite well on the open market. As clearly as
I could see, his politics completely undermined his aesthetics.

It is apparent to me that leveling charges of "dumbing down" is simply a way of asserting particular aesthetic preferences and a desire for social privilege. And the reactionary political agenda such charges routinely advance makes it virtually impossible to address matters of genuine cultural concern in our society in a civilized manner—questions like, How do we increase literacy and educate people for the society that awaits them in the future?

Ever since rock and roll first exploded onto the cultural scene in the 1950s, criticizing it has had more to do with anxiety about burgeoning social movements than anything remotely to do with artistic criteria. Responding to such critiques in his recent book, *Rock and Roll: An Unruly History,* critic Robert Palmer examines the musical sources of rock and roll and the aesthetic strictures of the Western classical tradition, and does not find a contrast between culture and decadence, but two different approaches to making music:

In traditional West African cultures, a piece of music is held to be satisfying and complete if there is sufficient rhythmic interest; to oversimplify, rhythm is as fundamental to African music as harmony in European tradition and melodic sophistication in the music of India. Indian music has no harmony as such, and nobody complains; much European classical music is rhythmically one-dimensional—one is tempted to say "primitive"—and you don't hear symphony subscribers complaining about that. But when pop music begins moving away from tin pan alley song forms and musical values and embracing the aesthetics of its African origins, suddenly our culture is seen as adrift, endangered, riven by decadence and decay. Some pundits write books bemoaning "The Loss of Beauty and Meaning in American Popular Music." Others assert that heavy metal, or punk, or gangster rap—whatever the latest pop-music bogeyman happens to be—imperils the very fabric of civilization! . . . It would help if these gloom-and-doom mongers could see the history of this music as a matter of cycles within cycles, or as a developing idiom that periodically refreshes itself by drinking from its own deepest wellsprings.

Does it still really need to be asserted after all this time that art—*all* art, classical as well as popular—does not float unsullied above reality in some pure, eternal, universal realm, but is instead created and understood amid the gritty struggles and forced compromises of history? It is no less satisfying, and certainly no less challenging, for that.

Anyone yearning for cultural certainty at the present moment must face up to the curse of living in interesting times. Entire university programs are devoted to popular culture, and gangster rap is written about with great seriousness in the pages of the *New York Times.* At the same time, opera and theater are performed for free in Central Park and MTV underwrites speaking tours by young poets.

Culture is no less a battleground than it ever was, but now both sides have aesthetics in their armory. As someone who has grown comfortable moving from the art house to the club, from classic to contemporary literature, from rock and roll to a wide variety of other types of music, I'm saddened by the hardening of those lines, and I fight to break them down.

But I live in history, too. And against the current climate of philistine defense of high culture, cynical attacks on perfectly legitimate popular art, and reactionary longing for cultural privilege, I'll happily, eagerly, staunchly take my stand.

PHILLIP LOPATE

The Last Taboo

Phillip Lopate, novelist, essayist, film critic, and Adams Professor of English Literature at Hofstra University, endures more screenings of contemporary films than nearly all the contributors to this book collectively. Nonetheless, he has still found time to edit *The Art of the Personal Essay* (1994), publish an elegiac and meditative novel (*The Rug Merchant,* 1989) set on New York City's Upper West Side, and fill the pages of his own volume of essays, *Against Joie de Vivre* (1990).

There's much less *joie* to be found at the movies these days, according to Lopate, although he maintains that with some effort, we can still track down the original, the delightful, the memorable film. But in this essay he points to a dismal conjunction of the aggression of marketeers with the violence of American society, and to the extinction of articulate language (which turned out—not greatly to our surprise—to be a preoccupation central to most of those writing for *Dumbing Down*). The expletive has almost prevailed over the nuanced, expressive, and carefully crafted compound sentence in the very form of popular culture where once it had wide scope, while irony slinks away, holding its battered head.

Lopate has never divulged the title of the worst movie made in recent times.

ONE DAY last summer my friend Lorenzo, an old pro screenwriter, called for some quick advice. He had been hired to do last-minute rewrites for a *Die Hard* sequel that was about to start shooting but still had script problems. One difficulty: how to get across with a line or two of dialogue that the mad bomber was brilliant. "Speaks five languages?" mused Lorenzo, thinking aloud. "That's old hat. Went to Oxford? Doesn't mean anything any more. Help!"

"There's always the chemical wizard approach. Like in *Blown Away:* 'That guy can make bombs out of Bisquik.' "

"Please. A total fiasco, it lost a pile. What are the marks—the stigmata of intelligence? Come on, you're supposed to be an intellectual."

"He reads Adorno in the original German . . . ? I don't know what to tell you." I offered a few other lame ideas. One reason my friend's request for a mark of brilliance was so difficult was that, as we both knew, true intelligence is an ever-renewing process, not an acquisition. By now, I sensed that Lorenzo had given up on me, and we turned to the more enjoyable part of the conversation. But afterwards, I thought: Has it really come to this? That the last refuge of intellect in films—the only one allowed to demonstrate a brain—is the mad-bomber character?

Of course, intelligence has always been associated with villainy (Mephistopheles, Iago), and simple minds with virtue. The audience for action movies pays to see its stand-in, the medium-IQ hero, get the better of the twisted genius through physical effort and fortitude. And Americans have long felt, as Richard Hofstadter argued in *Anti-Intellectualism in American Life* (1963), a mistrustful ambivalence toward the brainy. Yet some some sort of sea change does seem to have occurred recently: ambivalence's positive pole has dropped away.

Why is "dumb" such a powerful metaphor for the American mood? Conversely, why has it become so rare nowadays to see onscreen a lively, functioning intelligence—an articulate, educated, self-aware character with an inner life?

Granted, we have been passing through a particularly silly season. Film in 1994–95 has been dominated by (1) recycled versions of old television shows, such as *The Flintstones, The Little Rascals, The Brady Bunch, Lassie,* and *Maverick,* which are, above all else, presold packages testifying to the staggering unimagination and timidity of studio executives, who will only green-light a project with some built-in recognition factor, and who narcissistically overrate the nostalgia value of the TV fare they grew up with; (2) action movies wherein a mad bomber or terrorist holds a significant portion of the civilian population at risk *(Speed, True Lies, Blown Away, Die Hard 3)*, and the best of these pictures, such as *Speed* and *True Lies,* lavish considerable narrative intelligence and cinematic craft on entertainments that essentially bypass the cerebral cortex; (3) films about cretinism, which give us a choice between hapless morons *(Airheads, Dumb and Dumber, The Jerky Boys, Billy Madison)* and helpful ones *(Forrest Gump)*.

The comic idiot-film genre clearly points to audiences' needs to feel superior to others who seem stupider than themselves. Its demographic base is young teens, mostly male, who like to smirk at everything; perhaps self-contempt, as much as superiority, constitutes its emotional draw. I do not abhor this genre: it continues a legitimate vein of American film comedy, based on gracelessness, infantilism, and irreverence for authority. Its roots go back to Harry Langdon and the Three Stooges, its *maître* is Jerry Lewis, its cousins are the denizens of *Animal House,* Cheech and Chong, and PeeWee Herman. Sometimes it offers a vehicle for a wonderful talent, such as the rubber-limbed Jim Carrey, whose *Dumb and Dumber* is a mildly amusing comedy (if weaker than his innovative *The Mask*); sometimes it bogs down in interminable longueurs, like *Airheads.* Often, the characters in these films are not precisely stupid so much as arrested in childish behavior.

The idiot genre has been too decried by public pundits and columnists as an avatar of the decline and fall of American civilization. Myself, I am less troubled by its significance than by the anti-intellectualism I see in the high end of American movies: the independent, provocative, festival films such as *Pulp Fiction, Ed Wood, Natural Born Killers, Bullets Over Broadway. Forrest Gump,* one of the top-grossing films ever, is clearly a phenomenon: a feel-good tragedy for the Prozac generation. Well made for what it is, it is a smile decal plastered onto a depressive's grimace: Vietnam vets with blown-off legs, women dying of AIDS, a whole society coming unglued; but with the right attitude, you can come smiling through. "Whistle while you mourn," as film critic Carrie Rickey summarizes it.

In the forties, Jimmy Stewart represented the figure of the typical American, harassed and desperately trying to act with dignity without being taken for a sucker. Now our typical American, our neo-Capraesque, is Tom Hanks's Forrest Gump, a mentally "challenged" optimist who lands on top mostly by accident. He represents one pole, the holy fool, while the opposite pole is taken up largely by serial killers, hit men, drug addicts, and psychopaths.

What has been lost is the middle, in the form of that conception perhaps too easily dismissed as patronizing: the common man. In a 1945 classic, *The Clock,* two ordinary people, a soldier (Robert Walker) and an office worker (Judy Garland), meet in Grand Central Terminal and fall in love, and have to overcome various obstacles to get married before his two-day leave ends. Aside from the restrained beauty of the two performances and Vincente Minnelli's tactful direction, what lingers in the mind is the touching belief implicit in offering a story without melodrama about the problems of ordinary people.

In the Coen brothers' recent, smirking *Barton Fink,* the eponymous playwright-hero is shown to be a sap merely by expressing concern for social injustice and the plight of the common man. The movie takes the position, as film critic Jonathan Rosenbaum astutely observes, that "The very notion of the common man is fraudulent," first by setting up an embodiment of the common-man cliché (in Charlie, played by John Goodman), then by undermining it with "a contemporary cliche that's every bit as hackneyed. When Charlie turns out to be the serial killer, we are offered the revelation that people who chop off other people's heads are nice, ordinary people just like you and me—'common folks,' in fact."

A good part of the hip filmmaking of recent years, inspired by the stylistics of David Lynch *(Blue Velvet, Wild at Heart),* has set about to satirize the rancid, decadent, psychopathic underbelly of Middle America. This is wishful thinking. If only Middle America were so decadent. The older direction, to plumb the lives of ordinary Americans for stories about their daily struggles, seems no longer an attractive alternative to filmmakers.

I wonder to what extent the reasons are demographic—and racist. The increase in new immigrants and minority groups is met by an almost spiteful refusal to engage the premise of a common man. Historically, the common man in America has been white; and if the face of America seems to be turning darker-skinned, one impulse is to deny the very existence of a shared humanity by expunging the national archetype, the typical American. Part of this spite takes the form of an explosion in vulgarity (bathroom jokes, infantile silliness of the *Dumb and Dumber* variety) and silly characters, as though, unable to put forward a single adult model of commonality that would reflect the multicultural audience, there is an attempt to locate universality in a pre-adult child mind.

Never, I think, have intellectuals been so alienated from American movies as now; never has there been a period when they less expected to see in motion pictures a vestige of their own commitment to the life of the mind.

Intellectuals have always been drawn to film. Not, be it said, for narcissistic reasons, to see mirror reflections of themselves onscreen, but for the movement and erotic glimmer of the material world. (Wittgenstein was said to rush off to Betty Grable movies when the mental pressure became too great.) Movies have offered a quick, painless way for those devoted to refinements and "elitist" esoteric problems to participate in, or catch up on, the interests of their fellow men.

Nevertheless, before now there were always traces, subversive smugglings of higher culture and intellectual perspectives into American movies. Sometimes these would take the form of adaptations of the classics (now derided as overly literary, MGM parvenu). Or an intellectual surrogate, a model of mature intelligence, would be planted in the story: an older minor character who seemed worldly, cultivated, wise, like the aunt in *Love Affair* or the uncle in *Snows of Kilimanjaro*. Often, aspirations to higher culture would be asserted through a ballet sequence, or a scene of the family gathered around the radio, listening to an opera program. "Carnegie Hall" was a universally recognized trope; and numberless times a John Garfield type from the slums donned a tux to conduct some Rachmaninoffian schmaltz in the orchestra pit. Certainly, we can smile today at the clumsy culture-mongering of those interludes; but the very naïveté of these sequences reproaches us. For they point to a time in American movies when both high-culture and popular-culture references existed, whereas now only pop culture has the right to be alluded to.

I think one of the main reasons why so many cultural references (particularly to classical music) found their way into American movies of the thirties and forties was the large enclave of German refugees in the Hollywood film community. They missed Europe; they deplored the blandness of American consumer culture; and they found every opportunity to sprinkle their screenplays with references to the Louvre or the Vienna Philharmonic. They also wrote in countless minor comic roles for displaced European character actors, as violin repairers, Pushkin-quoting janitors, etc.

These homesick refugees were joined by a second group of "émigrés," the ex–East Coast writers who had deserted Broadway for the gold of Hollywood. Herman Mankiewicz, Ben Hecht, Dorothy Parker, Robert Benchley, and all from that tribe who saw themselves as cynical sellouts nevertheless managed to allude to the cultural life they had left behind (sometimes rather floridly, as in Hecht's *Tales of Manhattan* and *Specter of the Rose*). Joseph Mankiewicz, Herman's younger brother, never passed up an opportunity to insert a little speech about the importance of reading and English teachers!

Those leavening émigré populations are gone. What we have today are young would-be screenwriters and directors pouring out of film schools, who either have no cultural memory or repress it, who want to make a tidy little film noir about two greasers (he sports an Elvis jacket, she a Marilyn wig), stuck in a nowhere town, who meet cute, fall in love, and then find a gun. . . . The appeal of Nowheresville is especially ironic, given that many of these young filmmakers live on New York's Lower East Side or similar urban hangouts. They descend on the sticks for their six-week low-budget shoot, thinking they are being sympathetic to white-trash America when they are actually slumming. What the small-town setting offers, in *their* imaginations, is the allure of rural idiocy, of a pre-mental world, occupied by characters who have nothing in their brains but the indoctrinations of mass culture. (The serial killer just wants to be a star.) Believe me, I am not saying that intellectual life takes place only in big cities; but I *am* saying that the small town is appropriated precisely for its ostensible "emptiness," which sets into harsher relief the tale, enacted for the thousandth time, of sex, violence, and ersatz celebrity borrowed from the icons of popular culture.

One is entitled to ask: Why this narrow obsession with a few pop culture idols—Elvis, Marilyn, James Dean? How can it be that a complex national culture should have allowed itself to be stripped down to such few, barren archetypes? Take Jim Jarmusch: a very gifted, intelligent filmmaker, who studied poetry at Columbia, he yet makes movie after movie about low-lifes who get smashed every night, make pilgrimages to Memphis where they are visited by Elvis's ghost, shoot off guns, and in general comport themselves in a somnambulistic, inarticulate, unconscious manner. Quentin Tarantino, the great hope of New American

Cinema, writes a screenplay *(True Romance)* in which the main character is also obsessed with Elvis, talks to his ghost, gets involved in a life of crime, is chased by the Mob, etc.

His *Pulp Fiction*—admittedly an enormously inventive, entertaining, and polished work—is also a celebration of mindlessness and an assertion that nothing exists but pop culture. Hit men muse over old TV shows and cheeseburgers, between killings. The characters act entirely reflexively, without ever thinking: guns go off by mistake; the prizefighter dumbly returns to his apartment to retrieve a family watch, knowing that a Mob hit has been put on him. The one bit of "inwardness," Samuel T. Jackson's last-minute conversion to moral responsibility, seems a too-calculated plant to show that someone has a soul. *Pulp Fiction,* for all its tricky constructional surprises, is so filled with comforting allusions to old movies, TV shows, and movie icons (like the scene in the fifties-decor restaurant) that the audience can feel they are in on the joke, they are seeing something they already know. ("Look, they're quoting *Saturday Night Fever!*") Indeed, the movie exists in a kind of echo chamber of recycled pop culture.

It seems we are stuck in an ever-shrinking set of referents: a barroom with a juke box, a TV set, some movie posters, and some virile specimens of white trash.

In a *New York* magazine article about the takeover of "white trash culture," Tad Friend noted: "But now screenwriters are obsessed with the idea of the road-tripping, spontaneous, and often murderous poor. (It is ever tempting for Hollywood to impute authenticity to the ignorant—and to give them bodacious bods.). . . 'It's totally about sex,' says director John Waters. 'Extreme white people'—Waters' preferred term for the white under-class—'look incredibly beautiful until they're 20, and then they look about 50. It's a sexual fantasy for people in the movies, who don't meet those sort of people very much—it's the idea of the bad boy, the juvenile delinquent.' Movies give us an airbrushed dream of white trash: alluring and deadly."

I understand the attraction of this material, within limits, but what I don't understand is why there can't also be films which express more of the experience of the filmmakers' own lives—including their intellectual lives. The young French cineast and his or her American counterpart live fairly similar lives: they hang out in cafes, read, go to movies and classes, talk endlessly. Yet a first feature by a French director about young people is very apt to show characters sitting in cafes, quoting Nietzsche and talking a lot, while a first American feature (like ex-NYU student Katherine Bigelow's *The Loveless*) will more likely be about a lockjawed motorcycle gang that terrorizes a small town.

I refuse to believe that the answer is simply economic ("You can't show brainy characters onscreen because no one will pay to see it"), since the vast majority of independent American first features are distributed very narrowly, if at all, and lose money anyway. They might even stand a better chance of turning a profit if they reflected more closely their college-educated audience's experiences. No, it isn't just economics, it's a matter of choice and taste: people without brains are cool.

Does this have to do with the postmodernist antagonism to psychology—its disdain for motivation and characters' past backgrounds, its preference for actions that seem random and mysterious, as a way of asserting more freedom for the human species? Whatever its rationale, the suppression of psychological understanding results in cartoonishly impulsive characters living in the eternal Now, who perform one *acte gratuit* after another. Hence the preference for serial killers, drugstore cowboys, hit men, and their thrill-seeking, amoral molls.

One way to consider the dumbing down of American movies is to examine some recent portraits of intellectuals or creative thinkers on the big screen.

We can start with the figure popularly equated with intellect itself: Albert Einstein. On face value, it would seem daringly elitist to call a commercial movie *I.Q.* and use the famous physicist (ably mimicked by Walter Matthau) as one of its main characters. But, for penance, this Einstein is made to repeat a half-dozen platitudes that assert the heart's supremacy over the head. In other words, the great thinker must ritually offer his head to the audience's anti-intellectual prejudices. His scientist colleagues are portrayed as a bunch of desexed, impractical old ninnies who cannot even change a lightbulb; his niece's fiancé is an adenoidal, snotty academic. The only virile, attractive, capable character is a garage mechanic with a big pompadour who has lots of heart.

In the previously mentioned *Barton Fink,* a leftish playwright goes out to Hollywood to write screenplays. There are suggestions that Barton Fink has been based on Clifford Odets; however, Odets was anything but dumb, whereas Fink seems incorrigibly dense—a fool who grasps no more about the world around him at the end of the movie than at the beginning. The filmmakers sneer at his intellectual pretensions (and, by extension, the claims of the mind), while putting their main energy into a visual *exercise du style,* in the surreal *Twin Peaks* manner.

In Woody Allen's *Bullets Over Broadway,* the hero is again a playwright who proves to be an inept faker, and who is unable to apply a scrap of intelligence to the chaos of his private life. Unable to solve his play's script problems, either, he turns to a low-life thug, who naturally has all the narrative solutions at his fingertips. *Bullets Over Broadway* is, admittedly, uncharacteristic Woody Allen, both in its glib, impersonal filmmaking and in its anti-intellectualism. Usually, this auteur has at least provided one thinking man's role: for himself. Curiously, he cannot seem to write a cerebral, reflective character for another actor or actress. Hence, those Woody Allen films without Woody in the cast have lacked a self-reflective core, a judgmental consciousness. For most Americans these past twenty years, the one recognizable "intellectual" onscreen has been the Woody character. In *Bullets Over Broadway,* he shows again his unwillingness to share the mental laurels, while pandering to the audience's prejudice that writers and others who work with their minds are idiots underneath.

The creative intellectual's inability to learn anything of consequence from his or her experience is a constant in recent biopics, sometimes played for laughs, sometimes for bathos. Thus, in *Mrs. Parker and the Vicious Circle,* we are given a Dorothy Parker who may be clever enough to toss off *bons mots* but who is so pathetically self-destructive (drinking, chasing the wrong men) that all lesser brains in the audience are invited to feel superior to her. Poor T. S. Eliot, in *Tom and Viv,* seems so baffled by his marriage that you want to laugh at him. And Ed Wood, in the movie by that name, is championed for never learning, as though the inability to acquire craft and sophistication over time were an artistic gift. Wood, played with dimpled zest (and zero character development) by Johnny Depp, is as satisfied with his first takes on the initial day of shooting as every day thereafter, despite the fact that the results continue to be dreadful. He is another holy fool, a Forrest Gump with a megaphone, whose innocence is his strength and armor. As a movie, *Ed Wood* is ravishing to look at, another cinematic *exercise du style;* but again, one is asked to check one's brain at the door, identify with a character arrested in dim-witted self-admiration, and groove on the mysterious, ineffable, surreal charm of the pre-mental.

The one thing that is seemingly impermissible to show in American movies today is an intellectual possessed of self-insight. The struggle to lead an unillusioned life is nowhere visible on our screens. Again, I don't think the explanation is strictly financial: some utter follies have found their way into production, $30-million lemons, like *Toys* or *The Road to Wellville,* that make you rub your eyes and wonder what the studio was thinking of. No, the reason is that it violates the last taboo: we cannot have thinking people who aren't taken in by themselves.

So far I have been focusing on issues of character and theme to explain the dumbing down of American movies. But it seems to me that formal matters—recent changes in the very grammar of film, as it applies to the nature of a filmed image, a scene, a screenplay, the editing process—may cut deeper and provide more serious causes for this leakage in intelligence.

Much of what dumbs down movies today starts with the screenplay. Perhaps more than at any other time, screenwriting has become coded into a step-by-step convention. Workshops like those offered by Robert McKee, taken by thousands of wannabe scriptwriters, break down the screenplay into bite-sized formulae. Manuals like Syd Field's *Screenplay* dispense wisdom such as "The days of ambiguous endings are over," and decree with mathematical precision ("about 25 minutes into the film") where the first major "plot point" should occur. Tom Laughlin, of *Billy Jack* fame, offers a newsletter subscription guaranteeing you mastery over the nine plot points which will make a successful movie. Actually, much of what Syd Field and others like him say makes good sense. The problems occur when their prescriptions are applied too literally: the movie develops a homogenized, mechanical, predictable pace. Too many studio executives in Hollywood take Field's or McKee's ideas religiously; we were better off when the world was wired to Harry Cohn's ass.

The prevailing mantra in film schools is that movies are above all a visual medium: therefore, dialogue must be kept to a minimum, or you risk sounding "literary"; a voiceover is a "literary device" and a form of "cheating"; "literary" is bad. Translation: words and ideas are bad. The result is a fearfulness that creeps into the screenwriter's intestines whenever his characters start to speak up for more than two sentences.

One important result is that scenes are getting shorter. Sometimes very short indeed: in action movies, one character may say "Shit!" and another say "Duck!" and that is all she wrote.

The shorter the scene, the less chance there is for that tension between characters to reach the danger point where true communication can break out between them. As scenes grow shorter, too much pressure is put on the wisecrack, inserted between expletives and hot pursuit, to carry the load of character shading.

The art of writing movie dialogue has become less a matter of constructing scenes than of coining one-liners that can be quoted as marketing slogans in trailers and advertising campaigns. Dirty Harry's pioneering "Make my day" has become Schwarzenegger's "Hasta la vista, baby" and on down to "That guy can make a bomb out of Bisquik."

In domestic dramas, more and more inarticulate characters find themselves onscreen, like the eponymous hero of *What's Eating Gilbert Grape*, whose every scene with another character turns on the drama of his not being able to say what he feels. In action movies, the hero does not have to say much at all; he can grunt and swear. As W. H. Auden put it in another context:

> The Ogre does what ogres can,
> Deeds quite impossible for Man,
> But one prize is beyond his reach,
> The Ogre cannot master Speech:

About a subjugated plain,
Among its desperate and slain,
The Ogre stalks with hands on hips,
While drivel gushes from his lips.

The other night I was watching a 1939 Clarence Brown picture set in India, *The Rains Came,* on the cable channel American Movie Classics. I tend to watch AMC a lot, because of all the thirties and forties movies aired. Let's not overly romanticize that era: the 1930s and 1940s turned out thousands of clinkers, and *The Rains Came* is in many ways one of them. But what struck me was that, despite the wooden acting and the ponderous, artificial colonial backdrop, the characters were allowed to talk to each other! Scenes went on and on between them—taken verbatim, I assume, from the Louis Bromfield novel which the screenplay adapted—and in those confrontations one's sympathies would shift from one character to another, as each struggled to make clear his point, his perspective, his worldview.

This experience has been duplicated many times, as I watch an old movie and luxuriate in the ripening exchange, at the same time sensing the exact moment, like an internalized wince, when the same scene would have been chopped off in a contemporary movie. I can almost hear the producer saying, "Cut! Too much talk!" When studio executives see a large block of type (connoting a long speech) in a screenplay, they often dictate that it has to be trimmed without even bothering to read it.

The influence of TV sitcoms and stand-up comedians should also be noted in the reduction of screenplays to strings of one-liners. So we have arrived at the movie convention that conversation is a Ping-Pong match, zinging one-line ripostes across the net.

Formerly, our movies were allowed to breathe. They had hiatuses: atmospheric cutaways or comic-relief passages where the audience gathered its energies. (Howard Hawks, for instance, has been justly praised for the rhythm he developed of stress and relaxation in movies like *Rio Bravo.*) Today, we see increasingly a hyperkinetic type of movie *(Raiders of the Lost Ark, Terminator 2, JFK, Mississippi Burning, Speed)* which, well-crafted fun though it may be, is nothing but high points; all the "slack" has been squeezed out of it, there are no moments to pause, to reflect, we keep rushing up and down the roller coaster of sensations, and the movie suffocates for lack of breath, it is as though a plastic sealant had been applied to its surface. When we leave the theater we feel bounced around, black-and-blue, and strangely amnesiac, wondering: what was *that* all about?

JFK is a paranoid movie not only because it engages confusingly so many murky conspiracy theories, but because its bludgeoning montage technique, its avalanche of fragmented shots, does not allow you to take a step back and consider what part of its contents might be true and reasonable.

Underneath it all, the very nature of the shot is changing.

The pioneering films of Renoir, Welles, and Ophuls (among others) in the 1930s and 1940s had awakened a taste for a gliding, graceful camera that would track characters from room to room, exterior to interior. The 1950s may be seen as the golden age of this long-shot, deep-focused, extended-take, spatially complex image: what French critic Andre Bazin and his New Wave followers championed as the aesthetic of mise-en-scène. Partly because Cinemascope's horizontally forced a slower cut, and encouraged the camera to explore the sides and backgrounds of the frame before cutting to another setup, partly because veteran directors like Ford, Hawks, Walsh, Hitchcock, Sirk, Lang, Ray, Mann, Preminger, and Minnelli were all at the height of their powers during the 1950s, and were sympathetic to a composed, deep-focus composition, the result was a feast of maturely classical, "realist" moviemaking, which linked characters to their environments, in a formal (some would even add spiritual) wholeness.

The 1960s began the breakdown of this classical film grammar. Ironically, the very supporters of mise-en-scène, the New Wave directors like Godard and Truffaut, helped bring about its demise by their innovations: jump cuts and self-reflexive storytelling. In addition, new (or newly rediscovered) technologies like the zoom, slow motion, freeze-frame, and split screen began to be used like toys, puncturing the stately space of the classical composition. The era of fragmentation and rapid cutting had arrived. Television was certainly partly to blame, both for reducing the audience's attention span and for exerting a pressure on moviemaking toward quick close-ups and more shallow depth of field. Later, MTV would exert a specific influence in the direction of slick-magazine surreal, fricasseed visuals. Still, we might remember that, even without TV, "arty" film directors were moving away from the spatial integrity of classical filmmaking in the 1960s: Arthur Penn's *Bonnie and Clyde* (1967) employed numerous distancing and flattening devices, while Sam Peckinpah's *The Wild Bunch* (1969) used three times as many cuts as a normal movie, not to mention slow motion and special effects for blood.

In what way can I argue that the triumph of quick cutting, or montage, over a mise-en-scène aesthetic is somehow connected to the decline of intelligence in American movies? Well, it's like this: if we are no longer invited to enter an image on the screen and dwell there inwardly for more than three seconds; if our eye is not given the time to travel from one character's face to another's and then to the objects and scenery behind or to the side of them; if we are being presented with too many close-ups that show us a very small amount of visual information, which make one point and only one point per shot; if we are not encouraged to develop *fidelity* to a shot—then we do not make as deep a commitment to understand and interpret the material presented to us. A scene is no longer, properly speaking, a scene; a shot is less than an image. All is underselected; the necessity for rigorous composition is negated; we are in a perpetual, perspectiveless flux, a flux which defers judgment to a later, saner time, which never comes.

A case in point is *Natural Born Killers,* directed by Oliver Stone from a script by Quentin Tarantino. Not the worst film ever made, by any means; in fact, filled with talent and brio. But in the end this joyride (as in Stone's earlier movie, *The Doors*) leaves us bewildered, as the first half-hour's excitement gives way to utter indifference. Masses of shots, some lasting less than a second, are disgorged onscreen; the serial killer's hippie rationalizations ("I'm your shadow") are offered like serious insights; and the net effect is that nothing is real, all is presumably maya.

Thierry Jousse, editor of *Cahiers du Cinema,* wrote a piece in 1994 called "The Killers of the Image" in which he tried to understand the long-range consequences of such filmmaking: "Take, for example, Oliver Stone's film, *Natural Born Killers.* It's a child monster, a maelstrom of images, a whirlwind of colors and sounds, a sort of hash of gestures and movements, a magma of sensations and music. Can we speak here of the shot's composition? We need to find a new word to denote these incessant passages of images, simultaneously subliminal and convulsive—of electrons as much as projectiles. But decidedly, they're no longer composed shots. They're a space where everything is on the surface, like in a baroque sphere; where images never stop arriving, speeding into the eye and sliding over each other, in place of the old cinematic way, where the eye takes the road in order to scrutinize the shot. . . . It's a video environment, a big live show as well as a self-cannibalization of cinema by the media, or a sacrificial ceremony with the immolation of the frame and the invocation of new images."

Jousse goes on to say that the use of such images in Stone's and Tarantino's films approaches the sensation of a drug, a "film-trip." He likens the irresponsibility, the lack of consequences, in Tarantino's films to a cocaine high. "You could call it a stylistic exercise, but it's also the same sensation procured by cocaine, a drunkenness of the intelligence verging on the absurd, a feeling of superiority detached from reality. . . ." Ironically, Tarantino does not shun dialogue; in fact, his movies impress with their snappy talk. But the talk is designed to bounce back at us with a stylized "off" quality, a tinniness further detaching us from reality, the way you hears words when you're high.

Roland Barthes wrote an article in the 1950s in which he compared the old movie spectator with someone "lying prone and . . . receiving cinematic nourishment rather in the way that a patient is fed intravenously." He then went on to praise the different situation in which Cinemascope placed the spectator: "Here . . . I am on an enormous balcony, I move effortlessly within the field's range, I freely pick out what interests me, in a word, I begin to be surrounded. . . ." It seems that we are back in a prone position, only now they are using harder stuff in the IV.

Those friends active in the industry tell me that the problems with American movies today begin with the structure of studio bureaucracy and decision-making. There has been a vast increase of studio functionaries, few of whom know how to read a screenplay, they say. It takes forever to get a script approved; and, on the other hand, some projects are approved without even reading the script because a validated name—a star or proven director—has expressed willingness to make it. (The aforementioned fiasco, *Toys,* for instance, had Barry Levinson's and Robin Williams's guaranteed participation.)

More and more, I am told, action movies go into production without a final script; the gaps are patched over with last-minute wisecracks. In comedies, the whole process of screenwriting has changed drastically: it now resembles the method of the TV show *Saturday Night Live,* with teams of gag writers sitting around a table bouncing one-liners off each other. *The Flintstones* had thirty-five writers working on it, and the result was not so much a shaped narrative as a series of riffs. At its best, like *Wayne's World,* this can be refreshingly anarchic, a postmodernist reproach to the well-made play; at its worst, say, *The Flintstones,* you get an incoherent infomercial for marketed products masquerading as a feature film.

But we must pull back from these sour, dyspeptic thoughts. There is something in the discussion of the American movie industry as a whole that automatically distorts one's reflections in a pessimistic direction. Perhaps it is that the subject is too large to allow for nuanced discriminations. After all, films such as *Vanya on 42nd Street, The Hour and the Time, Schindler's List, Laws of Gravity, Quiz Show, Angie, Surviving Desire, Searching for Bobby Fischer, Fresh,* and *Before Sunrise* all demonstrate signs of intelligent life in American moviemaking.

One major source of intellectual complexity in American movies during recent years has been documentaries. I am thinking above all of the amazing dialogues between doctors and patients in Fred Wiseman's *Near Death;* of Erroll Morris's wry explorations of the Dallas justice system in *The Thin Blue Line* and Stephen Hawking's astronomical ideas in *A Brief History of Time;* of Ross McElwee's self-aware, probing, autobiographical exposures in *Sherman's March* and *Past Imperfect;* of Allen Berliner's bril-

liant family portrait, *Intimate Stranger;* and of Terry Zigoff's extraordi-
nary *Crumb,* about the cartoonist and his family. Good documentaries
tend to make psychological connections between past and present that
hip narratives shy away from: hence their more thoughtful, rounded
context. Take *Crumb:* we not only see R. Crumb, but we hear the testimony of his excruciatingly articulate brother Charles, his mother, his
ex-girlfriends, his children, and it becomes clearer how this hero of the
New Vulgarity turned out the way he did. Such documentaries—marginal as they may be commercially—at least ensure the survival of intelligence in American films.

We are still faced with an anomaly. Why are they so much less afraid
in Europe to make movies with intellectual discourse? Is it that the intellect is traditionally a less stigmatized, more alluring organ across the
Atlantic, or is it a function of government-subsidized cinema? Whatever
the answer, there can be no doubt that some heady films that tickle the
mind as well as the heart continue to be made abroad, with comfortable
audacity and without apology. For instance, Nanni Moretti's *Caro Diario*
(which showed in the States briefly) is a delightfully nervy personal essay,
in which the author muses on everything under the sun, like a modern-
day Montaigne, complaining of his ailments, critiquing other movies,
celebrating remnants of Roman urbanism. Moretti's film expresses his
worldview through his tastes (high as well as low culture—Pasolini and
Flashdance), which he defends in humorous or dyspeptic fashion. Eric
Rohmer's *The Tree, the Mayor and the Mediatheque* contains long arguments between characters about ecology and town planning, without
ever losing sight of the human drama. Indeed, the romantic sparks between a somewhat ill-matched couple (a provincial mayor and a Parisian
novelist) get expressed mainly through their intellectual disagreements.
The mind is perceived as an erotic organ, which requires its own stimulation, its own foreplay.

Rohmer has embodied for four decades a kind of happily intransi-
gent, thoughtful movie *(My Night at Maude's; Summer; A Winter's Tale)*
that permits extended dialogue, ideas, mental play. Equally important,
Rohmer established the model for a low-budget, psychological cinema—
restricted to a few characters, a few real locations, a contemporary story,
no costly special effects or costumes—which scores of European films
(*Un Coeur en Hiver; La Discrete;* virtually all of Jacques Doillon's and
Rudolf Thome's work) have followed. The Rohmer model has also been
taken up successfully by independent American filmmakers, such as
Steven Soderbergh *(Sex, Lies and Videotape),* Hal Hartley *(Trust; Simple
Men; Surviving Desire),* Richard Linklater *(Slacker; Before Sunrise),* and
John Jost *(All the Vermeers in New York).*

Moretti's idiosyncratic, personal-essay style and Rohmer's psychological chamber drama are two approaches that American filmmakers

might profitably follow if they are interested in seeing a less boastfully ignorant type of work onscreen. Or not. Maybe the solutions to this problem of cinematic brain-drain will not come from mimicking Europe at all, but from our filmmakers finally coming to terms with the persistence of American intellectual life, its valid concerns, and the specific, Emersonian nature of the American mind.

JOSEPH EPSTEIN

What to Do about the Arts

Joseph Epstein is editor of the *American Scholar,* where, under the nom de plume Aristides, he writes an essay every quarter, many of them strongly suggesting that while he is reasonably certain that we are not living in a golden age, we do manufacture a steady supply of golden calves.

As to his background, this citation lays to rest the canard that he ever attended City College or obtained his Ph.D. at Columbia University and maintains only that, in addition to being the self-described "extremely well-informed S.O.B.," to which he himself, his literary career, and his work attest, he is the author of the short-story collection *The Goldin Boys* (1991) and of eight books of essays, including *With My Trousers Rolled* (1995).

This essay was first published in *Commentary* in 1995. Since that time, the NEA has begun the process of meltdown, but poetry workshops still flourish in the academy, producing more poets than readers of poetry, more arts bureaucrats than gifted artists, while the union of cultural bankruptcy and poverty of means which Epstein observes here continues to play itself out under the grand rubric of postmodernism.

> Arts that lack a particular distinction or nobility of style are often said to be styleless, and the culture is judged to be weak or decadent.
>
> Meyer Schapiro

> "Art for everyone": anyone regarding that as possible is unaware how "everyone" is constituted and how art is constituted. So here, in the end, art and success will yet again have to part company.
>
> Arnold Schoenberg

Nobody with a serious or even a mild interest in the arts likes to think he has lived his mature life through a bad or even mediocre period of artistic creation. Yet a strong argument can be made that ours has been an especially bleak time for the arts.

One of the quickest ways of determining this is to attempt to name either discrete masterpieces or impressive bodies of work that have been written, painted, or composed over the past, say, thirty years. Inexhaustible lists do not leap to mind. Not only is one hard-pressed to name recent masterpieces, but one's sense of anticipation for the future is less than keen. In looking back over the past two or three decades, what chiefly comes to mind are fizzled literary careers, outrageous exhibitions and inflated (in all senses of the word) reputations in the visual arts, and a sad if largely tolerant boredom with most contemporary musical composition.

People who look to art for spiritual sustenance have been dipping into capital—they have, that is, been living almost exclusively off the past. In literature, less and less do the works created since the great American efflorescence earlier in the century seem likely to endure. (One thinks of 1925, that *annus mirabilis* for the American novel, which saw the publication of F. Scott Fitzgerald's *The Great Gatsby,* Theodore Dreiser's *An American Tragedy,* John Dos Passos's *Manhattan Transfer,* Sinclair Lewis's *Arrowsmith,* and Willa Cather's *The Professor's House.*) In visual art, the line is drawn—if not for everyone—at Abstract Expressionism, after which no powerful school or movement seems to have arisen, and so many reputations seem, as the English critic F. R. Leavis remarked in another connection, to have more to do with the history of publicity than with the history of art. In serious music, *performing* artists continue to emerge, but the music they perform is almost exclusively that of past centuries; the greatest appetite of all remains for the works created between J. S. Bach (1685–1750) and Maurice Ravel (1875–1937). True, dance, under such geniuses as George Balanchine and Martha Graham, has had a fine contemporary run. But no one, I think, would argue against the proposition that the only works of art capable of stirring anything like extensive excitement in the nation just now are movies, which, given their general quality, is far from good news.

In explanation, and partially in defense, of this situation it has been suggested that we are living in a time when sensibility has been fundamentally altered; and, it is sometimes also argued, advancing technology—the computer, the video—only figures to alter it further. The artistic result of this putative shift in sensibility goes under the banner of postmodernism. Although the word means different things to different people, generally postmodernism in the arts includes the following: a belief that a large statement, in everything from poetry to architecture, is probably no longer persuasive; a self-reflexiveness, a playfulness, and a strong reliance on irony which the advocates of postmodernism find a refreshing and fair exchange for spirituality in art; and a contempt for criticism traditionally understood as the activity of making discriminations, distinctions, and, especially, value judgments.

At the same time that some argue for a change in sensibility, suggesting in turn the need for a change in the nature of art, others feel that if art is not to lose its standing entirely, more than ever it needs to give itself directly to social and political purposes. We have driven around this block before, of course, most notably in the 1930s when novelists and poets, painters, and even musicians were scolded for insufficient engagement in the political struggles of the day. Then, these criticisms were directed by Communists and fellow-travelers; today they are made under the aegis of an ideology that finds its chief outlets in environmentalism, sexual liberation, a lingering anti-capitalism, and an inchoate but determined multiculturalism.

The paramount enemy for such people, then as now, is disinterested art that attempts to transcend political and other sorts of human division. This is art of the kind Marcel Proust had in mind when he wrote that it "gives us access to higher spiritual reality resembling the otherworldly metaphysical speculations of philosophy and religion." This is art which, among its other effects, seeks to broaden horizons, to deepen understanding, and to enhance consciousness as well as to convey the ultimately unexplainable but very real exaltation that is integral to heightened aesthetic pleasure.

By such measures, most contemporary art has fallen down badly on the job. Art still functions to confer social status on what today one might call the educated classes, as witness the large crowds that attend certain museum shows and operas and concerts given by performers who have been declared superstars. But high art (except the political kind) has more and more been relegated to a minority interest and is under attack for doing what it has always done best. Much of high Western art is now even judged, *mirabile dictu,* to be politically less than correct.

Some of this might have been predicted—and, in fact, it was. More than forty years ago, in an essay entitled "The Plight of Our Culture,"* the late Clement Greenberg wrote that "high culture has lost much of its old implicit authority." In that essay, Greenberg ran through those brutal simplicities—as he rightly called them—known as highbrow, middlebrow, and lowbrow.

Highbrow art, from Homer through Rembrandt to Schoenberg, had always made the greatest demands on its audience—and those demands, it had always been understood, resulted in the highest rewards, both philosophical and aesthetic. In its modern forms, highbrow art, wrote Greenberg, tended to be synonymous with avant-garde art, which made even stricter demands. Avant-garde art was often about itself, and the avant-garde artist, turning inward, was interested above all in solutions to the problems his particular art presented: problems of surface and perspective in painting, of tonality and dissonance in music, of language and depth psychology in literature.

Because of this it had become more and more difficult to admire a

*Commentary, June 1953.

modern artist's work apart from his technique. As Greenberg had put it in an earlier essay, as the avant-garde became highly specialized, so "its best artists [became] artists' artists, its best poets, poets' poets," and this, not surprisingly, had "estranged a great many of those who were capable formerly of enjoying and appreciating ambitious art and literature, but who are now unwilling or unable to acquire an initiation into these craft secrets."

Lowbrow art presented no difficulties of definition: it was mass art, produced for and aimed at the lowest common denominator, and promising nothing more than entertainment. But then there was middlebrow art, where the problems, for Greenberg and others, arose. Middlebrow art promised both to entertain and to educate, and attempted to pass itself off as highbrow by its appearance of seriousness. Yet the middlebrow was not finally serious; it was instead merely earnest, which was not at all the same thing. Middlebrow art was always teaching, if not preaching. (In our own time, it has been chiefly preaching political lessons.) And middlebrow art was responsible for deploying one of the most self-serving myths of our age, the myth of the artist as a permanent rebel against society.

Writing in a special issue of the British magazine *Horizon* in 1947, Greenberg called for a frankly highbrow elite that would help bring about an art characterized by "balance, largeness, precision, enlightenment." We have had, he wrote, "enough of the wild artist." What we need now are

men of the world not too much amazed by experience, not too much at a loss in the face of current events, not at all overpowered by their own feelings, men to some extent aware of what has been felt elsewhere since the beginning of recorded history.

Nearly a half-century later, all one can say of Clement Greenberg's aspirations for art is that none of them has come into being, whereas most of his worst fears have. Middlebrow art is taken so much for highbrow in our day that the very category of highbrow is in doubt. My own personal, shorthand definition of a middlebrow is anyone who takes either Woody Allen or Spike Lee seriously as an artist. And most of the country, it will not have gone without notice, does.

One of the consequences of the debasement of art is that fewer and fewer people are able to make the important distinctions which high art itself requires for its proper appreciation. An institution that has played a large role in bringing this situation about is the university. Formerly free from the tyranny of the contemporary—the tyranny, that is, of being up to the moment—the university now takes great pride in being a center for the creation of contemporary art. Over the past three or four decades, the university has become something akin to a continuing WPA program by furnishing an ever-larger number of artists—chiefly writers but painters and musicians, too—with jobs.

This might not be so bad, but, with all these artists on hand, the university now also provides a fairly strong diet of contemporary fare in its curriculum. Once, it was not thought necessary to teach the works of contemporary writers, painters, and composers; if a student was a reasonably cultivated person, or had the desire to be such a person, he could learn about such things on his own. No more. Some artists even teach themselves.

Although many universities continue to offer traditional subjects in the arts, the university has, at the same time, caved in to the demand for courses that fit the politics of a large number of the people who teach there: feminism, Marxism, Lacanism, the new historicism, deconstructionism, semiotics—"the six branches of the School of Resentment," as the literary critic Harold Bloom has called them. Thus, in the contemporary university literature and painting are often put through the meat grinder of race, class, and gender. This is well-known. What is perhaps less well-known is the odd way it has skewed the arts themselves.

To give an example of how the skewing works, the week before President Clinton's inauguration I was called by the (London) *Daily Telegraph* for my opinion of the poet Maya Angelou, who had been chosen to read a poem at the inaugural. I told the reporter that I had no opinion of Maya Angelou, for I had read only a few of her poems and thought these of no great literary interest. Ah, he wondered, did I know anyone who might have an opinion that would be interesting to English readers? I conceded that I knew of no one who read her. When asked how that might be, I responded that what the reporter had to understand was that in the United States just now there were a number of authors who were not actually for reading but only for teaching, of whom Angelou, who herself teaches, lectures for vast fees, and probably has more honorary degrees than James Joyce had outstanding debts, is decidedly one.

By teaching so many contemporary writers and simultaneously laying itself open to the political aspirations of multiculturalism, the university has had a serious hand in helping to discard the idea of standards, which is absolutely essential to high art. The politics of many university teachers have played a key role in this, with the result that today we no longer have in force the only distinction in the arts that really matters—that between the good and the bad, the well-made and the shoddy. Once one starts playing this particular game, the essential, the only really relevant, fact becomes not the quality of an artist's work but which category it fits into: black composers, women painters, gay/lesbian poets, and the rest of the multicultural mélange.

All but a handful of people who currently work in the arts—writers, painters, musicians, arts administrators, and patrons—seem to go along with this program. Multiculturalization has for many seemed a way out of the wrenching dilemma of wishing to seem as democratic as possible while knowing in one's heart that serious art is nothing if not thoroughly meritocratic and, in the best sense, finally and irremediably elitist.

"In art the ideal critical ethic is ruthlessness," wrote the music critic Ernest Newman. "The practice of art should not be made easier for the weaklings; it should be made harder, so that only the best types survive." Such notions are troubling to people of tender liberal conscience. The arts are now somehow construed to carry the message that they are themselves a means to progress, and progress implies encouraging the downtrodden; clearly, the last thing such people want to be caught acknowledging is that the arts are not—at least not necessarily—for everyone.

The misguided belief that art is one of the forms that progress takes is connected with the notion that the avant-garde itself is a kind of movement, or party, for progress—an appealing notion for people who wish the arts to do things they were never meant primarily to do: to fight censorship, to give groups pride in what is called their "identity," to increase the awareness of AIDS, to fight inequities of every kind. As Clausewitz said that war was diplomacy carried on by other means, so art is seen as social justice and political enlightenment carried on by other means.

The avant-garde of an earlier time, beginning in the 1890s and proceeding through the early decades of the twentieth century—the "banquet years" of French painting, music, and writing—was (again) an avant-garde of technique. It was impelled by a spirit of experimentation; it attempted to provide fundamentally new ways of seeing, hearing, and understanding: post-impressionism, atonal music, stream of consciousness, and free verse were names given to some of these experiments. Whether or not one admires the results, the utter seriousness as well as the aesthetic purity of the enterprise cannot be mistaken.

The practitioners of what must now somewhat oxymoronically be called the old avant-garde were true revolutionaries. They wished to—and often did—change the way we intuit and understand and feel about the world around us. They *truly* altered sensibility. For a complex of reasons, their revolution has been halted. While new experiments in style and technique continue, the avant-garde has largely turned away from technique and toward content.

Obscenity, homoerotic exhibitionism, sadomasochism, political rage—these have been the hallmarks of the advanced art of our day. In a way never intended either by Matisse, whose early paintings so upset the Parisian audience, or by Stravinsky, whose *The Rite of Spring* caused its audience to bust up chairs in the hall in which it was performed, the avant-garde artists of our day are knocking themselves out to be outrageous. An avant-garde magazine puts a woman's vagina on its cover and runs the tag line, "Read My Lips"; child pornography, if set out "tastefully," is not thought beyond the bounds of respectability; neither is a production of *Tannhäuser* with the title character as a TV evangelist and Venus as a hooker. If the political revolutionaries of an earlier day cried, "Burn, baby, burn!," the artistic revolutionaries of ours exclaim, "Squirm, baby, squirm!"

The targets for such art, it ought to be clear, are middle-class respectability, the family, heterosexuality, organized religion, and finally high culture itself. The aesthetic standard by which this art asks to be judged is the degree to which it succeeds in hitting its targets. As a panel for the National Endowment for the Arts (NEA) once put it, a work that is "challenging and disturbing . . . precisely . . . shows us that it is worthy of consideration." The more outrageous the art, the more worthy of notice and protection.

Consider by contrast how T. S. Eliot, a great avant-garde poet himself, saw the role of the artist:

The artist is the only genuine and profound revolutionist, in the following sense. The world always has, and always will, tend to substitute appearance for reality. The artist, being always alone, being heterodox when everyone else is orthodox, is the perpetual upsetter of conventional values, the restorer of the real. . . . His function is to bring back humanity to the real.

Yet the contemporary, putatively avant-garde artist is neither alone nor heterodox. He is today almost invariably part of a larger group—a feminist, a gay liberationist, or a spokesman for an ethnic or racial group—and his thought, far from being heterodox, is, within both his own group and what is called the "artistic community," more rigidly conformist than a Big Ten sorority. He is published in the fashionable magazines, exhibited by the toniest galleries, awarded Pulitzers and other prizes, given federal grants, and generally rewarded and revered.

The politicizing of art, setting it on the side of all the politically correct causes, has rendered it more acceptable even as it has become less artistic. A commercially successful painter named David Salle, a man with a good feel for the ideological winds, was quoted last year in *The New Yorker* apropos the politics of contemporary artists:

Because in art-politics to be homosexual is, *a priori*, more correct than to be heterosexual. Because to be an artist is to be an outsider, and to be a gay artist is to be a double outsider. That's the correct condition. If you're a straight artist, it's not clear that your outsiderness is legitimate. I know this is totally absurd, that I'm making it sound totally absurd. But the fact is that in our culture it does fall primarily to gays and blacks to make something interesting. Almost everything from the straight white culture is less interesting, and has been for a long time.

How could we possibly get into a condition in which what David Salle says, absurd as it assuredly is, can nonetheless be taken as axiomatic truth? We did it by accepting the quite false notion of the artist as an outsider and extending it to the point where the farther "outside" one represents oneself as being, and the more victimized, the greater one's standing as an artist.

I first came across the name of the dancer Bill T. Jones in an article in the *New York Times Magazine,* where he was described as the "HIV-positive son of migrant workers," which, in current *New York Times-*speak, means a man beyond any possible criticism. Recently Jones and what he represents have come in for some trenchant comment in, of all places, *The New Yorker,* a magazine where only a few weeks earlier he had been the subject of a fawning profile. Arlene Croce, the magazine's distinguished dance critic, wrote a powerful piece demurring from the general celebration and entering the opinion that "the cultivation of victim-hood by institutions devoted to the care of art is a menace to all art forms, particularly performing-art forms."*

Croce's article, "Discussing the Undiscussable," takes up the question of how the art of victimhood—so depressing, so manipulative, so intimidating, and ultimately so uncriticizable—has risen to such a high place in contemporary culture. She understands that some of its appeal is a combination of false empathy and real snobbery on the part of its audience: "There's no doubt that the public likes to see victims, if only to patronize them with applause." But she makes the larger—and, I think, valid—point that the behavior of government, specifically through the National Endowment for the Arts (NEA), has had a great deal to do with the situation she deplores.

In 1984 I was appointed a member of the National Council of the National Endowment for the Arts, a body on which I sat for six years. One of the most impressive moments I can recall from my years on the Council was when the director of the music program mentioned that a particular orchestra had had its grant reduced by something like $20,000 because of some "spotty playing in the cello section." I was much taken with how the NEA music panelists were able to pin down this fault, by the professionalism with which they went about the task of judgment. It seemed to me the way things ought to operate.

But outside certain select programs at the NEA, they seldom did. By the end of my term, every member on the Council had been appointed under either the Reagan or the Bush administration—and yet, despite this, the reigning spirit in the room, as among the staff of the Endow-

---

*See Terry Teachout's "Victim Art," *Commentary,* March 1995, for a discussion of the Croce article and the controversy it provoked.—ED.

ment generally, was preponderantly liberal-Left. Time and again, when arguments about standards and quality came up against what was taken to be democratic fairness and sensitivity to minorities, the latter inevitably won the day.

How could it be otherwise? Given our debased standards, how could one hope to make the hard professional judgments about modern painting or sculpture or literature, let alone mixed-media works? The chief problem with "the peer-panel system," as it was reverently called at the NEA—a system in which artists were asked to sit in judgment of other artists in their field—was that the sort of people who served on these panels were the same sort of people who applied for and received grants themselves. Like was giving money to like.

I could not help noticing, too, the special obligation which the people who worked at the NEA felt toward what passed for avant-garde or "cutting-edge" art. The cutting edge, almost invariably, was anticapitalist, anti-middle-class, anti-American, the whole-earth catalogue of current antinomianism. What was new was that the artists who wanted to seem cutting edge also wanted the government they despised to pay for the scissors.

Most people at the NEA and on its Council thought this a perfectly workable arrangement. If someone ever suggested that a grant application had all the earmarks of something too obviously political as well as boring beyond excruciation, the air would crackle with potential accusations of censorship and Cassandra-like warnings about slippery slopes heading into McCarthyism.

Those NEA grants that issued in obscenity and horror—Karen Finley smearing her nakedness with chocolate, Robert Mapplethorpe's photographs of men with plumbing and other appurtenances up their rectums, a man spreading his HIV-positive blood on paper towels and then sending them skimming over an audience—have given the Endowment its most serious problems in the press and on Capitol Hill. Yet the NEA's defenders are correct in saying that these comprise only a minuscule proportion of the Endowment's total grants. What they do not say—possibly because they are themselves unaware of it—is how mediocre have been so many of the artists who have received NEA grants.

Mediocrity, the question of what may be called quality control, was rarely discussed during my time at the NEA. It could not be. Most NEA panelists believed in encouraging the putatively disadvantaged more than they believed in art itself, and this made them prey to the grim logic of affirmative action. (Even the panels themselves were put together on an affirmative-action basis.) Add to this the assumption at the NEA that artists themselves were yet another downtrodden minority group, as "entitled" to their grants as other supposed victims. And then toss in plain old-fashioned politics in the form of Congressmen and members of the

Council who wanted to make sure that, say, Florida and Colorado got their share of grants. What we had was a fine recipe for spreading artistic mediocrity across the country.

Viewed from the middle distance of a seat on the NEA Council, the grants to individual artists seemed small potatoes. Most were for less than $20,000—an award which generally encouraged self-congratulation and the continued production of unnecessary art. What drained the spectacle of triviality was that the money was not "ours" to give away. No one felt too bad about this, for the NEA budget, generally hovering around $170 million, was, as government spending went, just above the level of walking-around money. Still, the spectacle was more than a little depressing.

The question of what is now to be done about the arts and arts policy in America is not one that admits of easy or persuasive answers. It is made all the more complicated once one concedes how hard it is to explain what, in any society, actually encourages the production of great art.

Traditions help immensely. In eighteenth- and nineteenth-century Vienna, the pressure of strong musical traditions along with a system of monarchical patronage played a part in fostering the magnificent music of that era. The splendid efflorescence of painting in nineteenth- and early-twentieth-century France can also be partially understood through the role played by French artistic traditions—and the reactions of artists to and against certain of those traditions. But how does one explain Russian literature in the nineteenth century, except to say that in Pushkin, Gogol, Dostoyevsky, Turgenev, Tolstoy, and Chekhov, God chose to create six geniuses who happened to share a geography and a language?

Since genius can never be predicted, one looks to institutions that might encourage art to set out in directions likely to be more rewarding than those of the past few decades. What, today, might such institutions be?

The first that comes to mind is criticism. Critics of the arts have traditionally functioned as gatekeepers, deciding what meets the mark and passes through and what does not and is therefore excluded. Some critics have also taken a much more active hand, preparing the ground for the acceptance of new and difficult art through explication and the main force of their authority. One thinks of Edmund Wilson who in *Axel's Castle* (1931) did just this for modernist literature, and, two decades later, of Clement Greenberg who did something similar for Abstract Expressionism.

Critics of this power are not on the scene today. Nor are there important movements in the arts that require such skills. Today our critics commonly function as doormen—or, more precisely, as cheerleaders.

Their job often consists in justifying the trivial, vaunting the vapid. Yet they seem quite happy in their work.

In part this derives from the fact that, like so many of our artists, many of our critics too are not merely university-trained but university-employed. As such they participate in the culture that has dominated academic life over the past few decades: they tend to disbelieve in the possibility of disinterested art; they condone the new multiculturalism and are willing to lower standards to make way for it; they are dubious about judgments of value; and they understand that "criticism" of the work of minority-group members, feminists, or homosexuals must be restricted to praise.

Criticism, then, is not an institution that can be counted on to help revive the arts of our age or in any serious way to arrest their decline—at least not for now. There are a few serious critics on the scene, but the best they can do is continue to remark that the emperor has very few clothes, and wears them badly.

Private foundations, on which many people in the arts depend, are also less than likely to help, for they, too, are hostage to the notion that art ought to be socially useful—that it is most relevant and vibrant when in the service of "social justice." The Lila Wallace–Reader's Digest Fund is fairly typical in this regard. Consider its program for resident theaters. According to the Fund, money for such theaters should be used

to expand their marketing efforts, mount new plays, broaden the ethnic make-up of their management, experiment with color-blind casting, increase community-outreach activity, and sponsor a variety of other programs designed to integrate the theaters into their communities.

Other major foundations—Rockefeller, Ford, MacArthur—are not differently disposed. All are committed to art for almost anything but art's sake.

That leaves the institutional linchpin of the arts in the United States, the National Endowment, now under fire from a Republican-controlled Congress. Supporters of the NEA, those who like the system as it now is, talk a good deal about the economic soundness of federal support for the arts. They trot out the following numbers: federal support for the arts costs the taxpayer only 64 cents a year, whereas the figure in Germany is $27 and in France and Canada it is $32. Every dollar awarded by the NEA in grants attracts $11 from state and local arts agencies, corporations, and private parties. There are 1.3 million jobs in the arts; if you add tourism, ticket revenues, and other money-making activities, this creates something like $37 billion in economic activity and brings in $3.4 billion in federal taxes. The arts, the argument goes, are good for the economy. So shut up, and eat your arts.

Not only have other nations throughout history supported the arts, NEA publicists maintain, but future generations will judge us by the extent to which we support the arts as "the finest expression of the human condition." (Ah, Mapplethorpe! Ah, humanity!) When, they remind us, Congress established the NEA in 1965, it noted:

An advanced civilization must not limit its efforts to science and technology alone but must give full value and support to the other great branches of scholarly and cultural activity in order to achieve a better understanding of the past, a better analysis of the present, and a better view of the future.

The arts, therefore, are not only good for the economy, they serve the purposes of moral uplift. So shut up and eat your arts.

To hear its advocates tell it, the NEA enriches community life, stimulates local economies, supports the promising young, makes culture available to the masses, works with "at-risk" youth, satisfies a deep demand for art among the American people—the NEA is in fact good for everything but growing hair. The arts are good for the city, good for the country, good for everyone. So shut up and eat your arts.

But—aside from all these magnificent side-effects—what, exactly, do the arts *do?* Here we return to the same old litany. Paul Goldberger, the cultural-news editor of the *New York Times,* a paper that has a great deal to say about what in contemporary art gets serious attention, answered the question by writing that "what art strives to do . . . is not to coddle but to challenge." In other words, painters who mock your religion, playwrights who blame you for not doing enough for AIDS, poets who exalt much that you despise, opera composers who make plain that your politics are vicious—all this is by definition art, and, whether you like it or not, it is good for you. So go eat your arts out.

The NEA might have been spared much anguish if someone truly knowledgeable had been in a position of leadership. But in its thirty-year history, it has never had a chairman with anything approaching an understanding of the arts. The specialty of Nancy Hanks, the first chairman, was charming Congressmen to support the agency it had founded in 1965. Her successor, Livingston Biddle, was a platitudinarian, who to this day likes to expatiate on his slogan that "the arts mean excellence"; one need only listen to him for two minutes to cease believing in art and excellence both. Biddle was followed by Frank Hodsoll, an intelligent and capable civil servant who, when it came to the arts, was clearly learning on the job. John Frohnmayer, the Bush administration's man, brought to the job enormous ambition exceeded only by ignorance of the ways of politicians and artists alike. The current chairman, Jane Alexander, an actress and hence technically an artist herself, has been running a rescue operation; she apparently thinks the way to do this is to talk about her wide travels in which she finds that the people of the United

States could not be happier with all the art the federal government has helped to pay for, and to remind everyone that the arts are good for our souls.

One cannot but wonder what it might be like to have someone in a position of leadership who knows what the point of the arts is. But who of any standing would want to take on the job? In the current political climate, he would find himself locked between radical artists shouting censorship and conservative Congressmen crying obscenity. His efforts could only come to grief.

That the future of the National Endowment for the Arts is in peril ought not to be surprising. What people at the NEA and those who accept grants from it have never seemed to realize is that they are sponsoring and producing *official* art, just as surely as the academic painters in France or the socialist-realist novelists in the Soviet Union produced official art. That our official art is against the society that sponsors it does not make it any the less official. But given the obscenity and the mediocrity and the politicization of so much of this art, government sponsorship of it has come to seem intolerable, and there is now talk of closing down the Endowment.

Should that be done? Any serious scrutiny of the NEA must begin with the stipulation that politically motivated art ought not to be underwritten by taxpayer money. (The argument that all art is ultimately political is greatly exaggerated; it is a question of degree, and everyone knows it.) Nor for their part should artists upon receiving a grant be asked to accept any condition that will inhibit them, such as not offending any segment of the population. Since these criteria cannot be satisfied in the case of grants to individual artists, and especially those on the "cutting edge," my own sense is that it would be better if all such grants were eliminated: better for the country and, though they are likely to hate it, better, finally, for artists.

In one of his essays the eminent cultural historian Jacques Barzun makes a distinction between "public art" and all other kinds. Individual artists, he believes, should fend for themselves, as artists have always done; I agree with him. But then there is public art, by which Barzun means museums, opera houses, orchestras, theaters, and dance troupes. "If as a nation," he writes, "we hold that high art is a public need, these institutions deserve support on the same footing as police departments and weather bureaus."

William F. Buckley, Jr., has supplied a corroborating argument derived, for conservatives, from the most impressive of all possible sources. It was Adam Smith who, in Buckley's words, "counseled that free societies are obliged to contribute state funds only for the maintenance of justice, for the common defense, and for the preservation of monuments." It is only a small stretch, Buckley suggests, to claim that a great many artistic works qualify as monuments.

I agree with that, too—but only in theory. In a different political-cultural climate—less confrontational and litigious—one could easily imagine a place for a federal presence in the arts. The government could contribute to preserving art: it could help to maintain the costs of museums in financial difficulty and ease the financial strain entailed in the performance and exhibition of established and often difficult art that does not figure to have a wide following. Some valuable art cannot realistically hope to survive in the marketplace, ever, and some of the good things the NEA historically helped to do are not likely to be done by private philanthropy—bringing in art from abroad, underwriting costly exhibition catalogues, helping small but serious local musical and dance groups get under way. There are other things, too, that the federal government would perhaps be in the best position to accomplish, if the political climate were not so deliberately abrasive.

Proponents of the NEA point to the fact that most West European governments do support the arts, without great tumult, for the perfectly legitimate reason that they feel a responsibility to their national cultural heritage and to culture generally. But there would not have been a great tumult in the United States, either, if the NEA's advocates, artists' lobbying groups, and artists themselves had not felt the need to justify the mediocre, the political, and the obscene. These justifications have even extended to the argument that *not* to receive an NEA grant is to be the victim of censorship. When Karen Finley and other performance artists were denied an NEA grant in 1990, they took their case to the courts on this basis, and won. As long as such things go on—and there is no reason to believe that they will not—the federal government would do better to remain outside the arts altogether.

When the abolition of the NEA is currently discussed, many people talk about turning the task over to the states. But the effect of this would most likely be to enlarge state bureaucracies, and art selected for support on the state level is likely to be even more mediocre, and no less political, than that selected on the federal level. The prospect of "devolution" is thus not one that ought to fill anyone with optimism.

It does, however, seem doubtful that, if government divorces itself from the arts, private philanthropy will pick up the whole tab. People who run large artistic institutions—museums, symphony orchestras—seem to agree that the new generations of the wealthy have shown themselves less generous than their forebears: the philanthropic impulse is not, evidently, a genetic one.

This is unfortunate. Although money has its limitations in the arts, there is no question that it also has its distinct uses. In my own time on the NEA Council I sensed that if an art was weak, there was nothing that the injection of money—which was finally all the NEA or any federal program had to offer—could do to strengthen it. If, on other hand, an art was strong, as dance was in the middle 1980s, money could help in small but real ways to support it in its vibrancy. Many dancers, for example, work a twenty-six-week season, or less, and hence are unemployed half the year; and, in a profession that almost guarantees injury, few dance companies are able to offer health insurance. Although nothing was done to rectify either of these situations during even the palmiest days at the NEA, the answer in both instances was fairly simple—money.

Other things that seem eminently justifiable are also not likely to be picked up by private philanthropy. The NEA has sent dance and theatrical and musical groups into rural and backwater parts of the country, so that people, and especially the young, could have an opportunity to see live performance, which, even in a television age, has its own magic. Arts education in the lower grades, which has been gradually yet seriously slipping in recent decades, is something that needs attending to. Private philanthropy is unlikely to step in here, too.

All that having been said, however, it still remains the case that if the Endowment were shut down, the arts would probably for the most part not be drastically affected. In some instances, fresh patrons would step forward to fill the financial gaps; in others, cutbacks in production and exhibition schedules would have to be made; in a minor number of cases, smaller institutions—literary magazines, design projects, local music groups—might go under. But much as the NEA and its advocates would like everyone to think otherwise, the presence of the Endowment is not crucial to the artistic life of this country. This may be a good time to lie low and have no arts policy whatsoever. After all, we had an artistic life—a much richer and more distinguished one—before we had an NEA.

Thanks in part to the NEA, we are now in an age of artistic surfeit. To provide only a single depressing statistic, I read somewhere that there are currently 26,000 registered poets in the United States. Where, it will be asked, do they register? With the Associated Writing Programs, I gather, which are chiefly made up of teachers of writing, who are even now busy producing still more poets, who will go on to teach yet more poets, who will . . . so that in twenty years' time we will have 52,000 registered poets. Degas, more than a century ago, remarked: "We must discourage the arts." What might he say today?

PART THREE

The Media

JAMES B. TWITCHELL

"But First, a Word from Our Sponsor": Advertising and the Carnivalization of Culture

James B. Twitchell is Alumni Professor of English at the University of Florida and is not as melancholy as this essay implies. If advertising serves to dumb down, the language of capitalism also has positive advantages, as he explains in *Adcult USA: The Triumph of Advertising in America* (1995). He is planning a book on the disappearance of shame in modern life. His previous books include *Carnival Culture: The Trashing of Taste in America* (1992) and *Dreadful Pleasures: An Anatomy of Modern Horror* (1992).

In the laboratory of his investigations, James Twitchell has discovered the very mechanism of dumbing down, and, like the Doomsday Machine, once activated, it apparently cannot be stopped. And if, in recent years, talk about the "end of history" centered on the final victory of laissez-faire capitalism, Twitchell points to this so-called victory as the same gloomy mechanism of which we speak.

High culture and commerce historically have had an uneasy relationship, going back at least to Juvenal's observation that the Roman masses preferred *panem et circenses* to the grander visions of the Republic. So in our own time the pursuit of happiness has become a daily collaborative obsession of corporate advertising and the American public. The terms of continued existence for previously protected areas of life—the library, the classroom, the museum gallery, the concert hall, the altar—have been reestablished: pay-as-you-go. Since most of us are cultural cheapskates, the piper who gets to call the tune nowadays usually wears a brand-name logo and is definitely not in favor of anything that might wrinkle the brows of the shareholders.

To oppose this, Twitchell offers the subversive idea of encouraging us to become faster and faster moving targets for the marketing sharpshooters whose fondest hope is efficiently to glimpse our vulnerable bodies in their corporate crosshairs.

WHENEVER a member of my paunchy fifty-something set pulls me aside and complains of the dumbing down of American culture, I tell him that if he doesn't like it he should quit moaning and go buy a lot of Fast-Moving Consumer Goods. And every time he buys soap, toothpaste, beer, gasoline, bread, aspirin, and the like, he should make it a point to buy a different brand. He should implore his friends to do likewise. At the same time he should quit giving so much money to his kids. That, I'm sorry to say, is his only hope.

Here's why. The culture we live in is carried on the back of advertising. Now I mean that literally. If you cannot find commercial support for what you have to say, it will not be transported. Much of what we share, and what we know, and even what we treasure, is carried to us each second in a plasma of electrons, pixels, and ink, underwritten by multinational advertising agencies dedicated to attracting our attention for entirely non-altruistic reasons. These agencies, gathered up inside worldwide conglomerates with weird sci-fi names like WPP, Omnicom, Saatchi & Saatchi, Dentsu, and Euro RSCG, are usually collections of established shops linked together to provide "full service" to their global clients. Their service is not moving information or creating entertainment, but buying space and inserting advertising. They essentially rent our concentration to other companies—sponsors—for the dubious purpose of informing us of something that we've longed for all our lives even though we've never heard of it before. Modern selling is not about trading information, as it was in the nineteenth century, as much as about creating an infotainment culture sufficiently alluring so that other messages—commercials—can get through. In the spirit of the enterprise, I call this new culture Adcult.

Adcult is there when we blink, it's there when we listen, it's there when we touch, it's even there to be smelled in scent strips when we open a magazine. There is barely an empty space in our culture not already carrying commercial messages. Look anywhere: in schools there is Channel One; in movies there is product placement; ads are in urinals, played on telephone hold, in alphanumeric displays in taxis, sent unannounced to fax machines, inside catalogues, on the video in front of the Stairmaster at the gym, on T-shirts, at the doctor's office, on grocery carts, on parking meters, on tees at golf holes, on inner-city basketball backboards, piped in along with Muzak . . . ad nauseam (and yes, even on airline vomit bags). We have to shake magazines like rag dolls to free up their pages from the "blow-in" inserts and then wrestle out the stapled- or glued-in ones before reading can begin. We now have to fast-forward through some five minutes of advertising that open rental videotapes. President Clinton's inaugural parade featured a Budweiser float. At the Smithsonian, the Orkin Pest Control Company sponsored an exhibit on exactly what it advertises it kills: insects. No venue is safe. Is there a blockbuster museum show not decorated with corporate logos? Public Broadcasting is littered with "underwriting announcements" which look and sound almost exactly like what PBS claims they are not: commercials.

Okay, you get the point. Commercial speech is so powerful that it downs out all other sounds. But sounds are always conveyed in a medium. The media of modern culture are these: print, sound, pictures, or some combination of each. Invariably conversations about dumbing down focus on the supposed corruption of these media as demonstrated in the sophomoric quality of most movies, the fall from the golden age of television, the mindlessness of most best-sellers, and the tarting-up of the news, be it in/on *USA Today, Time, ABC,* or *Inside Edition.* The media make convenient whipping boys especially because they are now all conglomerated into huge worldwide organizations like Time Warner, News Corp, General Electric, Viacom, Bertelsmann, Sony, and the like. But, alas, as much fun as the media are to blame, they have very little to do with the explanation for whatever dumbing down has occurred.

The explanation is, I think, more fundamental, more economic in nature. These media are delivered for a price. We have to pay for them, either by spending money or by spending time. Given a choice, we prefer to spend time. We spend our time paying attention to ads and in exchange we are given infotainment. This trade is central to Adcult. Economists call this "cost externalization." If you want to see it at work go to McDonald's. You order. You carry your food to the table. You clean up. You pay less. Want to see it elsewhere? Buy gas. Just as the "work" you do at the self-service gas station lowers the price of gas, so consuming ads is the "work" you do which lowers the price of delivering the infotainment. In Adcult the trade is more complex. True, you are entertained at lower cost, but you are also encultured in the process.

So far so good. The quid pro quo of modern infotainment culture is that if you want it you'll get it—no matter what it is—as long as there are enough of you who (1) are willing to spend some energy along the way hearing "a word from our sponsor" and (2) have sufficient disposable income possibly to buy some of the advertised goods. In Adcult you pay twice: once with the ad and once with the product. So let's look back a step to examine these products because—strange as it may seem—they are at the center of the dumbing down of American culture.

Before all else, we must realize that modern advertising is primarily tied to things, and only secondarily to services. Manufacturing both things *and* their meanings is what American culture is all about. If Greece gave the world philosophy, Britain gave drama, Austria music, Germany politics, Italy art, then America gave mass-produced objects. "We bring good things to life" is no offhand claim. Most of these "good things" are machine-made and hence interchangeable. Such objects, called parity items, constitute most of the stuff which surrounds us, from bottled water to toothpaste to beer to cars to airlines. There is really no discernible difference between Evian and Mountain Spring, Colgate and Crest, Miller and Budweiser, Ford and Chevrolet, Delta and United. In fact, the only difference is usually in the advertising. Advertising is how we talk about these fungible things, how we know their supposed differences, how we recognize them. We don't consume the products as much as we consume the advertising.

For some reason, we like it this way. Logically, we should all read *Consumer Reports* and then all buy the most sensible product. But we don't. So why do we waste our energy (and billions of dollars) entertaining fraudulent choice? I don't know. Perhaps just as we drink the advertising not the beer, we prefer the illusion of choice to the reality of decision. Else how to explain the appearance of so much superfluous choice? A decade ago, grocery stores carried about 9,000 items; they now stock about 24,000. Revlon makes 158 shades of lipstick. Crest toothpaste comes in 36 sizes and shapes and flavors. We are even eager to be offered choice where there is none to speak of. AT&T offers "the right choice"; Wendy's, "there is no better choice"; Pepsi, "the choice of a new generation"; Coke, "the real choice"; "Taster's Choice is the choice for taste." Even advertisers don't understand the phenomenon. Is there a relationship between the number of soft drinks and television channels—about 27? What's going to happen when the information pipe carries 500?

I have no idea. But I do know this: human beings like things. We buy things. We like to exchange things. We steal things. We donate things. We live through things. We call these things "goods" as in "goods and services." We do not call them "bads." This sounds simplistic, but it is crucial to understanding the power of Adcult. The still-going-strong Industrial Revolution produces more and more things, not because production is what machines do, and not because nasty capitalists twist their handlebar mustaches and mutter, "More slop for the pigs," but because we are powerfully attracted to the world of things. Advertising, when it's lucky, supercharges some of this attraction.

This attraction to the inanimate happens all over the world. Berlin Walls fall because people want things, and they want the culture created by things. China opens its doors not so much because it wants to get out, but because it wants to get things in. We were not suddenly transformed from customers to consumers by wily manufacturers eager to unload a surplus of crapular products. We have created a surfeit of things because we enjoy the process of "getting and spending." The consumption ethic may have started in the early 1900s, but the desire is ancient. Kings and princes once thought they could solve problems by amassing things. We now join them.

The Marxist balderdash of cloistered academics aside, human beings did not suddenly become materialistic. We have always been desirous of things. We have just not had many of them until quite recently, and, in a few generations, we may return to having fewer and fewer. Still, while they last, we enjoy shopping for things and see both the humor and truth reflected in the aphoristic "born to shop," "shop till you drop," and "when the going gets tough, the tough go shopping." Department-store windows, whether on the city street or inside a mall, did not appear by magic. We enjoy looking through them to another world. It is voyeurism for capitalists. Our love of things is the *cause* of the Industrial Revolution, not the consequence. Man is not only *Homo sapiens,* or *Homo ludens,* or *Homo faber,* but also *Homo emptor.*

Mid-twentieth-century American culture is often criticized for being too materialistic. Ironically, we are not too materialistic. We are not materialistic enough. If we craved objects *and* knew what they meant, there would be no need to add meaning through advertising. We would gather, use, toss out, or hoard based on some *inner* sense of value. But we don't. We don't know what to gather; we like to trade what we have gathered; and we need to know how to evaluate objects of little practical use. What is clear is that most things in and of themselves simply do not mean enough. In fact, what we crave may not be objects at all but their meaning. For whatever else advertising "does," one thing is certain: by adding value to material, by adding meaning to objects, by branding things, advertising performs a role historically associated with religion. The Great Chain of Being, which for centuries located value above the horizon in the world Beyond, has been reforged to settle value into the objects of the Here and Now.

I wax a little impatient here because most of the literature on modern culture is downright supercilious about consumption. What do you expect? Most of it comes from a culture professionally hostile to materialism, albeit secretly envious. From Veblen on, there has been a palpable sense of disapproval as the hubbub of commerce is viewed from the groves of academe. The current hand-wringing over dumbing down is not new. It used to be bread and circuses. Modern concepts of bandwagon consumption, conspicuous consumption, keeping-up-with-the-Joneses, the culture of narcissism, and all the other barely veiled reproofs have limited our serious consideration of Adcult to such relatively minor issues as manipulation and exploitation. People surely can't want, ugh!, things. Or, if they really do want them, they must want them for all the wrong reasons. The idea that advertising creates artificial desires rests on a profound ignorance of human nature, on the hazy feeling that there existed some halcyon era of noble savages with purely natural needs, on romantic claptrap first promulgated by Rousseau and kept alive in institutions well isolated from the marketplace.

We are now closing in on why the dumbing down of American culture has occurred with such startling suddenness in the last thirty years. We are also closing in on why the big complainers about dumbing down are me and my paunchy pals. The people who want things the most and have the best prospects to get them are the young. They are also the ones who have not decided which brands of objects they wish to consume. In addition, they have a surplus of two commodities: time and money, especially the former. If you can make a sale to these twenty-somethings, if you can "brand" them with your product, you may have them for life. But to do this you have to be able to speak to them, and to do that you have to go to where you will be heard.

The history of mass media can be summarized in a few words: if it can't carry advertising, it won't survive.

Books are the exception that *almost* proves the rule. Books used to carry ads. Initially, publishing and advertising were joined at the press. Book publishers, from William Caxton to modern university presses, have advertised forthcoming titles on their flyleaves and dust jackets. No doubt publishers would have been willing to bind other material into their products if only there had been a demand. While we may have been startled when Christopher Whittle marketed his Larger Agenda series of books ("big ideas, great writers, short books") by inserting advertising into what is essentially a long magazine article bound in hardcover, he was actually behaving like a traditional book publisher. When Whittle published William Greider's *The Trouble with Money*—94 pages of text and 18 pages of Federal Express ads—book reviewers turned away, aghast. But when Bradbury & Evans published Charles Dickens's *Little Dorrit* in 1857, no reviewer or reader blanched at seeing the bound-in ad section touting Persian parasols, smelling salts, portable India-rubber boots, and the usual array of patent medicines.

The reason why books were not an advertising medium is simple: there wasn't much to advertise, and once there was a surplus of machine-made parity items, there was a cheaper medium—the magazine. The death knell of book advertising is still being rung not by publishers, but by the postal service. Put an ad in a book and it no longer travels at fourth-class book rate but at third-class commercial rate. A prediction: advertising will return to books. UPS, FedEx, and the other commercial carriers make no such distinction about content, only about weight and size. In addition, since Dr. Spock fought Pocket Books to have cigarette ads removed from his baby-care book in the late 1940s, the Authors' Guild has advised writers to have a no-advertising clause inserted in the boilerplate of their contracts with publishers. What would it take to reverse this? Not much, I suspect. Put a few ads in, drop the price 10 percent, and most people would accept it. Of course, the real reason books are currently ad-free is that the prime audience for advertisers, namely the young, is functionally illiterate.

Here is the history of magazine and newspaper publishing on a thumbnail. All the innovations in these media were forced on them by advertisers. You name it: the appearance of ads throughout the pages, the "jump" or continuation of a story from page to page, the rise of sectionalization (as with news, cartoons, sports, financial, living, real estate), common page size, halftone images, process engraving, the use of

black-and-white photography, then color, sweepstakes, and finally discounted subscriptions were all forced on publishers by advertisers hop-
ing to find target audiences.

From the publishers' point of view, the only way to increase revenues
without upping the price, or adding advertising space, is to increase
circulation. First-copy costs in magazine and newspaper publishing are
stupendous. Ironically, the economies of scale are such that to increase
the "reach" of this medium and lower your last-copy cost, you also run
the risk of alienating core readership. This is not advertising-friendly.
What amounts to a Hobson's choice for the publisher has proved a
godsend for the advertiser. It means that papers and magazines will tend
to self-censor in order to provide a bland and unobtrusive plasma as
they, on their own, seek to maximize their profits. They dumb down
automatically. Look at the *New York Times* over the last decade and you
can see this operating in slow motion. The increase of infotainment and
the presence of movie ads, the inclusion of Tuesday's "Science Times"
section to showcase computer ads, the jazzy "Style" section of Sunday,
and, of course, the use of color, to say nothing of the appearance on the
front page of stories that used to be deemed tabloid-like and were therefore relegated to the back sections—all were attempts to find the
"proper" readership, not to find all that is "Fit to Print." If newspapers
want to survive, they will have to think of themselves not as delivering
news or entertainment to readers but delivering readers to advertisers.

One might even see newspapers and magazines, in the current baf-
flegab, as members of a "victim" class. They are remnants of a print
culture in which selling was secondary to informing. To survive, they had
to replace their interest in their reader as reader with the more modern
view of the reader as commodity. Still, print media might have maintained their cultural standards, had not radio and television elbowed
them aside. Ironically, print had to conglomerate, to fit itself into huge
oligopolies like Scripps-Howard, the Tribune Company, the New York
Times Company, News Corp, Gannett, the Washington Post Company,
Times-Mirror, Meredith, and the rest, in order to sell advertising space
profitably. As advertising will flow to that medium which finds the target
audience cheapest, the demographic specialization of print is a direct
result of the rise of Adcult.

This struggle to find targeted audiences has led to two interesting
extremes. On the one hand are magazines which are pure advertising,
like *Colors* from Benetton, *Le Magazine de Chanel*, or *Sony Style*, which
erase the line between advertising and content so that you cannot tell
what is text and what is hype. At the other extreme are magazines like the
reincarnated *Ms.* or *Consumer Reports*, which remain ad-free for political
or economic reasons. Meanwhile, the rest of magazine culture aspires to
the condition of women's magazines, in which the ratio of advertising

space to print space is about ten to one, and to the editorial condition of newspapers, which is as bland as vanilla.

The electronic media have turned the screws on print, have made it play a perpetual game of catch-up, have forced it into niches so that only a few national magazines or newspapers have survived. Broadcasting has forced print to narrowcast. Television is usually blamed, but the real culprit is radio. Radio started with such high hopes. It has achieved such low reality. Rush Limbaugh and Howard Stern are not stars of this medium by accident.

After World War I, Westinghouse had a surplus of tubes, amplifiers, transmitters, and crystal receivers which had been used during the war. So in November 1920, it started KDKA in Pittsburgh on the Field of Dreams ("if you build it, they will come") principle. It worked. Once transmitters were built, Westinghouse receiving apparatus could be unloaded. You could make them at home. All you needed was a spool of wire, a crystal, an aerial, and earphones—all produced by Westinghouse. Patience and a cylindrical oatmeal box were supplied by the hobbyist. By July 1922, four hundred stations had sprung up.

Rather like users of the Internet today, no one then seemed to care "what" was on as long as they were hearing something. When stereophonic sound was introduced in the 1950s, at first the most popular records were of the ordinary sounds of locomotives and cars passing from speaker to speaker. People used to marvel at the test patterns of early television as no doubt monks stood in awe in front of the first printed letters. However, in the 1920s great plans were being hatched for radio. Universities would take advantage of this new way to dispense their respective cultures by building transmitters. The government would see to this by allocating special licenses just for universities. This medium would never dumb down, it would uplift.

The problem was that everyone was broadcasting on the same wavelength. When transmitters were placed too close together the signals became mixed and garbled. AT&T suggested a solution. They would link stations together using their already-in-place lines, and soon everyone would hear clearly. They envisioned tying some thirty-eight stations together in a system they called "toll broadcasting." The word "toll" was the tip-off. Someone was going to have to pay. The phone company suggested that time could be sold to private interests, and they called this subsidy "ether advertising." The suggestion was not an immediate success. Secretary of Commerce Herbert Hoover, considered a presidential possibility, warned that it was "inconceivable that we should allow so great a possibility for service . . . to be drowned in advertising chatter" and that if presidential messages ever "became the meat in a sandwich of two patent medicine advertisements it would destroy broadcasting" (quoted in Barnouw, p. 15). Such Cassandras were uniformly ignored.

This would never happen. The universities would see to it by their responsible use of education.

In 1922 AT&T started WEAF (for Wind, Earth, Air, Fire) in New York. They tried all kinds of innovative things, even broadcasting live from a football stadium. They tried letting companies buy time to talk about their products. Such talk was always done in good taste: no mention of where the products were available, no samples offered, no store locations, no comparisons, no price information, and never, ever during the "family hour" (from 7 to 11 P.M.)—just a few words about what it is that you offer. At 5 P.M. on August 28, the station manager even let a Mr. Blackwell step up to the microphone and say his piece about a housing development. He only spoke once. This is what he said, and it is every bit as important as "Come here Mr. Watson, I need you," only a bit longer. It was to be the "May Day" distress call of high culture.

It is 58 years since Nathaniel Hawthorne, the greatest of American fictionists, passed away. To honor his memory the Queensboro Corporation has named its latest group of high-grade dwellings "Hawthorne Court." I wish to thank those within sound of my voice for the broadcasting opportunity afforded me to urge this vast radio audience to seek the recreation and the daily comfort of the home removed from the congested part of the city, right at the boundaries of God's great outdoors, and within a few miles by subway from the business section of Manhattan. This sort of residential environment strongly influenced Hawthorne, America's greatest writer of fiction. He analyzed with charming keenness the social spirit of those who had thus happily selected their homes, and he painted the people inhabiting those homes with good-natured relish. . . . Let me enjoin upon you as you value your health and your hopes and your home happiness, get away from the solid masses of brick, where the meager opening admitting a slant of sunlight is mockingly called a light shaft, and where children grow up starved for a run over a patch of grass and the sight of a tree. Apartments in congested parts of the city have proved failures. The word "neighbor" is an expression of peculiar irony—a daily joke. . . . Let me close by urging that you hurry to the apartment home near the green fields and the neighborly atmosphere right on the subway without the expense and trouble of a commuter, where health and community happiness beckon—the community life and the friendly environment that Hawthorne advocated. (Archer, pp. 397–98)

Three weeks later the Queensboro Corporation had sold all its property in Hawthorne Court (named for "America's greatest writer of fiction" who had clearly never been read by Mr. Blackwell) in Jackson Heights, Long Island. The genie was out of the bottle.

"Giving the public what it wants" had its price. Like television today, the messenger was soon being blamed for the message. Commercial radio broadcasting was "dumbing down" American culture with its incessant repetition of mindless humor, maudlin sentimentality, exaggerated action, and frivolous entertainment. Proving yet again the power of Gresham's law when applied to culture, radio programming by the 1930s was selling out to the lowest common denominator. Typical of highcult outrage was James Rorty, erstwhile advertising copywriter turned snitch for such leftward-leaning periodicals as the *New Republic:*

American culture is like a skyscraper: The gargoyle's mouth is a loudspeaker [the radio], powered by the vested interest of a two-billion dollar industry, and back of that the vested interests of business as a whole, of industry, of finance. It is never silent, it downs out all other voices, and it suffers no rebuke, for is it not the voice of America? That is this claim and to some extent it is a just claim. . . . Is it any wonder that the American population tends increasingly to speak, think, feel in terms of this jabberwocky? That the stimuli of art, science, religion are progressively expelled to the periphery of American life to become marginal values, cultivated by marginal people on marginal time? (pp. 32–33, 270)

But wait! What about those universities? Weren't they supposed to make sure the airwaves would be full of "the best that had been thought and said"? While there were more than 90 educational stations (of a total 732) in 1927, by the mid-1930s there were only a handful. What happened? Surely, the universities would never participate in any dumbing down. Alas, the universities had sold their radio licenses to the burgeoning networks—called "nets" or, better yet, "webs"—emanating from Manhattan. In one of the few attempts to recapture cultural control from commercial exploitation, the National Education Association lobbied Senators Robert Wagner of New York and Henry Hatfield of West Virginia to reshuffle the stations and restore a quarter of them to university hands. These stations would forever be advertising-free, making "sweetness and light" available to all. The lobbying power of the NEA met the clout of Madison Avenue. No contest. The Wagner-Hatfield Bill died aborning, defeated by an almost two-to-one margin.

One of the reasons the Wagner-Hatfield Bill floundered so quickly was the emergence of a new cultural phenomenon, the countrywide hit show. Never before had an entertainment been developed which an entire nation—by 1937 more than three-quarters of American homes had at least one radio—could experience at the same time. *Amos 'n' Andy* at NBC had shown what a hit show could do. NBC thought a "hit" was the way to sell their RCA receivers and they were partially right—more than 100,000 sets were sold just to hear the minstrel antics of "The Mystic Knights of the Sea." But CBS knew better. Hits could make millions of dollars in advertising revenue. Although not yet called a "blockbuster" (that would come with the high-explosive bombs of World War II), the effect of a hit was already acknowledged as concussive. One of these "hits" could support hundreds of programming failures.

In truth, CBS or not, television never had a chance to be anything other than the consummate selling machine. It took twenty-five years for radio to evolve out of wireless; it took only five years for television to unfold from radar. And while it took a decade and the economic depression to allow advertiser control of the radio spectrum, it took only a few years and economic expansion to do the same with television. Advertisers had rested during the war. They had no product to sell. No surplus = no advertising.

Even though radio not only survived but prospered during the war, the new kid on the block was too tough to beat. From the first narrow broadcast, television was going commercial. The prophetic Philo T. Farnsworth presented a dollar sign for sixty seconds in the first public demonstration of his television system in 1927. Once Hazel Bishop became a million-dollar company in the early 1950s, based on television advertising, the direction of the medium was set. It would follow radio. Certain systemic changes in both broadcast media did occur; most important, the networks recaptured programming from the agencies. Although this shift away from agency control took scandals to accomplish (most notably the quiz scandals rigged by advertising agencies, not networks), it would have happened anyway. Simple economics made it cheaper to sell time by the ounce than by the pound. The "nets" could make more by selling minutes than by selling half or full hours. Magazines maximized ad revenues by selling space by the partial page; why not television? The motto of this new medium became, "Programs are the scheduled interruptions of marketing bulletins." How could it be otherwise?

We need not be reminded of what is currently happening to television to realize the direction of the future. MTV, the infomercial, and the home-shopping channels are not flukes but the predictable continuation of this medium. Thanks to the remote-control wand and the coaxial (soon to be fiber-optic) cable, commercials will disappear. They will become the programming. Ditto: movies, perhaps. Remember, the first rule of Adcult is: given the choice between paying money or paying attention, we prefer to pay attention.

What all this means is that if you think things are bad now, just wait. There are few gatekeepers left. Most of them reside on Madison Avenue. Just as the carnival barker doesn't care what is behind the tent, only how long the line is in front, the pooh-bahs of Adcult only care who's looking, not what they are looking at. The best-seller lists, the box office, the Nielsens, the various circulation figures for newspapers and magazines are the meters. They decide what gets through. Little wonder that so much of our popular culture is derivative of itself, that prequels and sequels and spin-offs are the order of the day, that celebrity is central, and that innovation is the cross to the vampire. Adcult is recombinant culture. This is how it has to be if advertisers are to be able to direct their spiels at the appropriate audiences for their products. It's simply too expensive to be any other way.

Will Adcult continue? Will there be some new culture to "afflict" the comfortable and comfort the afflicted"? Will advertising, in its own terms, lose *it*? Who knows? Certainly signs of stress are showing. Here are a few. (1) The kids are passing through "prime-branding time" like a rabbit in the python, and as they get older things may settle down. The supposed ad-proof Generation X may be impossible to reach, and advertisers will turn to older audiences by default. (2) The media are so clogged and cluttered that companies may move to other promotional highways like direct mail, point-of-purchase displays, and couponing, leaving the traditional avenues open to us older folks. (3) Branding, the heart of advertising, may become problematic if generics or store brands become as popular in this country as they have in Europe. After all, the much-vaunted brand extension whereby Coke becomes Diet Coke which becomes Diet Cherry Coke does not always work, as Kodak floppy disks, Milky Way ice cream, Arm & Hammer antiperspirant, Life Saver gum, and even EuroDisney have all shown. And (4)—the unthinkable—mass consumption may become too expensive. Advertising can flourish only in times of surplus. Threats like the greenhouse effect, poisoned rivers, overflowing landfills, worldwide famine, and especially overpopulation may deplete surplus.

But by no means am I predicting Adcult's imminent demise. As long as goods are interchangeable and in surplus quantities, as long as producers are willing to pay for short-term advantages (especially for new products), and as long as consumers have plenty of disposable time and money so that they can consume both the ad and the product, Adcult will remain the dominant meaning-making system of modern life. I don't think you can roll this tape backwards. Adcult is the application of capitalism to culture; dollars voting. And so I say to my melancholy friends who moan the passing of a culture once concerned with the arts and the humanities that the only way they can change this situation is if they buy more Fast-Moving Consumer Goods, change brands capriciously, and cut the kids' allowance. Good luck.

WORKS CITED

Archer, Gleason L. *History of Radio to 1926.* New York: American Historical Society, 1938.

Barnouw, Erik. *The Sponsor: Notes on a Modern Potentate.* New York: Oxford University Press, 1978.

Rorty, James. *Our Master's Voice: Advertising.* New York: John Day, 1934.

SVEN BIRKERTS

Homo Virtualis

Sven Birkerts manages, in Arlington, Massachusetts, the paradox of being both a self-confessed Luddite and an unwavering enemy of deconstruction. He typed this piece, along with the multitude of essays and book reviews that have won him a Guggenheim and a reputation as a leading literary critic, on a Selectric 2.

Birkerts's most recent book, *The Gutenberg Elegies* (1995), reflects the passion for the printed word and the distaste for the abandonment of the "autonomous, bounded 'I' " which both he and Heather MacDonald observe in places hitherto unsuspected. (For Birkerts, the corpse of *Homo sapiens* may be lying just off the breakdown lane of the information highway.) Ironically, in an age which promotes the unfettered self, he worries that we may have lost the authenticity of the individual, for whom reading and writing are essential as "information" eclipses knowledge. The deluge of current communication may have left us drowned on the field of Babel, communally linked in cacophony. He directs our gaze to the on-line "neighborhood," a place potentially as desolate, as synthetic, and as empty of intelligent life as the theme-park malls which gradually replace real cities, the habitats of *Homo civilis* which we've forsaken.

Nonetheless, a number of people have persuaded Birkerts that the Internet is not entirely without its positive aspects, although he continues to avoid it.

"*T*HE INTERNET—" I said, on my way to a question. But already the red flag was up. My computer-savvy friend was shaking his head. "Nobody really calls it the 'Internet,' " he replied. "Just say the 'Net.' " Two words into my research and already I'm learning things. First, that there is no way that an outsider can talk to an initiate and hope to get anything right. A fierce territoriality, the expression of an us/them mentality, underlies most interchanges having anything to do with computers. Second, the fact that the Internet is already, familiarly, the "Net" tells us something about the velocity with which the whole phenomenon has infiltrated the culture: it has gone from breakthrough to buzzword in a few very short years. Suddenly everyone knows about the Net—the unlikeliest people announce to me that they are users. Already I have moments when I fear I'm the last man, the one to whom everything needs to be explained.

The Net. I see it defined every which way, often in terms of negatives. My favorite encompassing definition is given by science writer James Gleick: "It isn't a thing; it isn't an entity; it isn't an organization. No one

owns it; no one runs it. It is simply Everyone's Computers, Connected."
The Net is an ever-changing system of connections, options, and poten-
tialities, a newly fledged congeries of private links into larger provider
networks like Compuserve and America Online that all together brings
upwards of 25 million dedicated and sometime users together. *Together*—we will have to look at that word and some others. When I write
"together" in this context I mean virtually so—bringing them into potential electronic contact in a space that is brought into being and aug-
mented by the signals they pass back and forth from their computer
terminals.

The Net is a many-splendored thing. It functions variously as a high-
speed communication sluice (for E-mail and electronic bulletin boards);
a venue for recreational or professional on-line "chats" (where users
anywhere in the world can exchange views in real time, typing back and
forth to each other about polymers, politics, or perverse fetishes); a por-
tal to massive databases (like the catalogue of the Library of Congress);
and as a place to play out collective fantasy games (in MUDs, or "multi-
ple-use dungeons"). The Net is anarchic, grass-roots, ungoverned, and
unpoliced, except by self-appointed vigilantes, who take pains to remind
"Newbies," or newcomers, that there is a consensual "netiquette" to be
observed. Which does not, of course, prevent eavesdroppers, crashers,
pranksters of every description, and certainly does not seem to inhibit
"flamers" of every ilk—"flaming," as everyone must know by now, being
a vicious insult sent through the Net, often under cover of anonymity.

The range of the Net, then, is immense; it is at every moment the sum
of its active operations and the implicit condensation of its many possibilities. Like life. Its proselytizers, many and ardent, come in all stripes,
but I distinguish two fundamental orientations. There are the engineers
and there are the visionaries. The engineers are hands-on, interested in
specifications and intricacies of application. They love the computer—
and the Net—as a tool and are impatient with soft discourse. Many veteran hackers fall into this group.

Then there are the visionaries, the goggle-eyed futurists, all those
sci-fi dreamers and Trekkies who subscribe to *WIRED*, the *Rolling Stone*
of the electronic age, and heed the call-note of utopian desire. They
discern in the Net a larger future, one that stands in sharp relief against
the sprawl of codes and apparatuses described by the engineer. The Net
excites in these users a metaphor-making impulse. They readily speak of
it as a kind of massive nervous system, as the neural infrastructure of a
creation that may soon enough become greater than the sum of its individual impulse exchanges and attain a kind of animate identity. It may
not be a coincidence that the Net is growing all around us on the eve of
the millennium, for it is a millennial kind of excitement we register in
these quarters. A touch of New Age mysticism. We hear at times the

invocation of transhuman powers that derive not from deity but from the machine rendered transcendent through human guidance. Kevin Kelly, editor of *WIRED,* captures a hint of this when he sets down his image of the "collective hive":

A recurring vision swirls in the shared mind of the Net, a vision that nearly every member glimpses, if only momentarily: of wiring human and artificial minds into one planetary soul. . . .

The Net is an organism/machine whose exact size and boundaries are unknown. . . . So vast is this embryonic Net, and so fast is it developing into something else, that no single human can fathom it deeply enough to claim expertise on the whole.

The tiny bees in a hive are more or less unaware of their colony, but their collective hive mind transcends their small bee minds. As we wire ourselves up into a hivish network, many things will emerge that we, as mere neurons in the network, don't expect, don't understand, can't control, or don't even perceive. That's the price for any emergent hive mind.

Kelly's prophetic claims go way over the top for many. Longtime users, dedicated hackers, often think of the *WIRED* sensibility as Newbie—the dreamers are seen as being gee-whiz kids overawed by their toys. There is little conversation between the fantasists and those more oriented to concrete application.

The applied-science types have a point, of course. At present the Net is mainly a tool, an evolving resource. Fascinating, yes, with untold potential, but in the last analysis just wire and plastic and silicon bits. To get from the *here* of the present to the *there* that the visionaries are gushing about would require not just tremendous technological advances and unthinkable infusions of development capital, but also a collective will of the strength that founds new nations. But the visionaries—the ones I've read and talked to—are undeterred. They believe in the Net; they know that the experience is bringing thousands of converts over every day.

And the experience is hard to deny. The newcomer quickly feels the pull of it. How readily the curtain parts, how easily a few typed commands can lever us into a place unlike anything we know from daily life. Mastery brings increased rewards. I've watched more than a few users, seen the call response that kicks in between person and machine, studied the pinball fixity. There is clicking and pausing—flat, percussive rhythms—but otherwise a dense silence supervenes. Between eye and screen a swirling energy. Total absorption. Outside the cone of focus the clock hands move; inside, timelessness. And getting off-line is like coming down from a high. Reentry is hard, harder than leaving a friendly bar. When the screen finally dissolves into blankness you get the deflating balloon sense of everything out there going on without you. People often speak of it as an addiction; counseling is available.

The visionaries know that the center of balance has shifted, that the Net is moving from the fringe toward the center. Revolutionary scenarios are not nonsensical. The empiricists are looking at the phenomenon synchronically, their minds are tied up in minutiae. A diachronic time scan gives a whole other picture. Move the decades in and out of the viewfinder like a series of transparencies: 1950, 1960, 1970, 1980, 1990. . . . If we isolate just computer-related developments, our motion study resembles nothing so much as a dire proliferation of cells. A growth so rapid and inexorable that some sort of total conquest seems just over the horizon. A few decades ago there were a handful of select professionals and government operatives moving data along limited computer networks. Now there are those 25 million users. How can anyone argue that computer and Net are just tools, just ways to manage information and facilitate its transmission? The effect of massive individual and collective engagement must in some way alter fundamental human patterns. It must, in time, alter the humans themselves.

How can this *not* be the case? All human history is, in the last analysis, an account of change—evolution, if you will—from hard tribal isolation to ever more complex societal arrangements. Ours is significantly a history of technology freeing us stage by stage from the fundamental tasks of survival and changing the terms of existence in the process. The coming of the Net is but the latest instance of a development that began with the invention of the club, the wheel, and the stylus raking symbols into the mud.

It would be one thing if we did just make use of the computer as a tool, adding it to our repertoire. But we don't. We enter, instead, into complex psychological relations. We identify, we fetishize—we can't seem to help it. Sherry Turkle, in her book *The Second Self: Computers and the Human Spirit,* explores precisely this blurring of the line between self and computer. She discovers a slipperiness that has everything to do with the fact that computer processes and human mental operations share certain key features in common.

As Susan, one of the many MIT students Turkle interviewed, expresses it: "I believe that the mind is just a computer, but one of the programs that runs it gets to see the stuff that filters up from the dumber agents all of the time." She is echoed by her colleague, Mark, who affirms his view that "the brain can be modeled using components emulated by modern digital parts. At no time does any part of the brain function in a way that cannot be emulated in digital or analog logic."

Granted, Turkle is studying a select group of "tekkies," but these same ideas, in simpler form, are finding their way into mainstream thinking. As Turkle writes: "The computer, like a Rorschach inkblot test, is a powerful projective medium." Not only do people tend to see the machine as being like a mind, but they can even take the next step. They can confer upon it some of the aptitudes and potentials of consciousness itself. They extend to the computer volition, intuitive ability, even personality.

What we find at work at a deeper psychic level are, I suspect, some of the same subterranean needs and reflexes that millennia ago issued in totemic rites. There has been a gradual historic shift. We have seen the deified object shift from inanimate fetish to anthropomorphized deity. The widespread secularization of our age has not quelled those same impulses, but it has changed the forms they take. It is now common to find mature, educated people fetishizing the microchip and all of the operations it makes possible. The chip, rather than its engineers, is seen as infallible; it is a kind of wafer, affording if not redemption then transcendence—complete mastery over data.

Cultural context is everything here. Such projections upon something that is, finally, inanimate were once unthinkable—the machine's functioning was too obviously mechanical. The computer, by contrast, conceals its software much as the brain conceals the mind. There is an unfathomable gap between what we can grasp with the senses as cause and what issues as effect.

But the physical near-impenetrability of microprocessors and binary codes is only part of the reason we vest this technology with powers and attributes it does not yet possess. Every bit as important as our view of the computer is our changing view of ourselves. This is where context impinges. We are currently in the midst of a set of developments in the cognitive and psychological sciences, in the arts and in intellectual theory, and in artificial-intelligence research which are all transforming in a very profound way how we think about the world and our place in it. Indeed, about the very meaning of being human. The whole system of relations between self and other selves, and between self and nature, is being altered. This naturally bears on our understanding of the Net and a host of allied technologies.

And these developments? They are not any one thing, though what is striking, at least from a distance, is how kindred they are. There appears to be a strong fundamental connection between social constructionism in psychology—the theory that neither personality nor behaviors issue from a core self, but are constructed moment to moment under shifting societal constraints—and deconstruction, the aesthetic theory that works of art and literature are not coherent creations by individuals but are, rather, subtly masked ideologies and pillagings of the tradition. In these disciplines, the formerly bedrock premise of the self is subjected to a shattering pressure and the idea of an autonomous, bounded "I" is all but discarded. The self is refigured as a kind of locus, or site, where diverse energies and impulses converge.

Artificial-intelligence theory goes even further. Following a computational model of mental functioning, AI theorists assert that the brain is just "meat," a data-processing system that will one day be replicated, then improved, by machines. There is no place in AI, or in these other disciplines, for the sentimental idea of soul or spirit. That ennobling notion of self—self as connected to or embodying some higher mystery—is dismissed as silly. "Show me this spirit, this soul," says the disinterested scientist. And indeed, standing among plastic and wires, in front of streamlined screens, it does begin to seem that there was some mistake, that those old intuitions must have been wrong.

The whole business seems to come down to a basic change in paradigms—to a shift from a belief in a sovereign, bounded self (the Renaissance ideal) to a belief in transpersonal process. Discussing the AI community gathered around MIT's Marvin Minsky, Turkle writes: "For them, the suggestion that there must be an 'I' in order for thinking to happen is, as Minsky likes to say, 'prescientific.' That is, prior to scientific models of mind. The AI scientist belongs to a culture deeply committed to a view that thought does not need a unitary agent who thinks." Referring to a well-known debate between AI theorists and philosopher John Searle, she explains: "Searle sticks tenaciously to the primacy of things over process. He looks for a man in the room, a neuron in the brain, for a self in the mind. His AI opponents stick just as tenaciously to the primacy of process over things."

As the Net—computer use in general—keeps extending its empery, the basic AI model of cognitive functioning naturally gains in the marketplace. The intellectual climate promotes reliance on the technology, and the proliferation of computers and users intensifies the climate. The overall transition to computerized communications networks is made all the more likely by the assumption that mind and psyche and the chip-driven "neural" networks are in some way kindred. This should give us serious pause. After all, the horrifying thing about the Frankenstein creation lay not in its difference from us but in its skewed likeness, and in the fact that the electricity of "life" was circulating through formerly dead matter.

These are not thoughts from up close. We are not likely to think them when we are accessing needed information or sending an E-mail message to a faraway friend. But step away for a moment to ponder the whole phenomenon systemically and the dire perspective—or, for some, the exalting perspective—comes into view. Then it is possible to imagine it, the neural infrastructure, for what may in time acquire the character of Kelly's "hivish network," his "planetary soul." And we have to ask it: Are we not thrusting ourselves willy-nilly into an electronic collectivity that cuts against the very foundations of subjective individuality?

The idealized large-scale functioning of the Net—the Net once it actually becomes a high-performance info-sphere wrapped around our old Earth—will surely work in ways that are antithetical to selfhood as we have defined it through the ages. The user's time/space coordinates, not to mention his sense of boundedness, of subjective containment, must sustain a warping pressure. The Net essentially models the AI premise of the decentered nature of thought. The detached, open-ended communication that it fosters disrupts the formerly unquestioned sense of the self as a unitary agent who thinks. The user quickly grows accustomed to interchange that is web-like in its nature. Exchange is not bound by the old imperatives. Detached from time-and-space determinants, ideas and information are decontextualized ("liberated," say some), allowed to mingle in hitherto unknown combinations. This, too, is exalting, emancipating. The user is relieved of the crushing burden of having everything he says tied to a perception of who he is.

[You hear Xana's voice in your ear. She pages "hey."]
—Hey yoself, whacchu doin?
—Workin, stressin, needin a tickle really
—Tickle given, and another for good measure. The heat's a killin here. There?
—Here, too. Everywhere. I'm in hankie and flip-flops
—Where's the hankie? Lemme picture this
—South, movin north
—Ow. And you're tall and blond, right?
—In your dreams, soldier. I'm four-eight if I stand on a brick
—Then we're a match. I never went out for b-ball either
—Shame. But hey, tonight I'll be your purrfect stranger, what say? Or wouldja jes like to philosophize?
—Tell me about that hankie. Color? Present position?

All of this is theoretical, of course, and derives from a projection of greatly expanded and ramified use of the Net. But even used intensively, the Net will not straightaway rewire us. Fly through cyberspace as we might, we will still have to come back to attend to the laundry, to make dinner. But sustained immersion will exert gradual effects—it's bound to. It will change us just as the wheel, the rifle, and the telephone have changed us. And in this there are grounds for worry. Because the threshold of difference between computer process and certain mental functions is not high, and because we have been primed by countless prior adaptations to earlier technologies, we may without sufficient critical awareness slip into accepting the ersatz. We may take the abstraction of human exchange as a negotiable substitute for the real thing and allow ourselves to become accustomed to it.

We do not have to look very far to find evidence—this is already happening. On the front page of the *New York Times* (March 8, 1994), we find a story entitled "Strangers, Not Their Computers, Build a Network in a Time of Grief." We read about the death of David Alsberg, a well-known figure in the so-called electronic community, who was killed by a stray bullet fired in Times Square. As Peter H. Lewis reports, Alsberg "left behind a wife, a young son, and hundreds of grieving friends in both of the neighborhoods in which he lived: one in Astoria, Queens, and the other in . . . cyberspace."

The story is interesting not only for what it tells us about the public perception of the Net, but also for the language it uses to explore the phenomenon of grieving for an individual who was, in some still viable sense of the word, a stranger. As Lewis explains: "In a world where physical contact is impossible, Mr. Alsberg's cyberspace neighbors consoled each other over the senseless loss of a mutual friend. And in their collective grieving, they demonstrated an impulse for togetherness that is as modern as the digital age and as old as humankind. For as more people become citizens of cyberspace, they are forging relationships they describe as being as rewarding as their face-to-face friendships."

Describing these computer-based relationships, Lewis writes: "It is common to hear stories of people laughing or weeping while they interact with others through the computer screen, of people so attached to their on-line relationships—they become addicted to the Net—that they seek counselling." Though this is only a feature story—soft news—it does point us toward the deeper issue, suggesting that the boundary we draw between the real world and the proxy world—between actual and virtual relationships—can be alarmingly loose. So loose as to infect the language, playing havoc with the etymological sense of things. Though the article is perhaps intended to warm the heart, to suggest that cyberspace is not a cold and data-driven place but one that supports genuine relationships and carries emotional content, the implications seem to me chilling.

Consider how casually some of our most freighted terms are injected into this new context and weigh the assumptions behind the attributions. The on-line world is called a "neighborhood," and Alsberg's cyberspace neighbors are said to "console" each other over "the senseless loss of a mutual friend." Lewis speaks of "togetherness" and "relationships" without ironic inflection and betrays no surprise when he hears people describe their relationships as being "as rewarding as their face-to-face friendships."

I have to say that the first thing I think of is George Orwell's celebrated essay "Politics and the English Language," wherein he shows how language is routinely prostituted to serve political ends. Something similar is at issue here. We are not so much dealing with euphemism and concealment, the heart of Orwell's case, but we do see a similar pattern of language from the affective side of the spectrum being applied to what are, in the last analysis, abstracted phenomena. What is alarming is that so many people accept and even endorse the descriptions—they find "neighborhood" or "relationship" the adequate word for the situation.

Lewis is not an anomaly in writing thus. He is articulating a commonly shared set of attitudes. People *do* speak of chat- and bulletin-board contacts as friends and see nothing unusual about the idea of people grieving on-line over a person they've never met off-line.

Some of these notions, extrapolated mainly from reading and from discussions with Net users, were already finding their way to the page when I had to leave to go traveling. I was in another town, giving a paper on the related topic of reading in an electronic age, when I noticed a woman off to the side watching me very intently. She was in a wheelchair, and when the time came for questions and comments she seemed at the verge of speech, but more clamorous voices prevailed. Afterwards, however, she approached me and asked if we could arrange a time to talk. She said that she wanted me to see the other side of the picture.

I visited F. at her apartment the next day. As soon as she had ushered me in, she presented me with a thick sheaf of materials. She had taken the time to download an array of conversations and bulletin-board postings—a sampler from the Net. But before she would explain them to me, she wanted to tell her story. Two years ago, said F., she had been in an automobile accident and had nearly died. She had suffered massive trauma and had lost a limb. Normally an outgoing and active person, she had fallen into a deep depression. She stopped going out, avoided friends. She felt she had nothing of her former life and that there was no way back. Then, through a series of decisive coincidences, she found her way on-line and began to dabble in the Net. One contact led to another and she grew more fascinated. Finally she arrived at Lambda MOO (a MOO is a consensual community, a virtual place tenanted by a group of like-minded—or contentious—individuals). There, she explained, she found friends, playmates, and fantasy partners; there she discovered debate and an impulse to political engagement. F. is now a citizen of Lambda MOO and spends the bulk of her free time there.

"It saved me," confesses F. "I had all these feelings and needs—I *am* very sociable by nature—and I was not gratifying them out in what we call 'real life.' " Doubtless she guessed where my thoughts were tending, for she then cautioned me not to think of her life in Lambda MOO as unreal, as some simple fantasy compensation. "I heard what you were saying last night," she said. "You've got to stop thinking in terms of a black-and-white split, of real versus unreal. There are all kinds of realities out there. This experience is real, too—real in the way a dream is real."

F. then shows me what she has downloaded for me: transcripts of on-line chat, much of it familiar, breezy, not unlike what one might get if one copied telephone conversations between friends; some pages sampling what appears to be a role-playing game among a number of people, all of whom have fanciful handles; some poetry and prose exchanged by writerly MOO members; and then a hefty batch of postings on two issues currently under intensive debate: "mediation" (procedures for self-government by MOO members) and "rape."

Lambda MOO was first founded by one Pavel Curtis of Xerox Park. For a long time it was "run" by an oligarchy of "wizards"—decision-making moved from the top down. But now the wizards have abdicated (under what circumstances, I don't know) and with some 2,000 members and more coming on daily, there has been an initiative to establish a self-governing democracy. The most pressing question, apart from how to constitute an egalitarian on-line community, is what to do about new-comers. There are those who would seal the borders, denying admission to new people, and those who uphold freedom and openness as the fundamental tenets not just of the Net, but of Lambda MOO as well. The postings show, beneath an admirable facade of reasoned civility, a fierce struggle, a kind of German reunification in miniature. F. herself is deeply engaged. "This has taught me more about politics," she announces, "than I got from all my years of college."

Date: Sun Apr 10 15:58:02 1994 PDT
From: Sunny (#58292)
To: *Mediation (#27485)
Subject: Nancy / message 520 on *mediation

I find it untenable and unfathomable that we would ask people to re-spect and abide by a system whereby they can be held to account for alleged behaviors in front of people who, you claim would refuse to do "assigned reading and take a quiz"—to indicate that they understand and comprehend and are capable of the responsibilities of their weighty job—with responsibilities and abilities, e.g., @toad, @newt, etc., come expectations of illustrating one's capabilities to handle and carry out the expected tasks.

Being a mediator is not "required" for a player at Lambda MOO. It's a volunteer position. And because it carries powers of high impact to one's use of this MOO, I don't believe it is unreasonable to ask players to demonstrate their committment to the proper and prudent practice of it by doing some homework.

In real life, agencies that have authority over a citizen's life, professionals who one would consult (legal, medical problems), all have guidelines, standards of practice, ethics restrictions, education. We require this in real life as something tangible to rely upon if we are being asked for something in return. In this case, our compliance with the system and our physical presence, our "body's participation."

The suggestion of perhaps a mediator sponsoring another player seems like "the blind leading the blind." Who is vouching for those who already

ARE mediators and have no background, no training, no common understanding of their role?

But it is the debate over "rape" that seems to cut to the heart of the deeper philosophical questions raised by the Net and Net society. Rape in these precincts is defined not as a physical violation, but as a linguistic one—a community member trying to engage another in an offensive or violent or sexually undesired act of imagining; it can extend to nearly any unwanted sort of address. Reading through these postings I can't help recalling the public flap between journalist Carlin Romano and legal theorist Catherine MacKinnon. Romano began a review in the pages of the *Nation* by imagining that he was raping MacKinnon. MacKinnon then claimed that he *had* raped her, arguing that imaginative possession against her will was a violation of her rights. Mere words, one might contend, but in the age of the Net mere words have acquired a whole new valence. We have to rethink all questions of linguistic expression and accountability. Language has different consequences in virtual environments which are nothing *but* words. An understanding of virtuality will require a full reexamination of reality itself.

Message 39 on *Ballot: AntiRape (#60535):
Date: Thu May 5 14:12:22 1994 PDT
From: Kilik (#2819)
To: *Petition: AntiRape
Subject: violence! = rape wOOf!

I've haggled with Mickey about this, but have to strongly disagree with him (we've agreed to disagree). A rape necessarily is a non-consensual sexual act. Mere violence (mayhem) or humiliation (rudeness/slander) is not rape. Not to say they aren't offensive, but rape is very different, and in my opinion, much more acute. Rape is a kind of hate crime. It is intensely personal, and it plausibly hints at unwanted attention in real life. Being virtually beheaded by a stranger in the Living Room, while annoying and unmannerly, does not have the same bad karma. Not to say I'm for virtual beheadings. I disputed and won judgement against a player for writing beheading bonker-code, but it was not rape code.

If we are going to consider @toading for anti-social acts, then we must be careful to reserve it only for the most extreme cases where an overwhelming majority of us feel the line has been crossed. RPG attacks, bonker verbs and even virtual muggings don't in my dog-mind meet the test of extremeness. In the long run the danger we face is having a large range of impolite behavior be at the risk of @toading. When @boot was implemented, the provocations started out being unwanted moo-sex, but rapidly became less extreme.

Actually, my stand on moo-rape is quite extreme: I find it intolerable behavior, condemn it in the strongest possible terms and advocate zero tolerance. Since telephone lines are used to access the moo, moo rape constitutes telephone harassment and is IRL a violation of law. Maintaining the functional integrity of the moo requires that we not tolerate users who violate RL laws on-moo, and hence such users are subject to immediate @toading by anywiz that has even a hint of what is going on. While many moo-ers may not think the position I've stated is legally correct, it is legally plausible and that is enough to subject lambdamoo to risk.

It will not be long before RL law starts being made explicitly in this area, how we've treated this problem will likely be considered when drafting such law.

I left my meeting with F. in a state of agitation. My prior assumptions had been tested, in some ways undermined, and I was confused about my stand. Could one even *have* a stand on something as vast and inchoate as the Net? I had to concede that there was a good deal more energy and life in these unseen places than I had at first imagined—it was not all about nerds playing dungeon games. Interchanges on the Net so clearly filled real needs and brought diverse kinds of fulfillment. Indeed, some of these sites were home to a passionate and productive debate I rarely encountered . . . IRL. It would be willful blindness to ignore the private and social worlds that are at every moment being constituted through the wires. Suddenly Kelly's visionary scenario did not seem so far-fetched after all. I could readily imagine that as the outside world gets messier and more frightening, as circumstances propitious for genuine geographical community get harder and harder to sustain, *and* as the strands of the Net get more finely strung, then cyberlife might really begin to make serious inroads on the "real." Especially if people are willing—and able—to make the adjustment to proxy interaction and still believe that their basic human needs are somehow being met. Perhaps the next evolutionary development for *Homo sapiens* will be to become *Homo virtualis.* People may pull away en masse from the givens of nature, the defining constraints of place and time and immediate interaction, in order to carry on the business of living at one remove—virtually, without the impediment of immediacy, the confinements of gender, age, appearance, and perceived sexual status.

But we must proceed with great care. If there is a danger about our growing reliance on the Net it is this: that it levels a serious, if only barely registered, threat to our hitherto unassailable idea of presence. Unmediated face-to-face interchange, one "I" speaking to another, is the basis—the bullion, if you will—upon which all human communication is secured. A letter is posted as a representative transcript of speech—the signature vouches for the sender's presence. A telephone call is founded upon the identity that inheres in voice. Indeed, philosopher Walter Ong, in his book *The Presence of the Word,* has argued that the core of our spirituality is rooted in the immediacies (im-mediacy = without anything between) of the spoken—initially the speaking of the word by God, and later through our unfolding of our being to one another via direct spoken encounter. "Sound," for Father Ong, "is the special sensory key to interiority." It is through speech that we manifest what is concealed to the eye.

Significantly, interiority is the very thing we put at risk as we engage the electronic media. To plug into a system is to agree to behave according to the rules of that system; it is to direct the focus outward, away from the self. When the communication is not face-to-face, when it derives from an exchange of codes between terminals, a peculiar gain/loss formula asserts itself. The user attains greater access, greater reach, and can expedite message delivery in a way never before possible. But with this comes a sense of diminution. Perhaps it is as Bishop Berkeley long ago theorized: "To be is to be perceived." Our sense of our own presence in the world has much to do with our being the objects of other people's awareness. But on the Net awareness is only partial. The many people we communicate with know us not by sight, by voice, by aura, by anything except our typed comments. We exist for them, but in a lesser way. And no matter how far-flung is our on-line acquaintanceship, quantity cannot compensate us for the loss of this quality. F. acknowledged this as well. "The Net," she said, "can help in a lot of ways. But can it help in that deepest, most important way? I don't know, probably not."

The Net is finally about process, not product; it is about energy and message, not things. Yet the world we know as creatures of the senses has always been centrally, if not entirely, about things. Flesh-and-blood people, objects, places. This fact is not lost on hard-core Net users. Often they try to compensate for the barrenness of virtual sites by describing environments into being, creating rooms which they furnish, and—yes— planting gardens, building fences, devising neighborhoods. We read their careful detailings: "To the left of the knoll is a gnarled oak tree, next to it a worn patch of ground that still bears the traces of a recent picnic. . . ." There is pathos here. These users must know how forced this sounds. They must know that they cannot have it both ways. Go to a no-place, by all means, if that is what you need to do, but don't try to pretend that the no-place is actual, a home. It cannot be.

The Net is neural in its nature, and like all neural systems it requires that impedances be surmounted so that the impulses may flow freely. What we think of as the warps and eccentricities of personality—the recalcitrant stuff of selfhood—these are, from the point of view of the Net, impedance. Individuality appears to flourish, but it is a willed thing, just like the folksy orneriness of CB radio communiqués. Moreover, the Net has no purchase at all on meditative solitude. The time on-line is always Now—the zone one enters has little in common with the duration state that is the seedbed of all deeper reflection. Indeed, the system is not only inhospitable to the spiritual impulse, it works against it. In a world becoming increasingly secularized, the Net is the apotheosis of secularism. It threatens to become a non-spiritual substitute for deity. When the dream is finally realized, when every home is a node and all the nodes are connected, humming one to another, then we will have met the Nietzschean challenge: We will have become as God. But Nietzsche imposed his task upon the individual, whereas we will have done the deed collectively. On-line, we will be part of that entity named by the ancient philosophers, the one whose center is everywhere and whose circumference is nowhere. But this protoplasmic approximation of consciousness will not be the spiritualization of matter dreamed by Teilhard de Chardin. There will be no transcendent apotheosis, no supping on anything higher than ourselves. Brought all together we will, alas, just be what we are.

As I have been reading and speculating, channeling my energies toward the writing of this piece, I have also been carving out a counter-track for myself. I have been reading the novels of Cormac McCarthy and trying to figure out the source of their profound impact on me. I have been involved in his fictional world to an unusual degree, moving from novel to novel with a zealousness that has surprised me. At first I ascribed this simply to McCarthy's powers as a stylist and his darkly obsessive thematic focus. But now I grasp that it is something more—something extra-aesthetic. My immersion, I see, has been in part determined by everything else that I have been experiencing, reading, and thinking— that is, by my engagement with the Net. I have been using the novels as places of rescue, as sanctuaries. I go to them to regain a sense of proportion that I have feared myself losing. Another author might have served just as well, I can't be sure.

I have, at one and the same time, both incorporated my reading of McCarthy into my thinking about the Net *and* changed my reading by virtue of my preoccupations. I mean: When I conjure the world as it might become if the Net prevails, it is in part against the backdrop of the world as it is bodied forth in the novels. A world predicated upon the recognition of immemorial human solitude. Here, on the page (another virtual place, I suppose), are people caught in the implacable grip of their destinies. Their actions are played out in specific landscapes in a time that feels slow, very nearly palpable. In a time, that is, that knows nothing yet of the atomizing effects of modern technologies. And when I enter that world, it is with the piercing awareness of ways of being vanishing once and for all from our midst. Not just the moods and rhythms of some one prior epoch—these wane regularly as the world revolves—but ways that have governed human life from the first.

I don't know how better to establish this sense than by quoting. Here, very nearly at random, is a passage from McCarthy's *All the Pretty Horses:*

They ate by oillight at a small painted pine table. The mud walls about them were hung with old calendars and magazine pictures. On one wall was a framed tin retablo of the Virgin. Under it was a board supported by two wedges driven into the wall and on the board was a small green glass with a blackened candlestub on it. The Americans sat shoulder to shoulder along one side of the table and the two little girls sat on the other side and watched them in a state of breathlessness. The woman ate with her head down and the man joked with them and passed the plates. They ate beans and tortillas and a chile of goatmeat ladled up out of a clay pot. They drank coffee from enameled tin cups and the man pushed the bowls toward them and gestured elaborately. Deben comer, he said.

What I find here, what gathers around me as a kind of weather as I read, is a feeling about the primary components of human experience—the near presence of nature, the sensuous thingness of things, the unbroken quality of passing time, and a near-sacramental awareness of human beings which has everything to do with presence and, perhaps indistinguishably, boundedness.

This is so basic as to be almost unworthy of remark—yet of late it has become worthy. The conditions of modernity have gradually removed us from this. With every passing year we lose further these givens: the awareness of time, space, thingness, and other flesh-and-blood individuals. The awareness does not survive easily among the clicking of keys and the exchange of the myriad signals we use to guide ourselves through the new virtual space that encloses us. And as our electronic environment starts to feel like a new home, we lose our orientation to true north. We have to ask: Is human nature endlessly malleable, or do we accept modification only up to a certain point? My instinct tells me that we can only travel a certain distance from the world that our deepest instincts are programmed to. After that, who knows? A betrayal of the given must exact consequences. We may be risking an alienation unprecedented in our species history, an unbearable lightness of being that we will have no choice but to keep on bearing.

KENT CARROLL

The Facts of Fiction and the Fiction of Facts

Kent Carroll is the co-founder of the New York book publishing firm Carroll & Graf. For many years he was an editor at Grove Press and came to know firsthand the difference between publishing and the brand marketing that passes for it at present.

The annals of modern book publishing are filled with complaints of a continuous descent from a golden age into an age of bronze. What is rare is the opportunity to hear them preached to an audience other than the choir. Kent Carroll is a contemporary publisher who has no desire to tamper with the traditional formula for publishing: a sound mixture of commerce and the new, as classically exemplified in Alfred Knopf welcoming in poets at the front door while shipping Kahlil Gibran out the back.

But at least Alfred knew which door was which. Now, Carroll wonders, who is watching the watchman?

IT WOULD BE POSSIBLE to argue that, despite all the junk that is regularly published by New York trade houses who once took seriously their cultural brief to stand as custodians of the word, intellectual standards have not changed significantly in the past decade or so. This argument would be supported by all the good books that are released every year. And indeed, there is much evidence in support of this position. A list of all such books would be long and impressive.

But it is more fun to argue the opposite, namely, that there has been a decline in standards, or, more accurately, that shared and commonly understood values, and, yes, principles, have been replaced with a simple dictate that has the added benefit of providing an excuse. Simply put: publishers have no larger obligation than to make available what the public wants to read. So, if readers demonstrate an interest in artful fiction or the knowledgeable discussion of public affairs, we'll do a bit of that too. But what they most often want—crave, really—is miracles and magic, and sensation, confirmation that their worst suspicions or most extravagant hopes are true. So we'll give them heaps, stacks of the stuff. We'll even toss into the bundle some cheap laughs—check with the lawyers and make sure rural, southern whites don't have an anti-defamation group yet—and let's get *The Redneck Joke Book* onto the shelves.

The point is not just to assert that things have gotten worse but rather to identify what is being published and why. Conditions do not have to deteriorate to be judged deplorable. Just ask anyone over thirty-five who used to go to the movies regularly. The best evidence of what's going on is the best-seller lists, a generally accurate accounting of what readers are voting for. And here the junk outnumbers the good by, say, 100 to 1.

Consider a recent paperback chart ranking fifteen titles. In fiction there are five thrillers led by the inexhaustible John Grisham, five romances best represented by Danielle Steele, two mysteries, and three novels that could fairly be deemed of some quality. Among the nonfiction entries are four books designed to cure our spiritual malaise, which seems to have a lot to do with the possibility of dying some day. There are two books on how men and women might get on happily with one another (nobody ever seems to get this right); a lengthy observation on how your dog is more interesting than your neighbor; a humor book on life's easy pleasures as well as its ordeals (the latter included so you can grow as a person); an investigative report on the Clinton White House; an influential business book for corporate managers; a roaming history of theology; and two inspirational reminiscences by black women.

The most authoritative of these lists—that is, the one that affects both reputations and sales—comes from the *New York Times Book Review*. Next to their paperback hit parade are brief notices about new books specifically recommended by the *Review*. None of these titles is on the best-seller list. And none is likely to be. The same is true of a comparison between the hardcover list and the editors' choice of worthwhile reading. Does this discrepancy between the books the editors single out for their authoritative stamp and the ones book buyers so obviously prefer tell us anything? A bit, but not much that should surprise. People would rather read Margaret Truman (actually, Ms. Truman's ghost writer) than Edith Wharton; rather feel heartache than think about the difficulties facing the new democracies in Latin America; rather learn about serial killers than Mozart; rather understand the sad, short life of an AIDS-infected athlete than that of Charles de Gaulle.

Of the thirty hardcover titles ranked, there are two novels of wit and intelligence and four nonfiction books that make an honest, if overwrought attempt to address issues of current concern—from computers to plagues. It is doubtful, however, if any of these books, except, perhaps, the P. D. James crime story, will be read or remembered five years from now.

If we accept these best-seller lists as representative of what the reading public cares and thinks about, we can draw some conclusions. People clearly want to believe. Or find someone to blame: Are you thirty-seven and unhappy? Don't you know that it has nothing to do with the poor choices you've made as an adult? Ever consider it might all stem from something awful that happened to you *in utero?* Can't remember back that far? Have we got a book for you!

The current version of the self-help advice book of the past seems aimed rather at the self-absorbed. Such titles are now more often about asserting claims against family and society than they are about the rewards of discipline and learning. Still we call them self-help and, for our purpose here, include the inspirational and the confessional as well as the practical. What distinguishes these books today is that none is the least bit tentative. Nor do they even suggest approaches to the most complex problems we face, the ones that have vexed the minds of philosophers and resisted the experiments of science. They never, it seems, take up a question without guaranteeing to provide an answer. They are reasonably sure they have the Holy Grail and will let you into the inner sanctum for a look for just $22.95 ($14.95 in paperback).

Afraid of death? Worried that, after a divorce or two and a half-dozen failed affairs, passion and—dare we say it?—true love might not still be possible after forty? Can't locate the road to wealth on $30,000 a year? Lie awake at night because your four-year-old son turns every stick he finds into a gun? This sort of pablum has been around for some years. What is most revealing now is that (1) it has seeped over into fiction and (2) much of it is written by people who have little mastery of the language and very little talent for thought. Whether true or made up, the distinctions that used to separate the writer from the reader—things like surprise, originality, and clear, persuasive attempts to get at the truth—are collapsing.

As this is being written—and one suspects for many weeks to come—a remarkable best-seller is something called *The Celestine Prophecy.* The qualifier "something" is used deliberately. According to a magazine article published in the summer of 1994, when this self-published novel, already recording huge sales and devoted fans, was circulated to the managerial staff of its new licensor, Warner Books, most of the department heads believed it to be nonfiction. That is, after having read this simple tale of a quest (in Peru, no less) for the rules of spiritual enlightenment, they believed it to be true. It is not clear from the article if these career professionals thought it was a cure for all one's woes, or if they only bought the idea that the author had actually undertaken this journey. But given the reality that Warner then proceeded to republish the book in a deliberately ambiguous fashion—there is nothing on the dust jacket that clearly states it is a work of fiction—editorial judgment must at some point have given way to marketing strategy.

An observer might well wonder, if he has read this astonishingly silly book, how the good folks at Warner could possibly be confused. Isn't there a fundamental difference between fiction and nonfiction, a difference that is, well, obvious? Don't we evaluate the distilled information, moral lessons, and counsel available from a history, a biography, or a memoir in different ways than we thrill to the exploits and adventures of created characters in a novel, a short story, a fantasy? Are we not more likely to shape our values or change our behavior by learning about admirable things that are verifiable as compared to things conjured out of someone's imagination?

Great writers—Eliot, Dickens, Faulkner—created fictional worlds populated by characters whose lives and times impress themselves upon us and evoke emotional responses easily the equal of any actual biography. The difference, of course, between the yarn, no matter how well spun, and the real fact is how we choose to factor what is told into our judgments about matters that require choice. We only have le Carré's word for it that Karla surrendered, but though one can interpret Napoleon's strategic decisions in any number of ways, that he lost at Waterloo is not in question.

Given the degree to which these two modes of writing currently slop over onto one another and given the deliberate attempts to mingle established conventions for the unwary reader, as in the famous and self-labeled "nonfiction novels" of Truman Capote and Norman Mailer, and the interpretive biographies studded with invented dialogue by people from Erik Erikson to Joe McGinniss, we almost always make an attempt, or at least we did, to distinguish between the two forms. It seemed, in the days before those parodies of scholarship, women's studies and black studies, emerged, that it was important to do so.

But why, one might ask? Does it really make any difference that we honor the life and accomplishments of Lincoln by erecting statues and naming the places of our civic activity after him, but not, say, after Jay Gatsby, or after that old rapscallion, Huckleberry Finn? It should, but something has changed. If feminist historical theory can proclaim, imitating Henry Ford, that history is bunk, written by men to exclude the contributions of women, and if professors at reputable colleges can teach students attempting to learn about their African forebears that myth is superior to fact, opinion to accumulated evidence, the distinction between fiction and nonfiction may seem small beer.

That the influence exerted by words on the page is as often placed in the service of politics and commerce as it is in the service of art and knowledge is not entirely new. What seems original to our contemporary culture is the absence of gatekeepers who acknowledge the difference by withholding their approval of it.

Some of these cultural changes can best be observed on television, our principal source of information and entertainment, which are often one and the same. If daytime television is any gauge, the shameful carryings-on by a not insignificant part of our society captivate millions of viewers.

Much of what is being confessed to between lunch and dinner used to be the province of fiction—tawdry romances, crime stories, pornography. We knew the possibility that a middle-aged woman could seduce her teenaged daughter's inexperienced but endlessly enthusiastic boyfriend. But it was rare, wasn't it, and didn't it happen way over there? One learned of a woman whose love was strong enough to save the stranger who raped her, of men who were instructed by God to murder prostitutes, of wife-swapping honeymooners only in what were once called cheap novels. Cheap because they were low-priced, pocket-sized paperbacks and, of course, cheap because even though the evildoers get theirs on the last page, their purpose was to titillate by celebrating behavior no sane person would aspire to. Not anymore.

As real life, especially that variant that glows from the television screen, has overwhelmed imaginary life, the Jim Thompsons, the Grace Metaliouses, the anonymous writers whose scribblings were censored for two centuries have now been rendered pikers when compared to the perversity poured forth in mock horror by Jerry, Geraldo, Jenny, Maury, Montel, and Sally Jessy. It's not that pulp-fiction artists were above such cruel display of the worst in people. It's just that as storytellers, they knew they couldn't get away with it. It wouldn't work as fiction. What can any writer do with characters like these, whose acts were so casually insipid, so carelessly banal in their grotesque consequences—except perhaps shoot them early on? The men who brag about the sheer number of illegitimate children they fathered, the women who marry condemned murderers, the people "addicted" to love, sex, or shopping seemingly abound. There's no convincing motive here; no disguised intentions. The conflict that could propel a narrative line is missing. Once you're over the shock that anyone would publicly and voluntarily display such small, mean aberrations, not even surprise is left. These are not the materials from which 192 pages of suspense used to be fashioned.

And so, deprived of their natural materials, unable to compete with images and voices that are served up free on the TV screen, a segment of commercial publishing has turned elsewhere. And in doing so, they've stumbled on a kind of motherlode. They reason, if we can't do it on the outside with characters and situations the reader is unlikely to encounter, let's turn inside where there's some virgin territory to be mined. Let's do feelings. This has proved most profitable.

Another way to think about the enormous success of these suspect books—the celebrity biographies, the Kennedy assassination theories, the preposterous fantasies posing as thrillers—is to consider them as part of a cultural-democratization process. Why should talent be a requirement or a barrier? Readers now seem to identify as much with the author and with the idea of writing a book as once they identified with the characters. Only a fool would attend a play starring John Gielgud and exit thinking, Gee, I could do that. Not so with books. A remarkable percentage of people writing fiction, especially romances and mysteries, were former habitual readers who said to themselves, I can write as well as they can. And they can. Not as well as Ruth Rendell, surely, but in increasing numbers well enough to get published. Amateurs without benefit of training or the sober restraint of peer review write best-sellers interpreting our recent history; self-appointed activists seek out and find the source of all ills (it's usually a penis); movie stars claiming reincarnation offer solace and salvation from the wisdom they've accumulated since sailing the Nile all those many years ago.

Here book publishing goes to the movies. Never in the history of the world have there been so many self-described artists providing so little art as in today's Hollywood. This is a place where how you dress confers as much creative status as what you've done. Consider that the single indispensable person in the creation of the Academy Award–winning *Forrest Gump* is the author of the novel on which the movie was based. Yet the guy with the Oscar for best screenplay based on another source—that is, the novel—thanked everyone, including his seven children, but never quite got to Winston Groom. Maybe the kids made a bigger contribution.

What this screenwriter knows, what the movie industry has established as a law of nature, is that only success as measured in profit counts and that whoever gets the credit wins. There is a massive, indiscriminate audience out there who will spend lots of dollars for entertainment that promises no thinking will be required. A sizable part of this audience, of course, are thirteen-year-old boys who are unlikely visitors to bookstores. But the principle is the same. If you can tap into adolescent fantasies (in contrast, say, to Stephen Daedalus's uncreated consciousness), into make-believe, into enchanted thinking about love and immortality, and, always, into sex, there is a complicitous audience of millions.

Certainly these materials have always been employed by fiction writers. What has changed is their purpose. Where writers as disparate as Thomas Mann, Charlotte Brontë, and the Marquis de Sade challenged readers with the risk of unbridled passion, the sin of overreaching, or the chaos on the other side of convention's wall, current popular authors produce what might be called proscriptive fiction. Their characters don't take the risks for us so that we are able to learn and understand without having to undergo the danger. Now they offer us the dubious encouragement to emulate their characters. They are, after all, more and more like you or me and the familiar world we inhabit each day. These novels become, then, a kind of ersatz nonfiction. Since we suspect we can't really inflate to the size of a Cathy or Justine or even a Buddenbrook— their experiences of the heart and body are beyond us—and since what we really need is just something to get us through the weekend, give us characters our own size, familiar characters who can show us how we can transform our lives. If they can do it, so can we.

There is also a variety of nonfiction informed and made popular by this democratic leveling. Such works might be called noncognitive, for their central purpose is not to inform or instruct, but rather to administer therapy, of a sort that usually depends on a narcissistic or an aggrandized sense of self. Recurrent words in such texts are "unique" and "creative," especially as applied to the reader. And this flattery is successful. People need to think they are special, that they contain some godlike potential. Who can resist being told they have the power within to reinvent themselves? Bill Clinton can't. Here, experience and common sense seem to provide no shield.

There are doubtless many responsible self-help and inspirational books that offer sensible assistance in everything from investing money to growing flowers or providing comfort. But we are considering books that make the extravagant promise to assist people in discovering their wonderful selves, thus enabling them to blossom, to go forth, and to do—what? These books are not about living the good life in any Platonic sense. They are not in the wise American tradition of Emerson and Carnegie. They are essentially, overwhelmingly, about being selfish. Older, nobler goals that demand expressions of altruism, honor, and loyalty are foreign to their vocabulary. Such quaint beliefs are viewed, when noted at all, as obstacles, as direct barriers to self-actualization. This new breed of book is perversely democratic, tolerant beyond measure, utterly nonjudgmental. All values, ethics, or morality are supremely relative. No act is better than any other—if it makes you feel better, it's okay. Good, bad, right, wrong—these are precepts foisted on you by others. The culprits most often fingered are parents and husbands. Or if a college campus is nearby, add society and even Western civilization, a malignant collective that has somehow singled out decent middle-class Americans for the sole intent of making them unhappy. White men loom very large in all this, which gives you an idea of the dimension of the problem the authors have to overcome.

The techniques so effectively used in the feel-good books are also apparent in the critical studies that wear their ideology like a bright tattoo, the revisionist histories and biographies. Zelda could have been a contender, as great as F. Scott, if only her talent (unique and creative, one assumes) hadn't been stifled because she was a woman. The American political system was always corrupt, designed to be biased by race and sex. Witness old Thomas Jefferson, who refused to acknowledge his slave mistress and their progeny. That there is not a scrap of reliable evidence for this canard is beside the point. It's all in the effect, or rather in how effectively such nonsense can support current claims on society by arousing anger, sympathy, or group solidarity.

Few of today's publishers are agents of change. They are often the least likely people to predict a surprise best-seller. While the occasional book—one like Allan Bloom's *The Closing of the American Mind,* which appears to herald a reexamination of educational attitudes, or one like *The Bridges of Madison County,* which is tagged as the harbinger of resurgent romance—might have wide appeal in reality, far from being prophetic, they actually confirm something that has *already taken place.* As always, there are exceptions. The Free Press was regularly publishing books that dissented from the liberal orthodoxy long before Election Day, November 1994. Random House has now gotten into the act not, one supposes, because their politics have changed but because they want to tap the demonstrated conservative market. Modern publishing responds to public demand; it no longer creates a market for its goods.

Up until about fifteen years ago, the loose idea that governed trade publishing in New York was that editors controlled what was published and their greatest reward was not salary or community status. It was the chance to be the causal agent in the discovery and care of a great writer—to have a shot at secondary immortality. The historic model here was Maxwell Perkins of Scribner's, who edited Fitzgerald, Hemingway, Thomas Wolfe. Linked to this editorial ambition were the legendary publishers, men who believed, more often insisted, that what their houses published and the public read should be an extension of their personalities, their convictions. They were their companies. Their companies were them, with some begrudging nods to the editorial talent they hired: Roger Straus, Alfred Knopf, Barney Rosset.

Rosset is the most interesting of the lot. When he ran Grove Press, he embodied the concept of a publisher exercising his taste and belief. Rosset's instincts were essentially subversive. During the glory days of Grove, roughly 1955 to 1970, Rosset published such writers as Samuel Beckett, Jean Genet, Octavio Paz, and Kenzaburō Oe, and such books as *Last Exit to Brooklyn, City of Night, Games People Play, The Wretched of the Earth, The Autobiography of Malcolm X.* A stunning accomplishment and an impossible one to imagine any current CEO, as they insist upon being called, duplicating. He also understood sexual politics decades before the term was invented and unleashed on an unsuspecting America: *My Secret Life, Romance of Lust,* and *The Story of O.* He risked his company and his private fortune, and maybe his life, to fight to the Supreme Court censorship battles over *Tropic of Cancer, Naked Lunch,* and the movie *I Am Curious (Yellow),* successfully extending the reach of the First Amendment. In doing this, he changed not only what could be written and read, but the way we think about our private lives and public selves.

In much of the current publishing industry, editorial decisions have been usurped by the sales department; a publisher is primarily a marketing executive. And the only document that extols a vision is the profit-

and-loss statement that must be prepared for each title under consideration. In some cases, whether or not the author will sell on television is
decisive in acquiring or rejecting a manuscript. In the realm of popular
nonfiction, it outweighs both subject matter and nasty questions of basic
author literacy.

As publishing becomes more a corporate business—a mature, highly
competitive, and not very profitable business—control of what is published has shifted toward that which is measurable, quantifiable. And so
the old rules get eroded and the standards reassessed in response to
perceived reader interest. Who wants to be Max Perkins when, if you can
find the next Rush Limbaugh or Howard Stern, you could be Rupert
Murdoch's supereditor, Judith Regan. Nowadays, major publishing
houses owned by huge conglomerates abandon manuscripts already
contracted for when they turn out to be overly rude about such seemingly ordinary subjects as college basketball or Walt Disney. And here the
last vestige of editorial responsibility has been given over to the lawyers:
What, after all, is free speech really worth if it costs $250,000 to defend it?

If such tempests were confined to the local bookstore and branch
library with their mix of the sublime and the ridiculous, it would be less
cause for concern. But what we read and the writing we honor by reading
it do not exist in a discrete arena. They both reflect and reinforce the
larger culture. Just as there is now slight reward for risking investment
capital on books which do not bring with them a reliable readership or
service an identifiable need, there is no penalty for purveying the most
intellectually insulting rubbish. Publishers did not dream up this situation. They were taught. They learned from the communities in which
books play a central role: academia and politics. The lesson was that
standards are secondary to self-interest, forging a career, accumulating
power.

Moviemakers showed it was possible to run to the end of the rainbow
and dip both hands into a pot of gold. Television institutionalized the
allure of rumor, depravity, and dressed-up opinion, but the moral straw
that broke the camel's back of respect for an honorable tradition was the
capitulation to relevance and self-esteem (whatever they mean) by universities, and the substitution by the chattering class that influences social policy of self-righteousness for ideals, slogans for ideas. The gates
were flung open and publishers trampled each other to get through.
When we conceded in 1968 that it was fine for Eldridge Cleaver in *Soul on
Ice* to justify raping white women as a political act, was it not permissible
decades later to substitute Indian war chants for *Macbeth* in school curricula? When Shere Hite, aided and abetted by the latter-day house of
Knopf, can use statistically unreliable letters she solicited as the basis for
judging the sexual behavior of those beasts, American males, it is not
even passing strange that Gloria Steinem a few years later can cite the

astonishing figure of 150,000 as the number of young women who die each year from anorexia and none of her book's reviewers shout, "Stop the presses!" (For simple comparison, her figure is nearly three times the U.S. fatalities in Vietnam, four times the number who die annually on our highways, five times the current death rate for AIDS.)

The question is not ideology, as the attacks on the underlying requirements for honest discussion come from the Right as well as the Left. What has been set aside is common sense, the pursuit of excellence, the courage to engage uncomfortable truths, the responsibilities to the lessons of history. There is no future in this retreat. There is only an increasingly foreshortened present. And since publishers have rendered themselves much less influential than they would like to believe, why shouldn't they acquiesce to the Zeitgeist? If people are willing to be fleeced by the pseudo-pornography of Madonna's *Sex*, if they'll line up to purchase the goofy "sequel" to *Gone with the Wind*, if dieters—whose rate of recidivism is matched only by that of child molesters—scramble to get a cookbook by Oprah's personal chef, if *The Road Less Traveled*, inspirational music to the mentally deaf, can spend 600 weeks on the best-seller list, our public culture as represented by the publication of popular books has surely kicked over the traces that were once in place. And what we've trampled we will not easily resurrect.

For much of the twentieth century, publishers, like museum curators and educators, decided what would be available to edify and enlighten the public. They saw their role as arbiters as a privilege and a duty. Now they evoke the apology we sneered at when it was proffered by television executives: Don't blame me, I'm only giving the people what they want.

While it is false to say that all publishers are now gorging on their pottage, their retreat from elitism, and their unwillingness to assume the moral authority that that position demands, saddens. The historic American battle between the commitment to equality and the instinctive resistance to a dumb egalitarianism confronts an industry reluctant to defend its inherited role. Just as we don't have popular elections for Supreme Court justices, we should want those whose responsibility it is to regulate and enrich the marketplace of discourse to embrace the essential character of their enterprise.

PART FOUR

Public Life

GEORGE F. KENNAN

Egalitarianism and Diversity

George F. Kennan, for many years a Foreign Service Officer, was head of the State Department's first Policy Planning Staff in 1947–50 and ambassador to the Soviet Union in 1952. He joined the Institute for Advanced Study in 1953 and has written widely on diplomatic history and current affairs. Among his many awards are two Pulitzer Prizes and a National Book Award. The essay that follows is excerpted from Chapter 6 of his book *Around the Cragged Hill* (1993).

It is no surprise to find perhaps our wisest contemporary political elder looking back into the pages of Alexis de Tocqueville for the roots of commentary on the greatest source of contemporary tension in American democracy—the tug-of-war between the pursuit of excellence for its own sake and the pursuit of equality for all. Tocqueville saw clearly that it is easier to raze than to raise. Kennan gives us a spirited defense of why we must not let equality before the law be forcibly extended into arenas where a natural aristocracy of merit can produce far more creative governance than the opinion polling of "the public."

Tocqueville and Egalité

One cannot speak of egalitarianism without recalling, first, some of the conclusions of the man who gave greater attention to precisely this subject than any other thinker of the modern era: Alexis de Tocqueville. Born in 1805 into an aristocratic French family, Tocqueville, upon visiting the United States in 1831, became fascinated with the contrast between the hierarchically structured society in which he had been born and raised and the highly egalitarian society he found before him in America. This subject dominated his impressions of the United States; and while his great work, *Democracy in America,* the two parts of which appeared with a five-year interval later in the 1830s, referred to democracy in its title, the real subject of the book was equality—equality as observable in America: in the first volume, equality in general, in the second one, in America but elsewhere as well. Actually, he used the two terms "equality" and "democracy" almost interchangeably, because he regarded the equality of status of the members of the citizenry, socially and politically, as *the* outstanding feature of American democracy, overriding all others in importance.

The reason for this absorbing interest in the egalitarian aspects of American society was that Tocqueville was persuaded that this—the tri-

umph of the principle of equality over that of hierarchy and differentiation—was the wave of the future for all of the western European world
that he cared about. He saw all of European civilization as tending inex-
orably in that direction; and while this prospect saddened him, for it
implied the demise of all that he had come to love and to respect in the
position and the traditions of his own family, he felt very strongly the
necessity of studying it, of coming to understand it, and, finally, of coming to some sort of terms with it. He perceived positive as well as negative
features in American democracy, and did not fail to recognize the positive ones in his book, as short-term advantages of this form of government; but for the long term he had very serious reservations about it.
People, he thought, were more greatly attracted by the principle of
equality than by the principle of liberty; and confronted with a choice
between the two, as he thought they eventually would be (for he regarded the two as ultimately incompatible), they would choose equality.
He described the taste for equality, at one point, as a depraved one,
which would impel the weak to try to drag the strong down to their level
and would induce them to prefer equality in servitude to liberty in inequality.[1] He thought, too, that equality would lead to an unfortunate
centralization of power in the state and that this centralized power would
take the form not of any sort of personal tyranny or dictatorship but
rather of what he called "an anonymous despotism for which no one
person would stand as responsible." "What is to be feared," he wrote, "is
not a perverse individual, and not a maddened mob—it is a bureaucratic
tyranny that would make possible the weakness of the individual." This
tyranny, he envisaged, would not oppress the people in the classical
manner but would encourage passivity in them and hold them in submission by pandering to their thirst for the material comforts and for a
total social equality.[2]

Looked at from the perspective of more than one hundred and fifty
years, these fears of Tocqueville appear somewhat overdrawn, to be sure,
but not wholly without validity, at least so far as the United States is
concerned. In these intervening years the power of the federal government has indeed gained at the expense of that of the states. . . . And the
large proportion of Americans who, while continuing to demand of their
government that it assure their material prosperity, fail to exercise their
right to vote in the presidential and other elections would stand as a
good measure of confirmation for what Tocqueville perceived as their
indifference to the nature of governmental authority so long as it pan-

1. *De la démocratie en Amérique,* pt. 2, in the Robert Laffont edition of Tocqueville's major
works (Paris, 1986), p. 81.

2. Ibid., p. 418. In the French original: "Ce qu'il faut craindre ce n'est pas un individu
pervers ou une foule en folie, c'est la tyrannie bureaucratique qui rend désormais possible
la faiblesse des individus."

dered sufficiently to their material interests. It will be well, therefore, to hold these anxieties of Tocqueville's in mind as we turn to the egalitarian tendencies in the American society of this day and elsewhere. . . .

Egalitarianism in the United States

When we turn to the United States, we see that here, too, egalitarianism has had profound effects. The first great agency of this tendency has been the American governmental system itself, which is unapologetically and proudly egalitarian. All democratic governments have much of this quality, but in the American government it has particular importance. For while most of the European democratic governments have administrative structures through which laws can be interpreted, and their rigidity modified in the application to the individual citizen, we have, as interpreters of the laws, only the courts; and their interpretive judgments, like the law itself, have only a collective applicability, affecting alike all who come within their purview, and allowing no flexibility in relation to the individual citizen. This system, excluding as it does most administrative discretion and flexibility, gives to the law a position of unique and exclusive importance at the center of government—a situation reflected in the numerousness and prominence of lawyers in our public life and in the enormous amount of interpretative litigation with which our courts are burdened.

Now, because the law consists of great sweeping dicta prescribing the behavior of large numbers of people, and because we are, quite properly, all equal in the eyes of the law, the law constitutes the greatest and most authoritative of all the equalizing influences bearing on our society. And the scope of this equalizing effect is naturally enhanced by the growing centralization of government—by the growth of federal power, that is, in proportion to that of the states. Numbers of issues—such things as abortion, integration, and treatment of social or ethnic minorities—which at the outset of our independent national history would surely have been regarded (if they were seen as concerns for public authority at all) as proper concerns for the state governments, are now the objects of strident demands for treatment at the federal level, whether by legislation or by interpretation by the courts, or even sometimes by constitutional amendment. And every step in that direction, tending as it does to centralize in Washington the control over some of the most intimate details of personal or local life, is a step on the path to that total egalitarianism that loomed so unsettlingly on Tocqueville's intellectual horizon.

But it is not only in the governmental system that such tendencies are present. They are strongly represented in popular attitudes and expectations as well; and here they assume what, in the view of outsiders, must be seen as curious forms. First, there is the attitude toward wealth. Here, in contrast to the situation that seems to prevail in Russia, it has never been regarded as reprehensible to *make* money. To *have* it in large amounts is perhaps more questionable. It means, at least, that you should be more heavily taxed than others are. To have *inherited* it is, however, another matter. Thus George Bush can be seriously charged, by his political opponents, with having been born "with a silver spoon in his mouth," as though it were well established that to have been born to wealthy parents was, at least from the political standpoint, a serious deficiency of character. The politically ambitious person, it may be inferred, should be more careful in the selection of his parents.[3]

It is apparent, from these oddities in American attitudes, that where wealth is resented, the resentment centers not so much on the material comforts and luxuries it affords as on the incidental perquisites—the prestige, the privilege, the enhanced influence—that are seen as accompanying it. It is, in other words, the inequality of status that wealth is supposed to assure, rather than the inequality in wealth or income for its own sake, that arouses the resentment. And this is no doubt a reason why the egalitarian tendencies of the country have centered so sharply on the educational process. The more expensive the educational facilities, from the grade school up, the more they are seen as unjust channels of advancement to privileged status, and are resented accordingly. It matters not greatly whether, in any given instance, the parents skimped and saved and sacrificed in order to make possible the resort to these facilities or even whether the student himself took outside employment to make possible his access to them. Nor was the fact that in most instances they gave superior instruction allowed to stand as a redeeming feature. If such instruction could not be given to everyone, it should, in this view, not be given to anyone.

But it is important to note that the charges and complaints along this line find their expression primarily in liberal intellectual circles and in the press and media rather than among the people who, one might think, were the principal victims of these supposed injustices. It is not so much from the sufferers of poverty as from their intellectual protagonists that these complaints come. Much of this may be explained perhaps by the fact that the sufferers have, comparatively speaking, few possibilities for making their voices heard. But it is among the liberal intellectual circles that questions of status seem to be of greatest impor-

3. But even here, the matter is complicated. It is not a question of just being born anywhere to such parents. To constitute a serious mark against you, it must have been birth into something called the eastern establishment, where everyone is assumed to be wealthy. Birth to wealthy parents elsewhere in the country is less serious, if indeed serious at all. This curious distinction parallels an oddity of primitive Russian egalitarianism, which accepted the privileges of the party elite, regarded as the normal perquisites of authority, far more easily than it did the minuscule material advantages that might be detectible in the next-door neighbor.

tance; and one cannot evade the occasional suspicion that it is not so much sympathy for the underdog that inspires much of this critical enthusiasm as a desire to tear down those who preempt the pinnacles of status to which they themselves aspire. . . .

Elitism

The converse of egalitarianism, at least in many minds, would be "elitism." I must confess my amazement at the constant use of this term in a pejorative sense in so much of the public discourse of this country, as though "elitism" were something we had all agreed was reprehensible and abhorrent, so abhorrent, in fact, that anyone who could be plausibly charged with a partiality toward it was thereby stamped as irredeemably wrongheaded and deserving of consignment to outer darkness.

I am unable to understand such a view of the term. The word "elite" is simply a derivative of the word "elect" (*élire*, in French). Its meaning is little different from that of the noun "the elect," signifying those who are chosen or elected. In the United States, to be sure, it is often thought of, and the word used, with relation to some sort of a social elite, with all the negative connotations—undeserved privilege, conceit, snobbishness, disdain for others, and so on—that this term evokes. This, indeed, is what is suggested by the only definition of it given by *Webster's:* "a group or body considered or treated as socially superior." But it is not the original definition. The *Oxford English Dictionary* comes closer to the real meaning of the word when it defines an elite as "the choice part or flower (of society, or of any body or class of persons)." It is in this sense, as I see it, that the term should be used.

And what, pray, is wrong with this? What is implied is not a priggish sort of self-selection, or an assignment of undeserved privilege, but merely the recruitment, out of a general mass of people, of those best qualified to perform certain useful functions of society and the charging of them with attendant responsibility. Whoever rejects the possibility of that sort of choice flies in the face of the very principle of election on which our nation is founded. Surely, these self-righteous spurners of "elitism" are not recommending that we abandon the very idea of election—that we choose our public servants by some sort of lottery, and that the country be governed exclusively by gray mediocrity.

The simple fact is that in any great organization—government or what you will—responsibility has to be borne and the day-to-day decisions taken not by the mass of those involved but by tiny minorities of them, and sometimes even individuals, chosen from their midst. This is not primarily because the judgments of the mass would be necessarily inferior to those of the "elect" (although one of the reasons for choosing this "elect" ought normally to be the reasoned supposition that they would have superior qualifications and facilities for making the decisions in question). The primary reason for this sort of selection is the reality that a large mass of persons cannot, if only for purely physical and mechanical reasons, be organized in such a way that it could carry out a regular and systematic program of decision taking. For this, a smaller body is necessary. And since such a smaller body has to exist, what is wrong with trying to see to it that it is composed of those to whom might reasonably be attributed the highest qualifications for the exercise of this function?

Human beings, after all, may be born equal; and equal they should unquestionably be in the face of the law. But this is just about the end of their equality. Beyond this, they vary greatly in the capacity for being useful to society, or to any group to which they belong. And when it comes to the selection of small minorities of them to whom legislative or administrative or judicial responsibility is to be assigned, there the effort has to be made, at the very least, to find those best qualified to meet the responsibilities in question. The process of selection may be faulty; it may be dreadfully abused, as indeed it sometimes is. Human judgment is never perfect; and human institutions are at best never more than approximations of the ideal. But the effort to select has to be made. It cannot be avoided. And even those who are most vehement in their abhorrence of what they call an elite will have to accommodate themselves to this necessity.

The crucial question is not whether such things as elites must exist. The question concerns only the quality of the elite in question and, particularly, the standards and institutions by which it is selected. It does not have to be an elite of privilege, least of all of undeserved privilege. But we must remember that special responsibility, however imperfectly it is exercised, often requires special facilities—sometimes even special conveniences and prerequisites of authority. And superior position has the right to demand at least outward respect. Respect is due to the office whether or not the occupant seems fully worthy of it. All the world, as Shakespeare observed, is a stage; and those who hold high office (or lower office, too, for that matter) are merely playing their respective parts in a certain drama, usually as best they can. Outside the office or the public platform or the other outward manifestations of their responsibility—in the intimacies, that is, of home and family—the selected officials or legislators are, if you will, only human beings much like the rest of us: beholden to all the silly requirements of a physical existence, caught in the same turmoil of irrational emotions and compulsions that assails the rest of us, seldom much more successful than many others in coping with those imperfections of human nature. . . . But in the execution of their office, they represent something greater than themselves; and that something deserves respect.

For these reasons, I can find no patience for those who try to build themselves up in their self-esteem by denying respect for established authority and by trying to tear it down: for the students who fancy they have proved something when they appear in weird and silly costumes at their own commencement; for the journalists who think they have shown great cleverness and superiority by ridiculing highly placed persons for their personal foibles; for the persons who throw eggs at the limousines of visiting statesmen. Whoever is incapable of respect for others is usually incapable, whether he recognizes it or not, of respect for himself. By denying that anyone else could be worthy of respect, he confesses, unwittingly, his own unworthiness of it.[4]

Such, then, are the thoughts provoked in my own mind by the accusations (some of which I myself have not been spared) of "elitism." Let us by all means have an elite. Let it be an elite of service to others, of conscience, of responsibility, of restraint of all that is unworthy in the self, and of resolve to be to others more than one could ever hope to be to one's self. But in once having this elite, however far it falls short of the ideal, let us respect it and not pretend that we could live without it. Here, I stand unrepentant, in the unabashed pursuit of what others call my elitist tendencies.

Plebiscite versus Representative Government

And if there are forms of elitism the fear of which is overdrawn, there are forms of what might be called its opposite that are not sufficiently feared. And these are the plebiscitary tendencies now making themselves felt in American society.

Our political system was, as the founding fathers conceived it, intended to be outstandingly that of a representative government. The term was often used in contradistinction to the concept of a pure democracy. In a pure democracy laws were to be adopted by decision of the entire community of the citizenry, gathered in public assembly. This, plainly, was something that was feasible only in a very small and intimate community. This explains its usefulness in the institution of the New England town meeting and in the innumerable forms of neighborhood cooperation that exist in small American communities.

Under a representative government, on the other hand—something necessary wherever the size of the self-governing entity surpassed that of the small neighborhood community—laws were to be drawn up and adopted not directly by the public but by a representative legislative

4. I think, here, of Burke's stinging reproach to the radicals of the years of the French Revolution: "Respecting your forefathers, you would have been taught to respect yourselves."

body, or bodies, elected by the citizenry for this purpose. With this act of election, the public's active involvement in the legislative process was, for the moment, substantially completed. If citizens did not like what their representative was doing, they had the privilege of publicly criticizing it and, if their criticisms were ineffective, of voting at the next election to put someone else in his place.

While I am not sure that this was ever explicitly stated, it seems to me to have been implicit in this concept that the elected representative was expected, in the exercise of this legislative responsibility, to use his own personal judgment and to arrive at his own decisions. In doing so, he would, of course, also be expected to have in mind what he knew about the sentiments of those who had elected him, but he was not bound to be guided by these alone. He might, after all, have come to question their judgment. He might, in the very exercise of his legislative duties, have learned more about certain of the issues at stake in a bit of proposed legislation than was known to the general body of his constituency. In any case, he would have had the possibility of seeing his views refined by participation in the ordered and structured debate of the legislative chamber. His views must then have enjoyed the presumption of certain qualities above and apart from those of the constituents who had elected him. There was good reason, therefore, why he, once elected, should be guided primarily, in the exercise of his office, by his own knowledge and judgment of the question at hand. This was, of course, the ideal. The classic example for it was given by Burke, as illustrated in his well-known *Letter to the Sheriffs of Bristol*. As a member of the House of Commons, and aware that a position he felt bound in good conscience to take ran counter to the strong feelings of at least a part of his constituency, Burke wrote this letter of some fifty pages to explain to the constituents why he felt as he did about the issue in question and why he proposed to vote accordingly. But then, in order to make it clear that he intended to stand his ground, even if it cost him reelection (which it did), he added the following classic sentence:

If I were ready, on any call of my own vanity or interest, or to answer any election purpose, to forsake principles . . . which I had formed at a mature age, on full reflection, and which had been confirmed by long experience, I should forfeit the only thing which makes you pardon so many errors and imperfections in me.

This, I repeat, was the ideal. Normally, and particularly in this country, things have not worked quite that way. Seldom, one must assume, have representatives been prepared to fly as heroically as did Burke in the face of the opinions or prejudices of those who elected them, thus jeopardizing their own chances for reelection. But the ideal remains intact. And it still plays some part in the behavior of the American legislator, if only because he is frequently confronted with the need for decisions on questions with regard to which he has never had the opportunity or even the time to consult the feelings of a majority of his constituents, and is therefore obliged to use his own judgment, or because the issues involved, particularly when it comes to hectic last-moment adjustments of language in specific bills, are too intricate, and too urgent, to be taken in any way before his constituents.

And it is something else again when the electors are asked to express their opinions directly by means of some sort of an officially arranged plebiscite or referendum, or when private polls are taken of their opinions.

The idea of the passage or the repeal of legislation by direct popular vote rather than by regular parliamentary procedures marches under a number of names—plebiscites, public questions on ballots, direct democracy, and citizen legislation among them—but the idea is generally known in this country as "initiative and referendum."[5] In detail, it can take various forms; but provisions allowing for procedures of this general nature already exist, as I understand it, in the constitutions of some twenty-three states, most of them west of the Mississippi. And I have the impression that there is much lively, if not growing, sentiment in favor of setting up new such arrangements where they do not already exist, and of exploiting further those that do.[6]

In any case, I mention these tendencies here in order to express my strong aversion to them on principle. I see the idea of initiative and referendum as being in flat contradiction to the principles of representative government that have lain at the heart of our constitutional system from its very foundation.

The idea that legislation should be made or repealed by popular majorities involves, in the first place, the forfeiture of all those advantages of the system of representative government that were mentioned above, especially the presumptive superior knowledge on the part of the legislator of the issue at stake and its background, and the possibility of refinement of decision by means of ordered debate on the legislative floor or in the appropriate committee.

Second, the device of initiative and referendum invites all the evils of

---

5. There are many variations in the meaning given to these terms in the different states; but, in general, "initiative" is taken to mean the initiation and passage of legislation by direct popular vote, whereas "referendum" means the review or removal by such a vote of statutes already passed by a legislative body.

6. In the state of New Jersey, where these lines are being written, the question of an amendment to the state constitution, allowing for the possibility of legislation by initiative and referendum, has been before the legislature for some fifteen years; and the result of the most recent election would seem to presage an early favorable decision. I note, furthermore, that in this most recent election, in California, there were some twenty-eight questions of this nature on the ballot, which I take to be evidence of extensive enthusiasm for this method of legislating.

single-issue thinking and voting. There are literally no public issues involved in legislation that do not have implications for other issues as well. There are none that have qualities on the merits of which, alone, they can safely be treated. The elected legislator knows this. He cannot deal with any one question entirely in isolation. He is constantly being confronted not just with a single legislative question but with numbers of them. He is obliged to reconcile the position he takes on one question with those he takes on others. He has to balance the pros and cons, and he may never forget that what gratifies one constituent may offend another.

Not so the common citizen, asked to vote on a single public question. This question comes before him in starkest isolation, demanding an answer: yes or no. He is not asked or encouraged to take into account the wider implications. Nothing stops him, of course, from taking the trouble to inform himself on these broader implications; and some no doubt do; but there is nothing that constrains them to do it. The more common individual reaction is to give to the questions a relatively casual answer— an answer usually inspired primarily by whatever emotional nerves the question most intimately touches.

The voter-citizen has no choice, furthermore, but to accept the wording of the question as it is flung at him by whoever instituted the poll. He cannot modify it, amend it, or attempt to clarify it. He cannot respond by saying, "Yes, but . . ." or "Provided that. . . ." He is in fact at the mercy of whoever phrased the question. Yet anyone who has any knowledge of the role played by question and answer in public debate knows that the terms of the question often dictate a large part of the answer.

We have, finally, the fact that a decision once taken in this way, if it turns out to have unfortunate consequences, is relatively hard to change. A legislative body, faced with a similar situation affecting any of the laws it has passed, has much greater flexibility in this respect. It may rescind the law, or amend it, or pass another one in its place. For all this, nothing more is required than a simple vote of the body in question. To do any of these things with the decision of a popular referendum is far more difficult. Any change of this nature involves preparatory steps and procedures as cumbersome and protracted as those of the original measure itself. It allows very little flexibility, if any at all, in the recognition and correction of mistakes.

It will be argued that in our federal Congress as it exists today, some of the greatest advantages of the classical concept of formal legislative deliberation have already been forfeited in a number of ways: by the virtual abandonment of ordered and structured debate on the floor of the legislative chamber in favor of intricate political maneuvering in committee meetings; by the abject dependence of many legislators on the sources of their campaign expenditures; and by the penetration of lobbyists into the most intimate recesses of the parliamentary body.

True enough. All these evils exist, and cry out for correction. In certain instances they are even worse than the language used above would suggest. The admission of television cameras into the legislative chamber, in particular, is even worse than the mere abandonment of the use of that chamber for normal deliberation and debate. In the depressing spectacle of the individual legislator haranguing an empty house before the cameras in order to suggest to the folks back home that he is addressing a great legislative body hanging on his every word—in this you have one of the most pathetic examples of the triumph of the contrived image over the reality, a triumph inherent in the very nature of the television medium. . . . By this shabby sellout to the television industry, Congress has forfeited a large part of its own dignity and, with it, of the very function with which the founding fathers were concerned to endow it.

It will obviously be very difficult to achieve the correction of these distortions at the federal level. Some may even be already beyond the possibility of correction. To what extent it would be easier to avoid these same evils in smaller parliamentary bodies is impossible to predict. In any case, the proper answer is not, should never be, and in fact cannot be, plebiscitary democracy. The phrase is in itself a contradiction in terms. In the tendencies now running in that direction one has nothing less than the abandonment of faith in the democratically elected individual and the expression of a vain hope that a greater wisdom will be found to lie in the consultation of the faceless collectivity. This implies the loss of the very principle of personal responsibility of the elected representative, on which our governmental system was founded, in favor of an irresponsible and unreal anonymity of power. It leaves an open field to the backstage manipulator and the shameless demagogue. Neither will fail to take advantage of it.

No less symptomatic in this respect is the flood of unofficial public opinion polls recently undertaken (for their own commercial purposes) by the press and the media. No objection can be taken, of course, to this device, except where their results might influence an election already in progress. Such polls can be usefully informative for individual legislators as evidence of public reactions in matters with which they have to deal, so long as it is borne in mind that the polls are, after all, only one of the factors to be considered in the exercise of their legislative offices, and should never be viewed as substitutes for their own independent judgment on matters at stake. The public may, after all, be wrong, in the sense that the polls may reflect serious misapprehensions on the public's part which it is the duty of the legislative representative to expose and to set to rights rather than to accept passively. That is what leadership really ought to mean.

With these exceptions, there is, I repeat, nothing wrong about the sampling of public opinion in this way. But I cannot avoid the impression that the results of such samplings are often served up to the public by the pollster with the innuendo that there is, or ought to be, a certain unchallengeability and finality about them. "You see," the pollsters seem to be saying, "the public has given its verdict. That settles it." Particularly pervasive is this inference when polls are taken of the president's "popularity" at any given moment—of how many approve or do not approve of the way he is momentarily conducting his office—and all of this with the clear suggestion that here, in these undifferentiated and spontaneous reactions of the public, is the supreme and authoritative test of his performance of his presidential office, and the one to which his primary response is due.

It was pointed out above that the ultimate responsibility of government had normally to be borne by minorities, and sometimes even (as in the case of the American president) by individuals. The advantage of the American system has lain in the fact that the method of selection of such minorities or individuals, in the persons of legislative bodies or individual legislators, was regularized and their powers and responsibilities made clear.

What I particularly miss in all these plebiscitary approaches and devices is precisely the element of personal responsibility. This seems, in fact, to be a characteristic feature of all the egalitarian tendencies of the age. One notices that in the Scandinavian countries, where such tendencies find their most striking expression, it is hard to find any instance in which a single person can ever be clearly identified with any significant decision of public policy. Only collectivities appear in the capacity of decision takers; and these, very often, are bureaucracies. Because there is no clear allotment of personal authority, there is no allotment of personal responsibility. And the same anonymity of responsibility marks all the efforts in the United States to solve legislative problems, or to dictate the actions of executive branch officials, by the consultation of popular moods and responses in officially sanctioned initiatives and referenda or by means of the privately conducted opinion poll. Where personal decision lies buried, there, alongside it, lies personal responsibility. Where the role of the individual in public affairs is effaced, there, with it, disappears a good deal of the concept of public affairs that inspired the founding fathers of our republic.

Species and the Individual

I have reserved for mention at the end of this chapter, in view of the profundity of its implications, what I regard as the most significant of Tocqueville's doubts about democratic equality. In the body of the second part of his work, he had already complained of the tendency of the rulers of his age to concentrate on the great masses of their subjects and to neglect the individuals of whom those masses were composed.

In order to concentrate only upon the people as a whole, one is no longer accustomed to envisaging the individual citizen; in thinking only of the species, one forgets the individual.[7]

And then, again, in the fourth part of his work, in summarizing his final conclusions, he returned, in a different way, to this subject:

One might say that the rulers of our time seek only to do great things with men. I could wish that they would think a bit more about how to make men great; that they would give less importance to the work and more to the worker; and that they would never forget that a nation cannot long remain strong when each man is personally weak, and that one has not yet found either the social forms or the political combinations to make a nation strong when the citizens who compose it are pusillanimous and soft.[8]

It is true that Tocqueville, in this passage, did not refer specifically to equality or democracy. But he felt that many of the features of the egalitarian-democratic state to which his book was addressed were beginning to pervade European governments across the board, even in the constitutional monarchies. It was this he had in mind when he used, in the second of the above passages, the term "rulers." And the question he was raising was whether the pandering to the material comforts of great masses of people, which he saw as implicit in the egalitarian-democratic society, would not have the effect of depriving the members of the natural elite of that society of the discipline and challenge necessary for the emergence of true greatness among them. . . . .

7. *De la démocratie en Amérique,* in the Laffont edition of Tocqueville's major works (Paris, 1986), p. 448 (my translation). In the French original: ". . . on s'habitue à ne plus envisager les citoyens pour ne considerer que le peuple; on oublie les individus pour ne songer qu'à l'espèce."

8. "On dirait que les souverains de notre temps ne cherchent qu'à faire avec les hommes des choses grandes. Je voudrais qu'ils songeassent un peu plus à faire de grands hommes; qu'ils attachassent moins de prix à l'oeuvre et plus à l'ouvrier, et qu'ils se souvinssent sans cesse qu'une nation ne peut rester long temps forte quand chaque homme y est individuellement faible, et qu'on n'a point encore trouvé de formes sociales ni de combinaisons politiques qui puissent faire un peuple énergique en le composant de citoyens pusillanimes et mous."

DAVID KLINGHOFFER

Kitsch Religion

David Klinghoffer is literary editor at *National Review*. His writing has also appeared in the *New York Times, Washington Post, Wall Street Journal, Commentary*, the *Forward*, and the *New Criterion*. A native of Palos Verdes, California, he graduated from Brown University in 1987. He is writing a book about his religious evolution.

The landmark 1939 critical essay by the late Clement Greenberg, "Avant-Garde and Kitsch," cleverly transposed, here provides solid conceptual grounding for David Klinghoffer's examination of contemporary trends in mainline liberal Protestant, Catholic, and Jewish religion. In their frantic efforts to keep pews at least partially filled in the late twentieth century, American clergy have abandoned their strongest means of binding believers to their faith and instead have chosen to compete for audience share with other forms of entertainment far better fitted with deep pockets and strategic planners.

*W*HEN THE *New York Times* wants the opinion of respectable religion on an issue of the day, its reporter inevitably seeks out an Episcopal bishop, a Presbyterian minister, or a Reform rabbi; and so those Americans who rely on the Official Media for news can be forgiven for thinking that the liberal, "mainline" churches represent the mainstream of religious faith. At the same time, despite random signs of life—such as the ever-presence of Unitarian minister Robert Fulghum on the paperback best-seller list—there is a general sense among those who follow such things that liberal religion is on the decline, that in the marketplace of faith the more conservative denominations have achieved the upper hand.

This isn't what children growing up in liberal Jewish or Christian homes were told to expect. These children have long been taught that orthodoxy and fundamentalism are dying anachronisms—that, in the modern world, a "contemporary," enlightened view of God and man is the only viable stance. And yet that opinion has itself turned out to be an anachronism.

What has happened to liberal American religion? Though mainline Christianity and liberal Judaism are generally thought of as if one had nothing to do with the other, the declining fortunes of both suggest that, to be understood, they need to be considered simultaneously.

The numbers are not debatable. The fastest-growing sects in this country are typified by the Southern Baptists and the Mormons; whereas the mainline Christian groups—Episcopalians, Unitarians, Congregationalists, Presbyterians, Methodists—have been bleeding members since the mid-1960s, with millions defecting through the 1980s, so that by the beginning of this decade they had experienced losses in membership ranging from a fifth to a third. More depressing, from the perspective of the groups themselves, is that they have suffered this decline mainly among younger members. A study published in 1994, *All in the Family: Religious Mobility in America,* rated denominations on their ability to keep believers in the fold. Conservative Protestant groups such as the Southern Baptists and Assemblies of God did best, followed by the Catholic Church, while liberal Protestants were least likely to stay loyal to the faith they grew up in. Of men and women interviewed between 1988 and 1990, only 63 percent who grew up in a liberal church had remained there—compared with 83 percent among conservative Protestants and 81 percent among Catholics. Discussing mainline decay in the ecumenical journal *First Things* (March 1993), Benton Johnson, Dean R. Hoge, and Donald A. Luidens wrote about sitting "today in the balcony of a typical United Methodist church and look[ing] over a congregation of graying and balding heads."

I've had the same experience in synagogues affiliated with the liberal Reform movement and the misleadingly named Conservative movement in Judaism. (At its inception more than a hundred years ago, Conservative Judaism proposed to "conserve" the bulk of traditional Judaism; but since about 1950, Conservative leaders have parted ways with traditional Judaism on a variety of issues, resulting in the death of Conservative Jewish "law" by a thousand small cuts, so that today you rarely meet a religiously observant Conservative layman.) Walk into a typical Conservative synagogue in New York City, and you will find a small audience of senior citizens mixed with some middle-aged adults and a few thirty-something stragglers, all sitting passively, as if stunned, while the rabbi and cantor perform on a stage in front of them. Meanwhile, Orthodox synagogues overflow with fully observant Jews in their twenties, with young couples and their babies, the latter kicking up a racket throughout the long Saturday-morning service.

Though the Reform movement remains the largest body in Judaism, and frequently gains new members through intermarriage (when a non-Jewish spouse can be prevailed on to sit through a nominal "conversion" to Judaism), the only Jewish denomination that has been able to hold on to its young people against intermarriage and assimilation is Orthodoxy. In fact, many of the young Orthodox Jews you meet in stronghold neighborhoods such as Manhattan's Upper West Side grew up in Reform and Conservative homes but became disillusioned and made the surprising decision to embrace traditional Judaism.

If observers of the religious scene too frequently consider liberal Christianity in isolation from its Jewish counterpart, it is because they don't take the trouble actually to define liberal religion. If they did, they would find that liberal Judaism has a lot in common with the Protestant mainline. To remedy the problem, let me propose a three-pronged definition, which will become clear from an account of an exemplary event of religious liberalism: my bar mitzvah.

Taking place in 1977 at Temple Beth El, a southern California Reform temple, this event consisted of three main parts—excluding the mass expenditure of cash and credit by my generous father, which both preceded and followed the bar mitzvah itself. First came my reading of the Torah: a passage in Hebrew from Deuteronomy, beginning with the famous injunction, "Justice, justice, you shall pursue." Though I had spent three years in a typical Reform Hebrew school, instructed by a series of indifferent Israelis, all a Reform child really learns is to pronounce Hebrew letters; I understood hardly a word of my brief scriptural text.

Second came my bar mitzvah speech about the sad plight of "our Jewish brothers and sisters in the Soviet Union," an oration of little direct relevance to my Torah portion and written by my mother.

Finally, the third and main part of a Reform bar mitzvah: the party. This last had absolutely nothing to do with the ostensibly religious rite of that morning. Instead, at my insistence, at a nearby hotel in Long Beach called the Golden Sails Inn, I was the proud center of a living tableau of all that was most embarrassing about the 1970s. My guests danced to the Hustle, led by two specially hired lady disco dancers in brown suede jumpsuits. When the guests weren't hustling, a professional cartoonist wandered the large ballroom, drawing humorous caricatures. He drew me riding a surfboard on a large wave, though I've never surfed.

The differences between this and a traditional bar mitzvah illuminate the differences between liberal and traditional religions. An Orthodox boy reads a much longer passage from the Torah, and he understands all of it because he has been studying Hebrew as intensively as a Reform Jewish grammar-school boy might study Spanish or German. He also gives a brief sermon, or *davar Torah*, elaborating on themes arising from the chapters he's just read—again, because he has studied those chapters and understands their relationship to Jewish law, his acceptance of which is the whole point of the exercise. Then all adjourn to the synagogue social hall for pickled herring and a shot of whiskey.

So we see in what directions liberal religion diverges from the tradition it comes out of. I mentioned a three-pronged definition. Here it is.

First the matter of discipline and education. On turning thirteen, in traditional Judaism, a boy should be able to read and understand the Hebrew Scriptures from which the system of *halacha,* or Jewish law, derives, because on his thirteenth birthday the boy is suddenly responsible for carrying out that law. As a thirteen-year-old Reform boy, I was not asked to shoulder any new responsibilities. Though that morning I read from the Book of the Law, I didn't understand what I was saying, so I could hardly assent to it. (Actually Reform Judaism holds that Jewish law—in such biblically mandated specifics as Sabbath observance and the laws of prohibited foods—is no longer operative.) For the most part, liberal religion, whether Jewish or Christian, eliminates the concept of a *bar mitzvah,* literally a "son of the commandments," an individual on whom the responsibility falls to fulfill quite serious requirements imposed by God. Liberal religion upholds general principles of kindness and sympathy, but particular demands of the type familiar to previous generations have largely been booted out the temple, or church, door.

In researching their article in *First Things,* Johnson, Hoge, and Luidens focused on the Presbyterian Church and listed some of the traditional Presbyterian standards of behavior that have fallen into desuetude: "Rules against worldly amusements and immodest dress went by the boards after World War I, standards of Sabbath observance were widely ignored by 1940, and in many congregations old norms concerning alcoholic beverages had become obsolete by the early 1950s." The Presbyterian Church has also given up its opposition to abortion rights.

But among both Christians and Jews the most striking and symbolic evolution in ideas about proper conduct centers on homosexuality. Although, looking only at the text of the Bible, it is possible to imagine different definitions of Sabbath observance, there can be no similar quibbling about God's views on gay sex. Yet all the liberal religious groups have begun to collapse in their once unanimous opposition to that activity. Among leaders of the Episcopal Church, a debate proceeds, with a powerful faction advocating that the church endorse gay marriages and homosexuality in general. Openly gay Episcopal priests have been ordained. When homosexual Boy Scouts and Boy Scout leaders became an issue in the early 1990s, the Unitarians asserted their strong support of gay Scoutmasters and Scouts. In 1992, the major ecumenical organization representing the liberal churches, the National Council of Churches, just barely avoided, by a vote of 90 to 81, granting observer status to an avowedly gay denomination called the Universal Fellowship of Metropolitan Churches. Among Reform Jews, you find no such hesitation. When a gay and lesbian synagogue in Manhattan installed its first rabbi, the head of the Reform movement, Alexander Schindler, personally presided over the installation.

The first leg of my definition of liberal religion has do with a watering down of moral requirements, and the second is not unrelated. It is the substitution of politics for morality. To return to my bar mitzvah: Notice that, when the time came for me to comment on my Torah portion, I—or rather, my mother—chose to speak not about any of the *mitzvot,* religious commandments, that arise from the text, but about a political issue: the mistreatment of Soviet Jews. "Social action" often seems to be the principal concern of Reform Judaism. Nor are the liberal Christian churches uninterested in politics.

Don't be confused by the *rhetoric* of liberal church leaders, who in their public pronouncements often borrow the fire-and-brimstone style of stereotypical fundamentalist clergymen. It's striking, for instance, how frequently the word "blasphemy" comes up. During the 1992 presidential race, a group of twenty-three clergymen, who included the head of the Episcopal Church and officers of the National Council of Churches, objected to President Bush's assertion that the Democratic Party platform left out "three simple letters: G, O, D." This, they said, was a "partisan use of God's name," and thus "blasphemy." (Interestingly, the clergymen didn't appear bothered by then-governor Clinton's announcement, in his speech accepting the Democratic presidential nomination, of a "New Covenant," or his misuse of a quotation from Isaiah.) Just this year, another group of clergymen denounced the biotechnology industry for seeking to patent human genes. A head of the Methodist Church called the idea of gene patenting "blasphemy."

If you were handed a hundred public declarations by liberal clergymen, and a hundred newspaper editorials, you would not find it easy to distinguish one from the other. The issues that preoccupy these men of God are various. Take 1994. At the start of the year, the head communications officer at the National Council of Churches declared that violent crime was "at the top of the churches' agenda," with the head of the Council's Interreligious Task Force on Criminal Justice taking the occasion to attack the National Rifle Association with colorful references to a "bloodstained Constitution" and "closed doors of fear." In March a group called the Religious Coalition for Reproductive Choice, including heads of the Unitarian and Episcopal Churches, demanded that President Clinton's health-care plan provide funding for abortions. In April the National Religious Partnership for the Environment spent $4.5 million on an Earth Day campaign to endorse "eco-justice" and assail "environmental racism"—causing a skeptical Catholic priest to remind his liberal colleagues that "it is God, not Gaia, whom we will face on Judgment Day." Around the same time, a *New York Times* article produced a Reform rabbi who sells energy-saving lightbulbs and low-flow shower heads in his temple Judaica shop. As he put it, "the concept of the environment is central to Judaism"—though it's hard to see how that could be the case, given that biblical Hebrew contains no word for "the environment" or "nature," and that in Genesis God grants man mastership, not stewardship, of the nonhuman world. The year of liberal-religious activism concluded, in California, with Episcopal bishops urging priests and parishioners to oppose Proposition 187, the ballot initiative intended to discourage illegal immigration.

In seeking to explain the declining fortunes of liberal churches, conservatives often point to this obsession with politics and other non-spiritual matters. According to these critics, parishioners in liberal churches are, like most Americans, basically conservative. So they resent the political declarations of their leaders, with the result that these men and women have been abandoning the churches of their youth. I doubt it. At Temple Beth El during the Reagan administration, when the sermons of our own rabbi seemed to deal increasingly with the dangers of the arms race and the threat of nuclear winter, many of his congregants agreed with him. Meanwhile very few, if any, knew about the more radical positions being adopted by the rabbi's superiors at the Union of American Hebrew Congregations, where a portion of their dues money went each year. Had the well-meaning Jews of Temple Beth El known that the head of the UAHC's synagogue wing supported homosexual temples and homosexual rabbis, many would have been appalled.

The same goes for the rank-and-file members of liberal churches. After interviewing five hundred Presbyterians of the baby-boomer generation, Johnson, Hoge, and Luidens concluded that most of their subjects "know little or nothing about the policies promoted by denominational officials. . . . Our findings lead us to suspect that today's culture war within the mainline Protestant denominations is waged mainly by national elites and only rarely engages the attention and the passions of ordinary church members."

Which leads me to the third part of my definition of liberal faith. For some decades now the attraction of these churches has been religious only in part. Nor has it been political. It has been largely social. After all, the highlight of my bar mitzvah was the party—not my mouthing of foreign words nobody but the rabbi understood, or of words written by mother about Soviet Jews. My hunch is that, when a liberal church ceases to be a body concerned mainly with the dissemination of God's words, it can continue to function for a while as a social institution. As a child growing up at Temple Beth El, I didn't understand the ideology of Reform Judaism: a highly theoretical contraption asserting the existence of God while denying that the Jews or any other people possess a document containing clearly revealed instructions from Him. No doubt our rabbi sincerely believed the theories underlying Reform. He was, however, probably the only such person at Temple Beth El. In fact, I only heard about those theories many years after my bar mitzvah, when I had already decided that the sense of spiritual engagement and commitment I was looking for did not exist in Reform temples.

What it is in Reform that appeals to Jews now in their fifties and sixties is not Reform theories, but rather the Reform temple as a gathering place of friendly and socially similar adults. My parents' generation loves bar mitzvah parties, the *havurot* (groups of families that get together for outings to the zoo or the beach), the *kiddush* after services on Friday night (a brief benediction over some wine and bread, and an extended schmooze afterward with coffee and cake). As an adult, I realize what a nice group of people attended Temple Beth El. For my mother and father, these folks made solid, dependable friends. I can't think of another married couple they spent time with who did not belong to the temple.

If I'm right, this would at least partly explain why Jews and Christians of my generation have in such numbers dropped out of our parents' temples and churches. As other social organizations have discovered to their distress—fraternal organizations such as the Masons and the Shriners, do-good groups such as the American Jewish Committee and the Anti-Defamation League—young Americans today don't have time for them. We work too hard to spend Friday night at temple, Sunday morning at church, Wednesday night at the Moose Lodge—whatever—just to schmooze. For that, we can go to the gym, thereby accomplishing two objectives at once.

A few years ago I wrote an article for the *Washington Times* about the decline of the Masons. In the course of my research I interviewed some of the charming old men who maintain the archipelago of Masonic temples in the D.C. area. Behind the windowless walls of these awesome structures, redolent with mysteries of secret and ancient Masonic rites and doctrines, the old men gather for meetings. These consist mainly of procedural matters—taking roll, announcing the deaths of old members, occasionally inducting a new one—after which the Masons enjoy a repast of ice cream and cake: which, for them, is the main point. Like liberal Jewish and Christian clergymen, they can't understand why men my age aren't banging down the door to get in.

That, however, surely doesn't explain the whole phenomenon. After all, not everyone my age belongs to a gym. Critics offer different theories. A few years ago the dean of the Episcopal Cathedral in Washington, the Very Rev. Nathan Baxter, expressed his opinion that the decline of the Episcopal Church from the 1960s through the mid-1980s proceeded from its "inability . . . to shake [its] European identity." Rev. Baxter surely approves of his church's more recent conversion to multiculturalism—a conversion in which other liberal churches have participated, though without the hoped-for result of winning back the membership they lost under the old ethnocentric "European" regime. The Presbyterian Church, for example, doesn't seem to have attracted many American

Indians by opening its 1992 General Assembly with a pagan Indian ritual in which a pipe containing sage was smoked, to drive out evil spirits.

A more promising theory appeared recently in *The Churching of America, 1776–1990: Winners and Losers in Our Religious Economy* (1992), a startling book by two sociologists, Roger Finke and Rodney Starke. According to them, in the religious marketplace, churches rise in a direct relationship to the degree they impose disciplines of faith and action on their members. When a church eases those disciplines, it declines—as the mainline Protestant churches have done, and as the Conservative movement in Judaism has, too. (Since the Reform movement rejected the authoritative basis of Jewish law from early on, it doesn't fit into this analysis.)

Finke and Starke explain a lot, but not everything. Their view runs up against the event that led, however indirectly, to the formation of all these churches in the first place: the foundation of Christianity itself. Though it isn't obvious from the Gospels what Jesus himself intended, the apostle Paul asserted that Jesus wished to abolish Jewish law. Out the window, for the early Christian Jews, went Jewish disciplines ranging from circumcision to the prohibition against graven images—all of these *mitzvot* getting "spiritualized," in Paul's hands, to the point of nonexistence. Yet this didn't stop Paul from attracting followers. Eviscerating disciplines, then, isn't necessarily hazardous to the health of a religious body.

Thinking about the problem of liberal-religious decline, I came across a clue in an unlikely place. As far as I know, the art critic Clement Greenberg recorded no opinions about Reform Judaism. He did, though, provide the classic definition of *kitsch*. In an essay published in 1939, "Avant-Garde and Kitsch," Greenberg tried to distinguish avant-garde art, whether in literature or visual art, from another variety of cultural product called kitsch. As Greenberg saw it, art was real art, avant-garde art, if it refused to depict objects in the world, but rather worked within the constraints set "by the disciplines and processes of art and literature themselves. . . . These constraints, once the world of common, extraverted experience has been renounced, can only be found in the very processes or disciplines by which art and literature have already imitated the former. These themselves become the subject matter of art and literature."

In other words, real art refers only to other art. What exactly *that* means isn't important for our purposes. Greenberg's thoughts about kitsch, though, are very interesting. To appreciate real art is hard, but once the difficult contemplation of it has been done, it offers an enormous payoff, in the form of an aesthetic experience. Kitsch, on the other hand, makes things easy for us by taking the *form* of real art and, using techniques of its own, seeking to provide a simulation of aesthetic experience right off the bat. As an example Greenberg mentions *The New Yorker* (of his day, not Tina Brown's), a piece of "fundamentally high-class kitsch for the luxury trade, [which] converts and waters down a great deal of avant-garde material [fiction, mostly] for its own uses."

Discussing the difference between experiencing a Picasso, on the one hand, and, on the other, a painting by Repin, a kitsch artist who depicted dramatic historical scenes, Greenberg writes: "the ultimate values which the cultivated spectator derives from Picasso are derived at a second remove, as the result of reflection upon the immediate impression left by the plastic values [i.e., the picture itself]. It is only then that the recognizable, the miraculous and the sympathetic enter. . . . Repin predigests art for the spectator and spares him effort, provides him with a short cut to the pleasure of art that detours what is necessarily difficult in genuine art. Repin, or kitsch, is synthetic art."

Roughly speaking, liberal religion is synthetic religion, kitsch religion. In a religious system centered on an orthodoxy, the system asks the believer to subscribe to a set of faith principles, deriving from what it asserts as the Truth about God and the universe, from which also follow definite standards of conduct. After the believer has accepted these principles and sought to order his life by them, he gets the payoff: the experience of God and His transcendence. As Abraham Joshua Heschel acknowledged, that experience is fleeting, but it is the hope that all traditional religions hold out to their followers. Those religions disagree about what the Truth actually is and about the demands God makes on men; but their relation to the Truth, as they perceive it, doesn't vary.

Borrowing Greenberg's language, you might say that orthodox religion doesn't seek to reflect the world, but rather the Truth. Kitsch religion reflects only the world: its political interests, its desire to be free of troublesome moral obligations. The relationship to the Ultimate which the orthodox believer derives from his faith is derived at a second remove, as the result of reflection upon the immediate impression left by the Truth about God. It is only then that the miraculous enters. Kitsch religion, by contrast, predigests orthodoxy for the church- or temple-goer and spares him effort, claims to provide him with a shortcut to the experience of transcendence that detours what is necessarily difficult in genuine religion.

Historically, churches and synagogues have been the only organizations whose mission is to seek out and disseminate this Truth. If God exists, if He revealed His will to men at points in history, if His revelations can be found in the often ambiguous document called the Bible, then an institution is needed to explain that document—to tell us what God wants from us. In rendering decisions about the meaning of the Bible, rabbis and priests have relied on the authority of ancient traditions: the Oral Torah in Judaism, or the papal tradition in the Roman Catholic Church.

Now, say the liberal denominations, let the people decide! In place of these hallowed traditions, kitsch religion substitutes the prevailing opinions of the secular world. As a result, Reform Judaism is influenced less by the tradition of the Oral Torah than by the editorial page of the *New York Times*. The Protestant mainline churches increasingly reject the authority of their own traditions, allowing men and women to believe what they wish about virtue, sin, and salvation. After spending a year at Harvard Divinity School, the last word in tony, mainline decadence, Ari Goldman put it bluntly in his book *The Search for God at Harvard* (1991): "Religious truth did not seem to exist at the Div School, only religious relativism."

Of course many clergymen associated with liberal denominations do not practice kitsch religion. One critic of the Episcopal Church, the journalist William Murchison, himself an Episcopalian, even argues that his church's "commitment to social liberalism and permissiveness can be, and has been, exaggerated—through its own efforts, not just the media's." An important point. I've read about and spoken to Episcopalians who are every bit as evangelical in their Christianity as Pat Robertson, who oppose abortion with as much fervor as any conservative Roman Catholic. When I wrote a book review recently in which I made a few critical comments about the Reform movement, I got a call from a Reform rabbi at a New York temple who told me that he had lost faith in Reform, that on retiring he wanted to move to Israel and live the life of an Orthodox Jew. In my local Jewish newspaper, New York's *Jewish Week*, another Reform rabbi lamented: "We have become a vacuous, no-demand, no-standards, no-requirements, no-guilt, do-good enterprise of sloppy sentimentality: a liberal Protestant Christianity without Jesus."

Where you do find it, though, kitsch in religion seeks to do an end run around Truth, providing a feeling of "spirituality" without the requirement of orthodox belief and action. That is its downfall. From a strict marketing perspective, this strategy can never work for long. In the end, the problem is a simple one of redundancy. You can think of many nonreligious institutions in American life ready and willing to provide precisely the benefits offered by liberal religion. The New Age movement promises the feeling of "spirituality"—without God. Want to make friends? Go to the gym. A whole spectrum of political organizations provide the buzzing high of self-righteousness—without having to sit through an hour-long service. While striving to be relevant, the liberal churches have made themselves irrelevant.

The liberal project in religion has been tried before. In the Book of Numbers, the modern reader meets a curiously familiar character. While the Jews wandered in the Wilderness, a Levite named Korah concluded that the authority to interpret God's will should not rest exclusively with Moses and Aaron. Let the people decide! And so, with a group of followers, he rebelled. "All the congregation are holy," he reminded Moses and Aaron, "every one of them, and the Lord is among them; wherefore then lift ye up yourselves above the assembly of the Lord?" For their trouble, without even a moment to fret about "declining membership," Korah and his followers were swallowed up by a crack in the earth.

The columnist Don Feder quotes a Methodist theologian at Duke University: "God is killing mainline Protestantism in America," says the despondent mainliner, "and we . . . deserve it." I disagree. I don't foresee any cracks opening up in the earth. Very slowly, kitsch religion is killing itself.

CAROLE RIFKIND

America's Fantasy Urbanism: The Waxing of the Mall and the Waning of Civility

Carole Rifkind is an architectural historian whose books include *Mansions, Mills and Main Streets; A Field Guide to American Architecture;* and the forthcoming *Field Guide to Contemporary American Architecture.* An advocate for public sensitivity to the built environment, she has taught at Columbia University's Graduate School of Architecture, Planning and Historic Preservation and has directed educational programs for the Hudson River Museum, the Municipal Art Society, and Partners for Livable Places.

The malling of America must be almost over by now. And what are its fruits? Rifkind finds the mall a surreal arena built at five-eighths scale where First Amendment rights clash with Muzak and formatted shopping opportunities. She sees a diminished sense of citizenship everywhere constricted by the ascendancy of commerce over all other human values. And a subtler, diminished sense of self-worth seems to come in tow as well. Is a deep sense of lost community a fair trade for the maximum in shopping values and options?

*A*s THE CONQUEST OF space in the early 1960s turned science fiction into reality, the simultaneous rise of the shopping mall yielded new domains for the imagination. Surely, no fictional space habitat could be more fantastic than some of the far-out environments we've lately created right here on earth.

Horton Plaza demonstrates the kind of Technicolor dream world that today's designers are fabricating—vaguely familiar, yet totally improbable. It's as if Zanzibar, a Tuscan hill town, and Hometown, U.S.A., collided in outer space and fell to earth on a six-block site in downtown San Diego, where they were reassembled, painted all the colors of the rainbow, and lit up at night. Time, space, and substance are collapsed into a phantasm of towers, domes, and arcaded streets. We're in a never-never land, but it's also a workaday shopping mall, whose architect, Jon Jerde, has been beguiled by science-fiction writer Ray Bradbury. "Drama and theater are not special and separate things of life," writes Bradbury. "They are the true stuff of life."

The shopping mall is the non-downtown of America, the first suburban nation in history. For decades we have been fleeing our cities, with their minority and poor populations, aging infrastructure, and traffic and transportation problems. Most of us seldom venture downtown, preferring to spend our free time at the mall. There the greatest frequency of visits coincides with the most critical stages of our lives: as toddlers in tow with young mothers; as teenagers experiencing our first taste of independence; as young couples setting up households; as new retirees learning how to use up time. Having left real cities behind to decay, we have conceived an escapist environment, stuffed into a big, blank shoebox of a building. Where people look and behave like "we" do. Where nothing gets old or ugly. Where the weather and the time of day never change. The fantasy environment of the mall encourages Americans to think that they can avoid the societal and civic responsibilities of the real world.

The shopping center is America's contribution to twentieth-century architectural history, an entirely new building type generated by automobility, cheap out-of-town land, and the promise of profit. The form evolved rapidly in the post–World War II era, from an open, campus-like setting to a monolithic, introverted structure sited in a 50-or-so-acre parking lot. Of the 43,000 shopping centers built since the 1950s, some 1,500 are regional malls, varying in size from a ½ million to 3 million or 4 million square feet of enclosed space, which is more shopping footage than in the downtowns of many towns and cities. Typically in a dumbbell, X, or Y configuration, the regional or superregional mall contains two, three, or four major department stores at the ends, known as the anchors, and from 100 to 200 specialty shops stretched out between them.

Ironically, the concept of the planned shopping center originated in the idealism of the Modern movement, which valued large-scale, rational planning, land zoning that kept housing apart from commerce and industry, and traffic-free pedestrian zones. The first enclosed shopping mall was built in Edina, Minnesota, in 1954, designed by Victor Gruen, who almost single-handedly perfected the type. A wartime émigré from Europe, Gruen was an architect and city planner who saw the shopping center as a place for modern community life "like that of the ancient Greek Agora, the Medieval marketplace and our own Town Square." A stage director in his youth, Gruen was also the first to realize the potential for dramatizing the mall with lighting, color, and art, as if it were a stage set. In the 1980s, disillusioned by the loss of civic values that accompanied commercial real estate development, Gruen returned to his native Vienna.

Theatricality, illusion, pretense, manipulation, and artifice are the essence of the mall setting. The shopper must buy, although the operator feigns that it is otherwise. As Bruno Bettelheim has explained of children's play activity, there can be no goal other than the activity itself. Every possible design tool is aimed at behavioral control, to make the shopper visit more often, stay longer, and buy more. Pathways are contrived to require her to walk past the maximum number of shopping outlets en route to the planned destination, tempting her to suspend judgment and yield to impulse. Attention-getting banners, vivid signs, dramatic lighting, seductive color schemes, lush plantings, upbeat music, and soothing sounds provide intense sensations, alternately stimulating and relaxing the visitor until she is freed from normal constraints and caught up in the mood of buying.

The fantasy of the mall confounds the relationship between consumption and commodity, want and need. Standardized experiences are represented as unique. For example, the activities of craftspeople in mid-aisle kiosks—painting on velvet or carving wooden cuckoo clocks—pretend to bring our age of mass consumption and production back to a time of the handcrafted and precious. Local glee-club performances are surrogates for old-time concert halls or high school auditorium experiences. A make-believe tropical landscape substitutes for Wisconsin's bitter wintertime. A recent trend is to decorate this most non-urban of places as if it were a real city, with city-like storefronts, lighting standards, granite paving, park-like benches, and "landmark" clocks. The fantasy is that inside is outside, private space is public space, that you can find your way out as easily as you entered, that the transitory, mutable space of the mall will endure. The realities of social conflict, crime, poverty, unemployment, and congestion are out of sight and out of mind.

The mall is "the T.V. you walk around in," says William Kowinski, a mall maven who has paraded through dozens of them. A kaleidoscopic extravaganza of shopfront logos, copious piles of brand-name merchandise, New Wave music, sparkling lights, and rapidly shifting images, it's like watching television's insistent succession of can't-ignore images. Like the TV commercial, the mall can transform passivity into desire with only the sketchiest of images. A quick glimpse of the Eiffel Tower is enough to evoke romance and adventure. An abbreviated storefront is a prop signifying an entire Main Street where everybody knows everybody. "Television and the mall are in the same business," Kowinski reminds us.

The packaging of theme malls has facilitated mass production of mass-consumption settings. Ernest Dichter, the psychoanalytic marketing consultant, explained the shopper's selection of a designed package as a way of expressing her individuality. The theory surely lies behind the packaged shopping environment—a New York theater district in exurban Minneapolis, a medieval walled town in the Arizona desert, and parodies of historic Main Streets in every corner of the nation. Faux materials mock the real thing: simulated marble, wallpaper-thin granite, plastic palm fronds. Broad, mirrored expanses reveal improbable vistas. Pedimented shopfronts, actually little more than room dividers, are built at Disneyland's diminutive five-eighths scale to increase one's sense of importance and self-confidence. Anthropologists tell us that purchases of impulse items such as body lotions, T-shirts, compact discs, candle holders, and breadmaking machines bring the promise of a "transformed self." But it's an introverted self, based on your own opinion rather than on your value to others or on your reputation. Consumption replaces community as a means of identification.

Any mall developer will admit that the market doesn't need another shopping center. The drastic overbuilding of malls in the 1980s, the growing competition from electronic and catalogue shopping, and the diminished free time of working women have sent developers scurrying to jack up the entertainment quotient of the shopping mall. Today's malls encompass all manner of multiplex cinemas, video arcades, try-it-out gadgetry stands, sand beaches with tanning lights, ice-skating rinks, miniature golf courses, contests, demonstrations, and live entertainment. Sociologist Neil Postman has described Las Vegas as a "metaphor of our national character and aspiration . . . a city entirely devoted to the idea of entertainment . . . that proclaims the spirit of a culture in which all public discourse increasingly takes the form of entertainment . . . politics, religion, news, athletics, education and commerce have been transformed into congenial adjuncts of show business." He might just as well have been talking about the shopping mall.

Certainly, Disneyland has been a strong influence on the mall. On the model of the theme park, the mall is a false-fronted, set-aside universe, prettied up, polished to a shine, and heavily patrolled. Architect and urban critic Michael Sorkin has suggested that the theme park creates a "universal equivalence" of places, where "everyplace becomes destination and any destination can be anywhere." The mall and the theme park are also alike in their nostalgia for the past, optimism for the future, focus on consumption, and protection from diversity.

The shopping mall has antecedents in the market square, fairground, carnival, arcade, and department store. But perhaps most telling is its resemblance to the turn-of-the-century amusement park. In Coney Island's Steeplechase and Luna parks, Dutch architect Rem Koolhaas discovered the origins of the "Urbanism of the Fantastic." Like the contemporary shopping mall, its walls were relatively impenetrable, permitting "innocent pleasures" to be enjoyed on the interior, safe from the "corruption" of the world out there. Heightened imagination keeps harsh reality at bay. Like the amusement park, the mall is environmental theater, built like stage scenery, and just as easily modified. In the mall, nothing is permitted to appear old or obsolete. Few malls survive in an

as-built state for more than ten or fifteen years before being recon-
figured, repositioned, and repackaged to meet changing markets and
ever-more-aggressive competition. Renovation, in fact, has consumed by
far the largest part of mall construction budgets in the last decade.

It's surely no accident that the proliferation of shopping malls coincided with an explosion of leisure time. So important has the shopping
center become in American life that, for many, only work and sleep
occupy more time. The nation's bicentennial year saw the shopping experience conflated with heritage tourism when Faneuil Hall Marketplace, an age-encrusted wholesale food market on Boston's historic
waterfront, was scraped clean and spiffed up as an exotic food and
hometown craft boutique, shaking up conventional wisdom about shopping and how people like to spend their leisure time. Assisted by tax
credits, heritage tourism spread like brush fire, lighting up historic train
stations in Washington, D.C., and St. Louis, new-old markets such as
Baltimore's HarbourPlace and New York's South Street Seaport, simulated historic settings like Jack London Square in San Francisco and
Mystic Village on the Connecticut shore, and dozens of real old towns,
from New Hope, Pennsylvania, to Madison, Indiana, and Benecia, California.

Heritage tourism can be criticized for kitschiness, glorifying consumption over history, and falsifying reality. Venerable places become
mere "city tableaux," charges urban critic Christine Boyer, who mourns
historic settings transformed into "culinary and ornamental landscapes
through which tourists—the new public of the late twentieth century—
graze, celebrating the consumption of place and architecture, and the
taste of history and food."

In presenting itself as theater, the mall has turned us away from the
authentic drama that's played out every day on city streets, as sociologist
William H. Whyte has learned. In the 1950s, Whyte's *The Organization
Man* taught us about America's changing social values. In the 1970s and
1980s, Whyte's extended time-lapse photography of people's behavior in
public spaces—how they wait at street corners, greet friends, schmooze,
and watch others—discovered the street as the "river of life in the city,"
most fascinating, perhaps, for the activity of its "characters"—vendors,
entertainers, handbill passers, beggars, pitchmen, pickpockets, three-
card-monte players, and dope dealers. "Good performers and good
audiences," Whyte concluded. "These are the stuff of a good street life."

Like the shopping mall, the art museum has enjoyed mushroom
growth in recent decades. Insofar as they both provide sensual gratification, revere material objects over human interaction, create sanitized
environments, and exact standards of behavior above those maintained
by society as a whole, they are twin mirrors of our changing values. The
affinity of the mall and the museum was explored in a 1992 exhibit at the

New Museum of Contemporary Art in New York City's SoHo, *The Art Mall: A Social Space,* in which various artists challenged the connections between culture and commerce. Among the most provocative was Barbara Pollack and Grai St. Clair Rice's installation piece, *Modern Mecca: Shut Up and Shop,* which parodied the mall management's determination to control the shopper's behavior.

In museums across the country, blockbuster exhibits have exploited retail markets of their own, a practice that took off after the success of the Metropolitan Museum's Tutankhamen show some years ago. The visitor exiting the show, confronted by an engaging display of Egyptoid merchandise, could hardly be certain if some wrong turn had not taken her back to the beginning of the show. Increasingly needy for gift-shop revenues to help make up operating deficits, museums have doubled and redoubled the space and glitz of lobby stores and have hitched sales stands to individual galleries. They've even developed museum stores in shopping malls. Now there's no need to visit the museum, you can shop it in the suburbs.

Since antiquity, urban civility has been the test of the level of society. America's self-image as a democracy has surely been intimately related to our use of public space. The free assembly of citizens on Boston's Commons. Parades on Main Street. Sundays in Central Park. The "myriad-moving human panorama" Whitman describes on Chestnut Street in Philadelphia. We can no longer ignore the fact that the forward momentum of fantasy urbanism is more than coincident with the decline of the public realm.

The shared space of the public landscape is where we "lead the lives of free and responsible citizens," asserts J. B. Jackson, a preeminent cultural geographer. He explains the enduring features of the built environment—the boundary, the meeting place, the monument, and the public road—as critical for an awareness of one's social and political role in a democratic society. It is precisely in the distortion of these features that the mall's putative public space is revealed as spurious. While good fences make good neighbors, the wall of the shopping mall remains a virtually impervious barrier to social mingling; the kind of loitering that takes place around the courthouse or the post office is certainly impossible in the shopping center parking lot. The statuary and public art that enrich the culture of our cities with memories and inspiration are surely not equivalent to the mall's flimflam graphics and lighting tricks. It is in the denial of the public road—which Jackson regards as a social institution of particular importance—that the mall is most destructive of the public realm. At the dead end of the highway, the mall shows only its backside.

We don't like to remember that the mall is an exclusive, private, profit-making domain. The successful mall accurately targets very particular market segments, defined by age, income, lifestyle, and social values. No part of the mall welcomes the poor or the marginal. If it should happen—which it rarely does—that an "undesirable" finds the way to the mall, the private security guard will intimidate him and hasten him on his way. The relationship between teenagers and mall management is more problematic. To be sure, youths are paying customers, consuming mountains of tacos, hot dogs, egg rolls, and pizza slices and ringing cash bells on the sale of compact discs, T-shirts, cosmetics, and sports equipment. But they occupy the mall only by the sufferance of the management: a too-large crowd, rowdyism, and distraction to other shoppers are grounds for exclusion. The elderly, with time heavy on their hands, find the shopping mall a rare place to congregate these days and cause no trouble for the management. But their welcome is likely to be just as ambivalent. "We don't really want them to come here if they're not going to shop," one mall manager admitted. "They take up seats we would like to have available for shoppers." Management likes to promote the mall as the new center of community life, but banks on the fact that "having the perception of community feeling does not mean that it actually exists. . . . Perception is not necessarily reality."

Legally, the mall is likely to remain a battleground for constitutional rights of free speech and assembly. A 1976 decision by the U.S. Supreme Court found that shopping centers were private places where political activity could be muzzled. However, the constitutions of a handful of states provide for a broader interpretation of those rights, and a recent New Jersey decision may have cleared the way for a new series of challenges. Balancing free speech and property rights, the state's highest court noted the widespread displacement of downtown economic and social activity to suburban shopping centers, the centers' vigor in representing themselves as public places, and their generosity in providing spaces for meeting and talking and "hanging out." The court decided that "the flow of free speech in today's society is too important to be cut off simply to enhance the shopping ambience in our state's shopping centers." Complaining about the decision, a shopping-center industry spokesman wrote the *New York Times* to say that citizens can just as well "exercise their free speech rights on street corners, in parks, in bus terminals and in other places maintained by taxpayer dollars." Even if courts do eventually permit the quiet distribution of pamphlets, it's hardly likely that they'll tolerate parading, picketing, or vocal protest. The rights of citizens will remain very tightly drawn at the mall.

Of course, the mall is only one component of the ongoing convulsive privatization of the public realm. We're seeing local communities "selling" their schools to for-profit operators; municipalities leasing out their hospitals and sanitation services; state governments giving up their scenic highways for "adoption." Many cities allow developers to build extra footage up in the air in exchange for the provision of "public space" at street level, where close scrutiny by private guards is usually enough to discourage "those people" from entering. In New York City, so-called Business Improvement Districts permit self-taxing to pay for the sanitation and security services that the municipal government no longer provides. At this moment, there is serious consideration being given to the creation of a Neighborhood Improvement District that would permit well-to-do residents of the entire Upper East Side of Manhattan to hire private guards to patrol "their" city streets.

Fortunately, New York City's size and diversity enable pedestrian democracy to stubbornly survive. But other cities are less fortunate. The almost complete introversion of megastructures in cities such as Atlanta (Peachtree and Omni Centers, for example) and Detroit (Renaissance Center) has virtually vacuumed the streets clean of people. The retreat from the street is almost total in cities such as Minneapolis, Houston, and Oklahoma City, where skywalks and subterranean tunnels have ingested public space into private domains. But the prize for the most systematic destruction of public space, according to urban planner Mike Davis, belongs to Los Angeles, a city that has responded to its fear of Hispanics, blacks, youths, and the poor by "militarizing" civic territory. The city's publicly subsidized downtown office redevelopment has transformed an entire district into a forbidding "corporate citadel," whose architectural design and heavy arsenal of security systems ruthlessly discourage the poor from entering and enjoying the amenable open spaces that are provided to the middle class. Hollywood images that portray the metropolis as a prison *(Escape from New York)* or the streets as a setting for warfare *(Colors)* "are not fantasies," he charges, "but extrapolations from the present."

We can't imagine the future without shopping malls. People like and want them, and if they didn't exist we'd have to invent them. Certainly, they provide comfort, convenience, and diversion for people with plastic cards in their pockets. But let's not pretend, as some have, that malls will eventually mature into true community centers. And let's hope we'll wake up sometime soon and realize that citizenship is, after all, more important than consumerism.

WORKS CITED

Boyer, Christine. "Cities for Sale: Merchandising History at South Street Seaport," in *Variations on a Theme Park*. New York: Hill and Wang, 1992.

Davis, Mike. "Fortress Los Angeles: The Militarization of Urban Space," in *Variations on a Theme Park*. New York: Hill and Wang, 1992.

Jackson, J. B. "The Public Landscape," in *Landscapes*. Amherst: University of Massachusetts Press, 1970, from a lecture at the University of Massachusetts, 1966.

Koolhaas, Rem. *Delirious New York.* New York: Oxford University Press, 1978.

Kowinski, William S. *The Malling of America.* New York: William Morrow, 1985.

Postman, Neil. *Amusing Ourselves to Death.* New York: Viking, 1985.

Sorkin, Michael. "See You in Disneyland," in *Variations on a Theme Park.* New York: Hill and Wang, 1992.

Whyte, William H. *City: Rediscovering the Center.* New York: Doubleday, 1988.

JONATHAN ROSEN

The Trivialization of Tragedy

Jonathan Rosen wrote his first novel (forthcoming from Random House) while working as associate editor of the *Forward,* a Jewish national newspaper for which he
created the Arts and Letters section. His reviews and essays have been published
there, in the *New York Times,* and in *Vanity Fair.* In assuming a complex view of
institutions built with some good intentions, he undertook one of the most delicate
and difficult assignments in this book, but possibly one of the most necessary.

Rosen's arguments here are grave and troubling, proposing multiple pathologies.
Implicit in his piece is an indictment of the passing of true historical imagination—
the sustained effort to understand the past on its own terms. He declines the available props which we use as *aide-mémoire* to purchase the past, and we may well suppose, reading this, that we are all complicit in the acceptance of a formatted
simulation of experience over the meditative structures of memory. As we follow his
visits to the Holocaust Museum and to the Disney-sponsored re-creation of slavery
time in the Old South, we may be close to the virtual reality of the computer tour,
weeping readily but with dry eyes. These re-creations, Rosen has suggested, come
dangerously close to recreations, and any moral legacy appropriated by an entertainment industry may trivialize tragedy with its literalness, making amnesiacs of us all.
    Jonathan Rosen is one of the youngest contributors to this book, his presence
providing an unruly hope that rescue is still possible.

THE ONLY HATE MAIL I have ever received has been from survivors of the Holocaust.

"You must be mentally sick and insane," a survivor of Dachau scrib-
bled. "You should be thrown into one of those notorious gas ovens
which the Nazis used so successfully."

Another man wrote: "I feel sure that God, in his infinite wisdom, will
give you the harsh punishment you deserve."

What had I done to inspire such outrage? I had written an Op-Ed
piece in the *New York Times* suggesting that it was a mistake to construct a
Holocaust museum on federal land in Washington, D.C. My goal was not
to deny Holocaust survivors a real reflection of their tragic experience,
but to prevent Americans from seeing that reflection and mistaking it for
their own. This had something to do with the museum itself and a great
deal to do with contemporary American culture, which has a habit of
trivializing tragedy and adapting it for personal use.

The museum, of course, was opened with great fanfare despite my Op-Ed piece. President Clinton stood on its front steps and denounced evil in all its forms. Eli Wiesel spoke and urged President Clinton, in the name of the six million Jewish dead, to bomb Bosnian Serbs. The opening of the museum coincided with a march for gay rights on Washington and many chose to end their rally with a visit to the museum. Writing in the *Times Literary Supplement,* James Bowman reported finding the following messages in the Hall of Remembrance, which invites people to leave notes in honor of the dead. "I am a lesbian. It could have been me. It could happen again, and if it does this time it could be me. Never again." Another visitor recorded the observation that "AIDS is the holocaust of our era."

It is to take nothing away from the struggle for gay rights, or the horror of AIDS, to say that the Holocaust seems a hyperbolic emblem for the situation of homosexuals in America in the 1990s. But the museum planners were conscious of offering up a historical tragedy for convenient use by American culture. Two years before the museum was completed I spoke to Michael Berenbaum, the project director of the museum, for an article I was writing for the *Forward.* He told me that "the museum is based on the idea that you can take the bereaved memories of a parochial community and make them American life." It was the goal of the planners to graft a European-grown flower of evil onto the prickly body of multicultural America. "We're taking Jewish memories and speaking to the very heart and soul of the nation," Mr. Berenbaum boasted.

The claims of American relevance were no doubt necessary in the bargain the museum planners made for federal land—give us a place on the Mall and we'll give you an American experience. Obsessed with the details of the Nazi destruction—real hair from Auschwitz, a genuine cattle car—the curators' reassemblage of these disparate, though authentic, elements can't help but have an oddly spurious effect when reshaped by American mythic needs. The very placement of the museum in the civic heart of Washington, D.C., puts a symbolic burden on the catastrophe of European Jewry unsuited to the actual event.

Increasingly, Americans feel it is necessary to house history in buildings instead of books, which is unfortunate, since the more that history is embodied in buildings, the more historical events are turned into theatrical or symbolic moments stripped of the larger context that makes history valuable. As the written word itself is devalued, written records, however well researched and secure, are viewed as impermanent. In our new understanding, whoever trusts his history to a mere book is like the little pig content to have a house of straw. The first denier who huffs and puffs will blow the whole thing down. Museums are seen as the brick houses of history, and already battles are shaping up over the fight to create museums of slavery and of the American Indian experience in Washington.

Memory was not always so literally viewed. In her wonderful book *The Art of Memory*, Francis Yates tells a story that illustrates how memory rose out of literal bricks and mortar and into language, the opposite of our present trend. The story she tells is recounted by Cicero in "De Oratore," about the poet Simonides. A praise singer, Simonides was invited to a banquet by Scopas, a nobleman of Thessaly. In honor of the occasion, Simonides composes a lyric to praise his host, but he praises, as well, the gods Castor and Pollux. Scopas, insulted at having to share his honors, only pays half of what he promised to the poet. "Get the rest from Castor and Pollux," he tells Simonides. Midway through the feast, the short-changed praise singer is told that two men wish to speak to him outside. Simonides gets up from his place at the table and goes outside, where he sees no one, but, before he can go back inside, the roof of the banquet hall caves in, crushing all the guests. The bodies, including the nobleman, Scopas, are so badly mangled they cannot be recognized by the relatives who come to claim them. Simonides, however, remembers where every guest had sat. In his mind, he re-creates the order of the banquet and so is able to identify the bodies, which are borne off to the funeral pyre by their grieving kin.

Cicero goes on to say that Simonides became the inventor of the art of memory, pioneering the system, known as a "memory palace," used by the ancient Romans and later by medieval scholars for remembering speeches and manuscripts of tremendous length. In that system, a mansion full of rooms is imagined. In each room the orator deposits an idea. Then, during the speech, he revisits his imaginary palace, going from room to room in a set order and reclaiming the ideas he had planted there, thus delivering a speech, or recalling a manuscript of great length, without notes of any kind.

The home of memory, as Simonides and Cicero understood, is language. Simonides does not decide to rebuild the banquet hall so that passing Romans can sit inside and feel the fate of their fellows. The calamity did not befall them—or him, however close it came—and what separates Simonides from the victims is the story he can tell about it. The memory palace he goes on to devise lives in the imagination; its roof can never fall. The memory that grows inside the imaginary rooms, however, is real. Our own urge to bind history in mortar and brick seems driven by an opposite impulse. Our memory palaces, in this literal age, are real. The quality of our memory is another story.

More and more, museums are striving to re-create the mood of an original catastrophe and to provide an atmosphere that allows visitors to feel they are in the place represented. Some museums go so far as to make visitors feel that they are the people whose fate is on display. The Walt Disney Corporation recently had it in mind to build a historical theme park near the Civil War battlefield of Manassas in northern Virginia. Protesting in an August 1994 Op-Ed piece in the *New York Times,* William Styron quoted with disgust the words of Robert Weis, a proponent of the project: "We want to make you feel what it was like to be a slave, and what it was like to escape through the Underground Railroad."

Styron devoted several years to *The Confessions of Nat Turner,* a novel that, in his words, "was partly intended to make the reader feel what it was like to be a slave," and he was leery of Disney's ability to induce that feeling in the minds of distracted tourists out for a Sunday afternoon. Styron recalled his grandmother, who as a girl owned two slaves and, after their liberation by Union troops, mourned for them the rest of her life. Admitting that his grandmother's grief paled beside the suffering of slaves and those freed from slavery, he nevertheless wondered if a museum could ever capture the subtle intertwining of lives that slavery wrought over its 250 years on American soil.

"The falseness," Styron argued, "is in the assumption that by viewing the artifacts of cruelty and oppression, or whatever the imagineers cook up—the cabins, the chains, the auction block—one will have succumbed in a 'disturbing and agonizing' manner to the catharsis of a completed tragedy."

Partly because of protests like Styron's, Disney canceled its plans. But the spirit that inspired them seems here to stay. On Columbus Day, 1994, Colonial Williamsburg added a slave auction to the candle-dipping and bread-baking that usually go on. A pregnant woman was sold to a new master, separating her from her husband. A freed slave bought his wife. A carpenter and his tools were sold. Three thousand people, mostly white, attended. Many wept. Afterwards they clapped. Here, certainly, was the catharsis of a completed tragedy Styron had feared. For dramatic tragedy offers closure that historical tragedy never possesses.

Not that everyone was pleased. Jack Gravely, political action chairman of the Virginia chapter of the NAACP, said, before the auction, "We don't want the history of people who have come so far and done so much to be trivialized in a carnival atmosphere such as we have here." But later, Mr. Gravely, like Balaam in the Bible, changed his mind. He had come to curse. Afterwards, he praised. "I was wrong," he said. "Suffering had a face. Pain had a body."

But whose face? What body? "Living history" is the oxymoronic name some give this kind of interaction with the past. Certainly it stirs people up. Tourists, the same people Disney believed could feel "what it was like to be a slave," played their own weird part in the dramatization. Members of the audience called out to the actor portraying the slave owner, urging him not to separate a pregnant slave from her husband. The auction was scripted and the sale went through. But after all, to whom was the audience calling? The auction was based on a sale that took place circa 1773.

We would all love to shout down the evils of the past with modern voices of outrage, but we cannot. Tragic history is being treated increasingly like tragic theater, instilling fear, pity, and, ultimately, purgation. The strange ritual is becoming a kind of contemporary rite of atonement. This is not history but something else almost magical in its method and extremely ambiguous in its effect.

At the Holocaust Museum in Washington, each visitor to the museum is issued a kind of invitation to suffering. It is called an "identity" card and it carries the picture of someone who passed through the Holocaust. It might be a twelve-year-old gypsy boy from Romania or an eighteen-year-old Jewish girl from Vilna. You carry the card through the museum and on each floor punch it into a machine that "updates" your victim. The card is a ghostly guide through hell. By the end you learn what happened to your guide. Did he die in Auschwitz? Escape across the border? Allied to the fate of a single person, the theory goes, the museum visitor will care about the fate of a whole people.

The Holocaust Museum believes that identification with the victim is a good thing. To that end the museum itself, though in restrained fashion, echoes the claustrophobia of the ghetto, with narrow hallways channeling viewers uncomfortably together as they file past exhibits. The elevators, which move with excruciating slowness while an audiotape plays the voice of a survivor recalling his calamity, have been built to conjure associations with the interior of a cattle car or gas chamber. The walls are dark with riveted surfaces that suggest incarceration.

Identification and understanding are not the same. In fact, identification often comes at the expense of understanding. The Poles like to call themselves the Jews of Europe. That they should see their own fate in the fate of those they helped exterminate is one of those ironies so vast and subtle it almost defies explanation. It is also common. Jewish history is particularly fraught with such usurpations, and it makes the universalizing impulse behind the museum all the more disconcerting.

A perfect example of identification displacing understanding can be found in that handbook of intolerance, *The Autobiography of Malcolm X*. Malcolm X didn't like Jews, but he knew all about the Holocaust. Indeed, he used it as part of his attack on American culture. In his autobiography, he writes about the German Jews. Their tragedy, Malcolm tells his readers, is that they thought they were German. They believed they had achieved acceptance. "The Jew," Malcolm writes,

had made greater contributions to Germany than Germans themselves had. Jews had won over half of Germany's Nobel Prizes. Every culture in Germany was led by the Jew; he published the greatest newspaper. Jews were the greatest artists, the greatest poets, composers, stage directors. But those Jews made a fatal mistake—assimilating.

The Jews of Germany become the basis of his argument against integration. Whites hate blacks, he says, and the more blacks integrate, the more they'll be like the German Jews, disarming themselves against the final assault. Knowing about the Holocaust didn't diminish Malcolm's anti-Semitism, it merely refined his anti-Americanism. The Jews as Jews do not interest Malcolm X. He instead imagines himself into their place and views their fate as his fate. He makes a metaphor of their suffering divorced from the specificity of their time and place. He sees the Holocaust as a parable about America. He does exactly what Michael Berenbaum told me he hoped would happen. Malcolm took the bereaved memory of a parochial community and made it American life. It was because he was appropriating an experience that he hated most those to whom the experience actually belonged.

Unearned identification has become a pattern of our culture. Malcolm Little unmade himself into Malcolm X to eradicate the legacy of slavery. He has in turn been appropriated by hundreds of Americans collapsing the space between themselves and Malcolm X. At the end of Spike Lee's film *Malcolm X*, child after child stands up and proclaims, "I am Malcolm X." Whatever one thinks of Malcolm X, his experience, as hustler, criminal, preacher, was his own. He paid for his life with his life, and it is a cheap moment in the movie, and a sad cheapening of experience, when a chorus of Americans declare, "I am Malcolm X."

Something has changed in our understanding of what history is that makes us wish to conjure the past and have it perform for us. We seem to have lost respect for the sheer pastness of it, the elusiveness of anything gone. Perhaps television and movies have had a larger impact than we know on the way we perceive reality, for of course nothing in a movie or on television is ever lost. The central attractions of the Holocaust Museum are the video screens situated behind "privacy" walls (to prevent children from seeing over), giving them an almost pornographic appeal, where Nazi footage shows the dying endlessly dying.

At work, too, is a peculiar dimension of American spirituality best exemplified by Walt Whitman's haunting and egotistical declaration in "Song of Myself": "I am the man, I was there, I suffered." Harold Bloom examines this American Jesus in his essay on Whitman in *The Western Canon* and quotes a notebook fragment that makes Whitman's identification even more astonishing and telling:

> In vain were nails driven through my hands.
> I remember my crucifixion and bloody coronation
> I remember the mockers and the buffeting insults
> The sepulchre and the white linen have yielded me up

> I am alive in New York and San Francisco,
> Again I tread the streets after two thousand years.
> Not all the traditions can put vitality in churches
> They are not alive, they are cold mortar and brick,
> I can easily build as good, and so can you:—
> Books are not men—

For Bloom, this is a good illustration of the American religion he examined more closely in his book of that name, which he sees as "post-Christian" but emerging from Christianity. "The American Jesus," he writes, "is no First-Century Palestinian Jew but a 19th and 20th Century American," who feeds off the notion of the resurrected Jesus walking the earth. Without question, the trends Bloom identified have intensified. Just look at the number of near-death experiences, in which people die and come back to earth and then testify to the experience in print. It is nothing less than the personalization of the experience of Jesus: "In vain were nails driven through my hands."

This has a great deal to do with the planning of museums devoted to victims. "Incarnational theology works," Michael Berenbaum told me in my interview with him about the Holocaust Museum, and that is what identity cards, "personalizing" the experience of suffering, facilitate. That is what the Walt Disney Corporation wanted when a spokesman said tourists would "feel what it was like . . . to escape through the Underground Railroad." That is what Spike Lee was enacting when he filmed child after child rising and declaring, "I am Malcolm X," which is another way of saying, "I am the man, I was there, I suffered."

Whitman's poetic conceit, focused on a distant religious moment, has become a way of relating to all tragic occurrences. It may be strange to say, but the Holocaust Museum and others museums like it are the churches of the American religion: "I can easily build as good, and so can you." Walk inside and experience the suffering. Become, for an afternoon, the Jew on the cross. But inhabiting history is the opposite of understanding history.

Steven Spielberg fell prey to this trivializing tendency when he created *Schindler's List,* which, like the Holocaust Museum, fits secular history into a religious framework—an American post-Christian religious framework. The film has been adopted as the representative Holocaust movie, complete with grainy newsreel footage from the war spliced in to give it the feel of a documentary, but the story is not a small representative piece of the past. It is virtually the opposite of the larger history of the Holocaust. It is about a Christian man, a Nazi, who rescues Jews from the jaws of death, even marching into Auschwitz where he literally puts Jews back on a cattle car leaving the death camp. The horrifying image of *Shoah,* Claude Lanzman's epic examination of the Nazi destruction of European Jewish life, in which train after train rolls to the gates of the death camp, is undone in a kind of Indiana Jones moment of pluck and daring. The nails run through but they do not kill. The movie becomes a story not of annihilation, which the Holocaust was, but of salvation, which the Holocaust was not. That a real Schindler once walked the earth does not make him the emblematic man the film enshrines.

At the end of the story, his Jews saved, Schindler himself dresses in the outfit of a prisoner in order to escape. Jews yank gold teeth out of their own mouths and give them to the man still wearing a swastika button, to help him make his getaway. Schindler the savior descends, in a final act of martyrdom, into the despised form of those he has rescued. He is Nazi and Jew, hero and victim. He is the American Jesus, God and man, Jew and Christian, and something more than all of these. The swastika he wears in his lapel comes to seem a kind of cross, a symbol not of death but of life.

Like Spike Lee's *Malcolm X, Schindler's List* presents a coda, filmed in Jerusalem at the grave of the real Schindler. The actors, no longer dressed for their parts, lead the actual survivors they portrayed in the film to Schindler's gravesite. The fictional and the literal join hands, and the actor who played Schindler himself comes and puts a stone on his own grave, standing triumphant like the risen Christ.

It is hard to keep straight at the end of *Schindler's List* who is the savior and who is the saved, who is the soldier and who is the sufferer, who is the Christian and who is the Jew, who is an actor and who is a man, what is fiction and what is real. Spielberg, perhaps unconsciously moved to repair the break between Jews and Christians that the Holocaust so horribly implies, has created a fantasy inspired by history but whose mythic impulse overpowers the historic grounding of the film. Clearly Spielberg's own identification is with Schindler, the only full-blooded character in the film, and he allows himself to have it both ways by dressing Schindler, at the end of the film, like a concentration-camp inmate.

Hollywood, that ultimate homogenizer of history and fantasy, creates a Holocaust perfect for American audiences. Obsessed, like the Holocaust Museum, with real details (the Auschwitz scenes were filmed at Auschwitz), it recasts those details into an American mythic mold. Not only does *Schindler's List* have a happy ending, it is an invitation to identify with a charming hero, handsome and strong, who, however corrupt he may initially seem, becomes a savior. It is a celebration of the American Jesus, and it is fitting that it ends not at a place where Jews died but at Schindler's Jerusalem grave, out of which the movie rises to offer its viewers a soothing vision of redemption.

The Holocaust Museum in Washington follows a similar pattern. The first view visitors have when they enter the museum is from the perspective of liberating American soldiers. The first thing you see is giant photographs of concentration camps taken by American troops. Only then do you get your identity card that allows you to pass from the savior to the sufferer. Entering an American hero, you then inhabit the lowly role of the victim. The visitor, experiencing both, becomes an American Jesus.

That is why the frame of the museum, for all the imported evil within, is American. It is not a museum of Jewish life and culture before the war, for only the death of Jews fits the needs of the American religion. The justification for all the horror contained in the Holocaust Museum, and for the slave drama at Colonial Williamsburg, and for all the other museums of victimization in the works, is that these are teaching tools that eloquently argue the importance of democracy. Were there not some added mythical appeal to museums of suffering, particularly of the Holocaust, were they not constructed as churches of the American religion offering their strange promise of redemption through suffering, it seems unlikely they would be built.

Without understanding the American Christian mythic framework, it would be difficult to understand why so many people are convinced that the Holocaust can be put to practical use. That it is an agent of democracy. That images of hell necessarily frighten people toward heaven.

The arguments put forward are that the Holocaust Museum in Washington is a giant vaccine, a kind of inoculation against the evil contained within. This is American hopefulness neutralizing the dark knowledge of Europe. This is a view of tragedy that doesn't believe the gun in Act I will go off in Act V because it is the nature of guns to go off, of men to kill each other, of people to die. This is a view of tragedy that believes that the gun in Act I doesn't have to go off if gun-control laws are passed in Act III. This is a view of tragedy that believes it leads to redemption, not the dread conclusions of the truly tragic nature, which would challenge the optimism by which America functions.

At the same time there is a powerful and perhaps equally American desire to see and touch the evil of Europe, especially as it relates to the Holocaust, which feeds into American fundamentalist longings for apocalypse, for final confrontations, for Judeo-Christian resolution. I sincerely doubt that people are flocking in record numbers to view images of the extermination of European Jewry because they want to strengthen their ideas of democracy. There is an almost panting intensity to the tourists who come, a piety tinged with prurient titillation that has little to do with history. Would they come, after all, to see a museum of Jewish culture? Of Jewish life before the war?

Tragedy is what draws the tourists. They come to feel that calamitous events are somehow informing their own lives, enriching them, making them better. But that is not the same as learning what happened to particular people, in a particular place and time, and facing the honest consequences of those events. By all means we should, we must, study the Holocaust. But why should we assume that there are positive lessons to be learned from it?

Allow me to make a sinister suggestion. What if some history doesn't have anything to teach us? What if studying radical evil doesn't make us better? What if, walking through the haunted halls of the Holocaust Museum, looking at evidence of the destruction of European Jewry, visitors do not emerge with a greater belief that all men are created equal but with a belief that man is by nature evil? What if an appropriate response to touring the Holocaust Museum is to buy a gun? What if the message of the museum, of the Holocaust itself, is that the Enlightenment was an idle dream, that civilization itself is a cruel hoax? That there is something about Christian culture that feeds on death? That the death drive in all of us is more powerful than the instinct for life?

What if Christians, seeing Jews suffering the fate of the damned—babies burnt, bodies stript, corpses piled high—are secretly confirmed in believing that Jews are meant to be the burnt offerings of the age. After all, images of the suffering Jew were prevalent through 1,000 years of European civilization. Those images did not prevent the Holocaust. They may, indeed, have prepared Europe for it by making Jewish suffering seem a kind of inevitability, perhaps even in keeping with divine wishes.

Planners of the Disney theme park and even of the well-intentioned Holocaust Museum are letting Americans have it both ways, letting them savor irrational ugly evil and feel, at the same time, they are better democrats for it. You can watch men and women on the auction block—a spectacle in slave days, too—and feel good about yourself by yelling at the slave owners.

In my Op-Ed article criticizing the idea of the Holocaust Museum, I recalled a conversation I had with Lucy Dawidowicz, the pioneering Holocaust historian who died in 1990. Did she think the Holocaust should be taught in schools? I'd asked her once. She wasn't opposed to it, she told me, but it wasn't a priority. "I'd feel a lot safer," she said, "if they learned the meaning of the Constitution instead." She did not mean that the history of the Holocaust should not be taught, studied, preserved. She only meant that American decency isn't based on deep knowledge of the irrational indecency of the world but on positive principles of equality. The letters I received from Holocaust survivors—"I am sure that God, in his infinite wisdom, will give you the harsh punishment you deserve"; "You should be thrown into one of those notorious gas ovens which the Nazis used so successfully"—were the understandable expressions of people who hadn't just read about or seen evil but who had experienced it. For real encounters with evil so batter and bruise the soul as to misshape it forever. Who else broods so on the punishment of God?

Who else dreams vengefully of putting people into ovens? Those letters were smudged with the ash of suffered tragedy and it was bracing to receive them. Their authors wrote irrationally because that is what happens to people who pass through what the Holocaust Museum, which is only the shadow of a shadow, purports to represent. You do not necessarily emerge a democrat. You do not emerge singing that all men are brothers. More likely you emerge believing that Beethoven's Ninth died at Auschwitz along with the rest of German culture and who knows what else.

None of this is to say that teaching history is wrong or bad or, God forbid, that goodness comes from ignoring evil. It is only to say that the passion plays Americans have taken to putting on for one another in recent years do not necessarily end in redemption, and that the facile indentification with victims does not lead to better behavior. Victims don't occupy a higher moral plane. They've just suffered more. Which is only liable to make them, like the survivors who wrote me hate mail, full of rage.

ARMSTRONG WILLIAMS

"I Feel Good to Be a Black Male"

Armstrong Williams is the CEO of the Graham-Williams Group, an international public relations firm in Washington, D.C. He is the host of *The Right Side*, a program syndicated nationally on Salem Radio Network and on National Empowerment Television. This excerpt is taken from his book *Beyond Blame: How We Can Succeed by Breaking the Dependency Barrier* (1995).

Using the form of a series of letters to a young black American, "Brad," Armstrong Williams addresses his correspondent (who he makes clear is a real person) here on the subject of Brad's education and the attendant subject of role models. For Brad, feeling proud to be black is a valued outcome of his education; for Williams such an education, centered on self-esteem but lacking real achievements to support it, is for blacks the serpent in the garden of larger American realities. For Brad, Malcolm X represents a role model who points to a racist society and says that violence and retaliation are justified in the struggle for a viable identity—"by any means necessary." For Williams, a stronger means is the way of Dr. Martin Luther King, Jr.: "Dr. King and Malcolm X both realized that self-esteem comes from self-respect, and that both have to be earned through hard work and a dedication to living a moral life."

It seems clear that, if dumbing down is an option that society has seductively obliged too many black Americans to choose, we need both Malcolm and Martin to point the way to a solution: from Malcolm, the powerful sense of directing personal destiny; from Martin, the liberating sense that it is by giving that we receive; from both, as Williams notes, the realization that in life showing up just isn't good enough. Personal contribution is the way to achieve both goals—if the notion of personal contribution can be recovered and fostered in a culture that no longer appears to value it.

DEAR BRAD:

When we first met, you said you regretted your life as a street hustler and that you would make different choices if you could live your life over again. When I asked why you stopped hustling, you explained, "What really made me stop was the guys who kidnapped me." I guess I should be shocked at your reaction, but I am not. It was not until hustling became too dangerous for you that you stopped. You do not regret having used women; you are only sorry that you risked getting AIDS. Even when you talk of providing for your children, you seem to be motivated mostly by the fact that you are embarrassed. That is why I was so convinced that you were completely sincere when you said you wished to start a new life: you had decided that hustling is no longer in your best interest. From your perspective, the equation was simple: right equals whatever is good for Brad Howard. Today that means getting a good job and starting a career. Yesterday it meant selling drugs. Even now you can announce without irony, "I feel good to be a black male."

In some sense, I cannot fault you for your views. Like many other young people, you spent twelve years in school, but you got an attitude adjustment instead of an education. You were taught to feel good about yourself and to be proud of who you are, no matter what. On the surface, the idea seems sensible enough: young African Americans do not succeed because they are not taught that they can succeed. For the past thirty years, education experts have noted that young people like you are constantly bombarded by negative images of black men and women on television, in the movies, and in your neighborhoods. They have also pushed the idea that these images are holding you back. So instead of rewarding real success and discouraging failure, they decided to bolster your self-esteem. But rather than building self-esteem, educators have taught a generation of young people to parrot the phrases of "empowerment." Almost without exception, every young African American I have met says he is proud of himself. Even you are proud. And almost without exception, all of those young people cannot answer the simple question, "Why are you proud of yourself?"

Educators have ignored the obvious fact that real self-esteem comes only from real accomplishments. Without real accomplishments the phrases you repeat are just empty words. What is worse, words like *pride, courage,* and *respect* have lost their meaning to young people raised on a diet of self-esteem. Just as obscenities no longer shock, the vocabulary of self-esteem no longer inspires. With every accomplishment, no matter how small, now treated as equally important, young people are losing respect for real achievements.

The popularity of Malcolm X is a good example of what this education has done. In my previous letter, I referred to Malcolm's insights on street hustlers. I hoped that his ideas would carry weight because you, like most other African Americans, say you respect him. But let me suggest that you probably should not respect Malcolm, at least not for the reasons you think. I believe Malcolm X is the most misunderstood black hero in America. As one young looter during the LA riots said on *Nightline,* "King—King fought for peace, but you don't get nothing by just talking. I believe in Malcolm X's way. I don't believe in turning the cheek. We've been turning the cheek for far too long. Now it's time for retaliation." From political leaders to street hustlers to rap singers, Malcolm is lionized for one phrase: "By any means necessary." It has become the battle cry of every black hoodlum who wants to loot a store and the campaign theme of every black politician who wants to stir up his constituents. Although I disagree with much of what Malcolm believed, I am profoundly saddened that this man's life and all he stood for has been reduced to a slogan on a T-shirt and a way to justify violence.

There is much about Malcolm X's life that deserves respect. Like you, he began as a street hustler and a thief. But instead of making excuses for his behavior, he turned his life around. It is true that he talked of liberating African Americans "by any means necessary," but what were those means? He demanded abstinence from premarital sex and alcohol. He required his followers to study intensely. He did not tolerate drugs—either using or selling them; he called them poison. He condemned the lust for the material things you covet. Malcolm's message is perfectly clear: stop selling drugs, stop living in sin, take responsibility for your children, do not smoke or drink, work hard and study harder. As Malcolm would quickly explain, those are the "means" that are necessary.

Instead, Malcolm's misguided modern followers like to think he justified violence. To my knowledge, nothing Malcolm ever said or did could reasonably be used to justify the sort of street hustler violence that rap singers and high school cowards so admire. As I mentioned in my last letter, Malcolm wrote that your sort of violence "scared" him. I wonder if the young African Americans I see walking around Washington with Malcolm X's image on their backs have ever tried, or even know how, to live the kind of life he demanded. I disagree with many of Malcolm's views. He believed that America is a hopelessly racist country in which black people will never succeed. He believed it is better for black people to separate themselves from the larger culture and viewed the whole idea of integration as white scam. I know from my own experience that he was wrong on both counts. But I do know that he was right in first insisting that anyone who wants to improve society must first look at the man in the mirror. Humans are social creatures, and you are the element of society you are responsible for. How do you treat your neighbors? By selling drugs to them? Using them for sex? Occasionally offing one? You can't condemn the corruption or flaws of a society when you spend your time helping to destroy it. You can do the most to improve society by improving yourself.

The moral demands Malcolm X placed on himself and his followers are more than admirable; they are what is most essential to improve the lot of each black brother and sister in America. But it is also the most difficult thing in the world to change. It is much easier to point out the mite in the eye of the rest of the world than to deal with the plank in our own.

In many ways, he and Martin Luther King, Jr., had more in common that most young people realize. Like Malcolm, Dr. King was a deeply religious man who demanded much from himself and those who followed him. Dr. King and Malcolm X both realized that self-esteem comes from self-respect, and that both have to be earned through hard work and a dedication to living a moral life. How far we have moved away from those principles! Today the "civil rights establishment" is all about what kind of special treatment America owes blacks as a result of its racist past, rather than about what we can do to get beyond that. We push for a legalized racial spoils system called affirmative action, which, in principle, is just another shade of the old Jim Crow laws. We talk about "reparations." From whom? People who never held slaves. For whom? People who never were slaves.

Meanwhile, we set up our own children for bitter disappointment by trying to fill them up with empty self-esteem. We think that if we teach kids to feel good about themselves, perhaps real accomplishments will follow. That approach is exactly backward. Both Malcolm and Dr. King would have agreed that each of us should understand our own inherent worth as beloved children of God. Beyond that, both would measure a man or woman by how hard he or she struggles to follow God's laws and improve himself or herself. Esteem is a high regard or opinion for someone. Real self-esteem comes from making oneself worthy to be esteemed, but today it is in fashion to teach young people that just showing up is enough. Our children are in for an awful shock if we send them into the world with a baseless high regard for themselves.

I know that many black leaders disagree with me. Many believe that the history of victimization puts children at an emotional disadvantage that needs to be countered with as much positive encouragement as possible. They also believe that planting the seeds of self-esteem at an early age is necessary to counter the negative attitudes and experiences of racism they are likely to encounter. These people do have a point: many young black children have a hard time finding positive role models, and American culture is often willing to ignore the contributions African Americans have made. When I did a program on the D-Day invasion, for example, I had on my radio program my friend and mentor Senator Strom Thurmond, who had fought in World War II. Many people called the station afterward to criticize me for not bringing black war heroes on my show. At one level, I was distressed that so many of my listeners still see everything, even the anniversary of this historic day, in racial terms. On another level, though, I could appreciate their desire to publicize the accomplishments of black Americans. But even as I agree with this desire, I have to note that none of it makes a bit of difference when it comes to the philosophy of self-esteem.

Even if our history textbooks and newspapers were filled with the accomplishments of black Americans, it would not build genuine self-esteem among young African Americans. Imagine how silly it would sound if white people went around saying, "I am a personal success because I am white and Leonardo da Vinci was white." Anyone who made such a statement would be dismissed as an idiot by all of the white people I know. Yet this is precisely what black intellectuals have accomplished by teaching self-esteem to black children. Our young people are encouraged to believe that the heroic efforts of Harriet Tubman make them better people. Please. Harriet Tubman's accomplishments made *her* a good person. That is all. If we want young African Americans to feel good about themselves, we should teach them calculus in high school and reward them when they put forward the effort and perform to the best of their abilities. Worst of all, habituating children to maintain an unearned sense of self-satisfaction destroys the best incentive for real accomplishment and discourages the motivation that leads to all real achievement.

I am barely old enough to recall the time when we first heard that black was beautiful. In the early 1960s black America was just beginning to emerge from the legacy of Jim Crow. In the South blacks attended separate schools, drank out of separate drinking fountains, used separate toilets, and ate in separate restaurants. Whites made sure these accommodations were separate because they did not want to be soiled by the black people around them. Everywhere I turned were signs that America believed African Americans were dirty, unworthy, and somehow less than fully human. In the early 1960s, our parents' generation rebelled against these attitudes and asserted our humanity. Back then when black people began saying "Black is beautiful," they meant that black is no less beautiful than white, that we are all equal in the eyes of God. Today that phrase has been perverted to mean that being black is, in itself, enough to make you good and worthy.

I have often wondered why people of our race embraced this philosophy so quickly and completely. It is not as though some charismatic African-American leader persuaded the public that false pride was the true salvation of the black race. From Frederick Douglass to Malcolm X, every true black leader has stressed the principles of self-discipline and hard work. They have rightly objected to white America's refusal to acknowledge our accomplishments and virtues, but they never suggested that being black is a virtue. Perhaps the answer is as simple as your own life suggests: making race a virtue is far easier than trying to instill true virtues in our young people. Whatever the reason, the effort that began as a way to eliminate prejudice against African Americans has become the anchor of false pride.

This educational fad for self-esteem training, like so many other social and educational experiments performed on young American school children, has backfired. Well-intentioned people have used American children, and especially African Americans like you, as a proving ground for new ideas. I am sickened when I think about the criminal justice reform that dumped hundreds of thousands of violent criminals back into black neighborhoods in the name of rehabilitation, or the mental health reforms that dumped legions of former mental patients into those same neighborhoods, or poorly conceived and executed welfare programs that have encouraged the breakdown of poor families. Young African Americans are always the first to get free condoms in schools, free needles for drug addicts, and subsidized abortions for teens. It is as if society says to itself, "Why not try it in the inner city? After all, things can't get much worse there." But the experience of the past several decades indicates clearly that life can get worse even in the worst neighborhoods. You would be hard pressed to find anyone in America—white or black—who would not trade the illegitimacy rates of today for the rates in 1960, or the crime rates today for the crime rates in 1960, back when laws and attitudes were much more racist than they are today.

Political leaders, both black and white, have not been content merely to eliminate the obstacles to black success. They have sought to engineer our future—and just below all of that engineering lies the assumption that black people cannot handle this future without the help of government. It is this condescending "compassion" and enervating assistance, much more than overt hostility, that has sucked the marrow of black communities in America.

Through the curriculum of self-esteem we have made a policy of pretending that any accomplishment, no matter how trivial, is worthy of praise. In doing so we have undermined the value of real success. That same curriculum pretends that failure does not exist except in the most extreme cases. Your life serves as a clear, if unfortunate, example of this trend. Just by showing up to school each morning more or less regularly for twelve years, you received a high school diploma. I do not mean to offend you when I say that you should have learned a great deal more in twelve years of school than you did, and if you refused to learn you should have failed. Instead the educators who were paid to teach you academic subjects taught you that almost any fault can be overlooked and almost any effort is sufficient. No wonder you find it difficult to summon the discipline required to stay off the streets; you were never even required to finish your homework.

Sometimes this idea of hollow success produces some tragically ludicrous scenes. Each year, the mayor of Washington and other national luminaries hold a luncheon to "honor" a handful of girls who have "learned to practice self-respect and self-control" by agreeing not to have sex while they are enrolled in a program to promote abstinence. This past year the luncheon was attended by some of the nation's most influential women, including the vice president's wife, the wife of Virginia's governor, and the reigning Miss America. These 173 teen and preteen girls are being honored for the profound accomplishment of remaining virgins while they are in the program. I think many people must have been amused, as I was, by the entire spectacle. There stood the mayor of our nation's capital and many of the most important women in the nation appreciatively unveiling the last 173 teenaged virgins in the Washington area.

Talk about meaningless self-esteem! Now, teaching sexual restraint to kids is both admirable and necessary. But most professors of, say, physics are never honored with a luncheon organized by such luminaries. For young African-American girls, however, just keeping their pants on through high school earns them this honor. Honoring these girls undermines years of struggle against prejudice by admitting, in effect, that most young African Americans are no more able to control their sexual urges than most animals. The racist impulse in white America is reinforced by these displays. Once again, well-intentioned public figures had announced to the world that African Americans should not be held to the same standards of self-discipline and self-control we expect from others in our society. For blacks, they seem to say, retaining one's virginity through most (though not all) of their teenage years is nothing short of heroic, and it deserves the personal attention of Miss America, the wife of the vice president, and the highest elected official of our nation's capital.

If the curriculum of self-esteem robs young people of the drive to succeed, its twin, the philosophy of blame, provides them with an excuse for almost any failure. Together they comprise a philosophic outlook that says, "All my actions are worthy; all my deficiencies are the fault of others." Our culture of victimization has become so accepted that when it is occasionally put on public display, few people realize just how absurd it all sounds. I recall African-American leaders, such as Representative Maxine Waters, who defended rioters during the Los Angeles riots on the basis of "joblessness and despair." They agreed that the entire riot was unfortunate but a natural reaction to racism. During the NAACP's ill-conceived gang summit in 1992, Ben Chavis invited street hustlers and murderers to justify selling drugs as a natural reaction to their lack of "hope." Even child abuse in poor black families is excused as the result of the "frustration" poor African-American parents feel. If you are poor and black in America, there is no crime you can commit, no boundary you can cross, that cannot be excused on account of poverty, racism, or general psychological stress.

It does not take much for this philosophy to give way to the kind of selfishness I see in young hustlers such as yourself. After all, if nothing is your fault, then you have no faults. If anything you do can be explained and justified by forces beyond your control, then there is no reason to control your impulses. After a time, the idea that anything one does can be justified gives way to the notion that nothing you do even needs to be justified—at least not to anyone but yourself. It does not take long for the values your parents taught to vanish. This false pride is combined with the constant focus on the "self" in self-esteem to help create the sort of self-centered attitude I see in you. I have to wonder if your days as a street hustler are what those same political leaders have in mind when they proclaim that the eighties were a decade of selfishness and greed. Probably not.

As I look back on my own life, I realize that I was fortunate to have been raised as I was. I grew up on a farm in Marion, South Carolina. It seemed all we did was work. We were up at the break of dawn, feeding the cattle, slopping the pigs, or tending to the fields. I recall one summer day when I had to bring in the tobacco from the fields. It had rained the night before, and by midday the heat and the humidity seemed unbearable. My father had given me several rows of tobacco to finish. When I whined and told him that it was too much, he bent down and explained to me, "Those are your rows. They are yours to do. If you don't make it through those rows, you won't make it through life."

Those rows of tobacco seemed endless. But I knew my father, and I knew that he would not listen to any further complaints, so I got back to work. At that moment I hated the work, and I was angry with my father for making me do it. Between plants I would stop to rest for a few seconds, but that only prolonged my time in the sun. The dust clouded my eyes and got in my clothes. My hair was matted by the dirt and the sweat, and my head pounded in the heat. If it had been an option, I probably would have quit, but I did not have a choice. After what seemed like an eternity, I finally reached the end of the last row. I looked over to my father. He did not say anything; he just smiled and walked with me to the tobacco barn. I knew he was proud of me—not because I was able to work in the tobacco fields but because I did not quit.

That afternoon I learned that real self-respect grows out of little victories. My father was like that. He placed the greatest importance in the smallest things. From getting good grades in math to finishing my chores, he viewed almost everything in the context of a larger picture. Every life is made up of those small decisions, those little victories and defeats, that we deal with every day. Every little, unheralded choice is a piece of the bigger picture—the general direction your life will take. If we are not faithful in the little things, then we cannot be faithful in the larger things. That is why he did not cut slack for my little slips and failings. He felt a great responsibility as our father. As important, he had a keen insight into character—both how it is formed and the role it plays in our lives. It is this insight that he has passed along to me, and which I am now trying to pass on to you.

Getting up, going to work, giving everything your best effort: these are the foundation of real character and, consequently, real self-esteem. My work in the fields does not seem like much now, but the self-respect I gained by completing those rows of tobacco was genuine. Although I would never have finished my chore if my father had not demanded it, the accomplishment was still mine. Looking back on it, I think I felt better about finishing those rows of tobacco than I did graduating from college. In many respects, I think finishing those rows was far more important to the success I enjoy today.

I wonder how differently I might have approached my life if my father had said on that hot summer day, "Don't worry about it, Armstrong. It is good enough that you came out here to the fields to try. You should be proud of that." Even as I write those words, I realize how ridiculous they are. My father knew better. Yet every day teachers, parents, and politicians say those very words to people like you. When your father bought you a car and continued your monthly allowance even though you were hustling, he was telling you that just showing up was good enough. When your parents put up their house as collateral so they could bail you out of jail and then stood silent as you continued to deal drugs, they were telling you that just showing up was good enough. When your school gave you a high school diploma even though you can barely speak basic English they were telling you that just showing up was good enough. And when your girlfriend and newborn daughter stayed with you even though you were running around with other women, she too was telling you that just showing up was good enough. These people who never demand anything from you say they are trying to help, but all the while they are robbing you of an opportunity to earn even the most modest real self-respect.

While the philosophy of self-esteem prevents many young people from gaining self-respect, it also robs others of the respect they have earned. You said to me, "I had a lot of respect on the street." I would have laughed at that comment except that I have heard so many young people say they "respect" street hustlers. As Malcolm X observed of his time on the streets, the highest respect goes to the most reckless and vicious hoodlum—the "craziest nigger." The virtues normal society encourages in its members are twisted to fit the hustling lifestyle and then held up to younger or less reckless hustlers as a model. Courage becomes recklessness. Independence is reduced to contempt. Ambition and drive are transformed into selfishness and greed. Bravery becomes self-destruction. The words, and the world, are turned upside down, and many young people do not even know it.

In this world, there is no room to recognize real courage, drive, ambition, or independence. So while other young people you knew were busy admiring your fancy cars and your ghetto courage, they were ignoring or ridiculing people who worked in so-called dead-end jobs. Without a moral compass to help them distinguish between real and empty accomplishments, they looked only at the material results of each. Because so few young people are taught the real meaning of dignity, they think the peculiar power wielded by the street hustler has earned him respect. Young people see hustlers like you acting as petty lords: issuing commands, demanding homage from your lieutenants, even setting and enforcing your own legal code. As you bragged to me, you were able to have someone killed if you wished; you "had a lot of power." Thanks to millions of men who have abandoned their children, many young African Americans who grow up in the city will be exposed to your kind of power and respect, and it is the only example they will ever see.

You should have known better. Even while he was making it easy for you to do the wrong thing, your own father was living a life that deserves real respect. To this day, you say you respect your father. Why? What about him do you respect? Your father is just another working-class black man stuck in a job that is going nowhere. He has spent all of his life working, and what has he gotten for it? Unlike you, your father would never get the respect of your former friends on the street. Unlike you, your father would never have women lining up to win his affections. Unlike you, your father would never be able to tell someone in his "crew" to "take care of" one of his enemies. By the measure of the street thug, you, Brad, had a lot of power; your father has none. If he were not your own father, I think you might call him a chump.

Still, you are beginning to understand that his wasn't a dead-end job but an opportunity to provide an honest living. Even with all of your money and your "power," you could never earn his respect, and you could never re-create the dignity that he has. That, Brad, is why you and your brother were dead to him. You had lost his respect.

I think your young admirers would be surprised if they knew the truth about you and your father. He can see right through your false pride, your empty success, and your recklessness. Teenagers in the ghetto think that hustlers who carry guns and face death are courageous. Only you knew how scared you really were. You told me about it, but you could never tell your boys back home about it. For them, you have to put up a front, put on a show, because your life depends on the face you show. Living as a predator, living with predators, any sign of weakness is fatal. So you and all your friends live on the edge of the abyss day in and day out, never looking down, pretending not to notice. Inside, this life eats you up, which is why you said you wanted out. Yet looking back on your life, even you admit that you took the easy way out. As dangerous as dealing drugs could be, it was much easier to live for yourself, for the moment and for money, than to take responsibility for your actions and live as your father did: working hard, providing for your children, reining in your impulses. Even today, it is difficult for you to face the struggle and real sacrifices that such a life requires. Unlike carrying a gun and walking the streets, living a respectable life demands genuine courage.

I warned you in my last letter that you will not get much encouragement as you try to change your life. One clear reason is that by rejecting the false pride that has anchored you in the past, you are announcing to your former friends that they are not leading good lives. By changing, you are implicitly holding them accountable for still leading that life and condemning the damage they do. To make matters tougher, you must turn away from the streets in shame rather than victory. You should feel bad about the way you have lived. You should be ashamed of how you have wasted the opportunities people have given you. You should be ashamed and embarrassed by the way you used women. You should lose your false self-respect, and along with it you should lose forever the hollow respect you had for your street hustler friends. None of this is easy to do. It is a very hard thing to renounce your past, because you have to assume the heavy responsibility of your actions. But renounce it you must, if you are to have any future at all.

In so doing, you will have achieved one of those small victories I talked about earlier. Your decision itself is a real accomplishment. You have given up the streets so you can provide for your children. In exchange, your daughters will see in you a bit of the dignity you admire in your own father. That is no small reward. And if you manage to break from the streets completely, one day you will feel good to be Brad Howard rather than feeling good to be "a black male."

> Sincerely,
> *Armstrong*

[An additional excerpt follows from the book's "Epilogue: A Letter to the Reader."]

Telling a young person to behave as he ought to is far different from demanding that he live up to the standards of civility we expect from each other. Our nation sends two distinct messages to Brad: you should act like a moral human being, but we do not expect it from you. It is a message we transmit loud and clear every day. We transmit it in our classrooms when we instruct our teachers to tout the virtues of abstinence and then hand out condoms at the end of class. We transmit it through the afternoon talk shows that provide a forum for the most perverse and dysfunctional segments of our society and imply that they are typical. And we transmit it through the criminal justice system when we refuse to hold teenagers like Brad accountable for their crimes.

If Brad is cynical and suspicious of our institutions it is because we made him that way. Others have wondered what someone from another planet would think of our society if all they knew about us was what they learned from our television and radio signals. In many ways Brad's view of the world answers that question. What does Brad know of religion, for example? If his view were built around what he has seen and heard on television—and it largely is—Brad would believe that religions are run by crooks, crackpots, and child-molesting priests. How often would he have learned about the overwhelming majority of chaste priests or the legions of men and women who have dedicated their lives to ministering to the most needy? Would he have ever come in contact with the writings of C. S. Lewis or the religious writings of Dr. King? Probably not.

In thousands of small ways Brad would have been taught that living a sinful life is normal while living a moral life is an unrealistic ideal. You can blame the schools or the media or the parents or even the sixties counterculture, it does not much matter. There are virtually no places left where the old virtues are held up and morality is demanded. Nowhere, that is, except in the tens of millions of homes where parents quietly and often desperately push against a culture they cannot tolerate. Even as many of these parents find themselves willing participants in many of the worst aspects of that culture, they try to protect their children from it. In the end, I think that is the true challenge of this book: to help Brad become one of those hypocritical parents who demand far more from their children than they do from themselves.

To those of you who share my concern about his future I make the same promise I made to Brad more than a year ago: as long as Brad is willing to put his old life behind him I will be there to help where I can.

"Where I can." It is unfortunate that, even now, I am compelled to use that phrase. I began the previous sentence with the intention of making a sweeping powerful promise to both you, the readers of this book, and to Brad. But even in the few seconds it took to jot down the words I realized that such a promise is not possible for Brad. Instead it requires a qualifier, and the implicit disclaimer "you may well be beyond the ability of me or anyone else to help you." Neither my best intentions nor the best designs of all the outreach programs, mentoring schemes, or government programs can save all of the young men like Brad Howard. We will be lucky to save a few. Our prospects for saving his children are only modestly better.

That said, we still must try—not only for the sake of Brad or even for the benefit of his children, but for ourselves. Ignoring the millions of young people like Brad and his girlfriend diminishes all of us. In doing so we conspire to promote the attitude I have decided throughout this book, the attitude that tells Brad we really do not expect anything more of him. And if Brad is at least partly the product of the excesses of the larger culture, the larger culture is in equal measure becoming the product of people like Brad. When we do nothing to change people like Brad we are allowing their growing influence on our own children to expand unchecked. Changing Brad means helping him make a better life for himself and his family. It is not enough to say we will "stop" him, we must also show our children that our society will reward Brad if he strives to live as he should.

PART FIVE

Private Life

NAHUM WAXMAN

Cooking Dumb, Eating Dumb

Nahum Waxman, a former academic anthropologist and editor, is a culinary scholar and proprietor of a food-and-wine bookstore on the Upper East Side of New York City. A consultant to food writers, restaurateurs, and amateur cooks, he happily supplied us with his list of the ten most overrated eating establishments in the city and is convinced that cooking is too important to be left exclusively to the experts.

Not every food writer, in the opulent new world of gastronomy, could have taken on Waxman's subject here. Many would argue that in the food-revolution supermarket of balsamic vinegar, black pasta, and sophisticated menus concocted from the elaborate recipes he glumly (but genially) describes we now eat better than ever, skylarking around, high above a leaden past of meat loaf, fried chicken, and mere spaghetti. But when he scrutinizes a recipe, it's with the same astringency and focus on its deep intentions that I. A. Richards brought to a reading of Coleridge, and his practical criticism suggests bad news. Waxman, who understands and emphasizes the careful transmission of tradition and culture on which real preparation of food depends, has little love for the high-concept entree—or restaurant. Clearly he thinks we have lost more than we've gained in the cookbook universe of lark tongues, stony literalism, and dumbed-down, numbed-down late-twentieth century palates.

READ THIS RECIPE:

To Make Green Pease Porrage

Take of yᵉ youngest pease you can get, what quantety you please, & put yᵐ in a little more faire water then will cover them. Boyle yᵐ till they be tender. yⁿ take new milke & make yᵐ of what thickness you please. Let yᵐ boyle well together, yⁿ take a little flower and wet it with milke enough to thicken it, & put it in with some spearmint & marrigoulds shread small. When it is boyled enough, put in a good piece of fresh butter, a little salt, & some pepper, if you please, & soe dish [it] up. (Karen Hess, ed., *Martha Washington's Booke of Cookery,* New York, 1981)

This set of cooking instructions was handwritten in the early 1600s—perhaps a little earlier. The source of the manuscript was the family of Daniel Custis, the first husband of Martha Dandridge (later Martha Washington); it appears to have been given to Martha when she and Daniel married in 1749. The simplicity and charm of the recipe are apparent. Beyond that, one might note the quality of confidence that underlies it—confidence that the writer, in barely a hundred words, has said exactly what she wants to say and that anyone who reads those words will get from them exactly that they want and need. What is reflected is an impressive rapport between writer and user. That rapport is essential, whether one is reading poetry, cookery, or a handbook of equestrian technique. The readers of Alexander Pope knew what he was up to (and he knew that they knew) when he larded his work with the sorts of references that now send us headlong to our classical dictionaries. Pope knew what sort of education he could count on his public to have. Tom Wolfe resonates in the same way with his late-twentieth-century public; he speaks our language, for better or worse, and we his.

Although the sphere of activity of the Custis family women was probably not literary, the considerations are the same: they and the users of their offerings spoke the same language, they shared knowledge of food ingredients, of techniques, and of results desired. The main concern was in producing a simple account of materials to be used and of method; all the rest was assumed to arise from common experience and common sense.

This closeness of writer and reader accounts as well for the fundamental tone of civility in the presentation of the recipe. We see here not a set of instructions to a beginner of what *must* be done but rather a respectful statement of an idea and then an offering of guidance in executing it: "take new milke & make y^m of what thickness you please," "when it is boyled enough," "a little salt, & some pepper, if you please." This may be instructional literature, but it is also polite discourse.

Another brief example from *The Improved Housewife* by Mrs. A. L. Webster (Hartford, 1854):

Cranberry Sauce and Apple Sauce

To stew cranberries till soft is all that is necessary to make cranberry sauce. When soft, stir in sugar or molasses to sweeten it. Scald the sugar in the sauce a few minutes. Strain if you please—'tis good without.

Apples should be pared and quartered. If tart, you may stew them in water; if not, in cider. After stewed soft, add a small piece of butter and sweeten to the taste.

How large a pot? How much water (or cider)? What sort of sweetening in the applesauce? How soft is soft? When to strain and when not? Not a word. These are not prescriptions but helpful, over-the-back-fence suggestions, as if for someone who already knew how to make the dish but needed a reminder. How did she know? She had seen dishes, these and ones like them, made in her mother's kitchen when she was a child, she had quite possibly participated in the paring or the quartering of the apples or the stirring and the licking of the spoon when they were sweetened. She had probably seen other things as well—the varieties of apples selected as appropriate for the sauce, the picking over the cranberries to toss out green or spoiled ones, the way the sauces were stored. She most likely had a good sense of how the sauces were supposed to taste. She probably could have figured out how they were made, and it is possible she could even have made her own occasional innovations.

Recipes were memoranda of ideas and methods whose use was subject to the judgment of the cook. Sometimes they were barely needed. From an 1885 cookbook: "We almost hesitate to give a recipe for this, because everybody thinks he knows how to make it best; and indeed with good materials, it is not easy to go far wrong."

Recipes today are quite a different story. Those who write them and those who edit them are determined that nothing "go far wrong"—or, indeed, go wrong at all. What follows are a few examples from cookbooks or cooking magazine articles of the past dozen years or so. First, from a recipe for a Fresh Tuna Daube Provençal:

Rinse the anchovies briefly in cold water if they are very salty. Using the back of a fork, mash four of the anchovies to a paste.

In a mortar, crush the peppercorns with a pestle. Add the garlic and pound to a firm paste. Add the mashed anchovies and pound to incorporate.

And from one for Fusilli with Vinegar-Marinated Zucchini:

Soak the zucchini in a bowl of cold water for at least 20 minutes, then scrub them vigorously under cold running water with a rough cloth or a stiff brush to remove any embedded grit. Trim away the ends and cut the zucchini into sticks about 2 inches long and ¼ inch thick. Set a large colander over a bowl or in the sink and put the zucchini in the colander. Sprinkle with 2 tablespoons of salt and toss two or three times. Let the zucchini stand for at least 45 minutes. . . .

And some others:

Peel the avocados and halve them lengthwise, discarding the pits. Rub the avocados well with the cut sides of the lemon.

Lift the roulades from the sauce and remove the string.

Bouquet garni made with 5 flat-leaf parsley sprigs, 3 thyme sprigs, and 2 bay leaves tied in cheesecloth.

Discard the bouquet garni.

Lower the heat if the brown glaze at the bottom of the pan threatens to burn.

Those who know the idiom will recognize that there is nothing very unusual about instructions such as these. They are typical, not especially complex or involved. Their premise, however, is, to put it mildly, worlds apart from that of the Custis family recipe for pease porridge.

The writers and editors of the modern recipes from which these extracts are taken have *not* assumed community between writer and cook. They have not assumed knowledge of technique or of materials; they have assumed, in fact, practically nothing. Their ingredient lists are, for the most part, long and explicit, and their instructions are exhaustive. They tell us to crush the peppercorns in a mortar using a pestle—in case anyone might be tempted to try the reverse—and prescribe, helpfully, mashing the anchovies with the *back* of the fork or rubbing the avocado with the *cut* sides of the lemon. They presume that their readers have never before handled or cooked a zucchini. They try to make certain that they and their guests will not try to eat the cheesecloth-covered bouquet garni. The only assumption the writers make, in fact, is that the reader—the cook—comes to each dish without knowledge, without accumulated experience, without capacity for judgment—more or less a culinary *tabula rasa.*

While Martha Washington's in-laws and their forebears expected that she and those in her kitchen would understand what needed to be done, today most writers of recipes presume nothing of the sort. And what happens? Readers come to expect that the recipe will tell them everything, some following orders like good soldiers, the rest—the disobedient—risking the ignominy of culinary failure.

The fact is, we are living in an age of recipe dependency, of cooks who crave (and writers and editors who feed the craving) safe, reliable ways of guaranteed, error-free cooking. Both sides, writers and readers, are participating in a Faustian bargain, grasping success—or reasonable success—in exchange for the risky, even treacherous, chance-taking that comes from the exercise of free will. As always with such bargains, this is a bad one, because along with the surrender of control goes surrender of the knowledge that supports it. What we are really accepting in exchange for a culinary safety net is ignorance and dependency.

"The bad cook," says Nicholas Freeing, the respected writer of detective fiction who earlier in his life had been a chef, "who buys a bundle of recipes thinking it will turn him into a tolerable cook is in for a disillusion, and so are his friends."

As a seller of cookbooks the most dreaded question I encounter is not whether a book is inspired or adventurous or imaginative or informative, but rather, "Do the recipes work?" I dread the question because I must manage a restrained reply. The questioners must be told—gently—that it is not the recipes but rather *they* that must work. That they are expected to think, to apply intelligence and judgment to ideas and to the materials that will be turned into a dish. It is up to them to bring their own good sense to cooking—their ability to understand variability in ingredients, to recognize error in a written text, to acknowledge their own tastes and preferences, to not let themselves be intimidated by the food arbiters into dreary cooking-by-numbers. *They,* not the food writers, are the cooks, and while everyone likes a suggestion for a good, imaginative new cooking idea, a glimpse into the not-always-obvious secrets of a remote ethnic cuisine, a boost on a difficult point of technique, or a little bit of hand-holding, there can be no mistake that cooking should be an individual, personal activity, based on the sole consideration of making a bunch of unruly ingredients behave themselves, work together, nourish, and end up tasting good.

The path of American cooking, from the eighteenth century and earlier, when knowledge and control of the craft were still possible, to today's dependency on detailed written recipes, has been a long, complicated one. A major initiating factor, observes food historian and critic Anne Mendelson, was the loss in the 1830s and 1840s of domestic servants to the world of work outside the household. "A woman running a middle-class household," Mendelson points out, "was likely to be more isolated in it, and to rely on the printed word, rather than live examples, for a general idea of what she was supposed to be doing." As firsthand kitchen knowledge declined, "the woman of the house became justifiably convinced of her ignorance," and before long, with the arrival of new immigrants to America, who brought with them little knowledge of American food or ingredients, the need for cooking schools and for instructional cookbooks that made no assumptions about what people knew was well established.

Cooking, asserted the new generation of writers and teachers, was one of the "domestic sciences." By the turn of the century, the books and the classes were routinely employing the precise standards and precise measurements of science, the use of which, it was claimed, would surely provide a guarantee of success. Most famous of the teachers was Fannie Farmer, who from 1893 ran the influential Boston Cooking School, where she spiritedly espoused the use of level teaspoons, level tablespoons, and other standardized measurements.

Journalist and scholar Laura Shapiro's fine book *Perfection Salad* (1986) documents the growth of the domestic science movement.

"The only things I consider beyond my control," asserted one teacher, "are the wind and the weather." . . . If the housekeeper could be made to think of herself as a scientist, calmly at work over her beakers and burners in her laboratory, then every meal would emerge as she planned, pristine and invariable. . . . Most women . . . responded gladly to the promise of order and rationality that came with scientific cookery.

In the following decades, the recipes grew more and more specific. Oven temperatures appeared in the 1920s, and exhaustive step-by-step instructions became prevalent in the 1960s. Meantime, home cooks came to know less and less about ingredients and methods. Too unfamiliar

with the roots of kitchen practice and the reasons for the cooking operations they were performing, they began to substitute the swapping of
recipe cards and magazine clippings for the conversations about cooking
and cooking experiences that had educated them in the past. Thus they
fell further and further from the traditions of the only craft that, by this
time, any of them had.

Cut loose, as we are, from the example of our mothers (or occasionally our fathers), who showed us how to handle food and how to work
with it, and coddled by the printed recipes that encourage obedience
and conformity at the expense of knowledge and understanding, we have
become a generation that cooks but does not know *how* to cook. This
degeneration is, of course, not confined to food. Those things that make
us lesser cooks are not very different from those that are impairing the
quality of much of our lives—insufficiencies of the right kind of education, an unwillingness or an inability to move beyond the superficial, a
reluctance to endure risk, and a stupefying laziness for anything but long
hours at our jobs. What all these add up to is that, even in an era such as
ours, which is at least superficially sophisticated, we are cheerfully accepting mediocrity of judgment and mediocrity of performance. To be
sure, we do not encourage bad results; we rarely rouse ourselves, though,
to achieve superior ones. Ends rather than means are our guideline—
dependable outcomes rather than ventures that might take us astray.
Such a standard may sometimes be appropriate. We happily praise our
young offspring when they have correctly assembled a dollhouse or a
model aircraft carrier ("Insert Tab A into Slot A, fold tab back"). But
carrying it too far, we can find ourselves with children deficient in imagination, unresourceful, and ultimately unexcited by their world. Carried
into adulthood, such habits of mind are near-fatal to the spirit.

Perfection may be an outcome of rote performance, but excellence
virtually never. What is it then that enables us to rise above literalism and
the unimaginative reliance on directions? More than likely it is our capacity to recognize and to respond to variability. Just as biological evolution was incompletely understood until mutation was revealed as the
force that made the process possible, so diversity—its discovery, its en-
hancement, and the uses to which it is put—is near the core of the way we
live at our best.

The paper roll on an old-fashioned player piano knew only that E♭
was E-flat. Arthur Rubinstein, however, knew that E♭ was actually hundreds of sounds, varying in every imaginable reach of volume, intensity,
tone, color, duration, even in minifractions of pitch. And these variations
reflect, in turn, variations in the materials and tautness of metal strings,

of touchy, delicate soundboards and the sturdy woods used in the piano case, of the mechanism that moves the hammer against the strings, of the day's temperature and the height and direction of the barometer, of the characteristics of the stage floor and the auditorium, of the pianist's strength and disposition at a given performance, of a composer's intentions, and of the effects of adjacent notes in the passage. One could practically say that there *is* no E♭.

So, too, with food. There *is* no bouillabaisse, no chicken curry, no scrambled eggs, no roast beef, no Fresh Tuna Daube Provençal. Are there no mussels in the market? Is one of the guests allergic to clams? Does the chef have a heavy hand for garlic? Those conditions add up to one bouillabaisse—there are scores of others. Old chicken or young chicken? With bone or without? One combination of fresh spices carefully toasted and ground or another combination, perhaps taken right out of the supermarket spice bottle? The result: two curries that wouldn't know each other on the street. Old eggs or very fresh eggs? Whipped with water or not? Salt? Herbs? Cooked hard or cooked soft? A nation of scrambled eggs. Roast beefs in their legions, even the hundred daubes of Provence.

The fact is that the central element in good cooking is an understanding of the diversity of the substances we work with and the staggering range of possible outcomes. Food making is a product of mind and eye and skill applying themselves to materials as variable as the blessed caprices of genetics and environment and circumstance can make them.

So what's going on here that's dumb? We should look back to the recipes, look to the spurious precision that makes them traps rather than sources of inspiration. We should begin to understand that numbers—teaspoons, cups and ounces, seconds and minutes—are generally there for guidance, not to produce mechanical performance. It is common to claim that in baking, where the chemistry of ingredients is more important, those numbers, or at least those proportions, are critical. But even there we should know that variables such as temperature, humidity, barometric pressure, the vigor of yeast, and the quirkiness of ovens impose themselves on the most careful attempts to be precise. And when we cook, let us recognize that a tomato is not in fact a tomato—that tomatoes vary not only in size but in acidity, density, and ripeness; let us remember that some tomatoes have tough, nasty skins and some have soft lovely skins; that some tomatoes are two-thirds flesh and that some tomatoes are two-thirds water; that some have hard bitter little seeds, that others have soft plump little seeds so exquisite that they can almost be eaten on their own. We should keep in mind that asparagus tops and asparagus bottoms are different creatures with different preparation requirements and possibly different cooking times. And we should not forget that some melons must be given a squeeze of lemon or lime, while the perfume of others will be impaired by the use of acid.

To quote Nicholas Freeling once again:

The most wicked [cookbooks] are the dogmatic ones, which give quantities and times, peremptory stuff about giving your chop seven minutes on each side. The inexperienced cook, starting confident in his mentor, becomes flustered by strange gaps in the information, is confused, irritated, and finally exasperated—what should have been a nice meal turns out spoilt and it is the wretched book's fault, not the cook's. You cannot teach cooking out of a book any more than you can carpentry. No two stoves, frypans, ovens—come to that no two cooks—are the same. No good writer on food gives formal recipes. (*The Kitchen Book,* 1970)

So what has to happen if we are not to be dumb in our kitchens? We have to begin to think about foods and their properties—their handling characteristics, their seasonality, and their variability; we have to remember that although certain produce may be available year-round, it may not be best to use it year-round. Plain and simple, we have to understand the stuff we work with—the stuff we peel (or not) or chop or slice or bone (or not) or boil or bake or steam or poach or eat raw. To discover that a vegetable is properly cooked in butter or olive oil or ghee or bacon fat because these are all different substances with different flavors and different behaviors. To know enough about onions to decide, in making a particular dish, whether to use the onions whole or in quarters, whether to slice them thick or thin, or chop them, or dice them, or mince them, to know whether they should be cooked fast, or be stirred or not stirred. The idea is to inform yourself well enough to make choices rather than merely do what you are told. Once food is understood, recipe instruction begins to stand in clear relief, serving not as marching orders but as proposals for the good cook to accept or to alter—perhaps even to reject. That ability—to make choices and to control—defines the highest standard.

Needless to say, none of this discussion even begins to speak to the sector of the population that does not cook at all—those who have largely abandoned the kitchen, satisfying their needs with a hash of eating out, of ordering in, and of using prepared or semiprepared foods.

Although the experience of excellence may on occasion be achieved through eating out, too often going to a restaurant is merely a means of avoiding cooking. Of course, dining out is not only for feeding oneself. Clearly it has an important social component, involving entertaining and seeing and being seen. It also offers refreshing opportunities for novelty—eating in a different setting, perhaps even encountering new foods and, as a result, new sensations and often new conversation. At its best, it can be a stimulating and even an elevating activity, in which we get to know and experience the breakthrough talents of a brilliant, creative chef or perhaps the comfortable abilities of a cook who works with more common ingredients and flavors and produces admirable renderings of familiar dishes—a superb Tennessee barbecue, a handsome mess of fried chicken with greens and cornbread, fine New England clam chowder. Not the performers, to be sure, we become in such places an audience, who, like concertgoers, revel in and are rewarded by the talents of others.

Unfortunately, eating out is normally not at its best in America today, and while it is impossible here to even touch the surface of that subject, it is worth observing that not only has the level of both performance and expectation plummeted over a wide range of restaurants, there has also emerged a style of establishment in which food is barely the issue. Celebrity restaurants are one style—those with celebrity ownership and (often the same places) those with celebrity clientele. Perhaps fine food was at one point a part of their appeal, but in most cases that interest has passed; the food they offer may range from fairly good to execrable, but it is, in any case, not the reason we dine there. An understanding of food and a knowledge of cooking that goes beyond what may be chic at the moment are no part of our being there.

Another style of restaurant, also relatively indifferent to food, encompasses those places whose raison d'être is a theme—an organizing principle that has nothing to do with food. Old West restaurants, sports restaurants, Hollywood and TV restaurants, business and financial restaurants (the ones decorated with old ticker-tape machines and framed front pages from the *Wall Street Journal*), period restaurants (Gay Nineties, 1920s, 1950s "retro"), and dozens of other styles, limited only by the ingenuity of the promoters and investors who spawn them.

A second means of avoiding doing one's own cooking is the somewhat newer practice of "ordering in." Whether from regular restaurants or special establishments created for the purpose, this form of getting food usually involves switching the locus of activity to one's home; often the food is consumed just feet away from the place where one would be cooking—were one cooking. As a rule, this is very rarely food at the highest level, in part because of the limited range of food establishments that will offer such service, in part because the foods that travel well are themselves limited. The fact is that even those foods most commonly ordered in, Chinese food and pizza, are best freshly made and lose a good deal of their quality en route from source to consumer. Some take-out foods (pasta salad, Buffalo chicken wings, stuffed mushrooms, and other room-temperature dishes) do hold up but, it can safely be said, rarely represent high points of gastronomic experience. More to the point, the ordering-in process normally involves neither knowledge nor judgment on the part of the consumer; it involves a good deal of settling for what comes.

The same is largely true of another variety of "order in"—catered foods. Although caterers frequently cook with loving care, their menus are generally controlled by the exigencies of bulk preparation, the mechanics of transport, the demands of on-site maintenance ("holding time"), and the forms of service that will be employed at a particular event. These are generally limiting rather than stimulating, and imagination is frequently defeated by matters that have little to do with the creative process. Poached salmon, grilled chicken breasts, couscous salad, and ratatouille are the signature catering dishes of the 1990s, as much as anything for reasons of budget, transport, and service. Inspiration has little or nothing to do with it.

Third, and even further down in the scale, however, is that practical but dismal choice of millions of Americans—the use of prepared or semiprepared "convenience foods." Pounding on this kind of food—and the lifestyle it points to—is probably unneeded. The words have already been spent attacking the thousand other ways we have fallen from grace—from the erosion of our critical sense to our loss of skills. But a few observations that point to how this method of feeding ourselves fits in with the broader questions may be useful.

Fully prepared foods have been in cans and other ready packaging for well over a century—generally a single dish such as corned beef hash or baked beans. These are, in a sense, "safe" foods as regards any argument about excellence. They are neither foods of great stature nor, in many cases, could they have been radically improved had they been prepared at home with loving care. Even here, though, there may be arguments; the legions of cooks who make chili (con carne or otherwise) object strenuously to canned versions of the dish they love. So, too, do the home makers of minestrone or clam chowder or other specialties.

However, the issue has become more serious since manufacturers began making in the 1960s a wider range of "serious" frozen foods—yesterday's dreary TV dinners, today's gourmet selections: Chicken Alfredo, Fettuccine Primavera, Chicken Cordon Bleu, Deviled Crab Miniatures, Linguine with Bay Shrimp and Clams Marinara. There are also dried-ingredient preparations (just add water and microwave): Knorr's Vegetable Primavera Risotto in Creamy Sauce, Rice A Roni White Cheddar and Herbs, Marrakesh Express Sundried Tomato Couscous. Moving in moments from oven to table, these are pre-proportioned, pre-flavored dishes, most involving little more activity by the "cook" than is necessary to remove a candy bar from its wrapper. As has been widely observed, some clever manufacturers (or their home economics departments) figured that there would be those who felt guilty that they were not participating in the process, and so we see "creative suggestions" being made on the packages: Lipton's Kettle Creations' Chicken 'N Onion Soup with Long Grain and Wild Rice should, "like a traditional homemade soup . . . be cooked on a stove for best results." A cup of cut-up fresh or frozen asparagus or of chopped celery can be added for a "special touch." Betty Crocker's Stroganoff Style Hamburger Helper is apparently aided by such "great ideas" as adding a package of frozen peas and topping off the finished dish with packaged french-fried onion rings.

And on they come. Legume-brand canned Italian Polenta, Empire Bagel Cheese Pizzas, Hungry Jack Pancakes, frozen and ready to thaw, heat, and serve, Kellogg's Eggo Nut and Honey Waffles, a dozen flavors of sugar-glazed, corn-syrup-filled Pop Tarts. The parade of grotesques has, alas, just begun.

So just what is wrong with all this? Yes, of course, this is lesser food. Most of the products are made from ingredients whose major virtue is that they are cheap and filling; many contain astonishing additives for enhanced flavor, color, and shelf or freezer life. Nearly all represent the lowest common denominator of taste. And beyond that? Beyond that, they, along with restaurant food and order-in food, represent take-it-or-leave-it eating. All are prepared by someone else, who is making the decisions on ingredients, flavor, and texture. All three represent food making that is beyond our control. When we adopt these, or a combination of these, as a significant proportion of our diet, we are truly eating in ignorance. When we abdicate in this fashion, we surrender yet another sector of our lives—as surely as we debase our politics when we leave ourselves uninformed in our civic life; as surely as we cheapen our literature when we read it without knowing its traditions and without understanding its cultural underpinnings; as surely as we do whatever we do— and don't know how and don't know why.

Food may not be the center of the universe, although historically it has never been at the margins. The way we deal with it, though, signifies much about our approach to our world. Why have I held forth so insistently in this essay for doing our own cooking and for doing it with knowledge, resourcefulness, flexibility, and independence? It might be argued that the creation of a dish of homemade food reflecting the realities of the kitchen, the equipment, the ingredients, and the informed preferences of the person who made it does not signify that America's retreat from excellence has been stopped in its tracks. It does not signal that our minds and our spirits will be restored, that we'll write better plays and play better music. But the fact is that any steps we take in our return to competence and control should be happily regarded. If cooking leads the way, so much the better. It is a homely art, but one we could practice with benefit every day of our lives.

PAUL R. MCHUGH

What's the Story?

Paul R. McHugh is Henry Phipps Professor and director of the Department of Psychiatry and Behavioral Sciences at the Johns Hopkins University School of Medicine. He is the author, with Phillip R. Slauney, of *The Perspectives of Psychiatry*. This essay appeared in the spring 1995 issue of *American Scholar*.

American courtrooms and talk shows are the current most popular venues for the diagnostic powers of psychiatry. Whether the hapless patient is recovering from repressed memories of satanic-cult abuse or has just returned from a sexually memorable alien abduction, he or she is the dramatic protagonist of a "story," in Dr. McHugh's terms.

Unlearning the conventional urge to make each patient fit the Procrustean bed of a narrative preexisting out in the cultural ether is a task he sets his students to master. By keeping the unique symptoms and personality of each person in the center of their lenses, psychiatrists can avoid a basic problem of our larger culture—the urge to format and socially engineer all possible aspects of contemporary life. Replacing this reproductive impulse in his students with a more humane look at mental illness is an approach that deserves wide imitation in a society whose current emblem is the High Concept.

I TEACH PSYCHIATRY to medical students and residents by emphasizing fundamental matters such as defining terms, describing symptoms, and reviewing concepts—the ABCs, you might say, of this medical specialty. I choose this approach because, as all teachers know, most mistakes are with fundamentals. And, perhaps more important, what makes a point fundamental, makes it interesting.

Although I have taught this subject this way for more than twenty-five years, every spring I fret about the introductory lecture on psychiatry to the Johns Hopkins University medical students. I don't worry about my grasp of the material; I have covered it before. I don't worry about capturing the students' interest, because anybody can be lively when talking about insanity. My fear is that I will mishandle an almost inevitable argument with some members of the class over how to think about mental illness and that this will sour the rest of our time together. As it turns out, the issues I address are not simple. They challenge a deeply rooted supposition about psychiatric patients which students have absorbed from the popular culture and which they are loathe to surrender.

This supposition holds that psychiatric patients are fundamentally alike because people are similar in sentiments and psychological vulnerabilities. Their mental disorders therefore vary only in degree rather than in kind. Any distinctions in the symptoms of mental disorders depend upon burdens imposed by the biographical events, life patterns, and social settings where people do differ. This kindly intended "fellowship of mankind" idea that many of my students hold is one of those half-truths that cause me more trouble than any flat-out error.

The facts are that, although some patients derive their mental distress from life situations, many patients suffer from symptoms that are entirely distinct from normal psychological states, symptoms that rest upon bodily disease. Teaching students how to make this distinction and to appreciate its importance in treatment, prognosis, and research is the mission of my department.

I always show students a patient with this first lecture. At this point I am not trying to explain much. I just want to present an afflicted person and let his disarray speak for itself. This modest aim seldom runs smoothly.

On a typical occasion, I was sitting before one hundred students with a woman whom I encouraged to describe her thoughts and feelings. She stated that she was frightened because one of the NASA satellites had been preempted by the Freemasons to record her every movement. She believed that the satellite had been equipped to beam down an invisible, but powerful ray, forcing upon her blasphemous thoughts. She rejected any suggestion from me that this might be her imagination or the remnant of some nightmare. She was in the hospital because she called the FBI repeatedly. She wanted to meet the president and have him put a stop to this business.

With such a set of symptoms I felt safe in saying that she had an incapacitating mental disorder such as schizophrenia. After thanking her and helping her return to the ward, I began discussing her state. I noted that she was not afflicted by NASA or the Masons but by a delusion—an idiosyncratic, incorrigible, preoccupying false belief. I parsed that definition, emphasizing that psychiatrists underline the idiosyncratic features of delusional false beliefs to differentiate delusions from mistaken assumptions that might derive from a patient's social group or education. I emphasized that this helped distinguish the symptoms of an illness from ordinary errors.

A student shot up his hand. With disdain, he said, "That poor woman's beliefs would only be called false if you took a narrow view of them. You should consider them within her life of poverty, chaos, and neglect. Then you would see them differently. She developed thoughts about NASA and the Masons to make sense out of a frightening and perplexing world."

The student, a college anthropology major, elaborated on this theme, saying that the false beliefs of this person served the same function as the cultural myths and beliefs of other civilizations that give life sense and purpose in the face of mysterious natural forces. "Those beliefs," he said, "certainly are adaptive and no one thinks of them as symptoms of derangement or entitles them 'false.' "

I have learned not to interrupt such a student as he runs an indictment of me as both insensitive and narrow-minded. To do so would only encourage a glimmering notion amongst the other students that perhaps I *am* a social oppressor, placing an additional burden on the patient by calling her mentally ill.

But as I listened to his version—with its fashionable multicultural stance toward both the patient and me—I knew that I would have to put aside anything else I planned to discuss that day and concentrate on the issue of story explanations in psychiatry. The student was attempting to tell a story about this patient that, to him, made sense of her symptoms. If I hoped to teach him or anyone else in the class what they needed to learn, we first had to consider how stories worked sometimes to help and sometimes to hinder psychiatry and whether a story provided an adequate understanding of this patient.

II

So what's the story? Psychiatrists often use a story to make a patient's symptoms intelligible—capturing the array of symptoms within a narrative of settings and sequential events in the patient's life. The story is thus one of the clinical "tools" of psychiatrists. In fact, all psychotherapists eventually compose with the patient's cooperation some kind of story—a chronicle that reveals how psychological symptoms arise when such motivations as hopes, commitments, preferences, and fears collide with reality.

The "motive" theme distinguishes the psychiatric story from the standard medical case report, where the onset and progress of symptoms are also described. The medical report is an account of nature's power over human life through infections, neoplasms, genes, and the like. In case after case, medical reports describe the stereotypical progressions and characteristic effects of these natural processes.

The typical psychiatric story, however, replaces nature's power with human motives and suggests that distressing mental states emerge when a patient faces some conflict between purposes and events in his life, between expectations and reality. The story provides, through its narrative power, all listeners, especially the patient, with a compelling sense of insight into the symptoms as they relate to this conflict.

Psychiatric stories also work to persuade people to alter their habitual thoughts and behaviors—another distinguishing characteristic. No-where is this method more vigorously employed than in the therapeutic efforts of members of Alcoholics Anonymous. The central theme of the AA story is the bondage to alcohol—a powerful metaphor that weaves the different stories of drunken revelry into a common image, encourag-ing any new member of the group to begin to move from addiction to sobriety as one might move from slavery to freedom.

The narrative power of a story, however, can, as I have learned from so many encounters with students, blind everyone to other explanations of the patient's symptoms, such as the effects of disease or the contribu-tion of a patient's temperament. I was a student myself—an undergradu-ate, in fact—when I was first struck by the power of a story to create a dubious insight.

One bright day in the late 1940s, the poet John Ciardi substituted for our instructor, Mr. Ludwig, in English A, the freshman composition course at Harvard College required of those who had misspent their high school years and needed help learning to express themselves. Ciardi was not prepared to work on elementary matters that we, the backward fresh-men, needed. He wished to show us the future as he saw it written out in Sigmund Freud's monograph on Leonardo da Vinci.

Ciardi enjoyed himself that day. He exuberantly explained how Leo-nardo's dream about a great bird beating its tail against his face when he was a baby was a prototypical Freudian dream. As Freud explained them, dreams hid from consciousness by representing, in a disguise, an unac-ceptable impulse—in this instance, Leonardo's homosexual urges. "That long tail, don't you know."

Ciardi believed that the Freudian "discoveries" of dream mech-anisms and the dynamic unconscious unveiled the hidden motivations that lay at the heart of all human actions (not just pathological ones) and so by extension could explain the motives behind any of our behav-iors. He accepted Freud's view that the key to Leonardo's difficulties in finishing some of his monumental projects was hidden behind this child-hood fantasy. Ciardi became irritated when a couple of us—with little more than an offhand reluctance to accept his point without more evi-dence—challenged the argument. We thought the issue at hand had to do with the use of symbol and metaphor as explanations.

Several days before, Mr. Ludwig had emphasized, when teaching about figures of speech, that metaphorical images used by writers re-vealed as much about the authors' preoccupations as about the things they portrayed. That was, of course, a typical freshman composition con-cept, right from the syllabus you might say, but it was an idea that at the moment was big news to me. It was an "Aha!" moment, illuminating important distinctions in the images and language, such as those dif-ferentiating classical from romantic poetry.

And that's what we said to Ciardi. Freud has extrapolated a sexual image from a dream. That action, we suggested, may tell more about Freud's mind than about Leonardo's. But Ciardi had not come to listen to such talk. For him, Freud was a wonder and a source, not an author to be examined. "You must have some unresolved sexual problem," he said to me in particular, and thus provided my first (and far from last) exposure to the repression-resistance stratagem psychiatric storytellers tend to use against their critics. The class broke up into those persuaded by Ciardi's argument and those unpersuaded, with me a highly irritated member of the latter.

Ciardi was an established poet, an illustrious member of the English Department, a translator of Dante, a practiced expert on symbol and metaphor. Mr. Ludwig, I am sure, thought he was favoring us that day by finding such a distinguished replacement. But why did this gifted man come to have such confidence in Freud that he failed to work with what he knew from his own profession? What prompted him to bully us, the strugglers with language before him, rather than win us round with more information?

The story he accepted overlooked more plausible explanations for Leonardo's difficulties—especially Leonardo's efforts to push the artistic techniques of his time to the limit. Ciardi had found, within the license of metaphor, a warranty for dubious opinions. On many occasions since then with students of my own, I have been reminded of John Ciardi and how he was bedazzled by narrative.

III

The idea—that stories are compelling and therefore must be employed carefully in psychiatry—lay behind my argument with the beginning student who found in a story a way to make sense of the delusional patient. This student was disagreeing with me over what was important. I claimed that the patient's beliefs were delusional and therefore marks of schizophrenia—a disease that called for special kinds of help and for medication. He thought that her ideas were adaptive responses to a life of adversity that might disappear if she found some understanding and support from me in facing those adversities.

The student has mighty champions on his side. Freud would be there. He said: "That delusional formation which we take to be the pathological product is in reality an attempt at recovery, a process of reconstruction." Carl Jung is definitely in his corner. He said: "Closer study of [deluded individuals] will show that these patients are consumed by a desire to create a new world system . . . that will enable them to simulate unknown psychic phenomena and so adapt themselves to their own world."

These old warriors and their views are hardly unfamiliar to me. In fact, I know their value in enlarging the scope of psychiatry and in appreciating some of the responses of patients. Prior to their proposals, psychiatrists may have concentrated too much on description, diagnosis, and physical treatment of the patients in their care and may have slipped into habits of disregard for them and for the circumstances of their lives. These masters of psychotherapy encouraged psychiatrists to emphasize that patients are people—not simply objects of nature, but vital subjects like the rest of us with aims, purposes, hopes, and fears—in need of aid.

The problem was that these champions tended to overreach themselves. They extended their conceptions about psychiatric disorders so far as to depict them all as expressions no different in kind from the rest of human psychological life. In so doing, it must be said, they played a bit fast and loose with evidence in developing their opinions about human nature and the provocations of mental illness.

Freud was not bashful about this extension. He noted that "psychoanalysis [restricted to] psychiatry would never have drawn the attention of the intellectual world to it or won it a place in the 'history of our times.' This result was brought about by the relation of psychoanalysis to normal, not to pathological, mental life." And on another occasion, he wrote: "If we can temper the severity of the requirements of historical-psychological investigation we may be able to clarify problems which . . . merit our attention." Jung was unambiguous about his intentions and methods when he said: "I can only make direct statements, only 'tell stories'; whether or not the stories are 'true' is not the problem. The only question is whether what I tell is *my* fable, *my* truth."

Freud and Jung were certainly candid about their methods and aims. They were the most vocal proponents of the idea that all psychological symptoms arise from a patient's encounter with life and can be understood like the outcome of a story. They were also certain that such symptoms would dissipate when their provocations were understood and the patients—with the assistance of psychotherapists—found more adaptive ways of responding to their problematic lives.

These assumptions of Freud and Jung represent—as Auden said about Freudianism—"a whole climate of opinion." Jung has emphasized the importance of this aspect of his stories. A conceptual framework—that which he calls *his* truth and which comprises, of course, his assumptions—lies behind the tales he tells and makes them persuasive to him and to his patients. Psychiatric stories announce an author and what he thinks. My medical student's multicultural story and Ciardi's claims for Leonardo rest on their beliefs, their assumptions about how people behave, *their* truth.

Imagination and reality often coalesce in the assumptions of psychotherapists. The assumptions foster the stories the therapists tell and provide justification for claiming some events to be psychologically important and others trivial in a patient's biography. And because the eventual story is a re-creation of what the psychotherapist assumes, its very composition—the fitting of events together in a narrative form—reinforces the confidence of the therapist in the correctness of the climate of opinion from which he began. In psychiatry, this "hermeneutic round"—from assumptions to stories to assumptions confirmed for the more confident composition of further stories—can sweep hesitancy aside and produce a dominating orthodoxy in which all psychiatric disorders are seen as emerging from the inherent potentials of human beings when faced with adverse circumstances or unfriendly associates.

IV

I was first plunged into the steamy climate of this orthodoxy by two teachers at Harvard Medical School. They were professors of psychiatry who worked with narrative in explaining the illnesses of their patients and, in the process, they revealed implications embedded in their own assumptions.

Dr. Elvin Semrad was the Director of Residency Training at the Massachusetts Mental Health Center. He was a short, stocky man with a distant manner toward students. He had, however, a way that urged patients suffering from schizophrenia or manic-depression to talk about themselves. He encouraged them to describe their lives and their responses to the crises of the moment. His aim was to suggest to them (and those of us listening in) how they had found, in their disordered mental states, an escape from problems that beset them.

The patients were comforted by Dr. Semrad's attention. They resembled ordinary people in many ways. That was his point: much that is normal is to be found in patients with serious mental illnesses.

But that also was the problem. Dr. Semrad made so much of patients' normality that why they were ill became less obvious. These patients were hearing voices, they were driven by emotional states that did not abate, they had idiosyncratic false beliefs. They were different in some significant way, despite the many normal features they retained. That difference is what made them patients, and that difference needed explanation. Dr. Semrad's skill at unfolding their personal stories, and, while doing so, obviously comforting and encouraging them, permitted everyone to brush by that point.

After Dr. Semrad's death, admiring students gathered his remarks about patients into a book—a collection of maxims, mottoes, and adages. Stories usually produce aphoristic generalizations—words of wisdom—rather than scientific laws and hypotheses. Like the story itself, aphorisms tend to assert rather than prove a viewpoint. These particular maxims, however, are most useful because they demonstrate what Dr. Semrad believed—the assumptions from which he worked—and how these particular beliefs shaped the stories he told and the teaching he gave.

Examples of Dr. Semrad's axioms found in the book include: "Psychotic patients are no different than we are, just a little crazier." Or, "We're just big messes trying to help bigger messes and the only reason we can do it is that we've been through it before and have survived." Or, "Don't get set on curing her, but on understanding her. If you understand, and she understands what you understand, then cure will follow naturally." Dr. Semrad assumed—fundamentally from his allegiance to the story method and the prevailing Freudian climate—that the remarkable symptoms of the mentally ill were exaggerations of universal human problems and that these symptoms would disappear when everybody got the story right and set about helping the patient find a better way of adapting to life.

Dr. Semrad influenced a generation of psychiatrists, made them aware of the humanity of their patients, and for this he is warmly remembered. However, he not only failed to differentiate what was wrong with the patients, he skipped past this question with a set of plausible assumptions and epigrams that implied that every patient, like some lost child, was simply expressing distress in the only way he knew how. Dr. Semrad thought that what psychiatrists needed to help patients was not more knowledge of their disorders but more feeling for their plight.

My other teacher, Dr. Ives Hendrick, was a different sort of man. By the time I met him, he had let himself go. He looked seedy in a three-piece suit, down the front of which were food stains and burns from cigarette ashes. As he smoked and talked, he would flick his cigarette without drawing it far from his lips so that a regular flow of ashes spilled onto his chest and abdomen.

Dr. Hendrick's skill was in his grasp of theory. He could apply the orthodox explanation to any symptom, for he was saturated in the Freudian assumptions. He worked backwards from the patient's symptoms composing a story and weaving the symptoms into it, a story in which the patient could be pictured as attempting to adapt to stresses found in sexual conflicts and generating a psychological disorder in the process.

I once presented, to a hospital conference Dr. Hendrick was leading, a recently married young woman who was suffering from a classical condition. She was anxious about swallowing her food and felt that a portion often stuck like a lump in her throat. This condition, which goes under the term "globus hystericus," is often a problem for individuals of an introverted and perfectionist temperament and resembles other hypo-chondriacal anxieties over bodily function both in its characteristics and its provocations.

Dr. Hendrick saw a symbol in this patient's symptom that fit into his assumptions about the nature of mental disorder. He interrupted my presentation by stating that, as a case of globus hystericus, this patient's problem was obviousy conflict over oral sex and that the treatment plan should consist of trying to have her see this problem in the same way he did. He made these comments calmly to the audience of some ten to fifteen social workers and other counselors, all the while puffing on his cigarette and flicking ashes onto his vest.

His opinion was greeted with solemn noddings of heads by everyone in the room. I was floored. Was I really hearing a proposal at Harvard Medical School in Boston that would fit right into the sexual banter of my guttersnipe friends back home in Lawrence? Did the sexual images and obsessions of adolescence reach so far that even Harvard medical professors couldn't resist them?

I was also embarrassed for the patient. The proposal struck such a coarse, degrading note. Here was this grubby guy pontificating to a room full of somber and rather condescending people, all of whom acted as if some great truth had been uttered—before, I should say, an attempt had been made to interview the patient and consider what things other than sex might be troubling her. No duty to fact could withstand their ardor for metaphor.

These two psychiatrists were narrators of mental disorder and actu-ally had similar assumptions about the sources of psychiatric symptoms. They were both members of the Boston Psychoanalytic Institute, which was devoted to promulgating an orthodox Freudian perspective on men-tal life. True enough, they began at opposite ends of the story. Dr. Sem-rad began with the person and never quite reached the illness, having been waylaid by the fascinating details of normality. Dr. Hendrick began with the symptom and never quite reached the person, having recast the patient's worries into a symbol of carnal conflict and letting it go at that.

Neither doctor, though, seemed baffled by anything about the pa-tients. Both were confident that the explanations their stories provided were adequate. They were certain about their underlying assumptions and never questioned them. They presumed that the life events they emphasized for the patients were the most important features to under-stand. Eventually, they produced a psychiatry of categorical mistakes and narrative error, primarily because of the assumptive world to which they were too faithful and in which their final conclusions were hopelessly embedded.

V

In one sense, the Freudian era is over. The "climate of opinion" that envisaged human beings as puppets of the unconscious manipulated by such stirrings of sexual conflict as Oedipal complexes, castration fears, and penis envy no longer dominates the psychiatric profession. But, in another sense, an essential idea—of which Freudianism is simply one of the examples—lives on in the views and practices of many psychotherapists who restrict their explanations to the story.

These therapists assume that human sentiments are so alike, human vulnerabilities so identical, and human expressions of distress so similar that any psychological disorder must be an adaptive response to a misadventure, trial, or burden. The presumption is: where there is present smoke of mental illness, there must be, at the least, past fire of mishandling and probably mistreatment that distorted the natural course of the patient's psychological development. If these provocations are unappreciated or unremembered by the patient, then their implications and existence must be revealed to him through psychotherapy. The biography of the patient, therefore, must be explored until the damaging events are discerned and the real story behind the mental disorder—sometimes presented as a drama starring those quasi-persons, id, ego, and superego, that Freud invented—is understood by everyone.

Great implications that extend into attitude and action are tied to the view that psychiatric patients are essentially the same. For example, as the medical student rejects the categorical features of schizophrenia in the patient I presented and sees her delusions as a natural effort to adapt to life's adversities, that student must at least suspect the parents and other relatives of the patient as potential sources of the adversities that beset her and, *even before evidence can emerge,* will approach them in a suspicious way. Psychiatric stories based on the assumption that only life's burdens can produce disorder have in the past led to depictions of parents of schizophrenic patients as "double binding" or "schizophrenogenic," and parents of patients with early infantile autism as generating the condition in their offspring through cold and obsessional child-rearing practices.

These false views have been disastrous to everyone. They have put therapists and families at odds with one another at the very time when they need to cooperate in the treatment and rehabilitation of these afflicted patients. As well, the therapists' opinions delayed research into these conditions for years. By mistakenly presuming that the causes of these conditions were known and the family complicit in provoking them, physicians undermined any chance of a cooperative alliance with the family in research.

The assumption that something *must* have happened if a mental disorder is present has provided an entry for zealots and charlatans into psychiatry. There have been Marxist therapists, feminist therapists, and sociobiological therapists—all attempting to write their presumptions into an explanation for mental disorders without a comprehensive study of the conditions themselves. In the last few years, as we all might have expected from the presumption that only life's burdens can produce disorder, patients have been told by therapists that their mental ailments were expressions of (you name it) infantile sexual assaults, satanic cult abuse, space alien abduction, or even irritating remnants of problems "unsolved" in some prior life in other centuries. This is the story explanation gone wild, with immeasurable damage to public confidence in the standards of practice represented by psychiatry and psychotherapy.

It is simply not true that mental disorders are all of one kind, varying in degree but not in nature. To make this clear, psychiatrists must confront the half-truth that the kindly intended "caring" fellowship-of-mankind idea represents. Some mental disorders are expressions of bodily disease. Others represent the effects of body-based drives either innate, such as hunger and sex, or acquired, such as the addictions. Some disorders are, like grief, the understandable outcome of life events. Other conditions depend upon vulnerabilities within the patient's constitution, such as emotional instability or mental retardation. Psychiatrists are responsible for the treatment of all these different conditions and must distinguish them to do so.

There should be no mystery about the treatments these conditions entail. Psychiatrists seek to cure diseases, interrupt behaviors, comfort the grieving, strengthen and guide the vulnerable.

The psychiatric story—a narrative recounting of how a person's hopes, desires, purposes, and constraints influenced the direction of his life—fits into every one of these treatments, both those that rest on medicine and those that depend on talk. It provides a natural and coherent context within which to appreciate the patient and his troubles. An understanding of context—the way this individual is unique even as he suffers from symptoms common to all who have his mental illness—illuminates the diagnostic task, transforming it from a simple process of attaching a label to a patient into something more like portraying a person's misfortune.

Narrative details arouse everyone's compassion for the patient and mediate the alliance between him and his physician. The story uncovers how this patient's character and life plans were affected by the disorder and what responses come most easily to him as he and his physician attempt to deal with it. But—and this is the big *but*—the context of a life should not be confused with the cause of all mental disorders or made the sole focus of therapeutic attention as though guidance were always synonymous with cure.

The story method and psychotherapy work together most straightforwardly when the patient's problems truly are context-driven and tied to universal human themes—grief from loss, fear from threat, demoralization from failure or rejection. Apt stories that provide an empathic understanding of these themes are as many as the predicaments in life and the individuals who encounter them. Freud and Jung identified some of these predicaments, but most of them are specific to the patient at hand and come to light in the midst of psychotherapy, where the patient and the therapist work together to get the story right.

Story-driven psychotherapy also is a crucial part of the rehabilitation of patients afflicted by psychiatric symptoms from other sources, such as disease. For example, patients with manic-depression need medication for their illness, but they also need psychotherapy to understand their affliction and to find ways to live effectively despite its intermittent disruptive symptoms. Any psychiatrist with a knowledge of this illness, as well as the story of its specific intrusions into the life of an individual, can and should provide both the medicine and the psychotherapy to the patient simultaneously.

Psychiatrists who try to work without the story forgo a vital way of appreciating their patients' predicaments. However, psychiatrists who dwell only on stories to explain mental disorders often misinterpret and misrepresent them. If these psychiatrists teach others to impose narrative solutions upon clinical problems arbitrarily, prematurely, and without attention to evidence, they will cheat their students of the knowledge and experience needed to join the group advancing this medical specialty in the future.

VI

All of these thoughts are at work in my argument with the medical student at the first lecture. I am far from denying that story-based ideas have helped psychiatric practice. What I am saying is that sometimes the story is a fable and—despite the kindest of intentions—does not fit as an explanation. For example, when we are confronted by a patient suffering from the symptoms of schizophrenia, the patient's domination by illness can be obscured for a student who reaches into the contemporary fashions for a story that will make the patient's confusing presentation intelligible. The patient has become a character in a tale the student can imagine rather than a person afflicted with a condition the student must come to learn.

All medical students, and eventually the public, need to realize that stories are helpful tools in psychiatry. But if used without reflection on their potential to become myths, medically authorized stories can produce a prolonged misdirection for everyone—doctor, patient, and family alike. Physicians, because they can do much harm with the wrong story, are duty-bound—in ways that poets are not—to check the story against the facts.

Although my first lecture often is disrupted, and even occasionally produces more heat than light, there are other lectures to come and clinical experiences on the wards that I go through with students over the course of their education. Eventually, this teaching, tying the explanations and the treatments of mental disorders together and indicating how our narrative instincts can lead us astray, wins out with most of them—not with all, I have to say—because the patients are around to remind us continually of the numerous ways we can get things wrong and, happily, the illuminating occasions when things do go right.

MICHAEL VINCENT MILLER

Does Sex Still Exist?

Michael Vincent Miller is a clinical psychologist in Cambridge, Massachusetts. His practice there inspired the subject of his recent book *Intimate Terrorism: The Deterioration of Erotic Life* (1995). A writer with degrees in both psychology and literature, he began this essay on the trajectory of the F-word with the working title "Getting Fucked and Its Vicissitudes," a sly nod to the influence of Freud and the master's seminal work. The tug of his literary concerns, which enriched and enlivened the controversial *Intimate Terrorism* to the point of provoking a few outraged reviewers, won out and he settled at last on the title chosen here.

Reading Miller's essay on the fragile emergence, superabundance, and near-collapse of erotic life in twentieth-century language and culture, we suspect a bleak answer, with no easy consolation, to the quite unrhetorical question posed by the title. The secret coinage of the F-word, once confined to the streets, now circulates as common currency, and the implications of its grinding prevalence connect with other casualties in American life as we sink to an angry inarticulate halt. W. H. Auden concluded his poem on the death of Freud with the lines, "Sad is Eros, builder of cities / And weeping anarchic Aphrodite." Miller, too, seems to propose a similar link in his own inquiry into sex, sublimation, and the rise and fall of civilization.

HERE IS an elegiac little vignette from a bygone era. A friend of mine, the son of a Brooklyn Irish cop, is walking home from school one day in 1955. He is about seven years old. As he ambles along his well-worn route through the neighborhood, a classmate named Andrew pops out of a news and candy shop across the street and yells, "Hey Malley! You're a fuck!"

Two weeks later the school term is nearly over. My friend finds himself in the family car, as his parents make their way to the beach on one of those cloudless Saturday mornings. Although he has been squirming with curiosity about Andrew's new word, he hasn't mentioned it to anybody. He doesn't want to ask Andrew or the other kids, because this would make him out to be a loser. And he hasn't asked his parents because he senses something dangerous about this word. It just *sounds* dangerous. But now, lulled by the tranquil goodwill of a family headed for the beach, he decides to risk it. "Daddy," he pipes up from the back seat, "what does 'fuck' mean?"

The response from the driver's seat is electrifying. Without turning

around, the father delivers a swift backhand to the head that sends my
friend sprawling. "Don't *ever* let me hear you use that word again!" his
father adds. The blow is serious enough to rouse a rueful appeal from his
mother. "Oh Harry," she says, "the boy doesn't know what he is asking."

Only a few months later, Malley drops by the precinct station at the
end of the day to meet his father. They get on an elevator with one of his
father's partners, and the two men proceed to dissect a mutual acquaintance. "Coswell?" the colleague says with a note of contempt. "What a
fuck!" But when he sees the boy's eyes widen, he adds, "Oh, sorry,
Harry."

My friend Malley, a thoughtful individual, quickly concluded from
these events that adults had even more mysterious prerogatives, guarded
jealously, than met the eye. The question remained, of course, as to how
the precocious Andrew had managed to get access to one of these.

Back in those days that already seem so quaint, it would be hard to
find another word that could more efficiently lay waste to polite discourse (although in private it might be used by bolder spirits to heat up
intercourse). Under the pressure of strong emotions, even the mere mechanics of its delivery could accentuate its impact. It was launched from a
kind of held-back grimace, whether of lust or fury, front teeth grabbing a
piece of lower lip. And it ended just as suddenly, as if truncated, in an
animal slap, a thick sound like that of thigh against thigh. Yet it could
also have the force of a slap across the face.

It must have seemed nearly as charged in print, capable there, too, of
inspiring powerful opposed feelings. Cultural and legal conventions,
when they didn't ban it altogether, at least diluted it, so that at most it
was allowed to appear on the page only in silhouette, reduced to its outer
consonants. Spoken or written, "fuck" was not only among our most
forbidden but also our most impassioned words.

Why so strict a taboo against a short word for an inevitable human
activity? Freud's early follower Ferenczi suggested that so-called obscene
words have an almost magical power to cause instant regression: they
take people back to that period during infancy before there is much
difference between reality and hallucination. To say them or read them,
Ferenczi speculates, is tantamount to seeing or even doing what they
describe.

This bit of psychoanalytic dazzle has a certain intuitive plausibility.
But it doesn't altogether account for the peculiar doubleness of the word
"fuck," which is used to deliver an insult at least as often as it is used to
arouse desire. Andrew's salute to Malley seems a good deal more aggressive than sexy, though who knows exactly what was on his mind? And if
you tell someone to "get fucked," you are not usually wishing him God-
speed.

When taken seriously (as it barely is any longer), the word "fuck" had repercussions. It may have been regressive all right, in the sense that it penetrated our civilized veneer and gave us a glimpse of what lay below. It seemed to reach down and disturb some unfathomable darkness at the bottom of the human soul, a hidden well that most of us have mixed feelings about peering into very closely. It stirred excitement that is not easily distinguished from anxiety, because it rubbed our noses in our physical drivenness and vulnerability. It conveyed the mystery of sex but also the stink of decay.

Thinking this way about it brings to mind Freud's humbling reminder (borrowed from St. Augustine) in *Civilization and Its Discontents:* "inter urines et faecea nascimur," which translates roughly as "we are born between piss and shit." But notice that Freud turns to the dignified polysyllables of Latin, the language of priests and physicians, as even that daring explorer was wont to do when an idea started him tugging at his collar. Unlike "sexual intercourse," "coitus," or "fornication," "fuck," let loose with no holds barred, goes straight for the mammalian substratum, even in the overtones it picks up from words it rhymes with, like "muck" and "suck." No wonder it could produce either rapture or horror, depending on what was going on, a pure distillation of the sex act or a dire curse. Has there been any other word in English that covers in one fell swoop so wide a spectrum of primal things humans do to each other—from the consummate act of love to the most abusive exercise of power (and sometimes both at once)?

Nowadays, of course, nearly anyone can get instant access to the entire human spectacle, on-line or off. Taboos seem a thing of the past, although some legislators are trying to crank them up again. Young Malley forty years later wouldn't have to wait long to get an answer to his burning question. If anything, he would probably be assaulted before he had asked it with an overload of answers coming from all directions. (Paul Tillich once wrote that "to cast answers like stones at the heads of those who have not yet asked the questions is the fatal pedagogical error.")

The once-notorious "F"-word shows up all over the place—in talk, whether sexy, angry, or merely emphatic; in serious literature; in our popular arts and entertainments. True, there are still some restrictions in the media. "Fuck" in all its grammatical forms is still banished from family newspapers and magazines. Television networks aren't allowed to transmit it without interfering blips until nighttime when children are supposed to be in bed, and there are "R" ratings for films that contain "adult language" along with nudity and sex, though most kids I know get in to see them without difficulty.

The freewheeling ubiquity of such language reflects a major shift in our habits. There had been a long, often painful rebellion against restriction and censorship over the course of the twentieth century. Once the rebel forces prevailed, there seemed little more to do besides mop up the last of the opposition. This victory deserves our cheers, for the most part: can any thoughtful person seriously question our need for a culture that openly acknowledges our elemental animal longings and impulses? Nevertheless, so thoroughgoing a conquest raises a few troubling questions.

It raises them because American society tends to travel through cycles from repression to liberation to saturation. One can readily see how periods of repression limit understanding of the human condition. Our recurrent episodes of acute puritanism (Bob Dole, Jesse Helms, and their cohorts may be among the early symptoms of a new outbreak) stifle our wilder impulses by rendering them incommunicado. Since it is difficult to learn or teach what you are not allowed to articulate, the result is a narrowing of intelligence, especially the capacity to make intelligent judgments for yourself about passionate feelings.

What is perhaps less self-evident is how the post-liberation phenomenon I call saturation also succeeds in diminishing our collective intelligence. Saturation is, in its effects, a neat political trick, capitalism at its most adaptive, running the show with an insidious wink. America tames rebellious social movements by swallowing them whole and regurgitating them in the marketplace.

Twenty-five or thirty years ago, young men with long androgynous hair and unkempt-looking beards or stubble and young women with granny glasses and no bras represented a variety of radical threats to the established order. They wandered off the path of middle-class upward mobility. Taking to the woods, they played with consciousness-expanding drugs and engaged in cheerful sex without feeling dirty or guilt-ridden. They fought for civil rights and protested the war in Vietnam. Now they stare at us blankly from the pages of every fashion magazine. Whatever thought-provoking influence they may have once wielded has by now been reduced to mere style.

In a similar vein, the struggle to liberate forbidden sexual language began as serious criticism of official culture, whether directly or indirectly. In the early days of the psychoanalytic movement, the preferred cure for neurosis was frank sexual talk. The idea was that such conversation worked like draining an infection; it could relieve patients from the hidden pressure of their own fermented sexual wishes or thoughts. These thoughts remained secret even from the patients themselves because culture had banned them from consciousness.

In a related development, writers like D. H. Lawrence and James Joyce expanded the novel's frame of sexual reference to include censored animal and emotional realities. Probably the two most notorious works of serious literature that first took up the word "fuck" in a big way were Lawrence's *Lady Chatterley's Lover* and Henry Miller's *Tropic of Cancer*.

These two novels showed up festooned with the word in full bloom, all its letters untactfully in place. In Lawrence's novel, though, it doesn't put in an appearance till about two-thirds of the way through, when Connie Chatterley and her husband's gamekeeper, Mellors, finally get down to doing it. There is no such buildup in *Tropic of Cancer*. Miller strikes the modern note by introducing "fuck," "fucking," and "fucked" right off the bat in the opening pages, four times in two sentences, in fact.

Lawrence's and Miller's willingness to jolt readers with obscene words sprang from an ideological outlook that they more or less shared. *Lady Chatterley's Lover* and *Tropic of Cancer* were, in part, manifestos against modern society. They attacked it for mechanizing life; for cutting intellect off from feelings; for employing genteel conventions to disguise the pernicious exercise of power. Both authors feared that these developments would deliver a fatal dose to Western culture.

Lawrence, much more than Miller, used unacceptable language with therapeutic intent; he wanted to force society to confront more of the physical human animal. As Lawrence Durrell wrote in a brief preface to a 1968 Bantam edition of *Lady Chatterley's Lover*, its author "was out to cure, to mend; and the weapons he selected for this act of therapy were the four-letter words about which so long and idiotic a battle has raged."

In *Lady Chatterley's Lover*, Lawrence's emphasis on fucking, instead of, say, making love, is his attempt to reinvigorate the romantic myth by replacing its ethereal (and therefore more socially palatable) idealism with the body's needs. Yet Lawrence's new ideal of fucking still borrows from a venerable pastoral mode: Connie and Mellors fall in love in the cultivated forests surrounding her estate; they explore each other's naked bodies in his softly lit and broom-clean rustic cottage; Mellors by temperament and manners might well be a noble country gentleman, even if he was born into the working class. Their orgasms are enough to convert anyone to pantheism.

On the other hand, there are barely any programmatic ideals in Miller's novel—at most an ambiguous touch of art-for-art's-sake, a whiff of Far Eastern mysticism, a celebratory toast to sheer vitality. Miller admired Lawrence, but *Tropic of Cancer* draws nothing from the poetics of pastoral landscapes. Miller's nature is all human nature, an exuberantly foul and seething mass stuffed into 1930s Paris. Miller's portrayals of broke American Bohemians and down-at-the-heels European pseudo-aristocrats picking their way through the rubble of modern urban life, looking for anything to feed their hungers, are bitter and hilarious. His characters fuck and fuck, nearly devouring each other out of insatiable sexual greed. There is certainly no romance in sight. For Miller, the only

authentic social reality is pure physical energy, bodies groping for satisfaction, facts of existence which are neither good nor bad in themselves
but have to be reckoned with.

Both novels struggled against the censors, particularly in America.
But once they broke through—*Lady Chatterley's Lover,* unabridged at
last, in 1959 and *Tropic of Cancer* in 1961—there was no staunching the
flood of literary fucking that has followed, to be followed in turn by an
even greater tidal wave of fucking in the popular arts. Freedom from
censorship turned out to be good for business. It is less clear what the
sheer magnitude of this outpouring implies about the quality of our
erotic lives. As I wrote in a recent book, *Intimate Terrorism,* "There can be
pathologies of freedom as well as pathologies of authority. If nineteenth-
century intimacy suffered from too much repression, perhaps twentieth-
century intimacy suffers from too much expression."

Not that there can be any doubt that lifting bans against obscene
language has expanded both our abilities to understand ourselves and
our options for expressing ourselves. But as "fuck" and its derivatives
spread all over present-day culture like some breed of self-replicating
graffiti, are we still learning something useful from it all? When does
repeating something enough times cross over the line between gaining
and losing information?

If you say a word over and over rapidly, after a while it seems to lose its
meaning and turn into a nonsense syllable. Similarly, when you look at
something intently, it stands out sharply against a background, but if you
continue to stare at it for a long time, its distinctiveness fades, and eventually it sinks into the background. Obviously the object hasn't changed;
your eyes simply tire, your mind shuts down, and you tend to become
bored. This is a case where familiarity literally breeds contempt.

Such is the fate of the word "fuck" and its former magnificence.
Once a forbidden symbol of animal heat and mystery, it has just about
declined to the status of a nonsense syllable. Maybe not altogether just
yet, but it is working its way there through rampant overuse.

There are various ways through which society can succeed in dumbing itself down. One is repressive control of information; another is a
repetitive flood of information that numbs the soul. When the latter
occurs, we start to lose our capacity to notice subtle but important differences. Pretty soon, it is no longer a question of subtlety: The ability to
describe even the most dramatic emotions and events with vivid specificity joins the other lost arts. Whole realms of experience begin to blur into
one another.

The word "fuck" has always had rich, multiple meanings, but now it
is used to cover almost every sin and every virtue that emerge from either
eros or aggression. It has become our most popular all-purpose inten-
sifier. There are rap songs that include hardly any other words. And

Roseanne told *The New Yorker*'s theater critic, John Lahr, "I love the word 'fuck.' . . . It's a verb, a noun, everything, and it's just infused with intense feeling and passion, you know, negative and positive. And women aren't supposed to say it, so I try to say it as much as I can."

She and everybody else. One has to give her credit: She has seized upon just about the last bit of edge "fuck" retains to raise a hackle here and there. It may be that women are still less supposed to say it than men, but judging by recent movie performances turned in by a range of women, from Kathleen Turner to Linda Fiorentino, you almost wouldn't know it. The general question remains in any case: How much experience can one word continue to communicate intelligently?

I can't imagine a more ironical demonstration of cultural change than Roseanne's sentiments being aired in *The New Yorker*. Until a few years ago you would never expect to find "fuck" spelled out in full in the pages of that magazine, not to mention other four-letter names for erotic and excretory functions and sites. The old *New Yorker* had a singular gift for publishing sophisticated or even avant-garde fiction without straying beyond the bounds of middle-class gentility.

You know that things have changed when they change at *The New Yorker*. I, for one, still fibrillate a little when I come across a sentence like this one in a recent *New Yorker* story: "He looks at the pan on the counter, imagines dipping his hand into the grease, smearing it over Elaine's ass and fucking her." The setting is a suburban kitchen after a dinner party, and the grease fantasy is directed briefly by a philandering husband named Paul toward his wife, Elaine. It occupies half his mind (the other half being occupied with a liaison he has just made with a friend's date at the party) as he lifts her skirt and pulls down her panty hose, while she bends over the dishes in the sink.

But neither the thought nor the action has much to do with conjugal affection; he is alienated and angry. When it comes to anger, Elaine is no slouch either. A few minutes later, only half-mockingly, she draws a carving knife lightly across Paul's neck and draws blood. And the next night, while they are hurling particularly hurtful, sarcastic remarks at each other, Paul grabs her and "fucks her, using the sofa for leverage, his feet pressing against the armrest." To which Elaine responds tearfully, "I'm so bored it's not even funny."

This story, "Music for Torching," by A. M. Homes (a woman writer— is she not supposed to use that word?), exemplifies the phenomenon that gave my book its darkish title. "Intimate terrorism" is what happens when a relationship goes bad, and love between two people is replaced by a different kind of bond, one based on causing each other pain and anxiety for the sake of gaining control over one another. The sex act itself, as in Homes's story of an unspeakable suburban marriage, can readily become a weapon in the hands of intimate terrorists. Homes's use of the word "fuck" gets across her couple's horribly mixed motives. And at least she uses it sparingly, fully intending the blur of meanings.

Still, the fucking in this story is a verb that works awfully hard. It seems to stand for lust with little by way of love, for an attempt to overpower one another, for apologies for the wounds they cause each other, and for sadistic efforts to inflict further pain. Maybe sex has always had to carry so burdensome and confusing a load of psychological baggage, under whatever name. But one wants art to help clarify rather than heap it on more; life is already too tangled.

At least this much is clear: Homes's scenes may be pornographic, but they are not very sexy, unless your taste runs to hostile sex. Pornography used to be hot stuff—damp muscles and membranes, groans of people apparently beside themselves with pleasure, not primarily the groans of casualties. But then not very much sex seems to be about pleasure these days. It has been too much intimidated by fear of AIDS, de-libidinized by Prozac, discredited by charges of abuse or harassment, and infused with bitter games in marriages like Paul and Elaine's.

If "fucking" used to be visceral and organic, evoking our primitive wishes, our protest against the social, this is no longer very much the case. As Homes's story illustrates, many of our latest sexual performances, especially in literature and popular culture, have turned cool and mean. While our sexual temperature lowers, its links to violence are increasing, as though this connection is what we have to resort to in order to get back to passionate feeling. And if this is not yet enough to give people a sense that something intense is taking place, the kinds of imagery that used to be considered obscene or pornographic often take on an apocalyptic tone. The once marginal arts, marginal because tabooed, are beginning to occupy the center. But as they do, they now suggest less the encroachment of pre-civilization, the jungle beyond the chandelier's reach, than post-civilization, things coming apart. "Music for Torching" ends in a conflagration. Paul and Elaine deliberately set fire to their suburban home by spraying its outside walls with charcoal starter and kicking over the barbecue grill. Then they pack their kids into the car and go off to a restaurant and a motel as the house goes up in flames.

Consider a more flashy but not unrelated instance: Madonna's obscene exhibitions tend to be cool in mood, self-indulgently mean, and apocalytically spectacular. I can't imagine anyone's mucous membranes being much dampened or erectile tissue becoming engorged by watching her performances. What excitement there is comes from one's awe at her virtuosity in portraying a constant flux of sexual possibilities, blurring the lines between the obscene, the perverse, the violent, and what used to be considered normal sexuality.

What we have now, in the age of electronic simulation, might be called "virtual obscenity." Sexual presentation, with pleasure and power made almost indistinguishable, turns into montage, flashbacks, cascades of changing images, like those computer-designed portraits of faces that keep shifting emotional expression, gender, and ethnic type.

This high-tech obscenity simulates a certain kind of paranoid high, which may be an extrapolation of how a great many of us are feeling. It is a kaleidoscope of words or visual fragments, revealing scenes of sex and violence in the process of being torn apart and recombined in often chilling ways. It resembles a frightening state that some potheads and acid freaks used to experience once in a while. Doctors in the sixties called it "toxic psychosis."

All this does not add up to a good feeling. It makes one wonder whether what we are witnessing is the desperate reap of a society muttering fuck this, fuck that, fuck you, and who gives a fuck, as it begins to run out of breath.

The Editors

Katharine Washburn is a writer, translator, and editor in New York City. North Point Press published her Paul Celan *Last Poems* in 1986, and her essays, reviews, and fiction have appeared in the *New York Times Book Review, Pequod,* the *Paris Review,* and the *New Republic.* She is co-editor of *An Anthology of World Poetry,* forthcoming from W. W. Norton in 1997.

John F. Thornton attributes his own nagging unwillingness to abandon all his standards to eight years of Jesuit education. After graduate study at Columbia University he began a peripatetic career in the publishing industry that has included time as editor-in-chief of *Facts on File* and editorial director for the Book-of-the-Month Club. He currently works as a literary agent in New York City.